THE COLORADO RIVER SURVEY

Robert Brewster Stanton in Glen Canyon. Miami University Library.

THE COLORADO RIVER SURVEY

Robert B. Stanton and the
Denver, Colorado Canyon & Pacific Railroad

Dwight L. Smith and C. Gregory Crampton
EDITORS

HOWE BROTHERS
SALT LAKE CITY   CHICAGO
1987

published by
HOWE BROTHERS
editorial and shipping offices:
Salt Lake City, Utah

Manufactured in the United States of America

Typography by Donald M. Henriksen
*This book was cast in hot metal in Intertype Baskerville,
with hand-set Baskerville display type.*

The manuscript for this book was
originally submitted to the publisher in 1984.

LIBRARY OF CONGRESS CATALOGING IN PUBLICATION DATA

Stanton, Robert Brewster, 1846–1922.
The Colorado River survey.

Bibliography: p.
Includes index.
1. Colorado River (Colo.-Mexico) — Description and
travel. 2. United States — Exploring expeditions.
3. Stanton, Robert Brewster, 1846–1922. I. Smith,
Dwight La Vern, 1918–   . II. Crampton, C. Gregory
(Charles Gregory), 1911–   . III. Title.
F788.S845   1987   979.1'304   84-22530
ISBN 0-935704-24-8

CONTENTS

ILLUSTRATIONS

F<small>IG</small>. 1. All loaded and ready to go. Green River, Utah, May 25, 1889.
Miami University Library.

PREFACE

Robert Brewster Stanton's railroad survey through the canyons of the Colorado River, 1889–1890, stands as one of the remarkable achievements in the history of the American West. And the complete record of that survey, presented in this volume, is one of the fullest primary records ever made of the Colorado River from Grand Junction, Colorado, to the Gulf of California.

During his career as a civil engineer, Robert Stanton worked in railway and mining ventures in several exotic places in the world. But he regarded the canyon railroad survey as one of the most meaningful experiences in his life. He was the first after John Wesley Powell to make the long run through the canyons of the Green and Colorado rivers below Green River, Utah. His study and survey was the first with utilization as the objective. And his work greatly extended the scope of knowledge about Powell's "Great Unknown." The magnitude of the engineer's achievement as an explorer of the Colorado rests solidly on his daily record of the experience. The publication of the Stanton survey notes will assure their author of a prominent place in the river's long history.

Robert B. Stanton was engaged by the Denver, Colorado Canyon and Pacific Railroad to run a survey along the Colorado River to determine the feasibility of building a railroad from Grand Junction, Colorado, to the Gulf of California. Meticulously, he recorded with pen and camera the day-by-day progress of the exploration survey. Press coverage of the venture, prompted by his correspondence, interviews, and lectures, was extensive. Beyond a few contributions to professional journals, however, Stanton did not publish his complete story and thus secure his place in the annals of the river which he so justly deserved. It was not because he could not, for he was capable of gifted prose and he had the craftsmanship of the professional historian.

The on-the-spot records which he kept became the raw material from which he began to construct his account for publication. To round out his own inadequate knowledge of some aspects of the river and its story and to provide context, he began to investigate and soon became involved in a prolonged effort to put together the entire history of the river, including its geology and prehistory. As the sands of time ran out for him some thirty years later he had researched and written and polished and repolished over a thousand pages. If it had been published at the time, "The River and the Canyon," as he called it, would have been a monumental history of the river. Except for the chapters that summarize and narrate his own expedition (published as Dwight L. Smith, ed., *Down the Colorado*. Norman, University of Oklahoma Press, 1965.), his efforts are now largely outdated by decades of writings by others and by the river history that has been made since his death in 1922.

Under restricted usage, the New York Public Library is the principal repository of the Robert B. Stanton papers. Following his death, the collection was established by Mrs. Robert B. (Jean M.) Stanton, with subsequent additions made by his daughter, Anne Stanton Burchard. The Colorado River related materials include the manuscript of "The River and the Canyon" with correspondence and supporting documents; the "Field Notes"; the manuscript draft of the official report to the directors of the railroad company; a scrapbook of clippings, articles, and other memorabilia of the 1889–1890 expedition; as well as a partial collection of photographs. Topographic maps, "blue prints," and other materials occasionally referred to in "Field Notes" have not been located by the editors.

It is impossible to determine how much or what manuscript and other materials were burned in three fires suffered by the Stanton family. In 1961, Anne Stanton Burchard remembered the loss of Stanton's "lantern slides colored from notes Father had taken at the time of each," "the equipment that had been used on the River," "family heirlooms," and Stanton's father's library.

There is an assemblage of Stanton papers in the Miami University Library, Oxford, Ohio. In large measure these duplicate the holdings in the New York Public Library, but there are some unique items. As Stanton spent considerable time in ferreting out details or in revising his writings, some of the fugitive notes and marginalia appear in this collection. Copies of some of Stanton's papers pertaining to the 1889–1890 expedition are held by the Huntington Library, San Marino, California, and by the National Archives in Washington, D.C.

The surviving photographic record is an important dimension. In addition to the partial collections of expedition generated photos in these collections, Stanton assembled albums. One is deposited with the Engineering Societies Library, New York. Another, in the Institution of Civil Engineers, London, England, has a " 'temporary' lost" status. A collection of negatives and prints was given to the U.S. Geological Survey; it was later transferred to the National Archives. Together, the surviving photos constitute an important archive of Colorado River history.

The basis for the present volume is a basic document of the Colorado River exploration and survey. The "Field Notes" are contained in four manuscript volumes, labeled as Books A, B, C, and D, in which Stanton made daily entries on well over a thousand pages. Although they are a part of the diaries he kept for the fifty years of his adult life, they are much more than that. They contain an engineer's observations and records and reminders that he could use later for reports, lecturing, writing, publications, and other purposes.

Photo or facsimile reproduction of the faded penciled "Field Notes" entries would not be satisfactory nor of much utility beyond a curiosity. A faithful transcription would have little use because of the on-the-spot vagaries that characterize much of the manuscript. Given the value of the immediacy of Stanton's daily account, however, editorial discretion renders it readable and more meaningful without violating its integrity. Stanton was a harsh task master of himself when he converted research notes into formal reports and articles for professional and popular journals. This perfectionist inclination in research and writing is what kept his "The River and the Canyon" from completion.

In the Stanton tradition we have introduced sufficient editorial practices to render the "Field Notes" readable and meaningful. Logical divisions have become chapters, to each of which we have assigned a title and added an explanatory editorial paragraph. Sentence sequence is sometimes changed. Paragraphing, capitalization, expansion of abbreviations, and punctuation are introduced as needed. Daily barometric and thermometric readings, telegraphic notes as reminder to write letters, memory joggers, and other extraneous jottings and remarks are deleted. Occasional crude topographic profiles with abbreviated word sketches keyed to them are usually omitted. Rather than burden the text with editorial devices and explanatory footnotes, these matters are handled silently. We think Robert Stanton would have approved of our treatment of his text.

Our indebtedness is considerable and gratefully acknowledged. The late Anne Stanton Burchard granted us permission to publish her father's manuscript; she was a constant source of information and inspiration for the project.

The New York Public Library, the Miami University Library, the Engineering Societies Library, New York, and the Huntington Library, San Marino, California, gave ready access to the Robert Brewster Stanton manuscripts and related materials held in their collections. Editorial labors along the way were eased by the gracious assistance of the staffs of a number of other agencies and institutions: Museum of Northern Arizona, Flagstaff; Reference Library, Grand Canyon National Park, Grand Canyon, Arizona; Arizona Department of Library and Archives, Phoenix; Phoenix Public Library, Phoenix, Arizona; Arizona Historical Society, Tucson; Arizona Western College Library, Arizona Western College, Yuma; Century House Museum, Yuma, Arizona; Bancroft Library, University of California, Berkeley; California Section, California State Library, Sacramento; Colorado Historical Society, Denver; Western History Department, Denver Public Library, Denver, Colorado; Colorado Department of State, Denver, Colorado; U.S. Bureau of Reclamation, Lower Colorado Region, Boulder City, Nevada; U.S. Bureau of Reclamation, Upper Colorado Region, Salt Lake City, Utah; U.S. National Park Service, Lake Mead National Recreation Area, Boulder City, Nevada; Nevada Historical Society, Las Vegas; Special Collections Department, University of Nevada, Las Vegas; Marriott Library, University of Utah, Salt Lake City; Utah State Historical Society, Salt Lake City; Lilly Library, Indiana University, Bloomington; Purdue University Library, West Lafayette, Indiana.

Martin Litton, Grand Canyon Dories, Stanford, California, generously provided the means for on-the-water research through Grand Canyon.

Our research efforts have been aided by grants from Miami University, the Huntington Library, and the Research Fund, University of Utah. The Utah State Historical Society has permitted us to adapt for the introduction, the article, Dwight L. Smith, "The Engineer and the Canyon," *Utah Historical Quarterly* 28 (July 1960), 262–273. Footnotes for this book were prepared by C. Gregory Crampton.

Richard Howe, of Howe Brothers, publishers, shared our enthusiasm for the value of the Stanton "Field Notes" as a historical document that needed to be rescued from obscurity. He urged us to prepare it for publication and has given it an appropriate format in this volume. His encouragement and involvement makes him a welcome partner in the project. John Alley, General Editor at Howe Brothers, smoothed out the rough spots which are bound to occur when two editors working on the same book live fifteen hundred miles apart. Donald M. Henriksen, through his artful design and typography, provided a fitting format for the intricacies and special problems of typesetting an engineer's field book.

Three others deserve credit for their essential roles in the preparation of this volume for publication. Pamela J. Messer gave professional attention to the manuscript in its raw transcribed form, defaced by our editorial scratchings and scrawlings, and typed it into a laudably acceptable format. Jane D. Smith spent countless hours laboring with good humor and alert scrutiny on the demanding chores of collating and proofreading, catching en route numerous editorial inadvertencies. In the field from Lee's Ferry to the Mexican border, and in the libraries and archives, Mary Helen P. Crampton contributed essential research assistance.

DWIGHT L. SMITH   C. GREGORY CRAMPTON
Oxford, Ohio   St. George, Utah

INTRODUCTION

It was staggering to the imagination of an average person in 1889–1890; ninety years later it is still fantastic. In the heroic annals of the unfolding Southwest in the latter part of the past century is a too-little-known chapter of railroad history. In light of the sustained interest in the Colorado River, the Stanton engineering survey to determine the feasibility and worth of a railroad along the river from Grand Junction, Colorado, to the Gulf of California is of considerable historical importance.

The much publicized Powell expedition which navigated the Colorado River in 1869 led even engineers to conjecture the possibility of a low grade railroad line by way of the river from the western base of the Rocky Mountains to the Pacific. Major John Wesley Powell certainly removed some of the misconceptions about the river, but there was still much more to be learned about it.

The Powell report fired the imagination of a college junior, Robert Brewster Stanton, enrolled in Miami University. He envisioned "a vast plateau . . . through it a winding river that by corrasion had cut its way down into the solid rock, to a depth of a mile and a quarter, *forming a canyon with practically vertical walls from the water's edge to the level of the plateau.*" At the surface the chasm was perhaps a half mile wide. He dreamed of someday throwing "a single span railway bridge across that chasm!" After graduation he went into mining and railroad engineering and established quite a respected reputation. One of his ventures took him into the Southwest on an instrumental reconnaissance with the Atlantic and Pacific Railroad, then projected from Pierce City, Missouri, to San Diego; but because of financial stringency of the company, Stanton's party never reached as far as the Colorado.[1]

---

[1] Unless otherwise noted, much of this account is derived from three basic manuscripts, Stanton Papers, New York Public Library: "The River and the Canyon" and its appendices; "Railroad Report," his report to the directors of the railroad company; and "Field Notes." Stanton's narrative account of his trip on the Colorado has been published. See Dwight L. Smith, ed., *Down the Colorado* (Norman, University of Oklahoma Press, 1965).

S. S. Harper, a lone prospector in north central Arizona, had followed the line of the Atlantic and Pacific survey. Since it crossed so many mountain ranges, he called it the "saw-tooth route." With a very limited knowledge of the Colorado River, not including the Powell report, he conceived the notion of a line running from the western slope of the Rockies to the coast with a water grade by way of the Colorado. Harper, with his vaguely defined idea, found a ready audience in Frank M. Brown, a successful Denver real estate businessman who was looking for a scheme for investment. The Denver, Colorado Canyon and Pacific Railroad Company was organized March 25, 1889, to carry out the Harper-Brown scheme and to try to interest a syndicate in financing it.[2]

Under the supervision of Frank C. Kendrick, the assistant engineer, the actual survey began at Grand Junction, Colorado, on March 28, 1889, and continued down the Grand (Colorado) River to the mouth of the Green River in southeastern Utah.[3] Here the main party was to pick up the survey and continue on down stream. Headed by Brown, president of the company, and Stanton, chief engineer, the main party arrived by rail from Denver on the Denver and Rio Grande Western Railway and embarked on the Green River at Green River, Utah, on May 25, 1889.[4] They chose this route because of the relative ease of navigation down river to the terminal point of the Kendrick survey.

Sixteen men made up the party. Outfitted with clinker-built, thin red cedar keel-bottomed hunting and pleasure boats and an ordinary flat-bottomed skiff used by the Kendrick party, and medicine, instruments, and supplies for seventy-five days, the party soon reached the confluence of the Green and Grand rivers and then plunged into Cataract Canyon. It was planned to replenish provisions at Lee's Ferry at the end of Glen Canyon, and at Peach Springs down river near the end of the Grand Canyon division.

The expedition was plagued with disaster, and there was serious doubt as to whether the river could be mastered and the survey completed. Most of the cooking utensils and some of the supplies were lost when the cook boat was jammed between two rocks. Other accidents resulted in the loss of nearly all of the provisions. Bedding and clothing were frequently soaked. Two of the boats were totally destroyed and the others badly damaged. Finally, on June 24, the men reached Dandy Crossing at Hite, Utah, just below the mouth of the Dirty Devil River near the head of Glen Canyon.

[2] Brown expected the line to be open by May 1895. Ethan A. Reynolds, "In the Whirlpools of the Grand Canyon of the Colorado," *Cosmopolitan Magazine*, 8 (November 1889), 25.

[3] For Kendrick's notebook, see Helen J. Stiles, "Down the Colorado in 1889," *Colorado Magazine*, 41 (Summer 1964), 225–246.

[4] Letter of application for the position as chief engineer, Stanton to Brown, April 15, 1889, Stanton Papers, Box 5, Folder 2, New York Public Library.

Here the party split into two groups. One under W. H. Bush was to continue the survey. Brown and Stanton led the other on what was to be a rapid examination by making notes, sketches, and photographs of the lower canyons and on down the river as far as Needles. President Brown was anxious to make an "eye survey" to that point where the Atlantic and Pacific (later the Santa Fe) Railroad crossed the Colorado, since he had an appointment with a group of eastern capitalists who had expressed interest in the project. This advance party moved on to Lee's Ferry, and, after a delay waiting for supplies, started into Marble Canyon on July 9.[5]

The next morning one of the boats was upset and President Brown was drowned. A few days later another disaster: two more of the party were lost to the river. These accidents probably could have been averted had life preservers been used. The expedition carried none. Now in charge, Robert B. Stanton decided to quit the river and to return more adequately prepared. The instruments and supplies were cached in a cave at Point Retreat thirty-two miles south of Lee's Ferry; the party climbed out of the gorge and returned to Denver.

For the second expedition three sturdy boats of oak, with more spacious watertight storage compartments, capable of carrying heavy loads, difficult to upset, and equipped with other safety features, were specially built. Other equipment, including rubber bags and floatable kegs for storage of such items as rice and coffee, and life preservers, was expressly designed for the undertaking.

The Stanton party of twelve included only three of the previous expedition. Since it was not necessary to go through Cataract Canyon again, the boats were wagoned from Green River Station on the D&RGWRR to the mouth of Crescent Creek (North Wash), a short distance above Hite. Here the Stanton expedition embarked on December 10, 1889.

While running through Glen Canyon, they tested their new equipment, staked gold mining claims, and completed the last thirty-four miles of the instrumental survey. After celebrating Christmas in grand style at Lee's Ferry, the expedition moved into Marble Canyon again. On New Year's Day, while climbing to get a better vantage point, photographer Frederick A. Nims fell and broke his leg. It was a treacherous and harrowing task carrying him out of the canyon, and this delayed the survey. Besides, novice Stanton now had to assume the responsibilities as the expedition's photographer.

Slowly, laboriously, the railroad surveyors continued their voyage through Grand Canyon. Finally, on March 17, 1890, they passed the Grand Wash Cliffs and broke out in the open, 278 miles below Lee's Ferry. With notebook

---

[5] Brown said a fifty-million-dollar syndicate was interested if the engineer's report was favorable. After Brown drowned, no further mention is made of this group. A reorganization of the company took place, Stanton was elected to the board, retained as engineer, and instructed to raise the necessary money to continue the survey.

and camera Stanton records this remarkable passage in great detail. He counted 419 rapids. There was a smashup and loss of one boat. One man defected. The engineer found an alignment for the railroad through every mile and he was captivated by the grandeur of the canyon.

Once through the Grand Canyon, Stanton felt his mission was "virtually accomplished" and he pushed along rapidly. There were no dams yet but the marks of Colorado River pioneers were evident all the way to Yuma: ferries, boat landings, steamboats, river towns, mining camps, army posts, Indian reservations, railroads. When the expedition reached tidewater in Mexico on April 27, 1890, the grand voyage was over.[6]

The Stanton Colorado River notebooks, here published for the first time, are the on-the-spot record of a high adventure. But the engineer's goal was not adventure. It was business. Major Powell's voyages were undertaken in the name of geology and science. Stanton's objective was to find a way to open the canyons to commercial traffic. Even in the most trying circumstances he never lost sight of the railroad. The records he kept along the way were designed to demonstrate the practicability of the idea.

Detailed information of the lower canyon walls, the composition of the river banks, and the alignment and fall of the river was needed.[7] To this end, a continuous transit line was run for the first 355 miles, levels were taken, contour topography sketched, and photographs made. Shortage of funds did not permit such a detailed survey below Glen Canyon. During the Stanton-led phase of the project only an "instrumental reconnaissance" was made except where excessive fall, sharper grades, or other circumstances made greater detail a necessity.

A visual record was made by photography, because of the "inaccessibility of the country," and as indisputable evidence to convince skeptics that the statistical and other data was all that it appeared to be. Altogether, over two thousand pictures were taken, most in duplicate and some even in triplicate.

[6] The contract under which Stanton had worked was canceled by mutual consent at a board of directors meeting in Denver, April 13, 1891. Manuscript, Stanton Papers, Box 4, Folder 1.

[7] Since the canyons are so wide at the top, the depths involved have little relevance to the consideration of a water level railroad survey. As was suggested, if the upper two thirds of one of the canyons were sheared off the problem would appear to be much less impressive to the layman. And the magnitude of the problems involved here would be no greater than of those encountered on the other western lines.

See also Arthur M. Wellington's editorial, "Canyons and Railway Lines," New York *Engineering News and American Railway Journal*, September 21, 1889, pp. 278–279, in which he discusses Stanton's article, "The Denver, Colorado Cañon & Pacific Railroad Project," in the same issue. While applying to this specific project, it is an excellent general discussion on the subject.

Wellington's editorial, "The Colorado Canyon Survey," *ibid.*, October 18, 1890, pp. 349–350, discusses a subsequent Stanton article, "The Denver, Colorado Cañon & Pacific Railroad Project," which appears in the same issue. Other comments in this editorial are relevant to Stanton's conclusions.

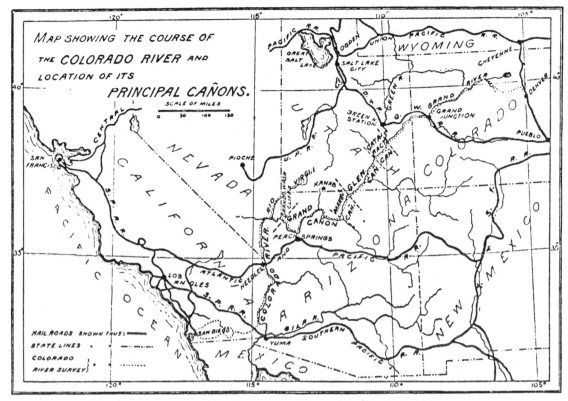

Fig. 2. Although he carried the DCC&PRR survey to the mouth of the Colorado River, Stanton argued later that San Diego would be the better terminus. To this end he made some faced examinations between the river and San Diego. The possible routes are shown on this map which accompanied his paper on the "Availability of the Cañons of the Colorado River of the West for Railway Purposes" presented to the American Society of Civil Engineers, and published by the Society, April 1892.

Only a very few negatives were lost or damaged, a remarkable record, even with all the precautions that were taken. The eleven hundred views are a valuable part of the records of the expedition.[8]

Preparation of a roadbed in the upper or canyon division from Grand Junction to the Grand Wash near the Arizona-Nevada border meant: two thirds "comparatively light work" in earth, loose rock, and talus slopes; one third "heavy" work in solid rock, cliff benches, and sloping granite walls; and two percent of tunneling and half-tunneling. While the average fall per mile

[8] Stanton offers a convenient summary and discussion of this phase of record taking in "Engineer with a Camera in the Cañons of the Colorado," *Cosmopolitan Magazine*, 15 (August 1893), 292–303.

in the Glen Canyon portion was less than in any other part of the division, the river was so extremely crooked here that a good line would require some eighteen tunnels.[9] In Marble Canyon one ten-mile stretch was the most difficult to locate on the entire river, and undoubtedly the most expensive to construct.[10]

The lower or valley division of the river, from the Grand Wash to the Gulf of California, generally is composed of broad valleys and sloping hillsides, but in places there are a number of short canyons. This part of the project would involve: three fourths earth and gravel work; one fourth solid rock work; one half percent of tunneling.

From the standpoint of the entire river, level bottoms with earth and gravel slopes could be handled by light plows and scrapers like similar work outside the canyon country. The high water line does not ordinarily reach these bottoms, and the roadbed could be adequately and cheaply protected by a riprap slope wall construction. Hillside and rough talus slopes were mostly side hill cuts which involved no waste to be hauled. These hillside slopes are generally not of loose rock slides, and the talus slopes are usually horizontal strata with but a thin top layer of debris. The tremendous width of the canyon area on top would lessen the damage potential of loose rock to a railway in the lower gorge area.

The principally solid rock work in the sloping hills or solid rock benches of sandstone, limestone, and granite would entail the least expensive kind of rock work. Excavation itself would almost entirely prepare the roadbed while the waste could be pushed into the river. Tunneling costs would only be high because of the inaccessibility of the area. But the twenty miles of tunnels would save about forty-two miles in distance and other difficulties so that the extra cost would thus be partially offset. New inventions, such as electrical drills, would further cut construction expense.

Most of the side streams and canyons enter the Colorado through deep and narrow channels of sedimentary rock or granite that could be crossed usually at elevations of fifty to a hundred feet above their beds. Although some are from three to six miles across on top, a hundred-foot, single-span bridge would

[9] See also Stanton, "The Denver, Colorado Cañon and Pacific Railroad Project," New York *Engineering News and American Railway Journal*, September 21, 1889, pp. 269–272. While reorganizing in preparation for a resumption of the survey, Stanton wrote this article in reply to what he regarded as misleading statements in a New York newspaper. His article contains data on the proposed railroad apropos to this study even though it is just a preliminary report.

[10] Even though "the canyon makes two almost complete right angle turns, a good line can be located by crossing the river — the only time in the whole survey — with a single span bridge, from marble cliff to marble cliff, at an elevation of some 200 or more feet above low water, and with a tunnel at either end." Stanton, "The River and the Canyon," II, 634, 640–641.

suffice at the railroad level. Where the mouths of the side streams had washed out into wide flats, ordinary bridge construction would suffice.

Adverse winter weather of hard freezing and snow that frequently handicapped the transcontinental lines through the Rockies, especially in the winter of 1889–1890 when the Stanton survey was under way, would have little or no effect in the canyon area of the Colorado.

Except for unusual situations, a railway line could be constructed with a grade not in excess of one-half percent per mile; and except for tunnels to take care of the sharper bends, the curves needed in the line would not be more than ten degrees. Where the average fall of the river was not more than twelve feet per mile, the roadbed could nearly parallel the high water mark.

If construction of a Colorado River line was possible only from both ends, time and costs would be unnecessarily increased. Stanton figured, however, that in the upper, or canyon, division, simultaneous construction could be carried on in perhaps as many as forty different locations by employing railroads (the Denver and Rio Grande, the Colorado Midland, and the Rio Grande Western on the north, and the Atlantic and Pacific on the south), existing and easily constructed wagon roads, jack trails, horse trails, ferries, flatboats, and steam launches. In the lower or valley division, that is from about the Arizona-Nevada line down, there was no real problem because steamboats were then running on the river and could haul the necessary supplies and equipment needed for construction.

Stanton was satisfied that the proposed line was "neither impossible or impracticable" and that construction and maintenance costs would be "reasonable" especially when compared with other transcontinental railways.[11]

The possibility of operating the entire line from electricity generated by the power of the river itself made the whole scheme appear even more attractive.

In themselves, however, these factors probably were not sufficient to convince investment capital in a venture such as a Denver, Colorado Canyon and Pacific Railroad which still sounded unrealistic and fanciful no matter what the cold calculations of an engineer revealed. Assuredly from an engineering standpoint it was possible. But what of the potentialities of traffic and profit? Stanton was convinced that this railroad scheme would be a profitable venture.

In the first place, the principal object of this Colorado River line was to haul coal from Colorado to the Pacific. Coal was expensive in California and most of it was imported from other countries. The projected railway seemed to be the answer. Because of navigation difficulties at the head of the Gulf of

---

[11] Stanton gives a detailed analysis of construction costs, section by section, in "Railroad Report." He estimated that the roadbed, "complete with all superstructures, ready for the rolling stock, of single track standard gauge," with stations, sidings, and terminals, to San Diego via Yuma, and with a branch line up the Rio Virgin, would cost about $60,000,000.

California, it was decided the road should go as far as Yuma and thence over the mountains to San Diego harbor.[12]

Assuredly there was much else for which the railway would be used. Counting on this sublime spectacle of nature as an attraction for tourists, this traffic itself should defray extraordinary construction costs. None of the other western lines had a drawing card of such magnitude. Its passenger traffic would be "in excess of all other lines across the continent." [13]

Potential freight traffic certainly was an important consideration. Competition in transcontinental transportation was becoming keener; and Stanton was confident that a thousand mile low grade year-round line through the mountain area would successfully meet this competition, as well as that of the then much talked about Nicaraguan canal. It would capture more than its proportionate share of the through freight traffic.

As other Western railroads were a boon to exploitation of natural resources and settlement, Stanton fully expected his line to have similar effects on the area through which it would run. The starting point, Grand Junction, was not only a western terminus of railroads that came into Denver from the East, and with connections to the West, but it was situated in a prosperous agricultural region and cattle-raising territory and within easy reach of large "inexhaustible" coal fields.

Although the canyon lands below Grand Junction seemed to have little to offer except scenery and thrills, there were large tracts of grazing land at the heads of the side canyons. Below that in Glen Canyon, there were almost continuous gold placer deposits, enough to support a prosperous mining industry, one which might be expected to last at least a century. Up some of the side canyons were other deposits of mineral wealth and coal and even petroleum.[14]

Existing wagon roads connected Lee's Ferry with agricultural and grazing lands in southern Utah and northern Arizona whose vast possibilities through irrigation were not yet dreamed of. In Marble Canyon, in fact in most of the canyons, a great variety of building stone awaited a railway to make possible the development of a considerable industry.

The Grand Canyon portion of the line was rich in deposits of silver, lead, copper, and iron ores, and even roofing slate. Here as elsewhere, besides taking out the ores, the railroad would bring in provisions, machinery, and other sup-

[12] In "Railroad Report," Stanton analyzes this idea and urges the board to consider it. He also suggests possibilities for another line from Las Vegas Wash, across the mountains, to San Francisco.

[13] Wellington, "Canyons and Railway Lines," 279.

[14] Dwight L. Smith, "Hoskaninni: A Gold Mining Venture in Glen Canyon," *El Palacio*, 69 (Summer 1962), 77–84; *ibid*., in K. Ross Toole, and others, eds., *Probing the American West* (Santa Fe, Museum of New Mexico Press, 1962), 125–132, 203–204; C. Gregory Crampton and Dwight L. Smith, eds., *The Hoskaninni Papers: Mining in Glen Canyon, 1897–1902* (Salt Lake City, University of Utah Press, 1961).

plies for the mining camps. And why not exploit the Kaibab Plateau timber for railroad ties, fuel, lumber, and other products?

The lower, or valley division had much to offer. Rich mineral areas of principally rock salt, gold, and silver flanked the Colorado. Many already established mines were inoperative because of the high cost of the coal which was needed to develop them. Others were waiting for favorable circumstances for establishment. The railroad would correct this situation. Prosperity to the mining industry would be accompanied by the development of agricultural areas with such products as grains and semitropical fruits, especially citrus.[15]

Coal was by no means limited to that obtainable in the Colorado fields. Probably even greater quantities were available from nearer points. To this end branch lines should be constructed to the various fields, especially one to the "practically unlimited" fields of the southwestern Utah area up the Rio Virgin.[16]

The market possibilities for coal were good. Mining and milling operations along the Colorado River would consume their share; the Atlantic and Pacific Railroad which crossed the proposed route at Needles and the Southern Pacific which crossed it at Yuma needed it for their own use and for shipping over their own lines; and their markets would welcome this new source of supply.

In 1889, Australia and British Columbia accounted for about nine-tenths of the coal received at San Diego; and British Columbia, Australia, and England supplied nearly two-thirds of the import at San Francisco. Stanton believed his own railroad could deliver coal and coke to southern California at from a half to a third of its market price. A cheap and unlimited supply would tend to make San Diego, with its connections with other roads to the north, the coal depot for the rest of California.[17] Ocean steamers using the proposed Nicaraguan canal would create further demand. San Diego would soon become the principal station exporting coal on the Pacific, and ocean traffic would increase considerably. Undoubtedly industry would be attracted to the area to take advantage of cheap ores, coal, coke, and ocean and land trans-

[15] "I am led to believe that this whole section through the Grand Canyon . . . will some day be developed into one of the most extensive and valuable mining districts of the Western States." Stanton, "Railroad Report."

[16] There were also iron fields that might be developed. Stanton urged survey for such a line to the board. *Ibid.*

Stanton prepared a paper on a railroad down the Rio Virgin, the Colorado, and to San Diego, in which he treats of the area and its value to the proposed line. Dwight L. Smith, ed., "Robert B. Stanton's Plan for the Far Southwest," *Arizona and the West*, 4 (Winter 1962), 369–380.

[17] Stanton figured that his line would be shorter from Denver to San Diego than any of the lines then operating. With existing connections, it would be shorter than all other lines, except one, from Chicago to San Diego. Generally not as much distance would be lost in the windings of the Colorado as was lost by other railways in crossing various mountain ranges.

portation facilities. The city would have tremendous advantages over other Pacific ports.[18]

With the attractive features of not-too-difficult or unusual or expensive construction, better than usual year-round weather conditions, a constant water supply, the possibilities of use of on-the-spot generated electricity for both construction and operation, cheaper rates, faster service, low grade line, a permanent road bed, the potential exploitation of mining, agriculture, and natural resources with plentiful markets, certainly the Denver, Colorado Canyon, and Pacific Railroad could successfully meet the competition of already established lines and indeed become a most prosperous venture.

Robert Brewster Stanton was convinced of the feasibility and practicality of the DCC&PRR, and he had collected convincing data to support his conviction. President Frank M. Brown was one of the casualties of the survey and the Colorado River had imposed delays and extra costs. With new and more attractive ventures to consider, the sponsors soon abandoned all interest in the project.

Although the DCC&PRR was never constructed, Stanton remained convinced. He continued to write and dream of the river and its potential development. In 1894–1896 he tried to promote a railroad from the Virgin River, along the Colorado River, to Yuma, and west to San Diego. He even talked to a group of investors about a Japanese-American shipping line which would use San Diego as a terminus.[19] In the closing years of the century, he was the prime mover in a placer gold mining enterprise in Glen Canyon.[20]

The Denver, Colorado Canyon and Pacific Railroad survey was, in itself, a considerable achievement. Stanton's "Field Notes" attest to that.

[18] For a detailed analysis of "the railroad connections and prospects" of San Diego, see the lengthy newspaper article by a civil engineer, Charles J. Fox, "San Diego's Railways," in the San Diego *Union*, March 15, 1891.

[19] Smith, "Robert B. Stanton's Plan for the Far Southwest."

[20] See note 14 above.

CHAPTER I

PLUNGING THROUGH CATARACT

Robert B. Stanton's diary of the survey of the canyons of the Colorado River began with his appointment as chief engineer of the Denver, Colorado Canyon & Pacific Railroad. The survey party, under the direction of Frank M. Brown, company president, embarked at the historical crossing of the Green River in Utah, and quickly floated to the confluence of the Green and Colorado rivers (now in the heart of Canyonlands National Park), where the instrumental survey was started. Almost at once the men were engulfed by the merciless rapids of Cataract Canyon. Riding without life preservers in frail skiffs, they soon lost supplies, equipment, and morale. The wonder is that no lives were given up to the killer canyon. Despite the hazards of navigation and the difficulty of moving about on land to make the actual instrumental measurements, the doughty engineer carried the survey along for fifty-four miles to Dandy Crossing at the upper end of Glen Canyon.

Notes of an Instrumental Examination of the Canyons of the
Colorado River of the West, for a Railway Line from the Coal Fields
of Colorado, to the Pacific Coast. By Robert B. Stanton, C.E.[1]

DENVER, COLORADO, FRIDAY, MAY 10, 1889. By instruction of Mr. Frank M. Brown, President of the Denver, Colorado Canyon, & Pacific R.R. Co. I prepared lists of necessary outfit and supplies for a preliminary survey and examination of a railroad route from Grand Junction, Colorado, to the Gulf of California and San Diego by way of the Colorado River and through the Grand Canyon.

Have devoted my whole time today to this work, though have not yet received appointment as Chief Engineer, for which position I made application, some weeks ago. I suppose, however, that the instructions given me today

---

[1] The Field Notes contained in four notebooks are labeled A, B, C, and D. This is the title page for Book A and can well serve as the title page for all four.

[11]

mean simply that the official appointment will be made as soon as Mr. J. C. Montgomery, the treasurer, returns from New York. He is expected tomorrow morning.

SATURDAY, MAY 11. Ordered instruments, etc. by telegram from New York and Philadelphia and completed lists and submitted them to President Brown.

MONDAY, MAY 13. Received appointment as Chief Engineer of the DCC&PRR with instructions to employ the necessary men for the party and purchase and ship to Green River the necessary outfit, with supplies, for the expedition.

My lists of supplies, outfit, etc., were all approved; but the list of men for the force was cut down [by] four men, leaving off all extra men whom I wished as *special experienced boatmen.* Mr. Brown saying that he and Messrs. Reynolds and Hughes, who are to be "guests" of the expedition, would take their places and keep the boats up with the survey!!!

FRIDAY, MAY 17. In conversation with Mr. Brown, he asked me how long it would take to make the instrumental examination from head of Colorado River as proposed with the force of sixteen men all told as now arranged.

I answered him promptly from *"six* to *eight months."* He was much surprised and said it ought to be made in from 60 to 90 days, and asked me if we could not with the two parties of 5 men each average ten miles a day.

I told him no, that I thought the best possible time would be an average of 5 miles a day when on the work; and that that would depend upon whether the boats were kept up; but that we would do the best we could, 15 miles a day if possible.

SATURDAY, MAY 18, 1889. Have been all the week getting our outfit ready. Have selected all the men and ordered all supplies. Had reported to me today the old trouble between *Banks* and *Bush.* After careful investigation decided that while Banks was not perhaps so much to blame, his disposition was such, as exhibited in our interview this evening when he came to my office with his wife and lawyer and *under the influence* of *liquor,* that it would be impossible to take him on this trip.

Got to bed at 11:30, tired out.

SUNDAY, MAY 19. Went with Mr. Woods to see Mr. Briggs, Chief Engineer D&RGRy., as to Mr. Bush. Mr. Woods talked with Briggs and then stated to me as he had before that Bush was thoroughly competent, but that his great fault was *whisky,* and when given to that he neglected his work.

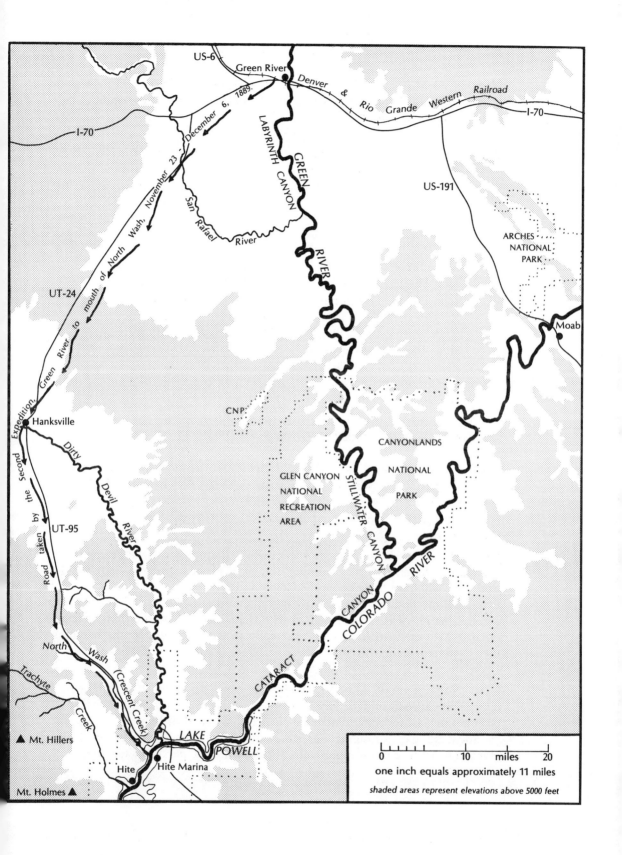

US-6

Green River

Denver & Rio Grande Western Railroad

I-70

December 6, 1889.

I-70

1889.

LABYRINTH CANYON

GREEN

RIVER

US-191

ARCHES NATIONAL PARK

San Rafael River

November 23 –

Green River to mouth of North Wash,

Moab

UT-24

CNP

CANYONLANDS NATIONAL PARK

Expedition,

GLEN CANYON NATIONAL RECREATION AREA

STILLWATER CANYON

by the Second

Hanksville

Dirty

Devil

River

Road taken

UT-95

COLORADO RIVER

CANYON

North

Wash

(Crescent Creek)

CATARACT

Trachyte

Creek

▲ Mt. Hillers

LAKE POWELL

Hite

Hite Marina

Mt. Holmes ▲

0   10   miles   20

one inch equals approximately 11 miles

shaded areas represent elevations above 5000 feet

Monday, May 20. Met Mr. L. B. France and Bush. Told them of my visit to Briggs, etc. And finally gave Bush place as first assistant on this trip but made no promises for the future.

Wednesday, May 22. Spent the last three days gathering together and completing our outfit. Think I have a good set of men. I have selected most of them from a large number of applicants, depending largely, after a few moments conversation, upon my ability to read character in the face.

We started from Denver by the D&RGRy. at 8:00 p.m. with the following party:

F. M. Brown, President	E. A. Reynolds, Guest
J. N. Hughes, Guest	W. H. Bush, Transitman
John Hislop, Transitman	G. Ed. Howard, Leveler
Ed. Coe, Leveler	F. A. Nims, Photographer
C. W. Potter, Front Flag	Geo. A. Sutherland, Rodman
H. C. Richards, Steward	G. W. Gibson, Cook

Peter Hansbrough missed the train and was left behind. Sent his ticket back and telegraphed him to follow by next train.

Thursday, May 23. Reached Green River, Utah, 11:15 p.m. Stopped at hotel.

T. P. Rigney joined us at Grand Junction and we found *Terry* at Green River. Green River Station, Blake P.O., is in Utah where the D&RGRy. crosses Green River.

Green River Station, Friday, May 24. Before breakfast we all went over to the railroad to look at our boats. I was awfully disappointed when I saw them. They are light brittle cedar hunting and pleasure boats, totally unfit for the work they will have to do down the Colorado River.

I shall say nothing now, for my position, and association with Mr. Brown will not permit of it. And I will go with these boats, though I think it really unsafe. Two of them have very large splits in their bottoms by the handling they have received in the cars.

Camp No. 1, Friday, May 24. Went into camp on Green River about 1/2 mile below railroad bridge. Had fine breakfast at hotel, trout, strawberries and cream. Our last for some time to come. Mrs. M. H. Beardsley.

Spent all day arranging our stores and separating them for the boats. Hansbrough came in on night train. So now all our party are together.

Have arranged our crews as follows:

Ward, No. 1	President Brown, F. M. Reynolds, E. A. and Hughes, J. N.
Mason, No. 2	Myself Howard, G. E. and Coe, Ed.
Mary, No. 3	Bush, W. H. and Hislop, John
Denver, No. 4	Rigney, T. P. and Nims, F. A.
Colorado, No. 5	Potter, C. W. Sutherland, G. A. and Terry, E. W.
Brown Betty, No. 6	Hansbrough, P. M. Richards, H. C. and Gibson, G. W.

Will be ready tomorrow to start down Green River for its mouth, which at its junction with Grand River forms the "Colorado of the West." [2]

SATURDAY, MAY 25. Completed repairing boats. Loaded all our boats and ready to start at 12 noon. Lunch, cold bread and water. Started 10 minutes before one. Found it impossible to load all our stores in boats as arranged with watertight compartments in center. Took *these* out, made them into a raft,

---

[2] The progress of the expedition was well covered by the press, especially by the Denver papers. As examples: covering the planning, organization, and start of the survey, see Denver *Republican*, May 14, 27, June 5, 1889; Denver *Times*, May 20, 1889. Technical periodicals also reported progress. See *Engineering News and American Railway Journal* (New York), June 8, 1889. Indeed, a complete history of the railroad survey would have to be based, in some measure, on reporting in the Denver press. See Dwight L. Smith, "The Nims and Czar Incidents in the Denver Press," *Colorado Magazine*, 48 (Winter, 1971), 49–58.

From Denver the expedition shipped on the Denver and Rio Grande Western Railroad to Green River station at Blake Post Office (later Green River P.O.) in Utah, the point of embarkation. Here, between two canyon systems, the Green River flows through an open valley. Building its line westward toward Salt Lake City, the railroad had bridged the stream in 1883, an important crossing known to Indians and for over fifty years to a succession of trappers, traders, settlers, and military explorers.

The boats were pitifully inadequate and there were *no life preservers*. Despite these serious deficiencies, Stanton did not feel he could overrule Frank Brown, the company president, and the expedition set forth. The plan was to float the Green River to its mouth and there tie in with the railroad survey which had been brought down the Colorado River to that point by Frank C. Kendrick. See note 6 below. Along the way, however, we see that the engineer made note of the possibilities of railroad building through the canyons of the Green River.

and loaded them full of stores and screwed down tight. All moved off smoothly. The postmaster took photo and about all the village, male and female, came out to see us start.

Boats all in good order, except *Brown Betty*, old boat, which is leaking all round her top lap. Gibson and Richards quite alarmed as they have the raft in tow. Old boat leaks badly. 1:30, hauled [it] up on shore and unloaded and carefully caulked the *Brown Betty*. Used flour and lard for *"dope."*

3 P.M., started again, at 4, came to our first small rapid. Five boats east side. Water shallow, rocks. *Denver* stuck on rocks and stove 3 holes in her bottom. All hands jumped into river and carried rest of fleet over safely.

Camp No. 2. Camped at 5 P.M. on left bank almost if not exactly in spot of Powell's camp July 13th '69.

President Brown not seeing us while repairing boat. Started back to find us. We passed him on opposite side of *Island*, so he came into camp late. President B. with the *Ward* ran rapids on west side of river. Came through safely. These are the "Whirlpool Rapids" or "Devils Corkscrew."

Open country, low bluff and good railway line on either side with light work on bottoms and flat *bluff* with long swinging curves. Beautiful alignment.

MAY 26. Left camp 8 A.M. Floated down river without incident except several very small rapids. All easy. Brown ran the *Ward* against gravel bottom in one shallow place. *No* damage. Noted all Powell's points as described in his book.

11:30, stop to take photo and eat lunch. 12 noon, started again. 1:30 P.M. at "Home Ranche." Four men at river. Stopped long enough to send order back to Denver for supplies to meet us at Lee's Ferry, and write short notes home. "Home Ranche" 1/2 mile below mouth of San Rafael River coming in from west.

About 8 miles further on passed "Trin Alcove Bend" opposite where Powell camped July 14, '69. In flat opposite Trin Alcove we started up 3 deer; 2 went in river and swam to talus below. Brown shot at them, and drove them back into river. My boat, *Mason*, came up and Howard killed one, as it came out of river onto talus, with his revolver.

About 4 miles below camped 5:30 on left bank opposite two huge amphitheaters in wall of canyon. This is *Camp No. 3* about 45 miles below Green River bridge.

All our trip today shows good railway line with long sweeps in bends of river, but would require heavy cuts or short tunnels at the *points* of bends to keep good alignment. Through the short canyons there are very few places where there is not a talus where a railway line could be easily constructed, with solid rock, easily taken from cliffs without destroying face of the wall. Quite a portion of the line would be on bottom land in the bends. A good alignment

FIG. 3. Camp in Labyrinth Canyon, Green River. *F. A. Nims.* Engineering Societies Library.

can be gotten by stealing part from the river and building with solid rock. Perhaps one tunnel could be used with advantage, but this can only be settled by survey.

Lunched at 11:30. Camped on sand bar at 5:45 P.M. River rose about one foot and covered upper end of bar and drove the cook from his kitchen and covered up his woodpile. Supper at 7:30. Camp No. 3.

MAY 27. We camped *last night, Camp No. 3,* at upper end of "Labyrinth Canyon." It is not well defined where canyon actually begins, but we were perhaps 5 or 6 miles in the canyon. Opposite our camp were two large amphitheaters. Camp on left bank of river.

Have been all day in Labyrinth Canyon. Nothing remarkable has transpired. Passed around "Bow Knot Bend" from noon to about 2 P.M.

The whole canyon offers a good railway line. Considerably best, as far as I can observe, on the left bank. Through the whole of today's trip there has been a good talus and always on the convex side of the sweeps of the river more or less of a sand shore line, and in many places this has been on both sides. Only in about 1/2 mile of distance have the cliffs come down to the water and in these places the talus at either end was such as to easily form a rock bank in the river. A very good alignment can be secured by stealing room from the river and thus being able to make long swings around the points.

At Bow Knot Bend of course some 8 miles can be cut off by tunnels but where they would be can only be told by actual survey; and whether bridges with the tunnels should be used can only be decided upon by careful location and estimates. Very few points on today's line requiring more than large box culverts for water ways.

Camp No. 4. See Powell, etc., for description of canyon and its scenery.[3]

TUESDAY, MAY 28. Breakfast at 6:00 A.M. Broke camp, 7:45 A.M. Nothing out of the ordinary happened today. All boats came along in good order. Killed one goose and one gosling and caught one large fish.

Our camp last night, No. 4, was about the center of Labyrinth Canyon. Today's ride, the country opens out, the river is broader, and the whole country is much more broken up. The general character of the banks of the river line is that of larger and more open bottoms with sand bottoms covered with willows on *both* sides of river for many miles and always on one side. The talus retains the same character as yesterday except that it is in many places further back from the river and thus with the large sand bottoms giving fine long swings for a railway line.

Tunnels: much distance saved. Quite an amount of distance can be saved by tunnels, when surveys are made. Two miles of cliffs. The whole line today has a fine talus except about two miles of real cliffs down to the water's edge. Part of this will be avoided by the tunnels above referred to and none of it

---

[3] Stanton refers here and previously to Major John Wesley Powell's *Exploration of the Colorado River of the West and its Tributaries Explored in 1869, 1870, 1871 and 1872* (Washington: Government Printing Office, 1875), which he carried along as a guide book. Powell's diary account of his important exploration of the Colorado River from Green River, Wyoming, to the mouth of the Virgin River, below Grand Canyon, takes up the first ten chapters of this book. Although the diary is dated 1869, Powell actually included much data obtained on his second trip through the canyons, 1871–72; he did not acknowledge the second voyage nor the men who composed it. He has been subjected to much criticism for the omission. Stanton himself later became one of Powell's critics.

As head of the first scientific party through the canyons of the Colorado, Powell named many natural features, and his nomenclature has largely been retained. Labyrinth Canyon was Powell's name for the sinuous gorge below Green River crossing. At Bow Knot Bend — a Powell name — the river winds about in a canyon twelve miles long to travel a straight distance of two miles.

difficult to overcome. One cliff is formed by white sandstone between Labyrinth and Stillwater Canyons.

Camped at 5:30 on windy point about 5 or 6 miles in Stillwater Canyon. Supper at 6:00 P.M. Camp No. 5.

Out of Labyrinth Canyon at *one p.m.* 1:30, saw "Butte of the Cross." About 2:30 entered Stillwater Canyon.[4]

N.B. As soon as we got into camp this evening Mr. Brown took me off one side, and went into a long explanation of the connection Mr. *Lawrence* had with the Company and then said that he was very anxious to push this survey through as fast as possible. That he thought it could be made to the A&PRR crossing in 60 days; and that if I would push it through to that point in that time he would give me $10,000. of stock as now capitalized which when the stock was increased to build the line would be quite large.

I thanked him for his offer and assured him that even without any such inducement I, and I believed all the men, would do our utmost to push the work along; but to accomplish it in 60 days was *utterly impossible.* I do not think Mr. Brown has the least idea of the difficulties before us, in getting our outfit over the rapids or the time it will take.

WEDNESDAY, MAY 29. Breakfast at 6:30. Broke camp at 7:30. In a few miles canyon narrows up. The top layer of vertical stratified red sandstone is far back from river, and white sandstone strata almost gone. Cliffs all formed of lower red sandstone and soon close in almost perpendicular to river. While there is not so marked a talus, there is in most places on both sides a narrow sand bottom; and the cliffs are much more rough all the way up thus giving an easy means of constructing embankment with rock from these rough cliffs and room stolen from the river.

10:00 A.M., formation changed back to that of yesterday with good talus on either side formed from lower sandstone ledge. 12 noon, lunch. 1:15, started again.

2:00 P.M., sandstone much harder and for a mile or two gives cliffs down to water with some overhanging. 2:30, another layer of softer sandstone comes in with talus as before. The river is much more in a real canyon than any we have had. And at 3:30 we reach mouth of Green and Grand and go into camp on right or west bank of Grand River. Probably from his description, the same spot where Powell camped on his trip in 1869. Camp No. 6.[5]

---

[4] Stillwater Canyon — another Powell name — adjoins Labyrinth Canyon. Together the two form one continuous canyon extending 120 miles below the railroad bridge at Green River crossing. Sailing along on the quiet water through these canyons, the Brown–Stanton party reached the mouth of the Green River in good time.

[5] Until 1921 the Colorado above the mouth of the Green was known as the Grand River. Feeling that it had proprietary right in the name, the Colorado State Legislature simply changed the name from Grand to Colorado. The Congress went along with the idea

MAY 30, 1889. Commenced survey of line down Colorado River this A.M. by taking true meridian from Polaris at 3:15 A.M. Breakfast, 7 A.M. Unpacked all boats. Left Howard, Coe, and Sutherland to overhaul and repair boats and Hansbrough to dry out and repack all provisions. Nims photographing points around mouth of rivers.

I took out rest of party, adjusted all instruments, triangulated the positions and courses of the three rivers during A.M. P.M. corrected lines with true meridian and started real railway survey on left bank of Colorado opposite Kendrick's Station 8489 + 50. Ran to 8524 +. The whole of this line is on smooth shore line from 50 to 150 feet wide. This shore is possibly about high water. Drift on lower edge. Good grass. Easy grading only necessary to raise embankment two or three feet. Drainage from hill very light. Flat at Station 8520 + ? Shows smooth sand channel and no wash.[6]

---

and wrote it into Federal Law July 25, 1921. The confluence of the two rivers marks the head of Cataract Canyon.

[6] Now in a flurry of activity, Stanton jumped right in to the business at hand. As noted, the railroad survey actually began at Grand Junction, Colorado. It was run down to the mouth of the Green River by Frank C. Kendrick, who set the first stake on March 28, 1889. He reached the Green on May 4. On a large "Red Sand Stone" on the "Y" between the rivers, Kendrick marked his last survey station this way:

Sta. 8489+50
DCC & PRR
May 4th 1889

Stanton tied in with this point (but started across the river on the left bank) and carried the "real" railroad survey on downstream. The Kendrick diary, edited by Helen J. Stiles, has been published, "Down the Colorado in 1889," *Colorado Magazine*, 46 (Summer, 1964), 225–246. Inscriptions on the rocks are part of the documentation of Colorado River history. Kendrick's marking on the "Red Sand Stone" was still visible in 1911 when the Kolbs saw it. (E. L. Kolb, *Through the Grand Canyon from Wyoming to Mexico* [1914], p. 126.) To complicate the record of the rocks, another inscription, deeply incised, identical in wording with the first, now weathered away, has been found on the right bank some 1250 feet downstream from the forks of the rivers. The distance between survey stations was 100 feet. See O. R. Marston, "For Water-level Rails along the Colorado River," *Colorado Magazine*, 46 (Fall, 1969), 287–303.

The sixth boat of the DCC&PRR fleet was the *Brown Betty*, a pine skiff used by Kendrick and his crew in the survey from Grand Junction. From the mouth of the Green the surveyors laboriously rowed and towed the boat upstream 120 miles to the Green River Crossing where it was pressed into service even though it was leaking badly (See entry for May 25). Only one member of the Kendrick party, T. P. Rigney, joined the Stanton survey crew.

To support their statistics with a visual record for those who might be skeptical about the practicality of building a railroad through the canyons, the DCC & PRR hired Franklin A. Nims to make a complete photographic record of the survey. At the confluence Nims sprang into action with his camera. The photographer's own account of his part in the railroad survey has been edited by Dwight L. Smith, *The Photographer and the River, 1889–1890* (Santa Fe, Stagecoach Press, 1967). Robert B. Stanton, "Engineering with a Camera in the Cañons of the Colorado," *Cosmopolitan Magazine*, XV (July, 1893), 292–303, details the value of a thorough photographic record. To insure this, three cameras were included in the list of equipment. Nims smashed one on June 3.

Back to Camp No. 6 for the night. Hansbrough caught 2 huge fish 20 to 25 lbs., and Brown caught two small ones.

MAY 31. Loaded all boats. I took all party, except Brown, Howard, Hughes, Reynolds, Richards, and Gibson, and resumed line at 9 A.M. Boats passed us about 11:30. River smooth but rapid.

FIG. 4. Looking downstream over the confluence of the Green and Colorado (bottom) rivers. The Kendrick survey ended at the "Y" between the rivers. Opposite that point Robert Stanton picked up the line and carried the survey down the left bank of the Colorado River (1963 Photo). *A. E. Turner*. Bureau of Reclamation.

Line up to Station 8672 on same formation as yesterday with good shore bank in some places 200 feet wide. Very light work. Earth and loose rock, with some large boulders. At one point line in river for 4 to 500 feet. Bank would be 25 to 30 feet high, material easily gotten. Station 8672+50. Cross stream(?) *Side canyon* will require 150 foot span through [broad?] beautiful bottom on south side of this creek, 1500 feet long, 200 to 400 feet wide. At point turned before crossing creek line will perhaps be very much improved by using short tunnel.

At about Station 8696 is head of long rapid. From this point as far as we have run today is a higher and very much rougher hill side, made of *slide* from cliffs above. This slide is cut through by washes, 8 or 10 in number, cut 20 to 30 feet deep and 20 to 50 feet wide on top. These all show very great force of water, and it must come from drainage on *top* of cliffs as we see them. Perhaps two 30 foot spans in this distance will take all the flow by cutting other drains above roadbed to them.

Our line today ended 1/2 mile below head of rapid. So we stop at 4:30. Walk back and cross in our two boats to where Brown has camped at head of rapid on west side. Reach camp at 6:30, *No. 7.*

N.B. Learn of narrow escape of Richards and Gibson and loss of our "float" and about one third of all our provisions in this wise. I instructed Gibson and Richards if they got into swift water and could not manage their boat and float to pull to shore as quick as possible. It seems that this was the case; and they had tied up the "float" and their boat in eddy above rapid, when Brown ordered them to take boat and bring float across the river, above the rapid where he had made camp. They tried to obey but were caught in the swift water when they both jumped out into the river and struggled hard to save the "float"; but finding that they and their boat were about to be carried over the rapid they cut loose the "float" and let her go, and saved themselves and their boat. *No* blame whatever can be attached to the boys.

SATURDAY, JUNE 1. Spend all day making two portages and run and let down by ropes [over] three rapids. The hardest day's work I've known for years. The whole party in water up to their waists half the time, and carrying heavy loads on their back the rest of the day. Went into camp at 7:30 P.M.

Several narrow escapes: While letting down Boat 3, with Hislop in it, the line was let go and Hislop went through the worst of the rapid. Hislop struggled manfully, lost his paddle and was drawn into whirlpool and spun around like a top; and then as if the water had shown what it could do he was thrown up and shot in towards shore. Coe and Howard went out after him in Boat 2 and brought him in safe.

Line broke at same point with Coe's boat but no damage except filled boat with water. I [was] pulled down by line, and knee cut.

7:30 P.M., all safe in camp but tired out. Camp No. 8.

SUNDAY, JUNE 2. In Camp No. 8, *resting*.

Noticed this A.M. that river fell some last night. Perhaps six inches. All the time since we left Green River Station the river has been rising from six inches to one foot each night and was much surprised to see the fall this morning.[7]

MONDAY, JUNE 3. Loaded up all boats and all hands got aboard and ran the rapid just below camp and in fine style landing on left bank. I then took Bush, Hislop, Potter, Nims, Coe, Rigney, and Terry and picked up line at Station 8723+. Mr. Brown took rest of men to move boats down to next camp.

About noon we came up to boats, and found Boat No. 5, *Colorado*, had run against a rock and sunk (no one in) and been under water one hour. Reynolds had swam out and saved the boat, but almost everything was lost, all of Potter's and Sutherland's bedding and clothes. Saved 2 sacks flour, black bag and medicine chest and some dried fruit. One other boat, 4 *Denver*, stove in.

[7] The railroad surveyors were now doing battle with rapids in Cataract, a narrow canyon forty-one miles long. The name is appropriate. The river in the canyon here has been a killer. Probably more people have lost their lives in this canyon than in any other in the Colorado River system. Some of the roughest and wildest water in the system is found here. On the average the river falls about ten feet to the mile, and there are over forty rapids, or more than one to the mile. The deepest of the Colorado canyons in Utah, Cataract measures about 1300 feet in depth at its head and nearly 2000 feet at its mouth. The waters of Lake Powell behind the Glen Canyon Dam have drowned all but the upper fifteen miles of Cataract Canyon.

At the head of the first rapid, four miles below the confluence, trouble began when the "float" was lost. The five cedar skiffs came equipped with water-tight compartments, but these took up room needed for supplies. Solution? Remove the compartments, fill them with supplies and tie them together in a raft to be towed by the *Brown Betty*. See entry for May 25. At best this must have been an awkward and unwieldy arrangement in quiet water. In fast water at the head of the rapid, the "float" got ahead of the boat and the boys cut her loose. The first rapid in Cataract is now called "Brown Betty."

Of course, with no compartments to keep them afloat, the cedar skiffs were highly vulnerable in rough water. After the narrow escapes on June 1 and the back-breaking labor of portaging and lining, the rest on Sunday must have been sweet indeed. The river flow on the Colorado (especially before all the dams were built) generally peaks during the first week or two in June. On June 2 Stanton noted the river level was beginning to drop. This may have been all to the good, since the lower water made portaging and lining somewhat easier. However, we do not know what the flow was at any time during 1889, since mainstream gaging stations had not yet been established. We do know that whatever the stage of water, Brown and Stanton were remarkably lucky to run through Cataract without losing a man. And only two boats were lost. In the unadorned language of his survey notes, May 31–June 22, 1889, Stanton has left us one of the best accounts of a Cataract run. See the literary version of this adventure in Dwight L. Smith, ed., *Down the Colorado* (1965), Chapter IV. The modern river traveler will find Bill Belknap and Buzz Belknap, *Canyonlands River Guide* (1974), with river maps and historic photos, an informative book to take along. The maps, from the head of Cataract Canyon downstream, are based on *Plan and Profile of Colorado River, Lee's Ferry, Arizona, to Mouth of Green River, Utah, and Certain Tributaries*, issued by the U.S. Geological Survey in 1921.

Fig. 5. Under way with the survey in upper Cataract Canyon. Land of Standing Rocks on the skyline. Canyonlands National Park. Miami University Library.

We stopped at 12 noon and helped with boats till 2 P.M. Returned to line at 2 P.M. and ran to 8838 +. Stopped to wait for boats. Nims' photo camera blew over the cliff and smashed up. We have two more.

The whole of the line we ran today has been either over or at the foot of "slides," loose boulders and rock of all sizes cemented together with wash; but judging from a few exposed places, solid formation is but a few feet under surface. Estimate that classifications would be 3/4 solid rock and rest loose rock. The drainage from above is very large, would not put in less than 30 foot openings; but several washes can be carried to one opening.

Quit work at 4 P.M. Waiting for boats. The river has been one continuous rapid now for two miles divided into 9 separate falls.

The damage to our stores by the swamping of one boat is quite serious. Besides the loss of all of Potter's and Sutherland's clothes and blankets, the loss of provisions is quite extensive so that our supplies are being rapidly cut off.

Camped *No. 9*, about opposite Station 8828.

TUESDAY, JUNE 4. All hands stayed with boats, to let them over the rapids with lines. Loaded up all boats and while we were finishing loading up cook boat Brown, Hughes, and Reynolds start off in advance to run the rapid. After going about 1/2 mile their boat, No. 1, *Ward*, was capsized in heaviest rapid and all thrown out. They clung to boat and went down some half mile when they righted her, full of water. Still clung on and were carried down about 1/2 mile when the eddy took them against right bank at cliff. They scrambled out and stayed on rocks, all day, drying out clothes, etc., and night.

Soon after this in swinging boat 5 around point, line broke. Sutherland in her and she was swept about a mile downstream through same rapid as above but went through safely, shipped very little water and landed on left shore. Sutherland quite frightened, but kept his head. Pulled in the loose line and only lost one oar.

One portage nearly all day. In Rapid No. 10 we swing around all the small boats safely, except 5, when the line of our cook boat the *Brown Betty*, being swung round in the same manner that the others had been, caught on rock under water and held her before she got into rapid. She was swinging into shore nicely when the line as mysteriously let go as it had caught, and let her down into the worst part of the rapid next the shore, and against a huge rock. She did not break at once but soon filled with water.

Rigney tied a line around his body and jumped into the boat and unloaded her as far as possible. Hislop also went over and helped. We saved a part of the cook's outfit, but lost all but seven of our plates, all spoons, pans and two camp kettles, the buckets, pans, etc., etc. Saved the three bake ovens, but only one cover, the flying pans and cups and a few sauce pans, etc. Lost nearly all our grub in cook's boat. Tried every way to save the boat but she broke all up and was a total loss.

After this accident we went into Camp No. 10 just 3000 feet beyond Camp No. 9, tired and worn out. Having all of us been in the water, some up to their necks *all day*, nearly everything was wet in one way or another. So we spread out our supplies to dry and found many of them *spoilt* by being wet and in the sun. Dried peaches spoiling. Hominy so bad we had to throw it away and everything in very bad shape.

The matter of supplies till we get to the Dandy Crossing begins to look serious. Had a talk this evening with Hislop and Bush and proposed that Brown and his crew take Terry and push on and get supplies at Dandy Crossing. They both said this met their approval and that they thought we would get along much better and faster if these men were out of camp.

Talked to several of the men and find a good deal of dissatisfaction among them as to the way Mr. Brown is managing the expedition and the way Hughes and Reynolds try to boss the handling of the boats. I will have a talk with all the men at breakfast tomorrow.

WEDNESDAY, JUNE 5. After breakfast, 7 A.M., broke Camp No. 10 and moved down river about a mile, and camped 2 P.M. about center of large flat, one mile long by 1000 feet wide at mouth of side canyon coming in from east. The water was not so bad, still we had to make two portages. Came through without serious accident. Two boats slightly damaged and *Mary*, No. 3, had end completely knocked off. Repaired her while making portages and repaired other boats after reaching camp.

By the boats leaking, *all* our provisions got wet again and I immediately on reaching camp spread everything out to dry and took stock. I find that we have still left about

> 4 weeks' supply of flour; 3 weeks' supply of bacon; 1 week's supply of sugar; 6 weeks' supply of dried fruit; and 6 to 8 weeks' supply of coffee. With enough salt, pepper, etc.

Camp No. 11.

As we started with 75 days' supplies of everything, this looks rather serious. I therefore went to Mr. Brown and proposed that he, Reynolds, and Hughes take one boat and Terry, who is utterly worthless except to eat up our grub, and go in advance to Dandy Crossing and get supplies ready for us. And we would push on as rapidly as possible. Telling him that the men were getting alarmed about our grub and I feared that when the men saw their supplies were getting so low they would abandon the survey, take what was left, and go down river.

He said he would think of it overnight.

Camp tonight is at head of small *rapid*, in large flat about one mile long and for a good part of the distance one thousand feet wide.

THURSDAY, JUNE 6. Mr. Brown told me this morning he could not go down river with one boat, but proposed to divide the party and go down with seven men to Dandy Crossing, get supplies for us, and start new survey there, and leave us to catch up. I told him this would gain nothing except get supplies and would cripple the party and in my opinion would be unwise and foolish; but that the whole object could be accomplished by his boat going on. Neither of us said anything more.

Breakfast at 5:30. Resumed railway survey at 6:30. Passed Camp No. 11 at 9:30. Ran today over 5 miles. Could have made more but stopped at 4:30 to go back to find boats. They were about 2 miles back and 2 miles below last camp. Water had been good to this point and they had come down without accident, except boats leak, more provisions and cook's bedding thoroughly wet. This is Camp No. 12.

The line we have run today has been over rough rock slide, with the exception of the flat at Station 8910 where was Camp No. 11. This flat about one mile long is formed by the wash from two side canyons coming in from east and for a good distance is 1000 feet wide. The greater portion of it is below high water; but I think it would be best to locate line near edge of river on embankment, 25 feet high, so as to reserve this fine piece of land for side track purposes, and by this means much better alignment can be secured. A wide opening must be left in this embankment for waterway for side canyons.

The remainder of today's line on side hill slide is over rough loose rocks and boulders. It does not appear that any solid formation is near surface under this but it is all slide. This will not be difficult to handle but will be classified fully 1/2 solid rock. The drainage over this debris shows a great deal of water at times. Numerous openings will have to be left through. Quite a number can be carried to one. Don't think it safe to make any less than 20 feet wide.

Second flat at Station 9000 and Camp 12 is similar to the former one.

Stopped line today at head of very bad rapid 2 miles below this Camp 12; but the water is very good from here to that point except small rapid just at this camp.

FRIDAY, JUNE 7. Resumed survey A.M. at Station 9078+ at head of bad rapid. Ran about 2 1/2 miles. Stopped at 2 P.M. Have had no dinner. 2:15, Hansbrough comes up with a bucket of bread, corn bread, and bacon, all worked into a mush by being under the river for an hour. We each took a handful of this mixture and "sopped" it up and started back to camp which we found 2 1/2 miles back at the point where we started line this A.M.

We learn that while Bush and Hislop came down from Camp 12 to this point safely early this A.M., when rest of party came down, the cook boat was upset. Lost *all* plates and wet their bedding. Reynolds was sucked down with his boat in whirlpool and Brown had his boat capsized. The only boat coming through safely was our No. 2, *Mason*, with Howard in charge.

Camp 13 tonight is Station 9100.

Our line today was all on side hill slide or debris, loose rock, and huge boulders. Similar to that of yesterday. The drainage is more severe, and will require more openings. It is a very curious fact the great difference in the two sides of the river as to the extent of the talus. While 4 or 5 miles from the head of Colorado River there was little difference though the wider *bottoms* were on left side. From that point on, the left bank has a wide sloping talus from one to four hundred feet wide and with slopes after leaving the immediate edge of river varying from 10° to 45° from horizontal, and in some few places there being an almost level stretch of debris.

On the right bank, however, the talus is very much narrower and in some places it is only 5 to 10 feet wide and the slope is almost always about 45° and in some places steeper. Of course there are some few places with small exceptions, but the rule is generally good down to where we quit work this afternoon.

SATURDAY, JUNE 8. I remained in camp this A.M. to write up notes. Rest of party took two boats and move down 1 3/4 miles and came back to lunch. In P.M. I went with other three boats and moved to same point, making five short portages on each trip. No mishap, all went smoothly except very hard work.

Camp 14 Saturday night is 200 feet up river, left bank, from Rapid No. 27.

SUNDAY, JUNE 9. In Camp No. 14. *Resting.* Mr. Brown's and Gibson's *birthdays.*

MONDAY, JUNE 10. All hands moved boats down river. Had very hard day. *One* long and *two* short portages. Howard and Coe repaired boats with rosin Hansbrough got from pines on top yesterday. Rest of party portage, very long one, of all stores.

Swung boats over rapids with lines. Boat No. 3 got loose, empty. Went down 3/4 mile. Brown caught it in eddy. Boat No. 2 swamped against rock when loaded. Filled with water. Wet all my clothes and blankets, will have to sleep tonight against a rock. Howard and Coe likewise. Lost one large sack peaches and large coffee pot. Other boats leak so got all stores wet again which I dried out so well yesterday.

Went into camp a little beyond the end of our line at Station [*blank*] at 4:30. Just before this Brown and Hughes not satisfied with good day's work attempted to push on over Rapid No. 31. Line got caught in oarlock; swung Boat No. 1 into current. They could not hold her and so she went down. A total loss, including $250.00, transit, 2 sacks flour, 1 keg vinegar, 3 sacks fruit, 1 sack beans, etc., etc.

Brown and Potter followed Boat No. 1 for 3 miles, but saw nothing of it. On the way found *one* of the *five* floats, which were lost June 1st. It was buried in sand in eddy about 30 feet from river, and contained 2 sacks flour, 2 cans tomatoes, soap, 2 sacks fruit, 1 sack meal, and some tobacco, all in pretty good condition. So we are about where we were before Boat No. 1 was lost.

This is Camp No. 15.

The rapids we are now going through are the heaviest we have encountered and are undoubtedly the very bad ones spoken of by Powell, where is the "75 foot drop" in river. Our levels will tell.

Four boats left, 1 down river which we got on June 14th.

TUESDAY, JUNE 11. All hands moving camp again. Brown, Reynolds, and Hughes stayed in camp all forenoon.

Made in all *five* portages today, two very long and 3 short. It was the hardest day's work we have had since starting; men completely worn out at night. All of the party including self in water off and on all day. In A.M. everything moved smoothly and we made good progress.

2 P.M., while swing boats around point, *Mason*, No. 2, was caught in current with so much force that it took the bottom out. Boat saved and can be repaired. Boat No. 3 swamped and my blankets wet again, nothing lost.

Distance made about one mile. Made Camp No. 16 more tired than ever before.

WEDNESDAY, JUNE 12. Reynolds and Hughes start after rosin for boats. All hands moving still further down river; but everyone is so stiff and sore that but little progress can be made. Brown, Howard, and Potter went back to repair No. 2, *Mason*. Finished by noon. I repaired rifle till ten A.M. All being ready I went with men and moved whole outfit 3/4 mile and went back to last camp for lunch because cook had *bean soup* for us.

Everything went smoothly in A.M. but about 2 P.M. Hislop let *Mary*, No. 3, get away from him against a rock and smashed her up pretty badly, loosing our last coffee pot, all but nine cups, all our dried peaches, and one sack of beans. A pretty bad loss in our present condition. We drew her up on shore and loaded up all rest of stuff in our two remaining boats and pushed on.

I went with Boat No. 4 and established Camp No. 17 at Station 9310 about 4:30 P.M. After being in camp 1/2 hour Gibson called out that Boat 5 with Howard was swamped just above camp. We went up and pulled out all we could save and came into camp. Summing up, found my blankets wet, but saved. Howard's sack gone. Caught below later. All bacon, beans, and fruit on No. 5 lost and my level box with medicines, etc., etc. Rather a bad disaster to wind up the day with.

Potter, however, reports finding two more "floats" intact and one broken up. At once three men Hislop, Coe, and Potter took boat and crossing river, went up 1 1/4 miles and brought floats to camp: 2 sacks flour, coffee, syrup, 2 kegs pickles, 12 cans condensed milk. A good find.

THURSDAY, JUNE 13. Breakfast rather late, 7:30. Survey party started back to resume line. Breakfasted on flapjacks, syrup, and coffee. Walk about 2 1/2 miles. Line resumed 9:30 at Station 9201 +. Worst line work we have had. Work to Camp No. 17. Dinner 3 P.M. Tomato soup, bread, apples, and coffee. 4:30, resume line and run 1 1/10 miles. Stop 6:15. Late supper, 8 P.M.

Line today is the heaviest work we have yet encountered. The heavy slides have been cut into by the river, and being so cemented together, stand in almost perpendicular bluffs and are very high above the river. They are also cut very deep by drainage from above the cliffs, thus making the work quite heavy. The river in some places has washed these slides out far back to the cliff. This again makes heavy work; but a good alignment can be gotten by making good banks through the bends or rather *bays* of the river from the material from the cuts through these high slopes.

The line of today was run too high. This on account of my supposing that these rapids were where Powell's "75 foot fall in 3/4 mile" came. But on getting the levels this evening I find that the fall is only about 55 feet in *two miles*, so that I can easily maintain my 16 feet per mile as a maximum grade.[8]

While in Camp 17 at dinner I with cook took stock of all provisions and found:

> No meat; 5 lbs. dried fruit; 6 sacks flour, when sifted will make *three* 150 lbs. and no more; 2 weeks' coffee; 12 cans condensed milk; 10 lbs. beans; 6 cans tomatoes; 30 lbs. lard; 2 lbs. baking powder; Salt, pepper, etc.

Coming home from work Sutherland found 1/2 barrel 1/2 full white *lump sugar*.

This is pretty slim for sixteen men and will not last even with *short* allowance for six days. Mr. Brown does not seem to grasp the situation *in the least*, but goes on as if we had two months' supplies in camp. He seemed much surprised when I started out after dinner, 4:30, to run more line and was thunderstruck when I suggested that he and the rest of the men go up river about 1/2 mile and bring down the *Mary* this evening. They did nothing more but at dark all howled for supper. This making *four* meals for Reynolds and Hughes today. Should have noted that Brown with Howard and Nims went up river and repaired *Mason*, No. 2, and brought her to Camp 16 about 4:15.

---

[8] By the time they reached Camp 17 (now at the upper end of Lake Powell at full pool), about 15.5 miles below the confluence of the Green and Colorado rivers, the Brown–Stanton party, one way or another, had passed twenty-five rapids, including two of the worst. One almost continuous series, beginning at 11.5 miles below the confluence, is now named "Mile Long Rapids." At another place, starting about two miles above Camp 17, within the distance of less than a mile, the Colorado falls about thirty-five feet in a series of three rapids collectively known to river men today as the "Big Drop." At this point Powell had written in his *Exploration* (1875), 62, that the river dropped seventy-five feet. However, in his 1869 journal written on the spot, and not published until recently, Powell gave the drop as forty-two feet, a figure closer to the mark. See W. C. Darrah, ed., "Major Powell's Journal, July 2–August 28, 1869," *Utah Historical Quarterly*, 15 (1947), 125–131. With transit and level at hand, Stanton had found an exaggeration in Powell's 1875 report. In later years, turned historian of the Colorado, the engineer was rather tediously critical of this and other distortions he found in Powell's writings about the river. See J. M. Chalfant, ed., *Colorado River Controversies* (1932, reprinted 1982), and footnote 7, Chapter X.

For the place Cataract holds in river running history, and especially that of its major rapid, the Big Drop, see R. O. Collins and R. Nash, *The Big Drops, Ten Legendary Rapids* (1978), Chapter Five, entitled "Satan's Gut," the name applied by river men to the third in the series of rapids in the Big Drop.

For the purpose of modern orientation, the Big Drop is directly on the imaginary boundary between Canyonlands National Park (upstream) and Glen Canyon National Recreation Area.

After supper about 9:00 P.M. I took Brown aside and explained the situation that we did not have six days' provisions in camp; and if we went on as we were and as he proposed — all hands stay in camp to repair boats and then move down together, etc. — that we would all be hungry before we got out of the canyon to the placer mines and Dandy Crossing. He was very much surprised and seemed dazed. I told him I would take 5 men besides myself, take our share of the stores, cooked, and put them on our backs and run the line to the placers, and leave him 10 men to repair boats and overtake us. Thus gaining a great deal of time for our work where the water was rough, etc., etc.

Brown seemed to wake up when he saw my determination, and said if I thought I was able, to go on and do as I thought best, and that he would stir up the rest of the men and "run us a race." I then went to the mens' beds and asked each one that I wanted if they would go with me and all said promptly "Yes." I will take Hislop, Coe, Rigney, Potter, and Hansbrough.

FRIDAY, JUNE 14. Up early. Woke cook 4 A.M. and ordered him to cook up at once 3/8 of all flour in camp. Brown and Howard went to repair boats after breakfast.

At 9:00 A.M. all was ready. We had 10 cakes of bread about 10 and 12 inches in diameter and 1 1/2 inches thick. This divided between 6 men gave 1 2/3 cakes to each man. At 9:00 A.M. we started with our packs on our backs, Hislop, Coe, Rigney, Potter, Hansbrough, and myself. We each stopped as we passed and took in our sacks some of the government sugar found on the river bank yesterday.

We reached end of line at 10 o'clock. Lost 1/2 hour by Potter mislaying his sack when he went to show Hansbrough his back sight. Ran 3 miles less 700 feet and camped in broad bottom. A great relief from the narrow canyon we were in all day.

Our rations being very short we lunched today on *three lumps sugar* and *plenty* of river water. For supper I took 1/6 of my loaf with a cup of hot water and condensed milk.

This camp we call *Bivouac No. 1*.

The line today has been through the narrowest canyon we have yet met. River from 200 to 300 feet wide. The talus on left side is still the largest and is best for a railway line. It is quite rough and some small cliffs come down near to the river making the work quite heavy. In other places the debris is cut by the river straight up and down like a cliff though it is composed of large and small stones and boulders cemented together, so that there would have to be some pretty heavy cuts to make a permanent roadway.

In about 2 1/2 miles from where we started this A.M., Station 9368+, the cliffs break away on the left leaving a large rough flat, mostly covered with boulders, about 1 1/2 miles long and from 500 to 1000 feet wide. About center of this flat a side canyon comes in, showing a very large waterway, 100 foot span bridge, and at end of flat river turns sharply to west.

As we came down we saw on other side of river the last "float." Left note for men with boats and discovered No. 1, *Ward* boat, on other side of river also.

SATURDAY, JUNE 15. After an early breakfast we started line just at camp. Breakfast consisted of 1/6 of loaf bread, 2 cups of coffee, and one lump of sugar. Ran 2 3/4 miles by noon. 2 lumps sugar and *plenty* of water for lunch.

Ran 1/2 mile and came upon an impassable cliff, i.e., an *almost* perpendicular cliff rising out of the water with a very swift rapid running at its base. Near the water line was a broken shelf undermined in the cliff. We tried to go along it but it was impossible. I then took the transit and level rodsmen and started to go over the top. There was no bench that was passable to pass along short of 300 feet high. Started 3 P.M. Wandered along cliff this bench till 6:00 o'clock before we found a way down. When after great labor and much danger we did get to the river.

Spring. We had not had a drink since one o'clock, when about 5:00 we discovered a beautiful cove, high up with beautiful shrubbery of all kinds and a fine living spring. We drank fully and starting down reached river 5:30 P.M. We then tried to go up river where instrument could see us. We found it impossible for we were below *Two Cliffs* and it was impossible to get down between the two so as to get in sight of our other boys. We therefore bivouacked on the river below the cliff by ourselves at 7:00 P.M.

Fortunately our level rodman brought his *grub sack* over the hill with him and we had our supper. In his sack he had brought a can of tomatoes. We ate them cold and famished as we were I never tasted anything better.

SUNDAY, JUNE 16. After breakfast this morning we make another attempt to get along the cliff to a point where the transitman can see us, but after working hard for two hours we give it up as impossible without a boat. We three Potter, Rigney, and myself then start back over the cliff to join the other boys. When on top we meet them Coe, Hansbrough, and Hislop coming to hunt us. We all go back to where instruments are and then decide to leave them there, and go back to where we saw Boat No. 1 on other bank of river, get her and then proceed with the survey.

When about 1 mile back, met Howard and saw various things, bags, blankets, etc., floating down river. Howard told us the whole party were about 2 miles up river, coming on, that Bush and Hughes had lost the boat *Denver* and he was after it. In its load was Bush's transit, and all sorts of other things including one sack flour.

Fig. 6. Sketch of cross section of Cataract Canyon at Camp 20. Miami University Library.

Meet whole party at our Bivouac No. 1, about noon. They had come down from Camp No. 17 in the last day and a half, with very hard work, making five portages on Saturday and three today. They had torn up the *Mary* in order to get material to repair the other boats. This affected Brown very much as the boat was named for his wife and he cried before the whole party. The men went over river and got boat *Ward*, No. 1. Found it little damaged. Went also for the last "float," but found it broken and *empty*.

Hislop got nice fish on beach which we had for supper. I was quite disgusted with the way things were going. Ordered cook to cook up at once everything in camp. And then sat down for a rest.

There is great grumbling in camp. The men threaten to take boats and leave down river for grub. After supper I divide all the grub between the men, and give each 1 1/2 loaf bread about 12 inches in diameter and 1 inch thick, with no baking powder or salt. One can condensed milk, a little coffee, and a handful of beans. They seem thunderstruck.

I determine to remain with this amount of grub and as many men as will stay, and finish the survey out of canyon, while Brown goes ahead and gets provisions to send back to us. This is Camp No. 19.

After supper, Brown called me aside and said he intended to have a confidential talk with me, and he believed this was the proper time. He then explained why he was in such a hurry to get the survey through, and why he had spoken to me before and *made* the offer [he] had, saying that he was under an engagement to be in New York by August 15th to meet a syndicate of New York men, who represented $50,000,000. who had agreed to take hold of the building of this road if the engineer's report was favorable. That they had agreed to wait in New York till August 25th before going on their summer trips in their yachts and hence it was of utmost importance on reaching Dandy Crossing to drop the instrumental survey and push on to the A&P Road so that I could make a report to these men from an "eye survey" of the remainder of the route.

I then told him I of course understood the situation and would push on after I had completed the survey to Dandy Crossing. But that I would recommend a separation of the party at that time. Leave Bush with four men to continue instrumental survey at least as far as Lee's Ferry and we with six men go through to the "Needles." I told Brown my determination to stay and finish the survey. He was very particular to say he would not ask me to stay, nor would he ask anyone to stay and work without enough to eat; but that if we did stay he would hurry back grub to us even if he had to carry a sack of flour on his shoulder up the river.

MONDAY, JUNE 17. Brown will go ahead for grub this morning with one boat and send us back supplies as quick as possible.

Had talk with Hislop and find men had conference last night and are nearly all determined to go out at once, and to induce *all* the men to go, so as to prevent *me* from staying in order to place upon *me* the responsibility of leaving the survey. Coe seems to be at the head of this attempt. Hislop says there is no need of being scared or leaving the line and will stay with me; and after inquiry I find that all will go except Hislop, Potter, and our two colored boys, Richards and Gibson. Some of the other men were very much chagrined at this finding they could not drive me out and did all in their power to get me to go. Sent Hansbrough to plead with me and went to my men, especially Potter, and tried to induce them to leave me.

All start about 7 A.M., we five to the line and the rest "running from hunger to grub." About noon we reach the cliff. We have one boat. Cross the river in two loads. Triangulate around cliff and go into camp early on sand bar opposite cliff. We made five portages today, last one at this Camp No. 20.

Brown and all the scared men reached this point a little before we did and in crossing river swamped one of the boats and lost 3 of the mens' sacks of grub. This seemed to frighten them more and they threw away almost everything they had, blankets, clothing, etc., etc., and started down the river like scared dogs with their tails between their legs!!

We triangulate around cliff as stated, this afternoon, turning angles to various points on the cliff so as to fix its position. It is 500 feet high perpendicular from water and then benches back in easy benches to the top. This is the first perpendicular cliff we have met more than 40 to fifty feet high. It will require a tunnel of from 1500 to 1000 feet to make good alignment but handling in this way will not be a difficult point. The material from tunnel can all be utilized on line beyond. Grade around this point must be kept quite high above high water as the canyon being so narrow here if filled up at all by railroad it will raise the water.

TUESDAY, JUNE 18. Start work at [*blank*], Station [*blank*] and reach Station [*blank*]. Camp No. 21 at Station 9868.

Everything went smoothly today except only having one boat we came near being badly caught. Potter and the two boys went ahead and after setting point beyond a long cliff in the river, could not get the boat back to us. So Hislop and I started up a side canyon and after a hard hour's work succeeded in climbing along the cliff 100 feet above river and got down to the boat. Having only one boat delays our work very much. Made *two* portages today, one carried boat around also.

Camped P.M. No. 21.

WEDNESDAY, JUNE 19. Camped last night on sand flat at mouth of side canyon on left bank of river, at Station 9868 + at Rapid No. 61, where Brown and party camped last night.

Up at 4:30. Pack up. Breakfast 5:30. Resume work at 6:30 while the men repair boat. Ran today good line. Station 9888 + to 10104, 216 stations.

Were delayed 1 1/2 hours by Hislop leaving his grub sack. All went smooth till we got to Station 10090 + when the river filled the canyon from side to side; and on our side the bottom part of the cliff about 100 feet high overhung the river. The only way to get our line run was by triangulation. This we did for one sight, 1333 feet; but on getting to that point we found it impossible to get any point further on, except to cross the river. At this point it would have been very dangerous with all our load, instruments, and five men, etc. So I determined not to do it, and went on down past the small rapid we were at, saying to the boys, "This ends the Survey." Everyone seemed quite sad. Potter's jaw fell in sorrow, and even the colored boys looked disappointed.

We drifted down with great care and in about 1/2 mile found good camp, No. 22, and at the same moment rounding a sharp point we saw what seemed to be open country ahead with the setting sun shining on the cliffs beyond. It was such a glorious sight after being shut up so long in the narrow canyon, that it seemed to inspire everyone; and Potter and the boys spoke up at once and said, "We will go back in morning and bring line down." We supposed the open place we saw was "Mille Crag Bend." Made one portage today. Camp No. 22.[9]

[9] Below the Big Drop the walls of Cataract Canyon become steeper and higher, and the river narrower. Stanton's confidence in the feasibility of building a railroad line through the canyon is certainly tested through this section where the cliffs, in some places rising directly from the water's edge, tower upward in a series of narrow steps nearly two thousand feet. The man's determination to carry on with the work is evident in every paragraph of his notes. On June 13, Stanton convinced Brown that the instrumental survey must be continued to Dandy Crossing even though the food was nearly gone, the crews were grumbling, equipment had been lost, and the boats were battered and broken. To save time Stanton would continue the line. Brown would repair the boats and catch up, and thus they would "race" to the crossing. Even when mutiny threatened on June 16, Stanton would not give

THURSDAY, JUNE 20. Immediately after breakfast Hislop, Potter, and I took empty boat and went up and across the river, to bring down our line. About a quarter of a mile above our camp, point fixed by transit later, I discovered cut in the solid rock of the canyon's side the following: "1836 D. Julien".

This inscription was cut in the deepest portion 1/4 inch deep. Was cut on the smooth face of the solid cliff at a point where the first bench of the cliff was about 30 feet high above the present water; and where it is overhung, the river [is] 6 or 8 feet. It was in a position where it could have only been cut there from a boat. It could not have been reached in any other way. It seemed to have been cut with a dull round ended center punch.[10]

We finish our survey to camp, load up and go on. All being happy at the fact of our getting our line along. Gibson started out early to hunt. When we got to the flat below we found it was not the end of the canyon but only a bend letting in the sun last evening; but we were well satisfied as we were getting along so well.

2 P.M., we come to very bad rapid. Find note from Brown. Run line as far past rapid as we could, and then took a point down the river to a rock on the bank. We then set up a pole with stadia marks on it 28 feet high, and left it to take sight on when we got to end. Made portage of stuff. Swung boats past worst part of rapid. Hislop and Potter took the boat down rest of rapid, which is very long and is undoubtedly the 1/2 mile chute with marble floor that Powell describes in his diary. But it was too high water to see it. 5:30 P.M., our provisions being so very valuable to us just now we will not trust them to the boat. So Richards, Gibson, and myself carry *all* the grub and instruments over the cliff past the rapid, which fills the river from cliff to cliff. Made 2 portages in all today.

---

up. Next morning, with four volunteers, each carrying his meager food ration in a sack, Stanton started out — "we five to the line" — while Brown headed up the rest of the party, those "running from hunger to grub." Brown would send back relief provisions from the crossing.

At Camp 22, 31.5 miles below the confluence, Stanton's survey party found itself beyond the gloomy, narrow part of Cataract Canyon. The rays of the setting sun on downstream cliffs, to all hands were glorious and inspirational. Mille Crag Bend was out of sight, farther downstream.

[10] The inscription discovered by Stanton has rarely been seen since. In April 1964, the late Otis R. Marston located it on the left side of the river thirty-one miles downstream from the confluence. D. Julien, who left his name inscribed at three places along the Green River, above its mouth has been identified by Charles Kelly, "The Mysterious 'D. Julien'," *Utah Historical Quarterly*, VI (July 1933), 83–88. The Julien inscriptions, all dated 1836, are documents of the fur-trapping era in the Rocky Mountains which reached its peak during the years between 1820 and 1840. That the trappers entered the great canyons of the Colorado after furs seems without question, though little evidence has been found to document this activity. Robert G. Cleland's *Reckless Breed of Men, the Trappers and Fur Traders of the Southwest* (New York, Alfred A. Knopf, 1952) is an excellent summary.

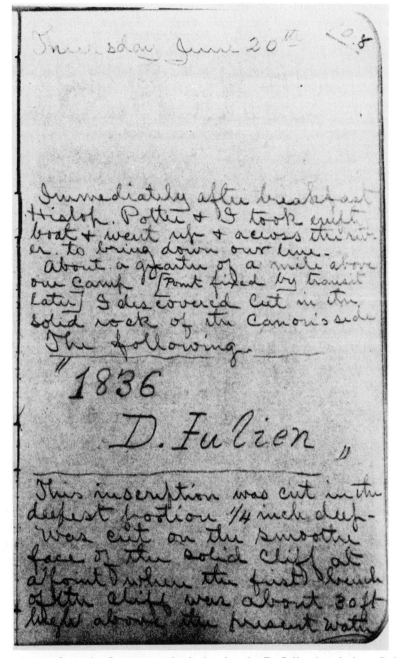

Fig. 7. A page from the Stanton notebook showing the D. Julien inscription. *Robert B. Stanton.* New York Public Library.

At 6:30 we come down the hill and meet Howard, who with Coe and Hansbrough have come back from Dandy Crossing, which they reached yesterday noon, with plenty of supplies. Howard is in great glee over plenty of "grub" but I feel sore over what passed last Monday and so remark that I don't care as much for grub as I do other things, which offends Howard. Hislop appreciates my feelings and we shake hands over our prospect of completing the line.

We go into Camp No. 23. Potter stuffs himself and is sick. Hislop is moderate. I eat two cakes, griddlecakes, and drink one cup of coffee, and go to bed.

FRIDAY, JUNE 21. We start early. Have now two boats, and so skip along. I ride nearly all day. Easiest day I've had since we reached the Colorado. Howard is glum all day. Go into Camp No. 24 at upper end of Mille Crag Bend.

SATURDAY, JUNE 22. Camped last night at upper end of Powell's Mille Crag Bend at Station 10580. Intended to take an observation on the North Star last night but slept too soundly so did not wake up.

It is rather curious, the effect of having as much food as one wants after living for six days on about *1/4 rations* of solid food for *six days*. At our first full supper Thursday night, I ate little, being very careful; but yesterday I ate all I wanted and last night and today I feel perfectly worn out tired and listless. It must be the effect of the stronger food getting into my system.

We resumed work at 6:30 A.M. About a mile and a quarter below, in upper end of Narrow Canyon, found two white sulphur springs. Warm spring on left bank and cold on right bank. Ran little over six miles and are camped tonight on right bank of river at two large sulphur springs and one iron, etc., etc., spring.

We should have made 7 or 8 miles today except that Hislop made mistake on one angle and we had to go back; and in P.M. Potter got rattled on account of signals. So in all we lost about 2 1/2 hours.

The cliffs today have been getting lower and lower and on account of the upper strata of sandstone coming down, the talus is much less, and the first bench of the cliff runs into the water in many places without talus. The cliffs are craggy and easily broken and there is always plenty of room in river for good line with easy alignment. All this work however will be solid rock classification.

Camp No. 25.

SUNDAY, JUNE 23. In camp at sulphur springs on right bank of river, about one mile above Dirty Devil River. Resting in Camp No. 25.[11]

---

[11] On June 20, Stanton and company passed the "very bad" rapid at the mouth of Dark Canyon, the last and one of the heaviest rapids in Cataract. Before the day was out, the

About 6 P.M. Mr. Brown came up from the camp at Dandy Crossing. Was very glad to see us. Had a long talk with him. Seems the men are pretty well demoralized and have been talking a great deal too much. I told him if he would leave the arrangement of the men to me I would straighten all out and for the best interests of all. He said go ahead.

MONDAY, JUNE 24. Up at 4:30. Breakfast at 5:30. On line at 6:00 A.M. Ran 7 3/4 miles to Dandy Crossing and quit work at 6:00 P.M.

Our camp last night was at sulphur and iron springs about 1 1/2 miles above mouth of Dirty Devil River, at end of narrow canyon. Passed this about 8:30. Ran line on high sandstone bench 40 to 60 feet above river on which we saw the first of the placer mines. These gravel beds are high and dry above the river. Must have been a former bed of river. The low gravel and sand bars now in river also prospect well.

We went across river to Hite City for Camp No. 26. Found all the rest of the men and mail from home.[12]

---

relief party arrived and the worst was over. Powell had named Mille Crag Bend (many high crags and pinnacles on the inside of the bend), a sharp, U-shaped bend in the Colorado marking the end of Cataract Canyon and the beginning of Narrow Canyon (also named by Powell), a short, narrow canyon about six miles long, ending at the Dirty Devil River. The towering cliffs of Cataract Canyon had now been left behind. The walls of Narrow Canyon drop down to less than 200 feet at the mouth of the Dirty Devil.

[12] The instrumental railroad survey through Cataract and Narrow Canyons to Dandy Crossing was a remarkable achievement. The Denver, Colorado Canyon and Pacific Railroad had hired an engineer capable of dealing with man and nature in all of their varied aspects, and with enough determination and fortitude to carry the job through to the end.

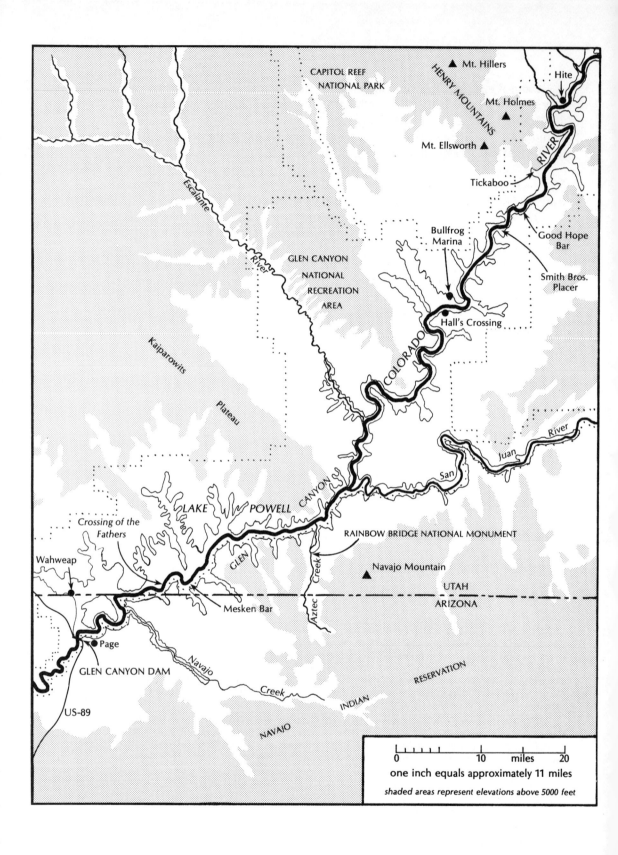

CAPITOL REEF
NATIONAL PARK

▲ Mt. Hillers

Hite

HENRY MOUNTAINS

Mt. Holmes ▲

Mt. Ellsworth ▲

RIVER

Tickaboo

Escalante

GLEN CANYON
NATIONAL
RECREATION
AREA

Bullfrog
Marina

Good Hope
Bar

River

Smith Bros.
Placer

Hall's Crossing

Kaiparowits

COLORADO

Plateau

River

Juan

San

LAKE   POWELL

Crossing of the
Fathers

RAINBOW BRIDGE NATIONAL MONUMENT

Wahweap

GLEN

CANYON

Creek

Navajo Mountain ▲

UTAH

Aztec

Mesken Bar

ARIZONA

Page

Navajo

RESERVATION

GLEN CANYON DAM

Creek

INDIAN

US-89

NAVAJO

0   10   miles   20

one inch equals approximately 11 miles

shaded areas represent elevations above 5000 feet

CHAPTER II

GLEN CANYON SURVEY

With the rapids of Cataract Canyon behind them the Brown–Stanton expedition arrived at Hite near the head of Glen Canyon, whose quiet waters extended from the mouth of the Dirty Devil to Lee's Ferry, a distance of 169 miles. Here there were food and supplies and other men to talk to. There were primitive roads in to Hite from both sides of the river and a crossing which Cass Hite, the canyon promoter, had called Dandy Crossing. Gold had been discovered in the riparian gravel bars in Glen Canyon and a rush to the new diggings was at its height in 1889. A post office had just been opened to serve the prospectors working along the river.

Brown and Stanton took note of these things and then with one crew they hurried on to "eye-survey" the railroad route through Glen Canyon. The other party was assigned to follow along after them carrying on with the instrumental survey. Stanton soon found that railroad building in Glen Canyon with its perpendicular cliffs and wide sweeping bends was going to be difficult and costly. In Cataract, by contrast, the comparatively straight course of the river and the ledgy, craggy walls of the canyon offered few obstacles to economical construction.

[Hite Post Office at Dandy Crossing, June 24, 1889.][1]

    Notes furnished by the men at Dandy Crossing:

    The placer mines are all taken up but no work is being done on them at this point. Men simply sitting down and holding their claims.

---

[1] The mouth of the Dirty Devil River, named by Powell in 1869, is the upper limit of Glen Canyon (another Powell name) extending downstream 169.5 miles to Lee's Ferry. The Glen Canyon dam, fifteen miles above Lee's Ferry, has formed Lake Powell, which has flooded the entire canyon above the dam, as well as all of Narrow Canyon and over half of Cataract Canyon.

Placer gold was discovered in the upper part of Glen Canyon by Cass Hite in 1883. A rush of prospectors soon followed and the excitement with some ups and down lasted until about 1914. The principal community in Glen Canyon was Hite, at Dandy Crossing of the

Everyone in this country is highly interested in the road.

We have been greatly surprised at what is told us as to the resources of this country that will give the road local business. It is stated, and from what I think with truth, that there are some 25,000,000 cubic yards of pay gravel that will net 25 cents per yard between the mouth of Cataract Canyon and the San Juan River. These bars are what are on the bluffs above the river and do not include the bars in the river.

The cattle interests: We are told that there are over 200,000 head of cattle from Little Grand Valley on the Grand River to lower end of Cataract Canyon within from 30 to 40 miles of the Colorado River. And they say that the rest of the river country is as heavily stocked. They estimate that there are now from one, to one and one half million cattle tributary to this river which would use this road, especially as it would be along a river so as to have plenty of water.

Government reports give the great extent of timber but it is remarkable to learn that the upper part of Dark Canyon is covered with sugar maple trees, and that last fall one man made 3000 lbs. of sugar from them.

Coal has been discovered in many places. In 15 miles of Dandy Crossing veins of from 6 to 22 feet thick are being opened.[2]

TUESDAY, JUNE 25. Since the men got here and have had nothing to do they have of course talked and seem to be very much dissatisfied. I talked with Bush and he talked like a fool.

Neither I nor Brown want Coe and Howard to go together with us any further. I want Howard. So in arranging for the survey I have given Coe the transit. Had a talk with Howard. Explained situation and asked him to go

---

Colorado River near the head of the canyon. The crossing was accessible from the west by way of the tributary canyons of North Wash and Trachyte Creek, and from the east by way of White Canyon. A post office had been established at Hite in 1889 just a short time before the Brown–Stanton party arrived. The gold rush to Glen Canyon is detailed in C. Gregory Crampton, *Standing Up Country, The Canyon Lands of Utah and Arizona* (New York: Alfred A. Knopf, and the University of Utah Press in Association with the Amon Carter Museum of Western Art, 1964). Crampton's "Historical Sites in Cataract and Narrow Canyons, and in Glen Canyon to California Bar," *University of Utah Anthropological Papers*, 72 (1964), describes the places now submerged by Lake Powell. Two additional titles by the same author, "Historical Sites in Glen Canyon Mouth of Hansen Creek to Mouth of San Juan River," and "Historical Sites in Glen Canyon Mouth of San Juan River to Lee's Ferry." *University of Utah Anthropological Papers*, 61 (1962), and 46 (1960), respectively, describe sites through the remainder of the canyon.

[2] Stanton's informants at Hite gave him ample figures. The best placer gold deposits in Glen Canyon were found on gravel-capped benches alongside the river ranging above it from a few feet to several hundred feet. It is doubtful if many placer deposits ran consistently as high as twenty-five cents in gold per cubic yard of gravel. The figures for cattle are too high. The sugar maple story was a yarn spun for one who was willing to listen. See Stanton's entry for July 3, and for similar information noted by Frank M. Brown, see note 13 below.

Fɪɢ. 8. Prehistoric ruin — Stanton's Moqui Fort — built by the Anasazi Indians in the twelfth century. *F. A. Nims.* Miami University Library.

with us and leave Coe with the survey. Promising him if he would do me this personal favor I would give Coe the transit and him the level in first party sent on location. In evening they declined to do it. Coe wants to go down Grand Canyon. So I will leave them both with Bush.

In afternoon went across river to see old Moqui Fort. This is the square building laid in mortar described by Powell. It was originally four walls about 8′×12′ inside; two stories about 6 to 6 1/2 feet with loopholes pointing every direction, varying in height, but those in lower room in two irregular rows, one 3′4″ and other 3′8″ above floor. The angles at corner of fort are very square and line of corner very straight; but the laying up of the walls is very poor, continuous joints within 15 inches of corner run up them to four feet although the walls are laid up with thin slabs of stone.

Many cliff dwellers' houses are in neighborhood, are very rude and show same defective work, etc., etc. The "mortar" spoken of by Powell is simply mud mixed with small rock.[3]

---

[3] Before flooding by Lake Powell there were many evidences of prehistoric man visible in the vicinity of Dandy Crossing. These consisted of petrographic art and structures in ruins.

In Camp No. 26 fixing up notes, letters, etc., to send to railroad by wagon from here tomorrow.[4]

Bush, Coe, Rigney, and Sutherland, running the line, on other side of river. Coe and Howard told Bush they would not be separated. I had long talk with Bush, told him they could then stay with him. But that under other circumstances I would settle all this trouble by at once discharging every man in the whole outfit. But as this is a peculiar trip and the future of the road is uncertain I will try to make things as smooth and pleasant as I can.

WEDNESDAY, JUNE 26. For the reasons explained by Mr. Brown, we will change our future plans. Rigney and Terry leave the party. Bush, Coe, Howard, Potter, and Sutherland will remain and carry survey as far as Lee's Ferry and then go out. Mr. Brown, myself, Hislop, Hansbrough, Richards, Gibson, and [Harry] McDonald, whom we have hired here, will take three boats, go to Tickaboo Placer 15 miles below here, repair them, and push as rapidly as possible to the Needles, making an "eye survey" for my report.

After fixing up matters as well as possible with the boys and getting all supplies we can at store we start, at 8:30, for Tickaboo!!

Wide bottom on right. On left, low bluffs coming to water's edge. Little talus but sloping back thus easy.

8:35 A.M., Rapid No. 79. Ran it. 8:45 A.M., Rapid Trachyte No. 80. Ran it.

At point to left just beyond rapid, bluff breaks up and looks like red *earth* bank, are soft sandstone, broken up in points and stand perpendicular at river. Low 30 feet to 40 feet, can be cut to any alignment.

The boldest and most imposing prehistoric building stood on a prominent bluff on the opposite bank and upstream less than half a mile from Hite, overlooking the mouth of White Canyon and the Colorado River. It was partly in ruins, but walls over twelve feet high still stood in 1889, and indicated that the building originally had consisted of two or more stories. The plumb line of the walls was remarkably true. In contrast to so many prehistoric structures in the canyon country of the Colorado which were built in obscure places, this one stood out on a bold headland and its interesting skyline arrested the attention of many river travelers from Powell's time onward. Stanton and others of the railroad survey visited "Fort Moqui," as it was called during the mining era in Glen Canyon, and John Hislop of the party inscribed his name and the date on one of the walls. See Crampton, "Historical Sites in Cataract and Narrow Canyons and in Glen Canyon to California Bar" (1964), 27-30, 88, for list of the many names inscribed on the fort and photograph. Stanton took a deep interest in the prehistoric ruins of the Colorado canyons, and he often jotted down valuable measurements and details as in this case. When he returned to Glen Canyon to undertake placer mining on a grand scale, he made some detailed drawings of Fort Moqui and other ruins. See C. Gregory Crampton and Dwight L. Smith, eds. "The Hoskaninni Papers, Mining in Glen Canyon, 1897-1902," by Robert B. Stanton, *University of Utah Anthropological Papers,* 54 (1961).

[4] News of the progress of the railroad survey was sent out from Hite. For some of the first press reports and letters, see *Denver Republican,* June 28, 29, 1889; Denver *Times,* June 27, 1889. Many of the newspaper reports cited in this work were collected by Robert B. Stanton for his *Canyon Scrapbook.*

This formation seems about 1/2 "earth."

9:20, Rapid 81. Ran it. 9:32, Rapid 82. Ran it. Small, choppy. 9:35, Rapid 83. Ran it. Rough and one bad rock.

The last formation continues on left, which is much best side, with more large rock and less earth and more even slope, 3/4 rock. Long sweep, beautiful. Right side would be heavier work with more cliff 30 feet high.

9:42, Rapid 84. Small and choppy.

10:00, at point where river turns to right is where tunnel line from "white" canyon would come to river again. Large portion of this part of the line would be stolen from the river, but it is wide with plenty of room, so this makes an *easy* line. Gravel beds on right 100 feet above river. Bottom on right but no use as if right side used the point would be tunneled further back.

Fig. 9. "Hite City" at Dandy Crossing in Glen Canyon. *F. A. Nims.* Engineering Societies Library.

10:25, for 2 or 3 miles back good, talus line on both sides, but better on left. Made better for high water mark is on about 8 feet above present stage. Left side of this continues back to tunnel site from white canyon. At this point, 10:30, immense gravel placer beds 30, 50, and 100 feet above river, and beyond bottom land 2 miles long and 500 to 800 feet wide. Beautiful ragged peak 3 miles ahead. Will photograph it from beyond.

10:45, at end of bottom on left is gravel Rapid No. 85. Very swift and choppy, running close under cliff on right. At this same point line on left bank under cliff, small talus, 30 to 50 feet high. Not difficult to make good line for this 1/2 mile as material above is broken up into easy working piles of earth and rock. On right line is very low cliffs and gravel beds, 30 feet and upwards above river.

11:00 A.M., half way down cliff on left as noted above commences large bottom on right 3 to 5 feet above high water with gravel beds further up towards cliffs. At end of above 1/2 mile cliff, left shore line has good sloping talus of debris with slaty appearing sandstone under debris.

11:25, bottom on right nearly gone and one come in on left probably right one 2 miles long. Left bottom 1 1/2 miles long and I do not think it overflows. It is 1000 feet wide at center and line on it riprapped would be perfectly safe. Beyond this earth slopes on both sides of river.[5]

11:40, long gravel Rapid No. 86. Ran it, not bad but choppy at point beyond last photos where river turns to left. Banks low and far back, thus line can cut some distance from the river.

11:50, long gravel Rapid No. 87. Ran this one also. Rough. 11:53, another just the same, No. 88.

12:05, *reach Tickaboo* placer mining camp. Camp 27, 15 miles below Dandy Crossing.

THURSDAY, JUNE 27. In camp repairing boats.

We are here within 12 to 15 miles of the Henry Mountains, covered with timber and said to abound in good coal. Hite tells us that good veins are now opened within 12 miles of this place.

This placer is very extensive and rich, paying on last clean up 55 cents per cubic yard. They have boiler and pump in place.[6]

[5] Although the average fall of the river in Glen Canyon was only about two feet to the mile, there were a few choppy riffles and small rapids. The biggest problem for the surveyor was the meandering course of the river. Stanton had carried the survey all the way through Cataract on the left side, but in Glen the rails might go on either side. The wide, sweeping curves of the river presented a serious alignment problem reflected in the many facts and figures which fill the pages of his notebook. Franklin Nims, the photographer who found so little time to work in Cataract, now appears busily illustrating Stanton's calculations with his camera. Nims's diary helps to clarify the activities of the surveyors in Glen Canyon. See Dwight L. Smith, ed., *The Photographer and the River* (1967), chapter 3.

[6] Within a year or two after his arrival in Glen Canyon in 1883, Cass Hite discovered gold placer deposits of some value along the banks of the Colorado at Hite and at the mouth

FRIDAY, JUNE 28. Still in camp at Tickaboo completing boats.

Just learned that while three of the miners from above Hite City were coming down this A.M. over Trachyte Rapid their boat filled and one man was drowned. He was helped to the boat 3 times but would not take hold, so badly scared he was crazy.

Mr. Hughes left us to go back to the mines and to Denver via Dandy Crossing and Green River Station. Embarked at 3:30 P.M.

The long flat opposite Tickaboo, 4 miles long, is the continuation of the broken ground at point turning to left as noted on Wednesday. The hills back of this flat are low and composed of crumbled rock as easy to work as earth; 3/4 of the work on this 4 mile stretch will be earth.

At point near where line stopped tonight, where we passed [the survey] party, line can be made tangent behind little bluffs at river without extra cost.[7] The bluff and breaks are very low for 1000 feet back. Just beyond this the largely but possibly not all above high water but line would be beyond this on good ground. This section of say 4 miles would be 3/4 *earth*. Above flat said to abound in good springs.

4:00, small Rapid No. 89.

Right bank of river gives good line but left is still better.

At end of flat for 3/4 mile, low earth and rock bluffs. Easy as D&RG near Littleton, 1/2 earth, 1/4 loose rock, 1/4 solid rock. This continues for one mile further with bluffs back from river. Then cliffs come nearer to river, with long sloping talus of earth and rock, same as any mountain debris. 4:30, stopped to wait for photograph opposite "Battery Point." Beautiful placid river.

Restarted, 5:20. 5:30, river turns to left. Very sharp good line on further side. Low bluffs and sand flats. Short tunnel at foot to save curvature.

---

of Tickaboo, or Ticaboo, Creek, fifteen miles below Hite. The "Bank of Tickaboo" was the name Hite gave to these diggings. The railroad surveyors traveled through Glen Canyon just at the height of the first phase of the gold rush. (See lengthy reports in the Salt Lake *Tribune* March 3, 1888; January 4, May 14, 18, 23, 1889) and Stanton became very much impressed with the potentialities of the mines. During the break at Tickaboo he had ample time to observe and to listen to Hite, who probably mined as much gold out of other people's pockets as he did out of the diggings. Within a few years Stanton was back to undertake the biggest mining operation in the canyon's history. Tickaboo Creek heads in the Henry Mountains, a laccolithic group of five peaks bordering Glen Canyon on the west. Coal is found in the sedimentary beds about the base of these mountains.

[7] Back at Hite on June 26, the Brown–Stanton expedition was divided. One group would carry the instrumental survey through Glen Canyon to Lee's Ferry. The other group, including Brown and Stanton, would push on rapidly and "eye survey" the canyons all the way to The Needles below Grand Canyon. After disaster struck in Marble Canyon, where three men, including President Brown, were drowned, this preliminary survey was abandoned. Under a reorganized company Stanton returned to the river to direct and complete the railroad survey. The new party put in the river in December 1889, and ran again through Glen Canyon where Stanton made further notes and calculations. Stanton refers here, and in the following pages, to photographs taken during the second trip. See his entry for December 21, 1889, and note 14, Chapter IV.

Beautiful perpendicular red cliffs on right bank with sand flats at bottom. On left bank beyond this for 2 miles, small talus of sand cliffs low, 200 feet, comes to water latter part benched and plenty of bottom land 50 to 150 feet wide.

At end of this stretch went into camp on left bank at 6:10 P.M. Made about 10 miles today. "Under the Garden Wall," Camp No. 28.

SATURDAY, JUNE 29. Broke Camp 28, 6:50. The bluffs in this neighborhood are almost absolutely bare of vegetation on top. With gravel beds as much as 500 feet above river.

Beyond point on which we camped last night, bottom widens out for 1/2 mile and then narrows to low bluffs 20 to 30 feet, with cliff 1000 feet back for 1/2 mile more, with placer gravel banks on top. "Silver Bell Placer." Perpendicular bluffs for 1 or 2 miles with good mountain slide talus with beautiful swing of river to right.

On right bank the formation is just same with gravel beds on low bluffs.

7:50, large island in river broad and 1/2 mile long. Does not overflow. Good bottoms on both banks with occasionally low rock bluff comes to river, 100 to 300 feet long. Side canyons come in frequently requiring bridges 30 to 100 feet.

8:00 A.M., more placers on left with low bluffs. Beautiful stretch of straight smooth river for 1 1/2 miles beyond.

8:15, reach Smith Brothers' Placers. This stretch with placers on bluffs. Small stretch of cliff perpendicular with talus either side. Whole extent, 2 places, about 1/4 mile. Material for these banks can be hauled in without disturbing these cliffs.

8:50, long gravel rapid, light but choppy. Beyond this point bottom 700 to 800 feet wide, low bluffs back covered with gravel beds. Beyond this, bluff 400 feet high comes down into water for 1000 feet at point where river bends to left from bottom, widest say 1500 feet, with gravel beds on low bluffs back. This flat makes easy curve for line and does away with necessity for tunnel at point. *River glassy smoothness.*

Since 9:15, passing line of cliffs on left 300 to 500 feet high and almost perpendicular, but with good talus, and for about 1/2 mile bottom level and flat running square up to bluff or cliff. Good scraper work. High water about 8 feet above present.

Beyond this 2 mile stretch straight, with low bluff on left and wide bottoms further down. Very light work, scraper earth and loose rock. Perhaps [tang?] whole distance. Appearance of gravel bed on hills 500 feet above water and said to exist so 3 miles back from river.

Last 1500 feet of the 2 miles is cliff. Average 30 feet high into water, top of which is covered with heavy gravel beds. At point beyond river turns to left.

Same cliff extends 600 to 800 feet around bend to wide flat. Best line is to cut cliff and make road partly in river.

10:35, long Rapid No. 90. *Bend left side.* Beyond point sandstone slopes 10° down to water (line when wanted) with gravel beds back. One mile distance. This ends bottom as river again turns to right.

Then 500 to 600 foot cliff 1/2 mile long with but little talus. Cliff so perpendicular, only way to handle it is to, with easy blasts, drop top of cliff into river and haul in material to finish from ends. High water only 6 feet above present. At point end of last 1/2 mile river turns sharp to left and cliff pulls out to right. To make good line make tunnel through this part, 300 feet. Bottom around point but think it too sharp.

Lunch, 11:00 A.M. Start again, 12:05 P.M. 12:15, long Rapid No. 91. Easy, 1/2 mile long. End of this 1/2 mile, river turns again to left with bottom land at point, with low bluffs and gravel beds for 1/2 mile beyond. At end of this repetition of cliff, etc. This cliff 1/2 mile, has much larger talus and part way flat in front of talus.

12:48, small Rapid No. 92, and at small side canyon cliff breaks up into low bluffs at water's edge and then turns into long sloping talus for some distance beyond, say 3/4 mile. This winds with 1500 feet of perpendicular cliff 500 feet high. This can be handled by 1/2 tunnel or by breaking from above and finishing from either end. This point ends same as those previously with low bluffs at extreme end with gravel beds back and small bottom next to ·river.

2:20 P.M., end of bend river turns to right. At this point 2:20 P.M., formation changes. Have been having cliffs of solid masses of rocks. At this point this mass rises rapidly and stratified sandstone comes in underneath.

So the next stretch is benched up from water, at further end of point broken cliff about 80 feet high for 500 to 600 feet. This commences just at Rapid No. 93.

2:28, quite a sharp Rapid No. 93. Beyond, sloping rock with small benches. 2:50, point at end of last too sharp for line. Tunnel start back about 1/4 mile. Tunnel would come out on benchy cliff with talus running to point where line can be carried round by cutting [a] short tunnel.

Red sandstone going rapidly up 3:15 P.M. and a few hundred feet beyond white sandstone comes up as rapidly; 100 foot cliffs, first of red and then of white, in little over 1/4 mile. This white sandstone is in easy benches and easily handled. It continues into long slopes, *mountain slides*, for 3/4 mile ahead.

3:45, white sandstone has disappeared and red in place again; but same long slope, mountain slide, continues as before for a mile ahead and almost a straight line. White sandstone is covered up by debris from above. 4:45, this same long slope of debris continued around point and for a mile down next stretch and is the same as far as can see ahead. Shore is of this nature on both sides of river, but left seems the *easiest*.

Camp on left bank at 5:45, Camp No. 29. We are supposed to have made 40 miles today.

SUNDAY, JUNE 30. Resting in Camp No. 29.

Note: since leaving Dandy Crossing the cliffs have been *really* perpendicular though not over 600 feet high. The rock is in one mass, not stratified, but it easily worked.

MONDAY, JULY 1. Up 4:00 A.M. Breakfast 4:30. Start 5:30.

First quarter mile from camp good wide talus. Then 2000 foot cliff sloping to river. This "sloping cliff" continues around point to left in beautiful long sweep.

6:00 A.M., pass Escalante Creek on right.

This same "sloping cliff" continues to next bend to right, without the usual swing in to left just before reaching it. This bend is the prettiest and easiest one we have passed. About every 1000 feet around this bend needs a drain, but as the bluff is low they only show small effects of water. Drains 6 and 8 feet would do, except last one. Then 40 foot span. The 1/2 mile or more beyond turn to right shows "sloping cliff" to water with slaty benches above rising to real cliffs above.

All work noted on *sloping cliffs* will be *solid rock*.

This sweep to end where river again turns to right. 6:50 A.M., is exactly same as last one described.

I think now road bed should cut entirely in solid rock on such slopes and not trust bank to catch on slope. Will examine further into it.

Side wash out little beyond end of this slope, 20 foot span. Latter end of swing and past bend of river to right is easy "mountain slope of debris," 1/2 solid rock, 1/4 loose rock, 1/4 earth.

7:20, at end of point where river turns to left is 300 foot steep cliff running into water, with nice bottom 150 feet wide at extreme point beyond. 7:35, high mountain appears ahead covered with timber to very top, *Navajo Mountain*. At this point river again turns to right and this stretch ahead is not so much mountain slope of debris but sloping cliff, an easy and cheap solid rock line. 8:00 A.M., end of stretch, river turns to left. Bluff low at point, 40 feet. Bottom off point.

FIG. 10. "Map of [the Colorado] River cut in rock at mouth of Escalante Creek, Glen Canyon." Miami University Library.

8:05, reach mouth of San Juan River, 200 foot span.[8]

Stopped till 8:50 to give Brown, McDonald, and Reynolds breakfast as they had come this far yesterday to hunt deer.

8:55, start again. About 1000 feet beyond mouth of San Juan River turns sharply to right. Cliff rises 500 to 600 feet, with 30 feet to 40 feet of stratified benches at bottom forming talus; 500 feet of straighter cliff into river near point. Material easily gotten. This point comes round to left too sharp for good alignment. Tunnel must start in before reaching "straighter cliff." About 1000 foot tunnel. Good place to come out on river below.

On right side of river wonderfully picturesque.

Beyond this tunnel, line is along high straight up cliff but with good talus in most places. This for 3/4 mile, and beyond this river turns sharply to right. The turn here is so abrupt that it looks as if river *ended* entirely under cliff. Some of this line has bottoms 50 to 60 feet and one hundred wide. Tunnel will be required if river turns again to left.

This point is cut by stream.

10:00 A.M., enter Glen Canyon proper, though Powell calls it all Glen Canyon from Dandy Crossing. Marked by point of stratified rock on right with small but perfect female head on top. From this place, few hundred feet beyond, the Navajo Mountain looms up on our left.

10:30, came to bad Rapid No. 94, formed by boulders washed out of stream from left, coming from the Navajo Mountain. On account of many boulders in stream and frail condition of our boats we concluded not to run it but let boats down on side. We find that the Crossing of the Fathers, "El Vado de los Padres," is at the point where we stopped to let boats over rapids.[9]

---

[8] With the instrumental survey following slowly behind, Brown, Stanton and company, sailed along rapidly. At the mouth of the San Juan River, the largest tributary in Glen Canyon, they had traveled 84.5 miles from Dandy Crossing. The precipitous walls of Glen Canyon, and the sweeping curves of the river, seem to have given Stanton little doubt about the feasibility of building the railroad. At least he expresses no doubt in his notes. Instead, we learn of prospective tunnels and bridges over side canyons. Long sections would have to be blasted in solid rock and in other places cliffs would have to be dropped into the river. Note how blithely he proposes to throw a 200-foot span over the mouth of the San Juan River.

The young engineer was a child of his time. At forty-three Stanton had already seen and participated in the spectacular railroad building era in Colorado. Railroads could be built anywhere, even through the canyons of the Colorado. Destruction of the pristine beauty of the canyon through railroad building may have crossed the engineer's mind, but it is not evident in his notes. But such thoughts were not characteristic of the times.

[9] Powell originally chose two names for the canyon which he later called Glen: "Mound" was the part above the San Juan River; "Monument" was the name given to the part below. At 10:30 *a.m.* the men lined their boats past the rapids at the mouth of Aztec Creek, a stream heading on the lofty slopes of Navajo Mountain, clearly visible to them from the river a mile upstream. Rainbow Bridge spans a tributary of Aztec Creek five miles from the Colorado. El Vado de los Padres — the Crossing of the Fathers — where the Spanish discoverers of Glen Canyon crossed the Colorado in 1776, was twenty-nine miles farther downstream.

11:10, start again below rapid. 11:15, Rapid No. 95 easy.

After tunnel comes out on lower side, bluffs are low and broken, and creek enters river from mountains. Keep tunnel grade as high as possible, which will shorten tunnel and make good crossing of creek, 50 foot span. This can be done. One-half mile or more beyond is perpendicular cliff with good talus at upper end with broad flat bottom at lower end of this cliff.

Lunch at 11:30 in cove cut out of solid cliff, right bank, by small stream from above. Whole cove nearly arched over with rock roof, 40 feet wide, 60 deep, 100 feet high.

Gravel bed on top of cliff over 400 feet high. Left side.

12:28, Rapid No. 96, 3/4 mile long. This rapid divides into three channels. In pulling hard to get away from the left, worst, channel we got too far for center channel and trying to pull back broke an oar and were drifted on to bar in center of river. All jumped out in river, lifted boat off into *right* channel and went through safely. Channel very crooked and swift.

After tunnel comes out through little creek, is 3/4 mile almost straight and perpendicular cliffs, 400 to 500 feet high, ending in point with large flat or bottom at extreme end. No talus of any account and will be handled by breaking down top of cliff. The point is easy for curve, except at extreme point. Tunnel 200 feet. Beyond this the river seems to be more straight.

Line is at foot of cliff with small talus. Point of this is about 40 feet above high water and juts out into river. Take line over this with 400 foot thorough cut makes good alignment to flat around point. Distance from 200 foot tunnel above about one mile. One-third mile of beautiful talus and flat covered with oaks. Then 1/4 mile cliff with rock slope at bottom. Bank to be made from top and finished from ends.

This point ends in low bluffs. Can be run over nicely before this point comes out in river. Short tunnel, say 200 feet.

One-half mile beyond perpendicular cliffs in river 100 to 400 feet high, some talus. Handle from above, finish from ends. Hardly any point at all. Line in river all the way around point. Two thousand feet rough round pointed bluffs in benches.

2:20, small Rapid No. 97.

One-half mile cliff in river some 800 to 1000 feet high. Some good talus can be handled from lower cliffs at ends, and flat beyond point. Think best way to handle this is to keep grade as high as possible and cut first part of low bluff heavy throwing line out on flat to make good curve. For 1 1/2 miles back better line on right side, but not enough to pay for crossing.

Next is low sloping bluffs to river. Easy line but all solid rock. These continue to 3/4 mile and then turn on long sweep to right of low bluffs, perpendicular into river with talus here and there. Bluff 60 to 100 feet high.

This stretch about 3/4 mile ends in lower cliffs, and large flat at extreme end. Three-fourths mile around it. This point is most difficult and expensive we have met. Too long for cheap tunnel. Line and cliffs all the way in water except on flats. Bluffs are 40–60 and 100 feet high. This same class of bluffs continues, with small talus here and there for a mile ahead. Good straight alignment. This same is continued 1 mile further, to where river turns to right. The only great difficulty in these low cliffs that rise perpendicular from water is where cliff is concave to river for short distances is to make good bank in river and provide waterways under, for side canyons, small ones, that continually come in.

5:15, another Rapid No. 99. Not bad.

Three-fourths mile further of line brings to point turning sharply to left. Same cliffs with occasional flats till end.

5:27, long gravel Rapid No. 100. Ran it and at 5:30 went into Camp No. 30. This will be my first night in *Arizona*. Made 40 miles today.

Have had all day, and all Saturday also, the heaviest and worst sections for railway purposes that we have met on the Colorado. The bends are sharp, the cliffs are *really* perpendicular and in some instances overhanging. Where the river cuts against these cliffs they are from 100 to 600 feet high, and almost always without talus. Here the line will have to be stolen from the river, and made by dropping top of cliff into river and finishing banks from either end. The sharp turns can be avoided by tunnels.

Fig. 11. Inscriptions left by the surveyors of the Denver, Colorado Canyon and Pacific Railroad Company at the mouth of Anasazi Canyon (1962 Photo). *C. Gregory Crampton.*

Through all these cliffs are cut water courses of drainage from above. These cuts are very peculiar being only 10 feet to 15 feet wide but cut down clear to river's level. They show but little severe water, no boulders or heavy gravel deposited at mouth, nothing but sand. A few exceptions are of larger creek that come from much further back, and in two instances must come from the Navajo Mountain with large amount of peculiar black boulders deposited at their mouth.

On account of very crooked river I have been carefully studying both sides of river. In a few places the right bank gives better line. But taking the whole line into consideration the left bank is the better line side, for these reasons. The banks above Tickaboo can have no comparison. Bridging the Colorado would be very expensive. Since entering Glen Canyon and for 40 or more miles above a good line can be gotten on either side, but taking the whole line there are a good many more perpendicular cliffs into the water on right side, and these clean cliffs are in most instances much longer. This to about 20 to 25%.[10]

No particular incident of our trip today except as noted above at Rapid No. 96. The wind has blown continually upstream all day making rowing hard. The water has been rough on account of wind. Whenever wind did stop for a few moments the water was almost glassy, though swift, until approaching a rapid.

TUESDAY, JULY 2. Up at 4:30 A.M. Breakfast 5:00 A.M. Broke camp 6:00 A.M. High water mark about 10 feet above present stage. River falling since June 2d.

The point beyond Camp No. 30 ends in low round bluffs and points, with very broad gravel flats in river. Line can be located behind some of these knobs. About 3/4 mile on, at end of last flat, river turns sharply to right, with perpendicular cliffs in river 300 to 400 feet high for 1/2 mile. No talus. Some of it overhanging. Then, 2000 feet, vary 20 to 40 feet, low broken bluffs with flat 50 to 100 feet wide in front. Then 1000 feet high perpendicular cliff in river.

Beyond this point 1 1/2 miles of lower cliffs, with flats, and good talus the whole distance, except about 200 feet.

The wide flat with high talus is about 300 feet wide. Lower end of this stretch shows about 500 feet more of clean cliff, hid by flat from above. This

---

[10] On a long day's run the surveyors had passed through the most spectacular part of Glen Canyon. Great sweeping curves are frequent and, although not continuous, sheer cliffs rise from near the water's edge to heights over five hundred feet. The cliffs are broken frequently by slot-like tributary canyons, the floors of which are at river level. Stanton's calm assurance of the feasibility of a railroad line through this section of the canyon is remarkable. However, he does admit that the part below the mouth of the San Juan River would be unusually expensive and difficult. See his entry for July 3. Camp for July 1 was about forty-five miles from Lee's Ferry, and 15 miles from the Utah–Arizona boundary.

1 1/2 mile stretch very low and broken bluffs, with magnificent flat 500 to 600 feet wide. Easy turn by cutting extreme point. Heavy. From point to end of flat 2000 feet to 1/2 mile. This flat will make earth work with say 1/4 loose rock. Next 3/4 mile is all perpendicular cliffs, 30 to 80 feet high. *Line all to be built in river.*

This whole distance, one mile, will be almost a tangent with two slight curves.

This point ends in *low* bluffs, with wide flat. The bluffs, low enough to keep grade up and come over top with not over ten feet through cuts on points. This continues long bend to left 1 1/2 miles round with "sloping bluffs." Line can be kept on top of these out of river. To make best line some cuts would be heavy. One-half mile more of sloping cliff, with wide long flat next river on which is mule trail and pasture. Runs down to where river again turns to right. This whole bend of over 2 miles would make good easy turn with line in solid rock cut, with slight fills all the way.

At end of this flat is long swing to right and straight stretch ahead, in all 1 1/2 miles. Cliffs perpendicular, 300 to 500 feet high, with talus and flats at bottom. Most of talus wide enough but not enough material above high water for bank. Top of cliff is broken and easily handled. About 1/4 mile of this has no talus.

This 1 1/2 mile ends in low bluffs, so that line can be kept on top of low portion. All through here left side of river vastly the better.

With use of low bluffs and one short heavy cut a beautiful line can be gotten round this point, to left, for 1/2 mile, as the low sloping rock extends all the way to where river turns again to right. This next sweep is to right under cliff as last one with same talus 1 1/2 miles long. Has one large creek about center cut down to river, 40 foot span; 300 feet without any talus.

For 1 1/2 to 2 miles on river straight. One-half mile beyond flat, cliff perpendicular in river. No talus.

Richards shot wild goose. First meat we have had for 3 days. High cliffs 100 to 150 feet back with flats and high talus for 1 mile. Then cliff is more rounded and not so perpendicular. For 1/2 mile with low rock bluffs at bottom.

At 10:30, long gravel slope with roar, but can hardly be called a rapid. At end of last 1/2 mile river turns to left with low bluffs and good point to come round except at extreme point where will be 100 to 200 foot tunnel. Beyond this cliffs broken with high talus for 1/4 mile. Beyond this low, 60 foot point of cliff can be cut to make straight line to long stretch of fine talus, equal to "mountain slope."

One mile down large creek comes in on left, 100 foot span. Three-fourths [mile] below this same slope continues. Lunch at this point, 11:00 A.M. Start again at 12:05 P.M.

The same kind of shore line continues one mile and a quarter to point where river turns left and around this long swinging point for 1 1/4 miles further. Around this point the talus is not so heavy but the cliff is rough and craggy and can be easily used. At end of turn to left is a 500 foot piece of "sloping cliff" into river. For 2 miles long sweep to right with fine high talus. About 1000 feet of this at end is cliff in river; but it has low bench easily worked. One-fourth mile more of good talus and benches.

Then come to point turning to left, 1000 feet high, 600 foot cliff in river. Line must all be stolen from river. Then talus and low bluffs in front of high cliff 3/4 mile to point where river again turns to right. Same class of line continues for a mile to point where river turns to left again. Very sharp point requires a 500 to 800 foot tunnel. Good place to come out on lower side, through creek that comes out 500 feet beyond point, 2:05 P.M. Then line is same as before, talus at foot of 600 to 800 foot cliff. Talus in most places sufficient, for 3/4 mile to next point turning left.

This point turns quite suddenly to left with flat in front of it. Perhaps 200 foot tunnel. Can't tell till go further on. This tunnel 200, or 300 feet. 1500 feet further on river turns again to left very sharply.

This next bend to right is sharpest, concave to river, that we have met on the whole trip, 1/2 mile. This will require quite sharp curve probably 10°. The above sharp right bend has very broad and regular talus, about 1000 feet. At end rough cliffs.

Next point turns to left and is easy low bluffs at foot of cliff, with great slopes of talus beyond, for 1/2 mile. Then river turns again to right. One-fourth mile to right, cliffs in river, but broken and benchy. Easy to handle.

Next point to left very abrupt and crooked and will require a *1/2 mile* to *one mile* tunnel.

It may be much better line than I have indicated can be found by running up side canyon even to the cutting, to cutting off two or more of the bad bends we have passed by a *long tunnel*. It is worth investigating.

From same point line turns easy bend to right on small talus but tunnel work would give plenty of material, about 1/2 mile. These cliffs very much broken by big washes coming in; they only show sand and *small* stones deposited. Two 50 foot spans. Good line along here.

Formation is changing, 4:10 P.M. Stratified sandstone coming in at bottom, with *cliff* all gone on left mountain slope all the way up for 1500 feet with low bluffs at river of broken up stratified rock with part of gentle slope down to river.

Canyon wall with cliff to river continues on *right side* for 1/2 mile. The whole left side is broken down for 1 1/2 miles further to point that turns to left. Line can be located back from river and thus shortening line and straightening alignment.

Fig. 12. Perpendicular cliffs of Glen Canyon, forty-five miles above Lee's Ferry. *F. A. Nims.* Miami University Library.

At 4:30 reach Lee's Ferry at mouth of Pariah Creek, where Powell camped the night of *August 4th 1869.* About 45 miles today. Camp No. 31.

Pa-riah [is] Pah-weibe (water-mud), [in] Paiute language [meaning] "creek of mud."

Went up creek 1/4 mile and found Warren M. Johnson's place. He was away. Beautiful field of alfalfa, corn, and all kinds of garden truck. Large apple and apricot trees in full fruit — pears, peaches, etc. Quite a little paradise after being for six weeks shut up in the rock walls of a canyon.

Great disappointment to us all to find that the stores ordered from Denver had not reached here.

This man Johnson is a Mormon and is said to have *five wives* though only one is here. He has eight children here. Supposed to be the children of this one wife. She is a very pleasant woman of moderate education and about 55 years old.

This point, called *Lee's Ferry,* is named after old John D. Lee, who was executed, by shooting, some years ago for his participation in the great *Mountain Meadow Massacre.*

July 3. Mr. Brown started early on horseeback for Kanab to get stores for our further trip. We will all stay here in camp till he returns, make oars, repair boats and try to get fat. They are killing a beef for us, and we are to have chicken, green corn, cucumbers, onions, and stewed apricots for dinner. Best of all, we had all the *buttermilk* we could drink this A.M.

We met here an old California "49er," one *Al Huntington*, who has told us all sorts of stories of this section, and has given me and promises to give me more Indian names connected with this country to use for naming stations, etc., on the road when it is built:

Tickaboo (Ute), "friend"

Wampebe (Paiute), "ash wood"

Nagadz (Paiute), "mountain sheep"

Mokiack (Paiute), "ouse apple," papaw-like, grows on vine. Name of Paiute chief at the "Grand Wash" below Grand Canyon.

Panzuck (Paiute), "The Otter." Name of Paiute chief at mouth of the Virgin River.[11]

---

[11] Another long run, through a canyon growing narrower as its walls grew higher, brought the surveyors to Lee's Ferry at the mouth of the Paria River and the end of Glen Canyon. Located 4.5 miles upstream from U.S. Highway 89A, Lee's Ferry is a place of major scenic and historic importance. Here the Colorado River dramatically breaks through the Echo Cliffs and sweeps out into the open briefly, with low banks on either side, before it tumbles over the boulder delta of the Paria River and is swallowed in Marble Canyon. The river was reasonably accessible here, the only place of its kind throughout the canyon system of the Colorado between Moab, Utah, and the lower end of Grand Canyon, a distance of over 500 miles.

Historically, Lee's Ferry became a prominent corridor between Utah and Arizona, and it became intimately identified with up- and downstream developments on the Colorado. Although others preceded him to the area, John D. Lee arrived late in 1871 and was the first permanent settler. He called the place "Lonely Dell" and established the first ferry in January 1873. Ferry service was continued until 1928. In 1877 Lee gave up his life to the firing squad for his part in the Mountain Meadows massacre which had occurred in 1857. Juanita Brooks, *John Doyle Lee, Zealot-Pioneer Builder-Scapegoat* (1962) is the standard biography.

Nearly all articulate river travelers from Powell's day have something to say about Lee's Ferry — the place, the ferry, the residents. Warren Johnson, who had two wives, was ferryman at the time of Stanton's visit. Al Huntington, scout, had been in the Lee's Ferry area as early as 1857. Along with other data, Stanton obtained from him information about Indians he might meet below the mouth of Grand Canyon. The Paria (a Paiute word, spelled variously and translated variously) River seldom runs clear. At times it appears to be liquid mud. W. L. Rusho and C. Gregory Crampton, *Desert River Crossing: Historic Lee's Ferry on the Colorado River* (1981) is a convenient summary and guide. E. A. Reynolds, who had signed on the first expedition as one of President Brown's "guests," left the party at Lee's Ferry. In an article, "In the Whirlpools of the Grand Cañon of the Colorado," *Cosmopolitan*, VIII (November 1889), 25–34, he describes the adventures of the surveyors in Cataract and Glen canyons.

General impressions of our railway line from head of the
Colorado to Lee's Ferry, at mouth of Pariah Creek.

In two things I have been very much surprised:

1st, in the easy and comparatively cheap railway line that can be gotten
through the Cataract Canyon; and

2d, in the difficulties of a line in Glen Canyon.

From the head of the Colorado to the San Juan a railway can be constructed with no more difficulty than along any mountain slope, and with
much less difficulty in some respects, for by stealing in some places the line
from the river, a most excellent alignment can be gotten with a grade not to
exceed 16 2/3 feet per mile or 3/10 of one percent.

The bridging and openings for side canyons and drains will be numerous
but not near so expensive as I was led to expect.

Estimates of these in detail are in my topography book. Two or three short
tunnels will be required on this portion of the line and at Dandy Crossing, perhaps one of a mile in length can be used by running up White Canyon, and
thus save four miles around the bend.

From the San Juan River to Lee's Ferry the river is *very* tortuous and will
require at least 15 tunnels. They will generally be short, from 200 to 500 feet,
but one or two will be one to 1 1/2 miles.

The cliffs in this section are really perpendicular and generally rise out of
the water. The high portions are from 500 to 800 feet high, and the lower
portions from 40 to 100 feet. These are given in detail in notes.

This makes the work in this section quite expensive, as the only [way] to
get material to make banks along the face of the cliffs, except by dropping the
top of the cliffs into the river and finish the banks from the ends.[12]

The following notes were in President Brown's Notebook
when he was drowned:[13]

Resources of the Colorado River Country

Cattle: Found cattlemen at first placers (Crescent) who assert that there
are over 200,000 head cattle ranging from Little Grand Valley to Dirty Devil

---

[12] Here we have Stanton's summary of the difficulties of building a railroad through the
canyons of the Colorado. As he sees it, with its sweeping bends and cliffs, Glen Canyon
would require the most work. Imagine, "at least 15 tunnels" and "dropping the top of the
cliffs into the river!"

[13] On July 10, Frank M. Brown was drowned in Marble Canyon below Lee's Ferry. His
body was not found, but by the rarest chance, at the time of the accident, Stanton recovered
Brown's notebook from the river. (See Stanton's entry for July 10, Chapter III). Like Stanton, Brown took notes of conversations with men he met as the surveying party traveled
through Glen Canyon. Since most of the information relates to Glen Canyon and the region
upstream, it is introduced here. Stanton had copied these notes into the back pages of his
Field Notebook "B".

River in a radius of 40 miles from the river on either side, beside extensive flocks of sheep. I was given a list of nearly 100,000 head running in that country, by C. L. Sanford. He made up the estimate from memory in five minutes. He only gave the largest cattle herders and stated there were numerous smaller herds. The cattlemen assert that the whole contiguous country of the Colorado is not overstocked, and will take care of from two to three times the present number of cattle. I am also assured, on the authority of men conversant with the country, that the whole Colorado region is as heavily stocked as the section described; and that the San Juan, the Little Colorado country, and the Kanab are even more heavily stocked; and that all that country will naturally ship by a road built down the Colorado; and they assert this would be the case where they would have to drive cattle from one to two days further. This advantage lies in the fact that the Canyon road runs near water where stock can be watered regularly while on many other roads water is hard to get.

Gravel Mines: The first Gravel bars of the Colorado in coming down the river [are found] a few miles above the mouth of the Dirty Devil River. The first bars are high up and scattered, but near the Dirty Devil they are near the Colorado and [are found] in extensive bars. The Crescent placer, three miles below mouth [of] Dirty Devil, embraces a bar of 320 acres. And [down] to this point, [there are] over 900 acres located and getting real work. Mr. Reynolds and Mr. Hughes prospected several of these bars, and Mr. Hughes individually quite an area of gravel, and report getting from a dozen to forty colors in each pan of dirt. The gravel ranges from a few feet to 60 feet in depth, and where cuts have been made and shafts sunk, prospects from top to bed rock.

Including the placers at Dandy Crossing (Hite City) where there are two bars, one 250 acres extent, there are between the Crescent placers and Cape Horn, about 8 miles below Hite City, over 600 acres of placer bars located. This averages about the same as Crescent in depth and is said to be rich. From Cape Horn to Good Hope placer, a distance of eleven to twelve miles, there is, including the Tickaboo placers, between 1000 and 1100 acres located. These bars are from a few feet to 60 feet deep, probably average 20 feet.

Considerable work has been done on Tickaboo placers. Steam pumps for supplying the placer with water have been put in. One run has been made and one of the owners, Mr. Cass Hite, tells me the gravel washed paid 55¢ gross to the yard. I have just finished washing a pan of gravel taken from the cut, the dirt was taken from bottom of cut up for 6 feet. I got about a dozen colors. The bottom of the cut is from 10 to 15 feet above bed rock. Two other pans were washed in my presence. One was taken from 7 to 8 feet above cut. This gave from twenty to twenty five colors. Another was taken from near top and gave 300 to 400 colors. Some of the colors were quite coarse heavy gold.

From Good Hope placers to Hall's Crossing, a distance of about twenty miles, from 1000 to 1200 acres have been located. Below Hall's Crossing and above the San Juan River there are several hundred acres located.

There is Mr. Mesken, a trapper, [who] tells me [there are] extensive bodies of gold placers west of Hall's ferry about twenty miles. Some of this gravel is so rich that it was packed to the river and washed. In the Henry Mountains, on North Wash, large placer diggings have lately been opened and over 1000 acres have been located to date. They are said to be rich.

Most of the placers described above, are high bars; and the river is as rich in gold as these high bars and is sure to be worked, and will return 10 to 50 times as much gross. Cass Hite asserts that the bars already located on the Colorado [cover] the greatest body of gravel unworked in America, that it [totals] over 25,000,000 cubic yards, and will net over 25¢ per cubic yard. We sailed for their home yesterday.

Left Tickaboo at 3 o'clock, and [traveled] all day today, the 29th June, through a big placer country. The dry bars occur near the river and on high bluffs back from the water, some near and others miles away. The area is very extensive, will run into thousands of acres.

Today, Sunday, we went up the Escalante Creek four miles and found several hundred acres of gravel bars. The shore carries as a rule a wide swell

Fig. 13. Smith Brothers' placer in Glen Canyon. *F. A. Nims.*

shore line. We are not stopped at the mouth of the San Juan. At this point there are high gravel bars, and we passed several between here and Escalante Creek, ten miles up. Mr. Smith has boiler and engine. He claims to net fifty dollars a day when he runs. The plant is very small and another, I understand, has been ordered.[14]

15 miles above the Little Colorado River, and 50 miles below Lee's Ferry several low canyons come in. Broken country. Up first canyon is large mineral deposits. It is within 3/4 mile of the river. Here granite commences and continues for 15 miles.

Timber Area: The higher mesas near Grand Junction on both sides of Grand River are covered with heavy forests of pine and other forest trees. The mesas just above Cataract Canyon are covered with a scattered forest of cedar, piñon, and pitch pine suitable for fencing and fuel; and some of the larger cedars can be used as ties for the road.

At the head of Dark Canyon, which empties into the Colorado about 30 miles below its head in Cataract Canyon, is an extensive forest of pine trees, cedars, piñons, and sugarmaple. This forest starts in from 15 to 20 miles from the Colorado and covers what is known as the Elk Mesa. One family made last year over 3000 lbs. of maple sugar in that region.

In the Henry Mountains which run down close to the river are large forests of pine, cedar, etc., fine timber for lumber. These forests cover a vast area. Caught a view today, June 30, of the Navajo Mountain. They show heavy timber and are close to the Colorado and south of the San Juan River. Had one view of them about five miles above the mouth of the San Juan.[15]

Coal Area: The hills about Grand Junction are underlined with coal, much of it being fine coking coal. This coal field extends up Grand River to Newcastle and embraces one of the vastest coal deposits of the world. It includes anthracite as well as the finest bituminous coal. It reaches down the Grand many miles below Grand Junction, so that the road will run through a part of it. When the survey was started from Grand Junction down the Grand about April first, it was not known that any body of coal existed nearer than forty

[14] Following some hearsay statistics on the grazing industry, Brown notes information on the Glen Canyon placer mines which he observed at first hand. See note 1 and Stanton's diary entries, this chapter, for additional information about the mines. Crescent placer, Hite City, Cape Horn, Tickaboo, Good Hope, and the Smith Brothers' placer were all early mining locations scattered along the Colorado from the mouth of Crescent Creek (North Wash) to Smith Fork, a distance of twenty-eight miles. There was some early prospecting along the foot of the Henry Mountains, near the heads of North Wash and Hall's Creek, but the diggings there were probably not as rich as Brown's informant indicated. However, Edward Mesken, trapper and prospector, was an early arrival in the Glen Canyon gold rush, and his words may have carried some authority.

[15] Except for the piñon-juniper forests so common in the canyon lands, only the high country — Elk Ridge and the Abajo, or Blue Mountains east of Cataract Canyon — support extensive forests (but not including the sugar maple) suitable for timber.

miles from the Colorado; but since then an extensive and seemingly inexhaustible coal field has been discovered in the Henry Mountains only 15 miles from the Colorado River. These veins range from 6 to 22 feet in thickness. An easy grade can be made to the mines. Coal on Last Chance Creek, 60 [50] miles up the river from Lee's Ferry, near the Colorado, 10 miles above "Crossing of the Fathers".

Asphaltum and Petroleum: Near Grand Junction [and] in both Utah and Colorado are vast deposits of almost pure asphaltum, and between Grand and Green Rivers are petroleum springs.

There is a large petroleum spring on the bank of the Colorado about 60 miles above the mouth of the San Juan River and half a mile up the San Juan from its mouth is another large petroleum spring.

Sunday, June 30th, we went up Escalante Creek four miles. In coming down, E. A. Reynolds noticed gas coming up through the water about half a mile up the creek. It readily ignited when a lighted match was applied, the blaze rising five or six inches above the water.[16]

Stones and Marbles: The canyons near the head of the Colorado possess different varieties of sand and limestone suitable for building, with some varieties of marble.

I have now traversed the river to the mouth of the San Juan and have found brown and grey sandstone the whole distance.

Agricultural Lands: There is a large area of agricultural land in and about Grand Junction with several valleys further down the river that will sustain a large population. Between the Grand and Green Rivers is a vast tract of land that can be covered with water from Grand River. This is being written at Tickaboo 70 miles from the head of the Colorado; and in Cataract Canyon there is little or no land suitable for cultivation; but from the lower end of Narrow Canyon to this point are numerous flats that can be cultivated. There are, I am told, small ranches east of the Colorado on the higher mesas, while on the west side at the head of Dirty Devil River are numerous and quite extensive ranches. At the headwaters of this stream is one of the finest and most beautiful lakes in the mountains. It is 13 miles long and about 2 miles wide. It is full of trout, as is the stream itself.[17]

---

[16] In Brown's day, we have to remember, the Grand River extended down to the mouth of the Green River, where the Colorado began. By 1889, coal mined from the lower elevations of the Henry Mountains was being used to fire machinery in the Glen Canyon placer mines. Last Chance Creek heads on the Kaiparowits Plateau and Brown's note is an early reference to the vast Kaiparowits coal field. Petroleum "springs" have been found in a few places in the canyon country. One, at Oil Seep Bar in Glen Canyon, twenty miles above the mouth of the San Juan River, was commercially drilled in 1920, but the venture failed.

[17] Below Grand Junction there is precious little arable land in the canyon country of the Colorado. Through the upper half of its course, the Dirty Devil is now known as the Fremont River. The stream heads in Fish Lake, once called Trout Lake, a mountain jewel five miles long and one mile wide.

Minerals: Above Grand Junction is situated one of the biggest silver and gold districts in the world. Below, until the placers are reached, no extensive bodies of the precious metals have been developed.

At this point 70 miles below head of Colorado are some good showings of cooper and iron; and in the Henry Mountains some good gold and silver bearing ledges have been found.

CHAPTER III

DISASTER IN MARBLE CANYON

After a good rest and good food at Lee's Ferry, and with new supplies at hand, the Brown–Stanton expedition started off on July 9 to resume the "eye survey" through Grand Canyon. Still using three of the shaken boats that had carried them through Cataract and Glen, the surveyors were poorly prepared to meet the rapids of Marble Canyon. Disaster was invited and it struck almost at once. Frank M. Brown was drowned the next morning and a few days later the river swallowed two more victims, Peter M. Hansbrough and Henry C. Richards. Saddened and dispirited, and unable to continue, the survivors climbed out of Marble Canyon through South Canyon, a tributary 31.5 miles below Lee's Ferry, and returned to Denver. If Robert B. Stanton entertained any thought of quitting the railroad survey, it does not appear in his notebook.

LEE'S FERRY, ARIZONA, JULY 4, 1889.[1] In camp waiting for supplies, before going on down the river. Of course it is the hottest day of the year, 132° in sun, and 105° in shade, north side of house, *Johnson's log house.*

FRIDAY, JULY 5. Severe sand storm all afternoon, and while we were eating supper. We have "sand" enough in us now to run any rapid or fight any Indians.

Hamilton [Huntington?] tells me of immense coal veins up Paria Creek 40 miles and others at other points 12 miles from river. With timber 20 miles by 60 miles, 60 miles up Paria Creek.[2]

SATURDAY, JULY 6. Taking up my notes again this A.M.

[1] This chapter forms the first part of Stanton's Field Notes, Book B.

[2] The Paria River heads in a spectacular amphitheater ringed around by the eroded cliffs of the high Paunsaugunt and Table Cliff plateaus. Part of the eastern face of the Paunsaugunt is enclosed in Bryce Canyon National Park; much of the surface of the plateau, which ranges upward of 8000 feet elevation, is timbered.

Fɪɢ. 14. Lee's Ferry, crossroads on the Colorado River (1951 Photo). Bureau of Reclamation.

After passing upper ferry on low slope as noted, line would cut through low cliff at head of Rapid No. 101 and build in river past rapid and then cut point just above lower ferry getting on face of slope of debris at ferry road.

We took boats today and moved down 1 mile to lower ferry to Camp No. 32. All of us running Rapid No. 101.[3]

[3] There were two principal ferry locations at Lee's Ferry. The upper ferry, over a mile above the mouth of the Paria River (the Paria has changed the location of its mouth on occasion through the years), was the main location; ferry service was in operation here from 1873 to 1928. Stanton's party camped somewhere below this place July 2–5, and on July 6 the men ran one mile down through the rapids at the mouth of the Paria River and camped at the lower ferry site. The lower ferry, at the head of Marble Canyon, was used during the winter months from 1873 to 1898. This route was developed to avoid crossing the eccentric

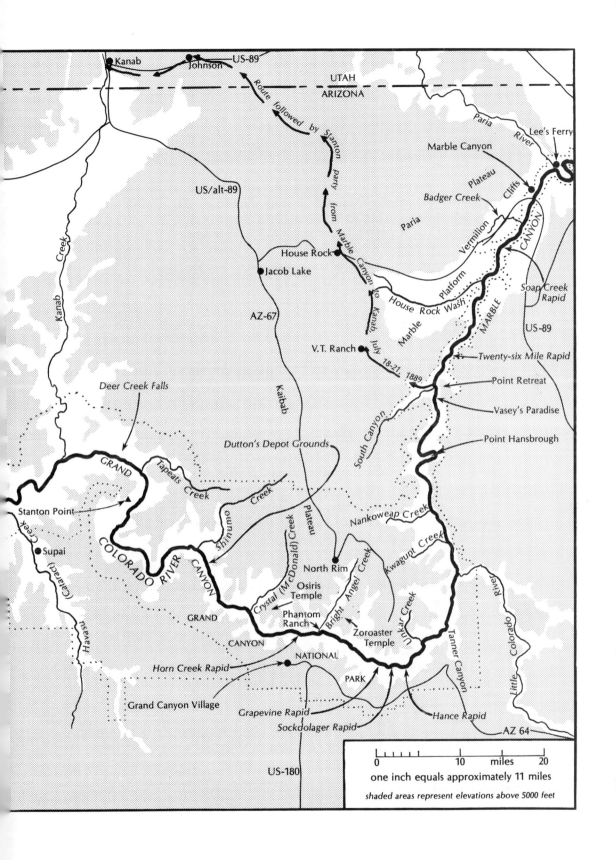

Kanab

Johnson US-89

UTAH
ARIZONA

Route followed by Stanton party from Marble Canyon to Kanab July 18-21, 1889

Paria River

Lee's Ferry

Marble Canyon

Plateau

Cliffs

Badger Creek

Vermilion

US/alt-89

Paria

House Rock

Jacob Lake

MARBLE

Soap Creek Rapid

AZ-67

Platform

Marble

US-89

Marble Canyon to House Rock Wash

V.T. Ranch

Twenty-six Mile Rapid

Point Retreat

Kaibab

South Canyon

Vasey's Paradise

Point Hansbrough

Deer Creek Falls

GRAND

Tapeats Creek

Dutton's Depot Grounds

Thunder Creek

Nankoweap Creek

Kwagunt Creek

Stanton Point

COLORADO RIVER

CANYON

Shinumo

Plateau

North Rim

Supai

Crystal (McDonald) Creek

Osiris Temple

Bright Angel Creek

Unkar Creek

Tanner Canyon

Little Colorado River

Havasu Creek (Cataract)

GRAND

Phantom Ranch

Zoroaster Temple

CANYON

NATIONAL

Horn Creek Rapid

Grand Canyon Village

PARK

Grapevine Rapid

Sockdolager Rapid

Hance Rapid

AZ 64

US-180

0   10   miles   20

one inch equals approximately 11 miles

shaded areas represent elevations above 5000 feet

Severe rain in hills up towards head of creek on right. After an hour or two quite a stream of heavy red water came down.

SUNDAY, JULY 7. Heavy wind and rain storm over us this P.M. First real rain since starting on the trip.

MONDAY, JULY 8. Load of provisions from Kanab reached camp at noon. Separated everything ready for starting tomorrow. Mr. Brown returned late in P.M.

Shall be glad to be on river again but sorry to leave this garden —

> green corn, string beans, cucumbers, onions, squash, apricots, apples, plums, watermelons, butter, eggs, milk and buttermilk every day, fresh beef and fish

Make a pretty good menu!! for camp life when well cooked, with other necessary concomitants.

TUESDAY, JULY 9. Up at 4:00 A.M. Breakfast 5:30. Loaded up and started 7:25 A.M.

From lower ferry cliffs are vertical with small solid talus. One-fourth mile to sharp bend to left. Talus is nearly all below high water but cliffs are ragged and easy to handle, about 200 feet high. Right side same cliff not quite so high and more of cliff in bend vertical from water. Point on left not so sharp as first with flat 50 to 75 feet around it. Drain, 30 foot span, 7:35.

7:45, Rapid No. *102*. *Ran* with two men and loads.

Left side continues with same cliffs 1/2 mile but with much better talus line easily built from ragged cliffs. Drain, 20 feet overhead. Right same, with side canyon requires 100 foot span. One-fourth mile from last is Rapid No. 103.

Next 1/2 mile 2–10 feet open possibly overhead. Cliffs with talus averaging same. Right side cliffs and talus same but cliffs higher. In next 1/2 mile are 2 side canyons, cut down to water level: 80 foot spans, or perhaps better 60 foot and one 40 foot open between. Cliffs have been perpendicular as far as first of these side canyons. Then the cliff commences to bench making construction of road much easier. No choice to right.

Line through this section can be good. Cliffs line as below. Necessary to cut points heavy and one 40 foot open between.

Paria River and the sharp ridge, known as Lee's Backbone, on the opposite side of the Colorado River. W. L. Rusho and C. Gregory Crampton, *Desert River Crossing, Historic Lee's Ferry on the Colorado River* (1981) is a summary history and a guide to the visible traces of the past.

High water shows 12 to 15 feet above present which is not far from *low*. Beautiful first bench on left about 30 feet above river. One-fourth mile on to point river turns to left. Good bench and wide talus.

9:07, sharp rapid with 3 huge rocks in center, No. 104. Just missed one rock, 2 feet. One-half mile on, large talus 60 feet high. Bench 30 to 40 feet above it. Fifty feet wide. At end of this, "overhead" drain, 10 foot span, comes over cliff, 1/4 mile to point, gradual turn to left. Talus increases in size and height, equals mountain slope of debris. Right side equally as good except alignment, opposite last noted point, side canyon, 80 foot span, forms.

Rapid No. 105. 9:30, stop to examine, and find rapid *very bad*. Perhaps this is Powell's 16 foot fall. It looks like it. No boat would live in it, so we conclude to portage loads and boats. This rapid is formed by the wash coming in from *two* side canyons directly opposite each other, hence the size of it. Brown says that one point is *Badger Creek*. Eighty foot span best. The one on left is larger and wider, say 200 foot span, without center fill. Both sides of this place have immense talus, equal to regular mountain slope of debris. Would require sharp cut in cliff above side canyon to make good crossing. After examining rapid we pull upstream on right side, where we landed, and cross river and drop down to within 20 feet of head of rapid. Unload boats and make portage of all loads and boats. Distance about 700 feet.

Fig. 15. On the rim of Marble Canyon overlooking Soap Creek Rapid (1921 Photo). *E. C. LaRue*. U.S. Geological Survey.

Lunched 11:40 A.M., after portaging boats, but before reloading. 12:45, reload boats in rough water and start again at 1:30 P.M. The same mountain slopes continue beyond for 2 miles, only very much larger, rising to 100 to 150 feet above river, giving good place to catch grade lost by rapid.

1:35, Rapid No. 106. Ran it with all loads and men. High waves but smooth, except one rock. This same "mountain slope" continues without break and for one mile in straight line and slopes increase to 200 feet high. The debris is underlaid with soft stratified rock only a few feet under surface. Splendid line and alignment. No large water courses. But must provide quite a number of say 10 foot spans.

2:10, reach Rapid No. 107. Land above on right bank to examine. Find it very long and difficult. The fall at its head greatest of any we have passed. Portage all goods for nearly half mile. Portage boats for short distance and then let them with lines down along shore. Completed portage by 6:00 P.M. and went into Camp No. 33.

The talus or "mountain slope" commences about 1/2 mile below Lee's Ferry and is formed by a softer section of rock in strata, bright red, of hard rock one to 2 feet in thickness with very soft rock, looking like red clay, between. This rises under the hard sandstone of lighter, yellow color, starting at nothing and gradually increasing at this point to nearly 500 feet in thickness and continues beyond.

Hansbrough caught fine fish.

The point on left at head of rapid is quite difficult. River turns sharply to left and has cut deeply into the soft strata so that it stands much more perpendicular. The rapid is formed by boulders from large side canyon on right and leaves wide space of sand and boulders. Railway line round this point.

By blasting out boulders at head of rapid in low water, channel can be changed and roadbed be built in present channel with solid rock from cliff above.

Rapid No. 107 has the greatest fall in less distance than any one single fall we have passed on the whole river. It is not far from 20 feet.

I think we made 10 or 11 miles today.[4]

---

[4] Probably no one but Powell had been entirely through Marble Canyon before them; and with his *Exploration of the Colorado River of the West* (1875) as their guide, the railroad surveyors began the long descent through Grand Canyon. Marble Canyon, named by Powell, extends from Lee's Ferry to the mouth of the Little Colorado, a distance by river of 61.5 miles. The walls of the canyon grew rapidly higher as they floated along; at 4.5 miles, where Navajo Bridge on U.S. 89A spans the canyon, they were in a straight-walled gorge over four hundred feet deep. They portaged Badger Creek Rapid (105) at the mouth of Badger Creek coming in on the right and Little Badger, or Jackass, Creek on the left. Powell had over-estimated the drop here at sixteen feet. The party went into camp below Soap Creek Rapid (107) about ten miles from the lower ferry site at Lee's Ferry. The expedition, still on the "eye survey," moved along as rapidly as possible. Parenthetical dates refer to data obtained by the instrumental survey through Marble Canyon, December, 1889–January,

Wednesday, July 10. Up at 4:00 A.M. Breakfast 5:00 A.M. Broke camp 6:23. Started in boats. 6:25 Rapid No. 108. Ran it.

My boat with Hansbrough and Richards struck the rapid head on in good shape intending to run all the way through, I telling Hansbrough who was steering to pull to the left of the heavy waves at the lower end of rapid.

Just as we got into the swiftest part at head of rapid I looked up and saw McDonald bareheaded on left bank running towards us with his hands in the air. I called to Hansbrough, "There they are waving to us we must pull out into the eddy." Fortunately we were going so fast we went head on through the heaviest waves and turned into the eddy, only shipping a few gallons of water. McDonald, continually calling to us, we heard say just as we got into the eddy, "Mr. Brown is in there." We realized in a moment that their boat had upset. I turned quickly and looked over the water. Saw nothing and then shouted to men to pull hard for shore, and just as we turned I saw Brown's notebook shoot up out of the water and float with the eddy. I called out "there's his notebook." Hansbrough picked it out of water as we turned through eddy. I jumped over Richards to shore with line and immediately looked over the whole eddy and rapid but could see no other trace of him, Brown. The whole of this did not take 1/4 of a minute, even much less.

I then called to men to unload boat which was done in a moment. By this time McDonald had reached us, and he and Richards jumped into our boat and pulled out into eddy close to rapid, and rowed all around but never saw any trace of Mr. Brown or his body.

When they came ashore, McDonald related the following: "We struck rapid head to all right. Just when we were in the swiftest part of water above breakers Mr. Brown said 'Mac, we want to make this eddy (McDonald was steering and Brown rowing) and look at rapid below. This is where Stanton wanted to stop and look at the rapid which he could not see.' I replied 'Alright' and turned the boat to come in. Just as we turned, in what seemed to be smooth waves, a heavy wave came up out of a whirl on upper side of boat and instantly upset boat, throwing us both into river away from the boat.

"We both went under. When I came up Mr. Brown was already up. I being in stern of boat was thrown into current and Brown being in bow was thrown in whirl between current and eddy. I was carried down and turning my head 'Hallooed' to Brown 'Come on.' He answered 'Alright' in a cheerful voice.

"I was carried by current and landed on point of rock in little eddy about 200 yards below.

1890. (See Chapter V this work.) Today's traveler on the river will find Buzz Belknap's *Grand Canyon River Guide* (1969), with river maps and historic photographs, an informative book to carry along. The maps, with mileages shown from Lee's Ferry, are adapted from the *Plan and Profile of Colorado River from Lees Ferry, Arizona, to Black Canyon, Arizona–Nevada*, issued by the U.S. Geological Survey in 1924.

"The boat, upside down, went down stream 50 to 75 feet ahead of me.

"As soon as I got out of water I climbed up on rocks and turned immediately and saw Brown still in whirl swimming round and at same moment saw Mr. Stanton's boat just coming into head of rapid not over two hundred feet above where Brown was.

"I ran up shore hallooing to Mr. Stanton, 'Mr. Brown is in there,' till I got up to Mr. Stanton's boat, which was then unloaded and immediately jumped in with Richards and rowed around whirls and eddies but could see no trace of Mr. Brown or his body and after some time searching went ashore. *This is correct.*"

Witness

Robert B. Stanton   Harry McDonald
R. M. Hansbrough   July 10th, 9:10 A.M.

Boat No. 3 with Hislop, Nims, and Gibson started from camp about 1/4 minute later than we did, but did not get out in good shape. Caught on rock and were delayed a little. They came down through rapid and into eddy at same point my boat did in safety. They passed us as McDonald and Richards were pushing off from sand beach.

From McDonald's statement and what I myself saw, our boat was at head of rapid, in the draw, when I saw McDonald first and he saw Brown still above water; and our boat was not over 175 feet from Brown. I paced this distance. We ran this distance in 5 seconds, no more, and reached the point where Brown sank not over 2 or 3 seconds after he sank for the last time.

His notebook he carried in his shirt and I suppose when he sank it escaped and shot up out of water just as I saw it.

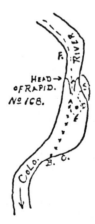

F_IG. 16. Sketch map of the river where President Brown was drowned. Miami University Library.

The whole accident happened inside of a minute and a half, for our boat was not more than 1/2 minute behind Mr. Brown's in leaving camp. We left camp at 6:23 and just before going into the rapid I noted time 6:25, as is my custom all through my notes. After the excitement of the first moment was over I looked at my watch again and it was 6:30 A.M.

As we were in the heaviest of the rapid, and all hands and eyes engaged in getting our boat through safely none of our boat saw Brown at all. Even if we had, it would have been utterly impossible to get to the place where he was any sooner than we did; but if we could have remained afloat till we got there we could have easily thrown him a line or reached him with an oar as our boat circled round the whirl of the eddy he was in. Mr. Brown's boat upset before we rounded point, though we might have been further on.

This we believe entirely correct

Robert B. Stanton   P. M. Hansbrough
Harry McDonald   H. C. Richards

and we know as to Boat No. 4 which was all we saw

John Hislop   F. A. Nims
G. W. Gibson   July 10th 1889

What Mr. Brown referred to, as examining rapid below came from this. Last evening while men were making portage I walked down river bank nearly a mile.

Line on left continues after rounding point on same mountain slope. About 3/4 mile below point side canyon comes in from left and forms Rapid No. 108. One hundred to 150 foot span as line will be so high both on account of fall of last rapid and the fact that the canyon, Colorado, is very narrow and *high* water mark shows fully 45 feet above present stage.

About 700 or 800 feet further on another washout, not canyon, on left side forms Rapid No. 109. This crossing would require 100 foot span. One-fourth mile below this is Rapid No. 110. Formed by washout from right bank and is quite heavy.

One change I note, a very hard stratum of sandstone commenced coming up, under the soft red stone. This is white and is split in layers vertically. Through this the river is cut and so makes a very narrow channel. At Rapid No. 110, it is on left side fully forty feet high, while on right bank it is not over 35 feet high. One-fourth mile on is Rapid No. 111. This is very narrow and swift, formed by heavy wash from right bank.

Beyond this point river is very much confined by the narrow walls. The hard slate of sandstone gradually rising.

Just above Rapid No. 111 high water shows, by heavy driftwood 75 feet above river. This does not interfere with railway line as being above high water. Puts line on the easy slope above first bench.

Fɪɢ. 17. Inscription chiseled on the rock by Peter Hansbrough who drowned five days later (1977 Photo). *C. Gregory Crampton.*

At about 11:20 today Hislop having gone ahead to look reported that he had caught Boat No. 1, Brown's, in eddy one mile below where accident happened. She was upside down and when righted, he found everything in her except McDonald's bag of clothing and the gold pan. McDonald's blankets were lost at first as they were loose in boat. As this boat came down so easily without losing a thing Brown's loss was only caused by his being in whirlpool.

Watched around eddy all morning and then left Hansbrough there and moved boats past Rapid No. 111, to where Boat No. 1 was and made camp; and Hislop, Nims, and myself on right bank examined river up and down for a mile and remained at place of accident with Hansbrough on left bank till 5 ᴘ.ᴍ.

Camp No. 34.

This has been a day of terrible experience. All started from camp in good spirits and in less than 5 minutes our good friend Mr. Brown drowned and gone forever was a blow to us all that no one can realize. In the depth of this lonely canyon and beside the roaring waters, which leaped and lashed and foamed without ceasing, we sat for hours utterly paralyzed. We watched eddy and whirl and then searched the banks for a mile and a half on either side in hopes of at least finding his body and giving it an honored burial place on top some high cliff, but all in vain. It is a common expression of those who know it, "This river seldom gives up its dead." [5]

THURSDAY, JULY 11. Up at 4:30 A.M. Breakfast at 5:30. Broke camp 7:45.

All hands got sorrowfully into our boats. Pulled across stream and landed on sand beach, about 600 feet below our camp on opposite side and examined water ahead. Saw 3 small rapids, concluded they were safe. So all got aboard, and at 8:04 ran small Rapid No. 112. Shipped a little water. 8:07, ran small Rapid No. 113. This was not so bad.

We then landed on sand bar and looked ahead. After next small rapid water was perfectly smooth for 3/2 [2/3?] mile ahead. All got aboard and ran at 8:15 A.M. Small Rapid No. 114. It was perfectly easy and safe. The canyon being so narrow, the water swirls from side to side so that at the foot of these little rapids our boats were carried first to one side and then to other.

At 8:20 we reached head of *roaring* rapid. This part of the canyon is called Echo, and the roar from this rapid is very loud. The perpendicular part of the cliff continues to rise, from Rapids No. 111 to No. 115, a distance of about *two miles*. At this point they are about 300 to 500 feet high, are perpendicular but ragged and broken into points which stick out into water, much more ragged and broken on left side. These form little coves with still water above rapid. In these we land catching on to points of the rock and stop to examine. The rapid is very much too rough to run. In fact as we now see it, it is a roaring cataract, with huge rocks in center, in which no boat could live.

After examining line carefully we attach 210 feet of small line to my boat and McDonald, Hislop, and I get in, push along, by catching hold of points of the rock, while rest of men hold line to keep us from being swept into rapid. We are, at start, about 200 feet above head of rapid. About 75 feet down we held to rock cliff, McDonald with his hands, and I by sticking oar in crack of rock, and Hislop actually scaled a perpendicular wall 20 feet high on which were only little points for toe and fingernail holds. When on top we threw him a fish line and he drew up our heavy line. Then with these two lines attached and pretty hard pulling against current which was rushing out from cliff, we were dropped around next point of cliff into little eddy about 75 feet above

---

[5] So often this is the case. Brown's body was sighted as it was floating down the river on July 17 (see Stanton's entry on that day), but it could not be recovered and was not seen again. The surveyors were still using those frail clinker-built boats. And *still no life pre-servers!* These deficiencies were remedied by Stanton on the second trip. The boats went through then (see the entry for December 31, 1889) at a lower stage of water, without mishap. The accident occurred in a rapid at the mouth of Salt Water Wash, a tributary coming in on the left twelve miles below Lee's Ferry. On a ledge overlooking the river, Peter Hansbrough chiseled an inscription: "F. M. Brown, Pres. D.C.C. & P.R.R. Co. was drowned July 10, 1889, opposite this point." For the contents of Brown's notebook recovered at the time of the accident, see Chapter II, this work. River mileages through Grand Canyon are computed from Lee's Ferry.

rapid. Hislop making our heavy line fast came across cliff above us and we cut loose our little line, which was pulled back to let other boats down. They came down easily as they had our heavy line, still attached to point where Hislop was. After getting last boat to point where we were we let them down in cove to about 30 feet of head of rapid where was a fallen rock in water and sand beach below. We then had line to them, and so McDonald, Hislop, and myself got in, swung out, and McDonald pulled us in hand over hand. We thus landed at 11:00 A.M. on sand and boulders which came out of little canyon on left which forms this Rapid No. 115. Sixty foot *span*.

All being tired out we stop for lunch in the shade under an overhanging cliff on left bank.

At 12:15 P.M. we made portage of all goods and swung boats down Rapid No. 115, and reloaded, about 200 feet below. The rough water continues 700 to 800 feet. We then dropped boats along cliff, after I had climbed along the points of rock close to water to find if it was possible, to about 1/4 of way to next rapid when we all got in and rowed to head of Rapid No. 116 which we reached at 2:00 P.M. From Rapid No. 115 to 116 is about 1000 feet.

Rapid No. 115 is undoubtedly the one Powell made portage at as recorded in his diary. But Rapid No. 116 has undoubtedly been formed since that time as it is made entirely of sharp angled rock fallen from the face of the cliff on each side and the places in the cliffs so fresh breaks as compared with other parts.

We swung our boats around this rapid full loaded with safety, and started again at 3:22 on smooth but rapid water. We ride at great speed for twenty minutes, is smooth water but filled with whirls which carry us from one side of the canyon to the other, and pass through the very swift draws shaped at the head like rapids but too smooth to be given such a name. When at 3:40 we land to examine new rapid ahead, we think it quite safe. So at 3:45 we all run Rapid No. 117. It is not heavy but we are all somewhat wet by the spray of the waves.

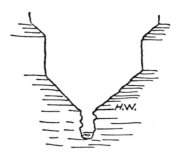

Fig. 18. Sketch of cross section of Echo Canyon with high water mark indicated. Miami University Library.

At this point two things attract my attention, the very quiet water and a break in wall of canyon on right through which the sun is shining on the water; and the two things put together mean a heavy rapid below, and soon we hear the warning roar, and at 3:54 we land on right bank just above a heavy rocky fall of 8 or 10 feet with long rapid below. This is No. 118. We examine it and find it will be necessary to portage not only our stores but boats also.

We unload, carry over the boats; and while the men carry the supplies, etc., the cook goes to getting supper and I sit down to write up my railway notes, by the roar of a foaming cataract. From the best estimate I can make we have traveled today between 4 and 5 miles.

The general conformation of the canyon all day has been same as yesterday, only the canyon walls are higher; but all day today these walls have run about parallel with the fall of the river, from 150 to 200 feet high.

Canyon very narrow, 250 feet wide. Just beyond Rapid No. 115 there seems to be a fault or slip in the whole rock and the lighter colored hard sandstone suddenly disappears and in its place brighter red sandstone, such as we had in Cataract Canyon; and I expected more broken walls hereafter, and so here at Rapid No. 118, 1/4 miles below. A new talus is forming at bottom of cliff next to river and canyon seems to be getting a little wider. And also the canyon cliff on left is getting much lower.

Through the whole section from Lee's Ferry to this point the river falls quite rapidly and as the canyon narrows up the high water mark shows so high it will be necessary to keep railway grade quite high. So that for a long distance the line could be easily constructed on the fine slope above canyon cliffs; but for 2 or 3 miles back from here to do this the work would be very heavy and expensive as the cliffs are too high to use slope above and keep good grade. But as this would only be a short distance, if the cliffs below keep low and they show from this point, this plan, by cutting off face of cliff at top and throwing into river, for these few miles, would be the best and cheapest plan.

But few side canyons come in on today's travel, the one at Rapid No. 115 on left and this one where we are on right. This last would take a 100 foot span. The drainage across a roadbed on this upper slope would have to be very large as all along drains show as coming down from the highest cliff and dropping on to this slope have worn immense gullies. If road was cut in face of cliff along here perhaps some "overhead" drains could be used.

Camp No. 35. We made perhaps 7 to 8 miles today.[6]

FRIDAY, JULY 12. Up at 5:00 A.M. Breakast 6:00 A.M. Load up and start at [*blank*] after spending some time repairing boats.

---

[6] Actually, about four miles, as he estimated earlier in the entry, though with two portages during the day it probably seemed like seven or eight miles. They were camped just below the rapids at the mouth of House Rock Creek seventeen miles below Lee's Ferry.

Noticing about 3/4 mile down river the sun shining through a side canyon on left, I expect another bad rapid there. While the men are loading the boats I walk down on right bank of river on talus to examine.

About 1/2 mile down is a very swift but not rough Rapid No. 119, formed by a wash over top of cliff on left side; and on going to the point where sun was seen I was much surprised to find two *small* rapids very close together formed by two washes which have not cut down so as to make canyons, and notice another about 1000 feet beyond. All on left side. First two 75 foot spans, third 100 foot span.

I wait here for the boats. They reach me at 9:00 A.M. being delayed in getting past foot of rapid. They ran No. 119. All got wet with the splash. I got in my boat and we crossed the river 9:15. Stopped to look at rapids. Started 9:20. All ran, Nos. 120 and 121. They are small but very crooked and required hard steering to keep out of whirls on each side.

Went ashore to look at No. 122, at 9:23. Started again at 9:25. Ran through. This is small. Only formed by huge boulder 100 feet wide, 80 feet long, and 40 feet above water. It is in center of river, the longest length across stream, thus forming two channels. The one we went through about 50 feet wide and the other not over 25 or 30 feet. We come into beautiful quiet water and at 9:30 stopped and Henry shot a duck. Here also is first tree on talus in canyon since leaving Lee's Ferry. The canyon walls do not continue low as noted in last night's record but are rapidly breaking up into benches, low and easy next to river.

One-half mile beyond the huge rock in river, the canyon turns sharply to the east. This point is very ragged and is cut through by 3 water courses, 50 foot spans. Beyond this for 1 1/2 miles the water is perfectly smooth but rapid. The canyon is wider 300 to 500 feet. The upper walls are growing higher and higher, but the benches next to river are growing wider and more in number.

Side canyon ahead on right side and at 10:15 we reach head of immense Rapid No. 123. The waves are dashing up 10 to 15 feet high. Of course we unload and make portage of everything. *Fifteen to 18 foot fall.* We push [into] the stream an old Indian dugout and time it going through the rapid. It went a distance of 1150 feet, I paced distance in 64 seconds. We unloaded and portaged the boats a distance 600 feet and then stopped for lunch at 11:30.

After lunch we reloaded boats and dropped them down to foot of rapid by 3 P.M. and waited for Hislop who went back for his instruments he left at camp, till 3:45.

We start again and in just 3 minutes ride are at the head of another huge Rapid No. 124. This one I think is of recent formation, as the slide on right that forms it is of sharp angled recently broken boulders. We drop our boats over this loaded, and cross the river to opposite side and in 1/2 mile come to a succession of three rapids all in next 3000 feet. Sharp and crooked and too heavy to run with our men in the state they are since Mr. Brown's death. These are Nos. 125, 126, and 127. We drop boats loaded around first and go into camp at 5:45 tired out with the day's work.

While the cook is getting supper I climb up on side of cliff with McDonald and am able to see down the canyon about 3 miles, though can only see the river a short distance. The shore line is getting much larger and the cliffs, benches, are in such shape that a railway line can be built on the shore line and the river makes bays and eddies so that the line can in places be stolen from the river and thus save expense and curvature.

Of course it is impossible for me to tell just what grade can be maintained along this rapidly falling portion but do not think the fall here is as great as in Cataract Canyon, where we can keep a 16 foot per mile grade. High water mark is so low along here and we have so much level water between rapids that I think the only difficulty of our line so far from Lee's Ferry is from Soap Creek at Rapid No. 107 to about No. 123. This portion of the canyon is very narrow and as noted the walls from water up to first bench run up in places 200+ feet high. The expensive part of the line will be cutting from top of cliff a bench down to grade, but through this portion grade will be *at least* 100 feet above river and perhaps can be made much higher to save work. But this question can only be settled by actual survey to find grade from these high cliffs down to the low benches and fine talus which form, as noted, further on. Of course line could be built along the 2 to 4 miles of difficult cliff work without cutting cliff from top but I think this the better plan.

Which is Soap Creek? That at Rapid No. 118 or that at No. 123?

I think we made between 6 and 7 miles today. Camp No. 36.[7]

SATURDAY, JULY 13. 5:00 A.M., everyone got up this morning utterly oppressed by the weather. Quite cloudy. Was waked up out of sound sleep at 4 A.M. by Hansbrough who had a pain in his toe and was thoroughly frightened. We had breakfast, all feeling very much under the weather.

At 7:30 we are loaded up and embark. Row across bay to head of Rapid No. 126, and swing boats down with lines. The three washes here will perhaps call for 50 foot-100 foot and 50 foot spans. At 8:10 we embark again and as we approach the next rapid(?), numbered last night 127, we find it so smooth that we shoot through it without stopping, and I conclude not to number it;

---

[7] In the sixty-one miles of Marble Canyon, the Colorado River on the average falls nearly seven feet to the mile. There were many rapids, some of them reminders of the heavy water in Cataract Canyon. During the days July 9–12, the surveyors had lined, or portaged, some of the most difficult rapids: Badger Creek (Stanton's 105), Soap Creek (107), House Rock (118), North Canyon (123), 21 Mile (124). Soap Creek at all stages of water, is one of the worst in the canyon.

Fig. 19. Frank Mason Brown, President, DCC&PRR, drowned in Marble Canyon. Miami University Library.

and we pass through three others of the same kind which are simply very swift draws. Numbers are only given to rapids that tumble and roar and shoot up white foam from their breakers.

Three-fourths mile further on side canyon comes in on left, and forms small rapid. We stop to examine, 8:22. Find the rapid small and smooth on left side and conclude to run it. The little canyon that formed this is not cut down to river but forms a basin back in cliff 75 feet above.

We start at 8:25 and at 8:26 are through Rapid No. 127, and first see *marble* on our left; and at 8:30 stop at head of very bad Rapid No. 128 which compels portage of everything including boats. Just below this rapid the marble shows about 15 feet high on right. This rapid is not caused by a distinct side canyon or wash but by a general smash up of the cliff on left side for 1/2 mile and requires 4-50 foot spans for water way. Beyond this point the lower cliffs on both sides of river are very much broken up, and talus of debris is formed as far as I can see, 1 1/2 miles, 100 to 250 feet high, while high water only shows 35 to 45 feet up, making an easy road bed construction equal to any mountain slope except the drainage.

This portion of the line and perhaps back for 2 miles would perhaps be classified 1/2 loose rock and 1/2 *solid* rock. Though if slope under this debris is solid as it shows in some places, the classification would be still higher.

We immediately go to work and portage the stores about 150 feet past head of rapid, and as the rocks are very high and hard to carry over we construct a tramway of driftwood on top of rocks and slide boats over on their keels, and into water just below head of rapid. Load each one up as it is brought over and tow it down to smooth water.

At 10:45 we reached next rapid 1500 feet distant, No. 129, and swing our boats all round; and at 11:25 are at head of Rapid No. 130, distant from last about 1500 feet, and stop for lunch. This rapid is over 1/2 mile long and is very crooked in shape with the water piled up high in center of current. We call this Lone Cedar Rapid from a large cedar tree under which we eat lunch. We take long time rest as men are all tired and worried out and this is the most oppressive day we have felt. All our work is done in the sun at 132°.

A few hundred feet beyond where we are eating lunch, the marble cliffs show on both sides of the canyon about 40 feet high and I conclude to call this the "Head of Marble Canyon". Heavy rain after lunch. At 1:30 P.M. we start again and swing boats over Rapid No. 130 nearly the half mile of its distance. Hansbrough is sick and so we are one man short; and with the excessive heat progress is very slow.

At 4:00 P.M. we embark and sail about 3/4 of a mile through one chute of very swift water, and then into a bay of glassy smoothness which of course means another rapid. At 4:10 we reach it. Large and terrific with huge boulders all over the upper part. With great care and success we swung the boats around this Rapid No. 131 and at 5 P.M., after a row of about a half a mile, went into camp at the head of Rapid No. 132. Camp No. 37.

To this point the railway line is described in notes written at noon. We only made 3 miles today.[8]

[8] To boat through Marble Canyon is to descend through the colorful strata that compose the distinctive profile of Grand Canyon. Trending southward the river has cut through the massive beds of sedimentary strata which have been tilted gently northward. Thus, as he moves downstream and crosses the several strata, the voyager may observe at close range the configuration of the canyon. One of the most distinctive formations (and easily identifiable from the canyon rims) is the Redwall Limestone, a hard cliff-forming stratum about 500 feet thick. Impressed by its sheer cliffs and hard, polished surfaces, Powell called it the "marble" and named the upper part of Grand Canyon after it. The Redwall first appears at river level at mile 22.6 where Stanton observed it (at his rapid 127). July 13 was a hard day for the explorers. They portaged or lined around a series of rough rapids. A careful study of the Stanton Notebook, together with the U.S. Geological Survey River maps (1924) suggest this

SUNDAY, JULY 14. Resting in Camp No. 37. Raining in showers all day.

MONDAY, JULY 15. Up at 4:30. Breakfast 5:00 A.M. Break camp and start at 6:40 A.M.

We at once come to Rapid No. 132. The channel at head is full of immense boulders which cause breakers and side waves which it would be impossible to run. Some of the boulders are very near shore and others further out. We let boats down with lines, twisting the boats around between the boulders. Stopping them every 50 to 100 feet to change and get them down quite easily without getting out into the main current.

No. 1 *Ward* boat is driven sidewise as she passes through one narrow place and knocks off her stern piece on a rock. We row down about 1500 feet to good sand beach and at 8:00 A.M. stop to repair the boat. This is at head of Rapid No. 133 and it is as bad as the last.

This side canyon is quite interesting. In years back the torrents have cut an opening through the cliffs 300 feet wide between walls, leaving slopes to the bed of the water course which is 80 to 90 feet wide.

Just in center of its course is a portion of the original marble cliff which has withstood the storms of ages and stands 80 feet long, 70 feet wide, and 40 feet high with a well proportioned cutwater at its upper end. This is in direct line of railway and will serve as an everlasting center pier for bridge of 2-100 foot spans which will be required.

Between Rapid No. 132 and 133 is little side wash on left. Requires 30 foot span, and across big wash that forms Rapid No. 133 will be required 80 [foot] span.

We swing our boats around the point of Rapid No. 133 and were ready to start at about 10:20. There were no waves below here but the current was swift. McDonald and Gibson went first. Did not go out far enough in current and stopped about 200 feet below to start again. They went down to point below. With some hard pulling reached sand bar below in safety. Just before they started Richards remarked, "Let's all go together." But I and McDonald thought and remarked while there was no danger it was best to let McDonald go ahead and the rest of us see how he went through.

The first boat started as stated above and as they were going Richards said, "We better drop our boats down"; and Hansbrough with the oars in his hand coming towards the boat said, "Why, Henry, that's all right let's pull through it," or very near those words. I then spoke up and said, "Boys decide it for

as a possible identification of the rapids on this stretch of the river where rapids are almost continuous: 24 Mile (Stanton's 128), 24½ Mile (129), 25 Mile (130–"Lone Cedar"), a rapid at Mile 25.2 (131). Camp 37 was made on the left side at the head of Cave Springs Rapid (132) at the mouth of "Marble Pier Canyon." Between 24 Mile and 26 Mile rapids, a distance of 1.7 miles, the river profile shows a sharp drop of forty-six feet.

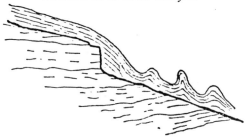

FIG. 20. Profile sketch of a rapid in the upper part of Marble Canyon. Miami University Library.

yourselves. I don't think there is any danger, but you must decide yourselves." Hansbrough then, "Why let's go, Henry"; and Richards replied, "Well, if you say so we'll go that way," and sat down to take off his shoes; and Nims heard him say, "That's a bad place to smash a boat, but of course there's no danger to us."

They got into the boat and I helped them push off remarking as I did, "Your safest course is to keep well out in the current way outside of the rocks." Hansbrough answered, "Yes, we will," and they started.

For the first few hundred feet they went down nearly out to the center of the stream. When all of a sudden we saw them turn towards the cliff and in a moment they were against the cliff at a point with an overhanging shelf of about 3 feet. They, as quickly as possible, put up the oars in the boat, and commenced shoving the boat out; and as I watched them I saw Richards get his end out from the rocks clear into the stream and Hansbrough had his head out from under the shelf. He was pushing with his paddle on main cliff and Richards his hands on the shelf. I remarked to Hislop, "They are all right now," and expected to see them pull out into the stream, when all of a sudden their boat turned over, and both went into the water. Hansbrough was never seen to rise by any of us.

I screamed to McDonald and Gibson who were below and they pushed out into the stream with their boat towards Richards who was swimming down the current; but he sank before they could reach him. He sank in what was swift but perfectly smooth water. Hansbrough we never saw from the time we saw the boat upset. Hislop and I ran over the cliff but by the time we got there all was quiet and both men gone forever.

What an experience. I am too much affected to write further. Gibson is so affected at Henry's death that he is crying like a child; and it is all we can do to keep him from starting right up over the cliffs back to Lee's Ferry.

After our lunch which was a little sugar and a cup of water we swing by Rapid Nos. 134 and 135 and go into camp at 5 p.m. on small wash of rocks and sand on right bank of river, Camp No. 38. These rapids 132 to 136 are from 1500 to 2000 feet apart, so we have not made 2 miles today.

We camp, No. 38, on right bank on small bench of sand and rocks about 50 feet wide in the river. All are in a very sorrowful and depressed mood, especially Gibson, who is utterly in despair, he feeling that he is responsible for Henry's death as he sent for and asked him to go on the trip. I sat down on Gibson's bed, after he had gone to bed, and talked a long time with him to convince him he was not in the least responsible for the accident. The marble cliffs here are in places 150 feet high and we have all, except Gibson, made our own beds in a marble cave 30 feet above the river.

This portion of the river is very much confined and the debris from side washes come in on both sides and the current changed by each one of these piles of rock shifts first to one side and then to the other making navigation very difficult.[9]

Nims' watch.

TUESDAY, JULY 16. Up at 6:00 A.M. Start at 8:50 A.M. We slept fairly well last night.

After breakfast we had a consultation and after talking the whole matter over we all, except Hislop, came to the conclusion it was best to try to go out through the Nankoweap Valley towards Rock House. Hislop said he was willing but rather thought the Little Colorado was better. We concluded then to go to the Nankoweap as quick as possible, stop and then decide what to do. We then looked over our stores and left everything we could spare so as to lighten our loads for portages. And with very sorrowful faces we started down river. The water is very turbid from heavy rains above.

We load up boats and swing them around point of Rapid No. 136, and at about 9:20 we embark and have good sail for 1 1/2 miles over smooth but swift water, and at 9:35 reach Rapid No. 137, formed by side canyon on left. This is very wide at top but very narrow where it is cut through the marble, 80 foot span. This rapid is very severe with wave in center 10 to 15 feet high. No boat could run it. We portage our goods and drop empty boats over with success. Long and tedious getting below rocks on to what is undoubtedly Powell's "marble pavement 1 mile long." High water mark 50 feet high here.

At 11:40 we embark and run across river to where we saw our Boat No. 5. This morning when we reached here, Rapid 137, we find only the vinegar keg. This delays us 5 minutes and at 11:45 we embark again and in 10 minutes land on left bank just above Rapid No. 138. This is but a small rapid and easily run under any other circumstances. As we land we discover our boat No. 5, across the river in an eddy. McDonald and Hislop take an empty boat, go across, and secure her.

[9] Tragedy struck a second time. The explorers lined Cave Springs Rapid (132) and then Twenty-six Mile Rapid (133). The accident occurred in the fast water below 133. When Richards and Hansbrough attempted to push away from the rock wall, the boat flipped in the heavy water and both men were quickly sucked under. No life preservers!

12:40, they have returned. They found everything of the load in the boat, even to the Winchester which was simply stuck under the straps, except the two loose kegs, 1 of which we have and the other is floating in eddy below, and my sack in which was my coat and vest, underclothing, etc., and what we had saved of Mr. Brown's clothes. The boat is stove in at both ends and so is useless. Out of the rest of the load we will pick what we need and leave the remainder.

We drop past this Rapid 138 and stop for lunch. The marble along this part of the canyon is from 100 to 200 feet high. Taken as one cliff it is not perpendicular but is benched. At this point the second bench is forming, and as we go down to Rapid 139 we see three benches in it. The lower benches are not wide but on top of the marble is a very wide [one]. The top stratum of marble is not so hard as the lower ones and is cut through by water courses. These can be handled by overhead drains, and this whole section can be handled same as the difficult portion described just below Badger Creek.

We start from lower side of Rapid No. 138 at just 2 P.M. We run one mile and stop a few minutes to examine and start again and run 1 1/2 miles through swift but smooth water to Rapid No. 139, 2:40. This we swing the loaded boats around and start at once and run the next rapid which though small has waves high enough to send the spray over our heads. This is No. 140, and at 3:50 P.M. we reach Rapid No. 141, formed by short side canyon on left bank. We stop to examine ahead, and climb up the marble cliff, and as the whole country seems broken up beyond, we wish to explore and so conclude to camp here. About 1 1/2 miles from last distance. Side canyon at No. 139, 80 foot span. Side canyon at No. 140, 50 foot span. Side canyon at No. 141, 80 foot span.

We climb up side of canyon at this point. It is very much broken up. The marble is also much broken. The first bench is only about 50 feet up and is flat and easy to locate upon. After climbing up 800 or 1000 feet we find that on both sides, the country seems much broken and that there is a large canyon coming in on right, about 1 1/2 miles down river. This we suppose to be the Nankoweap, and as it is so far back to top conclude to go back to camp.

Going down I have a long talk over the whole situation. They are both very loyal to me and will do anything I wish. Hislop does not want to go out at this point but wishes to continue down and go out at the Little Colorado.

Camp No. 39.

WEDNESDAY, JULY 17. Up at 6:30. *Drizzling rain.* Breakfast 8:00. Packed and start 9:00.

It rained most all of yesterday afternoon. So last night I climbed up about 40 feet on the side of the marble cliff where I saw a hole and found a little cave about 8 feet long and 2 to 2 1/2 feet wide with half of it open to the river and the shelf above projecting out 3 or 4 feet. It was hollow at bottom and full of fine dry sand. I spread this out and made my bed comfortable and dry while it rained hard all night. I had a good night's rest, only waking during a heavy thunderstorm at 12 midnight. And how the thunder reverberates between those marble cliffs. The lightning lit up the canyon with such vivid brightness followed by such awful darkness; and as peel after peel of heaven's artillery was echoed back from marble cliff to marble cliff, and died away in distant murmers as they rose among the ragged sandstone peaks above the marble 2500 feet above my head, was an experience of grandeur and awfulness not soon to be forgotten.

We leave camp at 9:00 A.M. Run down 1/2 mile to Rapid 142. Small. Through it and to Rapid No. 143 which, both of them, are small. Ran through No. 142, and reach the mouth of the side canyon at 10:45 and land on upper side of wash. We find the creek running quite a stream of red muddy water into the river. Through the marble the water has cut a very narrow channel 10 to 20 feet wide, which is the only outlet for the valley above which is very large.

About 1/4 mile below we notice beautiful green vines, ferns, and bushes and go down to examine it. There is quite a spring coming out of the cliff and there are several patches of rich soil lodged on a bench of the marble and watered by these springs are covered with rich grass, ferns, flowers, and bushes. We gather bunches of ferns and flowers to take home to remember this place which is Powell's "Vasey's Paradise," as at this point the river turns square around to the east.

And between the bend and the mouth of the side canyon are two large caves in the marble rock.

This is something the shape of the point opposite the Nankoweap and as we are to leave the river here I hope [it is] only till we can get new boats and finish the examination. *I name* this *Point Retreat*. Note, this *is not* the *Nankoweap* but a wash north of the Kaibabs [Kaibab Plateau] that *heads up near House Rock*. Point Retreat will require a tunnel about 1 mile long and it has a splendid approach on upper side; and as well as I can see there is an easy exit on lower side.

I have always expected that it would be necessary to cross the river and go through the Grand Canyon on the west side of the river. If that shall prove to be correct after examination further on this will be an excellent point to cross.

The marble cliffs above this point are very low and broken from 50 to 100 feet above the water and an approach to the tunnel can be made in any direction with ease, so as *I think* to put this tunnel all on a straight line. Perhaps through all this Marble Canyon, expense can be saved and alignment bettered by using some number of short tunnels, though there are no very difficult points of alignment from Lee's Ferry to Point Retreat.

High water mark shows here 25 feet.

About noon as we were returning from Vasey's Paradise I looked up the river and saw something large and white like a large bundle floating down. As it came a little nearer we all saw it was Mr. Brown's body. McDonald and Hislop jumped into a boat and at the risk of their lives attempted to get it; but it was impossible as it was so near the head of the rapid. They came near going over the rapid among the rocks with their boat. I followed the body along shore for some distance and saw it go around the big bend, through another rapid, and float on down the river. It was very sad. I had so hoped when I saw it that we could give it burial in the pretty little spot called "Vasey's Paradise."

After dinner McDonald, Hislop, and myself climbed up on marble about 50 feet above river and found a whole row of cliff dwellings with many pieces of broken pottery all over the cliff. And also a very old trail out on the (Nanko-weap) side canyon. We followed it till we could see up the canyon and re-turned to camp to prepare for our tramp tomorrow.

We have cached all our surplus supplies in a cave in the rock, in the first opening *above* mouth of the Nankoweap. Except the keg of rice which is on slope nearly down to Vasey's Paradise and boats which are useless. They are as follows:

210 feet 3/4″ rope, new; 1 saw and 1 screw driver; 1 brace and 2 bits; 1 drawing knife; 1 axe; 1 hatchet; 1 hammer; 2 *old* boats, *old* lines attached; 7 *old* oars; 4 *old* paddles; 40 45×70 cartridges; 1 No. 38 revolver; 3 sacks flour, not good; 1 pint tincture arnica; 1 4 gallon keg rice, good, 1/2 *full*; 1 4 gallon keg coffee, good, 3/4 *full*; 1 4 gallon keg sugar, good, 1/2 full; 1 coffee pot; 1 14 inch Dutch oven; 1 fry pan; 1 saucepan; 1 bread pan; 1 coffee mill, old; 5 knives and forks; 6 *old* spoons; 4 good cups; 4 double blankets, *common*.

This retreat is certainly a great disappointment to me and as much so to Hislop. But of course it would not only be unwise to attempt to go further with our present outfit, but would be impossible as we have not enough men to portage our boats. Hislop wants to go to Little Colorado River, but Nims has expressed to me a fear of the Indians that are said to be camped at the mouth of that river. Gibson is utterly overcome and broken up over Richard's death and has but one idea, to get away from the river. I have concluded not to risk anything more, but to go out here, if we can get out.[10]

[10] After these tragic days, Stanton moved the expedition down the river and went into camp (40) at the mouth of South, or Paradise, Canyon, 31.5 miles below Lee's Ferry. Vasey's Paradise, named by Powell after a botanist friend George Vasey, a short distance downstream from South Canyon, is a mass of ferns, shrubbery, and annuals watered by springs gushing from the Redwall Limestone. The Colorado River bends sharply to the east just below South Canyon. The towering canyon wall on the inside of the bend was named by Stanton Point Retreat to mark the place where he planned to leave the river. South

THURSDAY, JULY 18. Up at 5:00 A.M. Breakfast at 6:00 A.M.

Start 7:00 A.M. Climb up old trail by old cliff dwellings and course around on top of marble till we come in to bed of creek at junction of marble and sandstone. At this point we found a very large blanket vein of mineral lying between the marble and sandstone. It is from 10 to 15 feet thick where it is cut through by the wash, and is exposed for several hundred feet.

We go a mile or two further up canyon and stop to rest. Great storm comes up. Streams of water and *rock* pour down sides of canyon in every direction. Shelter behind a leaning rock. This storm shows great care with which the drainage *above* the road must be provided for. This storm in the side canyon was a wonderful sight, and a great revelation to me.

As the rain commenced to fall we heard some rocks roll down the slope behind us, when we looked up, and it seemed as if the whole slopes of the gorge had begun to move at the top. Little streams of water came over the top, and in a moment they changed into streams of mud; and as they came down they gathered strength and turned to streams of mud and rock, undermining larger rocks; and starting them they plunged ahead, and in a few moments the whole sides of the canyon seemed to be moving down upon us with a roar and awful rumbling noise; and as the larger rocks plunged ahead of the streams, they crashed against other rocks, breaking into pieces; and the fragments flew in to the air in every direction, hundreds of feet above our heads; and as these came nearer the bottom where we were, it seemed as if we were to be buried in an avalanche of rock and mud. But the rain soon ceased, and the whole canyon resumed its deathlike stillness except for the noise of the little stream of muddy water running in the creek bed at our feet.

It is a noticeable fact, that before today, in all the weeks we have been in these canyons we have never heard as much as a pebble drop or roll down from the sides.

Canyon heads on the eastern slope of the Kaibab Plateau. Nankoweap Canyon, also heading on the Kaibab, was twenty miles downstream.

Amid all the strain and mental anguish during the run through Marble Canyon, Stanton never lost sight of the prospects for the canyon railroad. All the way from Cataract through Glen and down to Point Retreat, his engineering eye favored the left bank location for the rails. If downstream surveys favored the canyon's right side, then Point Retreat would be a good place to bridge Marble Canyon.

Stanton notes the discovery of prehistoric ruins along the cliff above their camp. These ruins, which may still be seen by river travelers, are possibly a thousand years old, dating from the time when there was extensive occupation of the Grand Canyon by the ancient Anasazis, or Pueblo peoples. But even before the coming of the Anasazis men had occupied the South Canyon area and other places in Grand Canyon. In one of the caves mentioned by Stanton, archaeologists have found evidence of man dating back approximately 4000 years. The site is now known as Stanton Cave. See Robert C. Euler, "The Canyon Dwellers," *American West*, IV (May 1967), and J. Donald Hughes, *In the House of Stone and Light, a Human History of the Grand Canyon* (Grand Canyon Natural History Association, 1978), chapters two and eight, for the Indian history of the Grand Canyon.

Fig. 21. Point Retreat, where the first railroad surveying expedition ended. Supplies were cached and the men climbed out of Marble Canyon through South Canyon (center) and walked to the settlements (1967 Photo). *C. Gregory Crampton.*

After our lunch we resumed our march and reached the top at 4:00 P.M. The most difficult part of the climb was the last 200 feet at the top. This was over an old mountain sheep trail and was at about a 30° slope from perpendicular. We had to go up this one at a time to keep from rolling down rocks upon the others; and it was with great difficulty we were able to get up at all and keep from pulling huge rocks down upon ourselves as they were loosened by the recent rain, especially as each of us was loaded with 40 to 45 lbs. of blankets, food, and notebooks, etc.

We found some good clear water at top in rock pockets, and after a little rest pushed on straight across the mesa towards where we believed House Rock to be. At 7:00 P.M. we found a little pool of water on the plain and stopped for the night. I think we have made 10 to 12 miles today. The whole mesa we have crossed today is covered with fine grass and is a wonderful cattle range.

FRIDAY, JULY 19. Up at 5 A.M. Camped last night on top of the mesa in little draw, by a hole of water 10 feet long and 4 wide, with cow dung in one end of pool. Slept awfully cold. Got up at about midnight, built a fire of sage brush, and laid down beside it on rock and slept.

Started on our tramp 6:15 A.M. Walked about 9 miles and came to "VT" cattle ranch where they are building a new stone house, at 9 A.M.

Slept till 11:30 and at 1 P.M. we started in wagon and two mules for House Rock. Reached House Rock, 20 miles, about 6:30 P.M. Will stay here all night.

(S. W. Taylor, *House Rock*, Via Johnson P.O., Kane Co., Utah.)

SATURDAY, JULY 20. Up 6:30.

Stayed at House Rock last night. Mr. S. W. Taylor has charge of the "VT" cattle. A very pleasant and kind man. He hitched up his team and took us today to "Johnsons," about 12 miles from Kanab.

Reached Johnsons 9:30 P.M. Distance 40 miles. They received us very kindly and gave us a splendid supper of light bread and milk, and in preference we will sleep on the haystack.

This seems to be a great cattle and sheep country. All the stock is now on the summer ranges along the Kaibab (Buckskin) Mountains and these low lands and valleys are covered with the finest grass, which is the winter pasture. If these valleys and mesas had sufficient water for irrigation what an immense population southern Utah and northern Arizona would support.

SUNDAY, JULY 21. Slept late this morning, for we had a splendid bed among the haystacks. Mr. Johnson took us out before breakfast and showed us his fine gardens, and large fish ponds, etc., and told us all about his place. Barley and beets are raised here without irrigation, one beet 42 lbs.

His name is W. D. Johnson, Johnson P. O., Kane Co., Utah.

Had family worship and [say] grace at table. Elegant breakfast.

Started on our journey to Kanab. Reached Bishop Lawrence C. Mariger's at about noon. Went to Mormon Church at 2 P.M. Elegant dinner at the bishop's at 4:00. The kindness of these people. The bishop opened and turned over for our use the Tithing House and everyone has been the kindest with sympathy and good dinners.

E. D. Woolley, President, Kane Co., Utah.

Lawrence C. Mariger, Bishop, Kanab, Kane Co., Utah.

Alonz L. Steward, Kanab.

At 5:30 P.M. as soon as the telegraph line was open, the bishop sent the following telegram for me.

Kanab, Utah, July 21st, '89.

J. C. Montgomery, Clayton Block, Denver, Colorado.

President Frank M. Brown was drowned in the Colorado River, in Marble Canyon, July 10th, by his boat being capsized while running a rapid. He was thrown into a whirlpool and unable to get out of it, while the other man in the boat was thrown into the current and carried down about six hundred feet and landed.

All the other boats of the expedition went through the rapid safely and my boat reached the point where Mr. Brown was thrown a very little more than 1/2 minute after the accident happened and less than five seconds after he sank for the last time.

Five days after, while working our way down, another boat was driven against a cliff; and in pushing it off it was capsized and the two boatmen Peter M. Hansbrough and Henry C. Richards were both drowned before assistance could reach them. It was impossible to recover any of the bodies.

Robert B. Stanton, Chief Engineer.

I also sent telegram to my wife, to the *Engineering News*, New York, and to Henry Richards' family in Kentucky.

I have arranged with Bishop Mariger to send us with his team to the railroad tomorrow. With the exception of going to church we have spent almost all our time eating fruit, of which there is the greatest abundance.

This town of Kanab is the most southern settlement of the Mormons in Utah. It is situated in a beautiful valley just outside the hills and near the head of the Kanab Wash, which enters the Colorado River about the center of the *Grand* Canyon. It is quite an old settlement, has about [blank] inhabitants, is well laid out, with shade trees on all the streets, with good gardens, filled with fruit trees, and abundance of all kinds of fruit. The houses are good frame houses, except Mariger's which is brick. The people are engaged in farming, outlying farms, and in cattle raising.

While the whole place shows great care and energy in laying out and building up *at first*, this thrift has not been *kept up*. The shade and fruit trees have died and not been replaced. No pruning has been done for years. The whole appearance of the place is as if the last few years everyone had lost all interest in anything except mere existence. We're only staying here, expecting soon to move away. This is the impression made upon me by all Mormon settlements I have seen, except that of W. D. Johnson's where we stayed last night; and yet he with all his thrift and energy is talking of moving to Old Mexico.

KANAB, MONDAY, JULY 22. Kanab's elevation is about 4500.

This morning I telegraphed to J. C. Montgomery, treasurer of the company, saying I would draw on him at sight for $600.00 to get home with. Have received no answer. Bishop Mariger says it is not necessary and that I can have all the money and supplies I need to get home with, without any other security than my order on the treasurer.

After breakfast I went to Mariger's store. Got bill of groceries. Arranged for his team for $50.00 to take us to railroad at Milford and after settling up with Taylor and all other bills, Mariger gave me the balance of $600.00, some 500, in cash. We concluded all business by 11:00 A.M. Had lunch at Bishop's house and at 12:30 P.M. bade them all good-by and started in the wagon for the railroad. We have young Stewart, brother of Al. Stewart, for driver. We follow up Kanab Wash into the hills and camp about 18 miles from town.

TUESDAY, JULY 23. We start early this morning and cross range of mountains, elevation 6790 feet. Pass some good timber. We reach town of Panguitch about 7 P.M., elevation 6025 feet.

The bishop gives us the Tithing House yard to camp in, and the hay mow to sleep on. Get plenty of fresh milk and eggs. Panguitch is quite a nice town, mostly of brick houses, not many shade trees. Beautiful clear water in the ditches. It is too high to raise fruit so they say. It is situated in a fine large open valley of splendid pastures and fine hay. The principle industry cattle, butter, eggs, and cheese. Considerably higher, some 1500 feet, in the hills, is Panguitch Lake. Here everyone takes their butter to keep during the summer and sell and ship in the fall and winter.

WEDNESDAY, JULY 24. This is Mormon "Pioneer Day" on which they celebrate their first arrival in Salt Lake Valley. We were awakened this A.M. at daylight by a salute from a small cannon, Panguitch, and at sunrise the Stars and Stripes were raised on new flag pole in the churchyard.

Had a good trip over the mountains, 7890 feet high, today. Passed near town of Beaver, 5 miles distant. Looked like a thriving place of 2000. Fine trees. Said to raise all kinds of fruit. Elevation 5300 feet. Beautiful valley highly cultivated. Brick houses, and all looking well.

Camped about 10 miles below town on Beaver Creek. Made nearly 50 miles today.

THURSDAY, JULY 25. Left camp 7 A.M. Followed down Beaver Creek for some 21 miles and reached Milford, a station on the Utah Central Railway at 12 noon. We take it easy during afternoon, smoking and eating fruit brought in by Mormon team from Beaver. Milford is only a little one horse railway station at the foot of the grade [*blank*] miles below Frisco a mining town at the end of this railway.

At 7:30 P.M. we take the night train for Provo, where we will get the D&RG train from Salt Lake to Denver. Am much disappointed that I have not received word by wire from home.

FRIDAY, JULY 26. Provo, Utah. Reached this place for breakfast. D&RG train late. Excursion from Denver. Meet Mrs. Cresswell who tells me my family are in Denver and well. This is the first word I have heard from them since May 22d. Reynolds and Cass Hite come from Salt Lake at noon. Reynolds half drunk. Am glad he is not going with us.

Take train at 12:30. Passengers much surprised that such a rough looking set should come into pullman car. Make two pleasant acquaintances, ex-Governor Grey of Indiana and M. A. Anderson of Camden, New Jersey.

Denver, Colorado, Monday, July 29, '89. We reached Denver by the D&RGRy, Saturday evening *July 27th '89*.[11]

---

[11] Climbing out of this 2000-foot-deep Marble Canyon by way of the tributary South Canyon, and through a summer cloudburst, the explorers found themselves on the open, grass-covered Marble Platform. With the arching slopes of the Kaibab Plateau on their left, the men headed northward, reaching the V. T. Ranch headquarters, an outfit running cattle on the Arizona Strip. From House Rock they traveled to Johnson's and Kanab, pioneer Mormon communities in Southern Utah, and thence by way of Panguitch and Beaver Creek to Milford and the railroad.

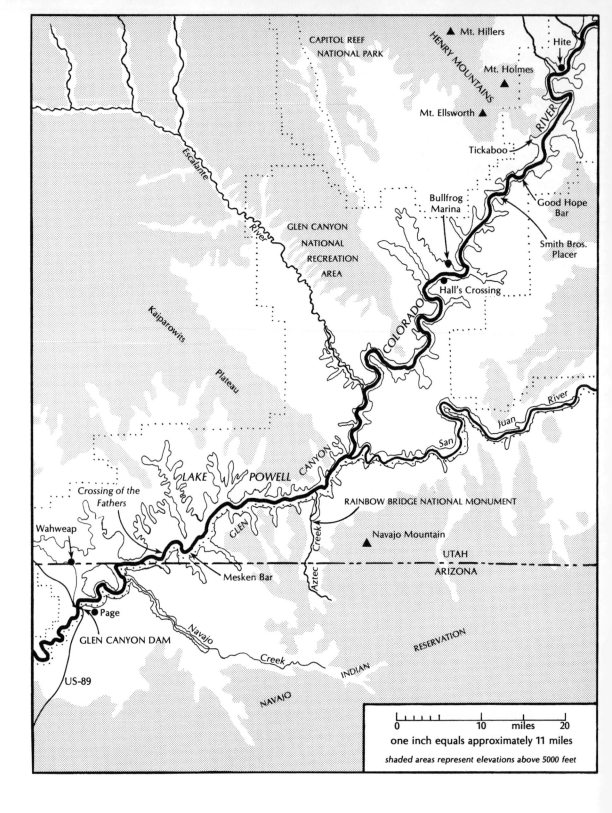

CAPITOL REEF
NATIONAL PARK

▲ Mt. Hillers

Hite

HENRY MOUNTAINS

Mt. Holmes ▲

RIVER

Mt. Ellsworth ▲

Tickaboo

Good Hope
Bar

Bullfrog
Marina

Smith Bros.
Placer

GLEN CANYON

NATIONAL

RECREATION

AREA

Hall's Crossing

COLORADO

Escalante

River

Kaiparowits

Plateau

River

San

Juan

River

CANYON

LAKE   POWELL

RAINBOW BRIDGE NATIONAL MONUMENT

Crossing of the
Fathers

GLEN

Navajo Mountain ▲

Wahweap

Mesken Bar

Aztec

Creek

UTAH

ARIZONA

Page

GLEN CANYON DAM

Navajo

Creek

RESERVATION

INDIAN

US-89

NAVAJO

0   10   miles   20

one inch equals approximately 11 miles

shaded areas represent elevations above 5000 feet

CHAPTER IV

BACK TO GLEN CANYON

Stanton now emerges as the prime mover in the operations of the Denver, Colorado Canyon & Pacific Railroad. New boats and safety equipment were built to his specifications. With contract in hand, and enough money sub- scribed to complete the railroad survey, the energetic engineer headed up the second expedition made up of four river veterans and eight new men. To save time and to avoid the hazards of Cataract Canyon, the party traveled overland from the railhead at Green River, Utah, to the head of Glen Canyon. On the run through Glen Canyon, the new equipment was tested, gold mining claims were staked, and the last thirty-four miles of the instrumental survey was com- pleted. After a memorable Christmas dinner at Lee's Ferry, the expedition made ready to tackle Marble Canyon.

Skeleton record of events from July 29th '89 to the starting of the second expedition from Denver, November 25th '89.

During this time I kept no regular journal and the following is compiled from notes and letters and minutes of the several company meetings.

On arriving in Denver, the members of the railroad company much de- moralized by the death of President Brown, and most of them ready to drop the railroad project, particularly Mr. J. C. Montgomery.

I was desirous to complete the work and at once set about to try to raise the necessary funds. In [order] to be more closely connected with the company and have some share in its management I bought on August 2d '89 Mr. Mont- gomery's stock and paid him $650 in cash for the same.

Mr. Montgomery resigned from the board of directors and I was elected in his place. I then set to work to raise the funds and was partially successful. Mr. T. C. Henry subscribed $10,000; H. B. Chamberlin 2,000; and S. S. Har- per 1,500. This made the work possible but was not enough.

I however went east, taking Harry McDonald with me, and ordered our new boats built at Waukegan, Illinois, and left McDonald there to superintend their construction. I went to New York where I remained for some weeks and got much encouragement from Mr. Arthur W. Wellington, C. E., editor of *Engineering News*.

In the meantime Major Powell had published his interview in the *New York Tribune* ridiculing our railroad project, and I published my answer in *Engineering News* of Septemter 21st '89.

Later I returned to Denver and not getting any more money, on November 20th '89, I signed a contract with the railroad company to complete the survey. A party having been secured and the boats shipped to Green River, Utah, we left Denver November 25th '89, on our second expedition.[1]

---

[1] The "skeleton record" appears in the last few pages of Stanton's Field Notes B.

The disaster in Marble Canyon and the reorganization of the DCC&PRR was much publicized in the contemporary press. For example: Denver *Republican*, July 23, 28, 30, Sept. 5, Nov. 2, 1889; Denver *Times*, July 22, 1889; Salt Lake City *Tribune*, July 23, Aug. 4, Nov. 24, 26, 1889; Phoenix *Herald*, Oct. 10, 1889; Chicago *Railway Age*, Aug. 8, 23, 1889; Los Angeles *Miner and Artisan*, Aug. 24, 1889; New York *Engineering News and American Railway Journal*, Aug. 31, 1889. In an interview in Washington, John W. Powell stated that Frank Brown had underestimated the perils of the Colorado River and he called the railroad scheme "quite impracticable." New York *Tribune*, Aug. 18, 1889. Clarence E. Dutton, who had been associated with Powell in studying the high plateaus of Utah and the Grand Canyon region, had already said in the Denver *Times*, June 14, 1889, that the railroad plan was highly impractical. In response to Powell, Stanton offered up a defense of "The Denver and Colorado Canyon & Pacific Railroad Project," *Engineering News and American Railway Journal*, Sept. 21, 1889, 269–272.

FIG. 22. Ready for the long haul overland to Glen Canyon, the second expedition starts out at Green River, Utah, November 27, 1889. *F. A. Nims.* Miami University Library.

NOVEMBER 1ST 1889. Supplies for Second Colorado River Survey:[2]

3 boats, 22′×4′6″; extra oars, paddles, etc.
lines: 3-250′, 3-50′, 3-30′.

straps for boats:

6-6′0″ long for center	12-12″ long for side lock
6-7′0″ long for center	6-48″ long for boxes
6-18″ long for cook outfit	12-40″ long for kegs

3 large sponges; 6 fastenings for boat seats; 12 life preservers; 3 life rings.

photographic supplies:

2 6 1/2×8 1/2 Albion cameras	12 6 1/2×8 1/2 rolls ⎱ C&H
4 extra front boards	12 4″ rolls ⎰
1 extra tripod	12 cans for rolls
1 detective camera	24 cans for rolls ⎱ S&S
12 6 1/2×8 1/2 best rolls	12 cans for rolls ⎰
1 8×10 WA lens ⎫	soldering outfit
6 ground glass ⎪	1 extra roll holder ⎱
1 yard ruby cloth ⎬ Davis	24 extra reels ⎬ express to GR
1 sole leather case ⎪	1 extra rubber slide ⎰
1 dark tent ⎪	
1 dark lantern ⎭	

rubber goods; tents, etc.; hardware; cook's supplies; groceries; medicines; instruments; ammunition; notebooks and paper, stamped envelopes; prospecting pick and pan.

personal outfit:

2 pairs heavy blankets	1 extra pair shoes
1 rubber blanket, pillows	1 wool overjacket
1 duck wrapper	1 cap
1 neck scarf	personal medicines
2 wool overshirts	sewing materials
2 suits heavy underclothing	blankets and straps
1 extra pants	scissors
1 rubber coat	buckskin needles and thread
1 overcoat	big coat buttons
6 pair wool sox	piece buckskin
2 pair wool gloves	safety pins
2 extra hats	

[2] This list of supplies and equipment is relocated here from the front pages of Stanton's Notebook C.

medicines:

[rryonia?]	mercurous	pellets
aconite	arsenicum	veratrum
camphor	ipecac	pulsatilla
belladonna	laudanum	podifilum [podophyllin]
cuprum	sepia	hepar sulphuris
nux	sponges	

DENVER, MONDAY, NOVEMBER 25, 1889. Clear and cold. Snow on ground. Left Denver 8:15 A.M. By the D&RGRy for Green River, Utah, with second expedition for the survey of the Colorado River.[3]

Party consists of:

Myself as Chief Engineer	Elmer Kane, Boatman
John Hislop, Assistant Engineer	L. G. Brown, Boatman
F. A. Nims, Photographer	Arthur B. Twining, Boatman
Harry McDonald, 1st Boatman	H. G. Ballard, Boatman
Langdon Gibson, Boatman	W. H. Edwards, Boatman
Reginald Travers, Boatman	James S. Hogue, Cook

The whole party came to [Denver on] time and everything starts off in good shape.

At Pueblo. Clear and warm.

TUESDAY, NOVEMBER 26. Clear all day.

Reached Green River 11:30 A.M. The men spent the afternoon in preparing wagon beds for the boats and I in fixing up accounts and writing letters. Our route from here will be by wagon across the sandy desert to Graves Valley on the Dirty Devil River, about 35 to 40 miles above its mouth. Then to the head of Crescent Creek at foot of the Henry Mountains and then down Crescent Creek Canyon to the Colorado River at Crescent City, about 4 miles above Dandy Crossing.

No snow. Bright sunshine.

WEDNESDAY, NOVEMBER 27. Clear all day. Completed loading boats. Freight arrived from Denver. Rubber goods from New York and so all supplies are here. Everything was ready to move by noon. But our Mormon teamsters are a terror. They were not ready till 4 P.M. Got into camp about one mile below here at 4:30. Supper quite late. Quite a jolly campfire. All the boys in a good humor, and the new ones seem to be good and reliable men.

[3] The remainder of this chapter coincides with part 2 of Stanton's Field Book A.

THANKSGIVING DAY, THURSDAY, NOVEMBER 28. Lazy Mormon teamsters did not get to camp ready to start till 10:30 A.M. I remained in town till noon and finished up my writing. Cass Hite gave me a pony and I overtook the wagons at 2:30 P.M. Went on and camped on the San Rafael River at 7:00 P.M. Distance 18 miles. One 4 horse team with load of supplies. Three 2 horse teams with the three boats.

Clear and crisp all day.

FRIDAY, NOVEMBER 29. Clear all day.

Started from camp at 9 A.M. Heavy sand. Camped on lower end of Iron Wash. Distance 10 miles.

SATURDAY, NOVEMBER 30. Clear all morning. Cloudy P.M. Rain 6 P.M.

Started at 7 A.M. Went up Iron Wash for 3 miles and then up on mesa, and 5 miles across to Cottonwood Creek. Stopped at 11:30. Teams played out. Have to haul water 2 1/2 miles. Distance 8 miles.

SUNDAY, DECEMBER 1. Rained and snowed all night. Showers all day.

In the midst of a sandy desert, without wood or water, so moved on. Distance 12 miles.

MONDAY, DECEMBER 2. Clear all day. Up at 5 A.M. Breakfast at 5:30. Start 8 A.M. By 8:30 met 4 horse team from Graves Valley. Put part of each load on new team and went on much easier. Stopped at 11:30 for dinner, about 12 miles from Graves Valley. Very heavy sandy roads. I rode ahead to store in Graves Valley. Bought crackers, bread, and cheese. Came back to Muddy Creek and met party. Camped 7:45 P.M. Distance 13 [miles].

TUESDAY, DECEMBER 3. Clear and cloudy by turns.

Started out early. Crossed Muddy Creek at mouth and Dirty Devil River. Stopped at Thompson's for beef. Stopped at store for grain, onions, bacon, etc.[4]

11:30 A.M. Started again. Long march over dry but good roads. Some sand. Mac and I went on ahead. Built campfires near head of Granite Wash. Camp 8:00 P.M. Drizzle rain all night. Distance 20 miles.

---

[4] Stanton's plan was to embark on the second expedition at the head of Glen Canyon and thus avoid the hazardous rapids of Cataract Canyon. From the railhead at Green River, or Blake, where the first expedition had begun the down-river trip back in May, Stanton loaded the boats and equipment on wagons and hauled them across the San Rafael, or Green River, Desert to Graves Valley (later called Hanksville), a green spot in an otherwise barren desert near the junction of the Muddy and the Dirty Devil rivers.

WEDNESDAY, DECEMBER 4. Rain all last night. Showers all day. Very wet march all day. My horse broke loose last night so I am afoot. Miserable walking in the mud.

Made 14 miles and stopped on head of Crescent Creek about 1 mile below where road turns off from Dandy Crossing road. Stopped because it was too dark to go down the creek road. Tired, wet, cold, and hungry.

THURSDAY, DECEMBER 5. Stopped last night on the north fork of Crescent Creek, at about 7 P.M. Dark and raining. Made pot of coffee and cooked some rice and went to bed.

Rained nearly all night. Got up this morning. No wood and little water. Hitched up without breakfast except a cup of coffee. Started 8:30. Went 3 miles down wash to junction with main Crescent Creek, 10:30. Stopped and cooked breakfast and dinner together. Ate at 12 noon, dried blankets, and fed teams.

Started again 1:30 down Crescent Creek Canyon. It is getting deeper and deeper. The formation is soft red sandstone just like that in Glen Canyon. Stopped at 4:45 P.M. at 2 miles above mouth of side canyon coming in on left. Stopped here because there is plenty of grass for the teams.

Yesterday and today have been very trying days, but all the men have behaved splendidly. But how the slow teams and lazy teamsters have tried me.

Rained nearly all night with wind.

FRIDAY, DECEMBER 6. Clear with flying clouds all day. Commenced rain 10 P.M. Rained by showers all last night. Cleared up early in A.M. Beautifully clear all day. Hislop and I slept last night in cave. Some of the men drowned out by the rain at 3:30 A.M.

Moved on down canyon at 7:45 A.M. Road not half as bad as I expected. It is really good. Everything moved smoothly. No damage to the boats whatever. Lunched on corn meal mush. Men all well filled.

Reached Colorado River at mouth of Crescent Creek at 4:30 P.M. As soon as we reached the river, we raised a pole with the U.S. flag and my own pennant, and the boys fired a salute of 13 shots, gave three cheers for the flags and three cheers and a tiger for myself. We unloaded the boats and stores. Pitched our tents and ate supper and went to bed, well satisfied that at last after 9 days tramp we had reached the river.

Camp No. 41. I have concluded to number our camps from our last camp on the river, No. 40, in Marble Canyon and give no numbers to those from Blake here.

SATURDAY, DECEMBER 7. Beautiful bright clear sunshine all day.

Spent all day rigging the boats, unpacking our supplies, and putting out in sun to dry. Little damage done to them by the rain. All goods came through in good shape, except our keg of pickles. Only thing forgotten seems to be the acid for the solder which Jones forgot to pack. Launched Boat No. 1 and I named her the *Bonnie Jean.*

Paid off the five teams and they started back about 10 A.M. At 3:30 P.M. two of the teamsters came back to camp and told us that about 3 miles up Crescent Canyon they met in the narrowest part a storm and flood of water 3 to 4 feet deep which upset their wagons and horses and threw them all into a mess, carrying them down some 200 yards and drowned *two* of their *horses.*

Distances from Green River Station D&RGRR, Utah, to Dandy Crossing by wagon road:

Green River Station to San Rafael	17 miles
San Rafael to Iron Springs Wash	8 miles
Iron Springs Wash to Cottonwood Wash	7 1/2 miles
Cottonwood Wash to Gilson's Buttes	7 1/2 miles
Gilson's Buttes to Thompson's Store	16 miles
Thompson's Store to Burr's Ranch	17 1/2 miles
Burr's Ranch to North Wash	12 1/2 miles
North Wash to Trachyte Creek	9 1/2 miles
Trachyte to Dandy Crossing	14 miles
	109 1/2 miles

SUNDAY, DECEMBER 8, '89. Charming bright sunshiny day. In camp, resting all day.[5]

MONDAY, DECEMBER 9. Cloudy. Rain till 8 A.M. Cleared up 12:45 P.M. Hailstorm, lasted one hour.

Spent all day in completing the rigging of the boats, and packing all stores in the rubber sacks made expressly for the purpose. Launched the other two boats. Hislop named No. 2 the *Water Lily.* Twining named No. 3 the *Sweet Marie.*[6]

[5] From Graves Valley the expedition traveled across the open desert east of the Henry Mountains and dropped down into the canyon of Crescent Creek, now called North Wash, through which it reached the Colorado River at a point about five miles above Dandy Crossing and Hite. Spirits ran high at the embarkation point, the beach at Crescent Creek. The boys ran up the colors together with Stanton's pennant. A thirteen-shot salute. Three cheers for the flags. Three cheers and a yell of "tiger" for the expedition's leader. Notice that Sundays were rest days. Stanton rested his oars on those days, as well as his pen. He seldom wrote very much during the weekly rest.

[6] The equipment provided for the second expedition was far superior to that used on the first. Stanton designed and had built, three boats made of oak, twenty-two feet long, four-and-one-half feet beam, and twenty-two inches deep. Each boat was equipped with ten separate air-tight compartments, and a lifeline was rigged to go entirely around the gunwales.

I had hoped to break camp this afternoon and move down to Dandy Crossing, but finding it would be so late concluded to complete everything in good shape and start quietly tomorrow. The boats leak almost none at all even after their 120 mile wagon ride.

Our crews will be as follows:

No. 1: Myself; McDonald; Gibson; Kane.
No. 2: Hislop; Travers; Edwards; Nims.
No. 3: Twining; Ballard; Brown; Hogue.

TUESDAY, DECEMBER 10. Clear and bright all day.

Broke camp this morning and started down the river on our second expedition at 10:10 A.M. Stopped for photos and reached Dandy Crossing at 11:30. Lunched.

Restarted at 2 P.M. after taking photos. At about 2:15 we came on to Trachyte Rapid. McDonald was entirely undecided which channel to take. Started for the main channel on the right and then changed his mind and started down the center channel. We had not gone more than 200 feet when we commenced bumping on the rocks, and in a few moments we were stranded on the head of an island. Our boat behaved splendidly. Would not be upset, and withstood all the bumps without a leak.

Boats 2 and 3 were close behind us and went bumping over the rocks but did not stick. They each bumped over the bar and got into the main channel but in doing so were turned round and went down stern first. Both Hislop and Twining behaved splendidly and steered their boats well. Stern-to all the way down, and landed safely on left bank. We were obliged to unload before we could get our boats off. After 2 hours work we got her off into main channel, without damage. Reloaded and started on. No. 2 boat sprung a small leak.

All the boats show their strength by the rough usage they had today. All the men behaved well except Brown who was so frightened that he dropped and lost both his oars and commenced pulling off his shoes.

We all went on and at 5 P.M. camped on island in the river 2 1/2 miles above Tickaboo. Camp No. 42.

WEDNESDAY, DECEMBER 11. Clear and bright all day after 8 A.M.

Broke camp No. 42 at 7:30 A.M. and at 9:00 A.M. reached Tickaboo going through Rapids No. 87 and 88. Left Nims and Brown off on shore to go back and complete photo work.

Each boat carried a cork life buoy and line. Cork life preservers, designed by Stanton, were provided for each man. All stores and provisions were packed in water-tight rubber bags made expressly for the expedition. Photographic equipment included three cameras and 2000 rolls of film. Writing later, Stanton described outfitting for the second trip in detail. See Dwight L. Smith, ed., *Down the Colorado* (1965), 94–101.

FIG. 23. "DCC&PRR Survey, the Fleet and Crews. Mouth of Crescent Creek, Dec. 10th, 1889. Twining, Ballard, Brown, Hogue — Hislop, Travers, Edwards — McDonald, Gibson, Kane, Stanton. DCC&PRR Survey, Photo No. 104. By F. A. Nims." [Stanton's caption for the embarkation at North Wash.] Miami University Library.

At Tickaboo we found, as I expected, G. W. Holdrege [and] R. C. Cushing who are looking at Cass Hite's placer mines with a view of putting machinery on them. Had a long talk with G. W. H. He released me from that part of my agreement to locate placers below here, as Hite's, if they take it, will be all they want. But they wish me to locate any placers I can find near the "Needles" on my own account and bring to them and they will consider them.

Remained at Tickaboo all day. Camp No. 43.

THURSDAY, DECEMBER 12. Broke camp 9 A.M. Cloudy and sunshine.

Passed through Rapid No. 89. Camped at lower end of Good Hope Bar. Spent the afternoon panning out gold. Wrote report and sent same to G. W. H. by leaving it under rock for Hite to get tomorrow.

FRIDAY, DECEMBER 13. Cloudy most all day. Sun 3–5 P.M.

Broke camp at 7:40 A.M. Nothing of any note happened in A.M. Stopped under the garden wall and took photos. Sailed on, and just above the California mine going over riffle our boat and No. 2 scraped on the rocks.[7]

One mile below Good Hope Bar is good low bar in river on right, not taken, and just beyond Battery Point on left is 20 acre *low* island of gravel, not taken.

Lunched at 12:30. 1:30, took more photos. Started at 1:50 P.M. and at about 2 P.M. was hailed by a man on shore asking us for tobacco. Went ashore a little below at the Smith Brothers' placer and gave the man a plug of tobacco and found it was Old Jack Sumner, Major Powell's right-hand man in 1869. I had a half hour's talk with him; and he gave us great encouragement and good cheer and advice simply to go slow and carefully; and we would be all right.

We took his photo, bade him good-by and pushed on. Another shallow riffle. Ran down to the second bend below Smiths' placer and camped on island at 4:45. Camp 44.

Jack Sumner, December 13th '89. Evening: Besides what's recorded on last page, I asked Jack many questions about the river below, particularly about the cataract where the three men left the party and going out were killed by the Indians, telling him that was the one rapid and the one place on the whole river, from Major Powell's account, that I was afraid of. He assured me there was no such awful difficulties at that point and encouraged us in every way. But I said, "Jack, Major gives a long detailed account of your experiences at that rapid," and read it to him from the copy we had. Sumner turned away with an air of resentment and disgust and said, "There's lots in that book besides the truth." I don't understand this, but Sumner wouldn't talk any more about it.[8]

---

[7] Stanton became interested in the Glen Canyon gold placers during the first expedition. See his notes made at Hite and Tickaboo, June 23–28, Chapter II. It is now apparent that he has taken on active interest in the mines. En route to Lee's Ferry he staked several claims in the lower part of Glen Canyon, and within the decade, Stanton returned to the canyon to undertake placer mining on a massive scale. See Crampton and Smith, eds., "The Hoskaninni Papers" (1961). As noted elsewhere, Cass Hite was an active promoter of his own mining interests in Glen Canyon. Good Hope Bar and the placers at California Bar were notable mining sites. The Garden Wall, one of the most imposing cliffs in Glen Canyon, is now known as Tapestry Wall.

[8] John C. Sumner was one of Powell's men on the 1869 voyage through the canyons of the Colorado. At Separation Rapid in lower Grand Canyon, three men left the expedition. Walking out, they were killed by Indians. Powell's account of the separation, which Stanton read to Sumner, is in his *Exploration of the Colorado River of the West* (1875), 97–100. This meeting with Jack Sumner probably did much to stimulate Stanton's interest in the history of the river, an interest that led him into extensive research which in turn caused him to question some of the statements in Powell's works on the Colorado River. See Stanton's own account (March 13, 1890) of his passage through Separation Rapid, Chapter IX.

SATURDAY, DECEMBER 14. Cloudy and raining by light showers all day.

Broke camp at 7:20. Sailed on without special incident. Took photos at Hall's Crossing and other points as noted.[9]

At about 1:30 P.M. we came to Rapid No. 92 over which we ran last summer without difficulty. Today the water was so low that we got through with great difficulty. No. 1 went through without touching but No. 2 struck several times and No. 3 stuck on the rocks. No. 2 rowed back and pulled her off.

We then found we were in a mess of shallow water formed by flat shelves of rock running across the river, and down. For 1/2 mile we attempted to land on right bank, and finding it very difficult, on *Mac's* advice crossed the river, and landing, went down to examine below. We found the water so shallow, that we could not get our boats through loaded. At 2 P.M. we commenced unloading. Made portage of 800 feet. Mac and Gibson ran the boats through light and at 4 P.M. we went into Camp No. 45 for Sunday.

SUNDAY, DECEMBER 15. Rained by showers all last night. Cloudy and showery all day. In Camp No. 45.

This afternoon Mac, Gibson, and Travers took No. 1 and went out to examine the channel. They found we could not get our boats with loads over the 1/2 mile shoal below, which will necessitate a portage of all our stores for 1/2 mile and running our boats down empty.

MONDAY, DECEMBER 16. It rained hard during the evening and early part of the night and at 12 midnight cleared up; and this morning the sun rose without a cloud. Bright sunshine and warm all day.

Commenced our portage at 7:00 A.M. and completed it and ready to start at 10:30. Distance of portage 2475 feet, or counting extra walks 1/2 mile. Each man averages 4 round trips or 4 miles each. This is the longest portage we have ever made; but it was good smooth level walking and hence was not so hard as some very much shorter ones made in Cataract Canyon.

Started at 10:45. Sailed for about 4 miles, stopping just below Anderson's placers to take photos, and at 12 M. came to head of long shoal, which on our

---

[9] A ferry was operated at Hall's Crossing, forty-three miles below Hite, 1881–1884. It served as a substitute for the Hole-in-the-Rock crossing, a much more difficult one, thirty-five miles downstream. Apparently Stanton did not see the historic Hole-in-the-Rock crossing, opened by Mormon pioneers in 1879–1880, as a route to reach southeastern Utah; he passed by it on July 1 and again on December 17 without mention of the place. David E. Miller's *Hole-in-the-Rock: An Epic in the Colonization of the Great American West* (Salt Lake City: University of Utah Press, 1966), is a scholarly and detailed account. A detailed study of the several historic sites along the middle reaches of Glen Canyon, see C. G. Crampton, "Historical Sites in Glen Canyon, Mouth of Hansen Creek to Mouth of San Juan River," University of Utah *Anthropological Papers*, 61 (December, 1962).

last summer's trip was simply swift water. Stopped for lunch and at one P.M.
we started out boats with only three in to make them lighter. No. 1 went
through the first 3/4 mile without grounding, but No. 2 and 3 both grounded
on gravel and worked for some time to get off. Succeeding at last, all hands
got aboard, and we started down the remaining 3/4 mile. In about 1200 feet
all boats got stuck on flat shelf of rock, and after various efforts, with two men
in the water, we got under way again at 3 P.M. below this 1 1/2 mile shoal.

This work is very hard, fatiguing. These shoals seem to occur now where
we had simply swift water before. The rapids that I remembered are nearly
the same except they are less swift, with more rocks exposed and longer. We
ran on with various riffles, and through Rapid No. 92 without incident till
4:45 when we camped on left bank of river opposite "large bottom" of
June 29th. Camp No. 46.[10]

At nine o'clock took No. 1 and pulled up to gravel bar 1 1/2 miles above
San Juan River and surveyed the "San Juan" placer claim. Stake No. 1
marked thus, "The San Juan Placer Claim. Stake No. 1." "We claim 15 acres
of placer ground southeast from this stake No. 1. December 18th 1889.

> Robert B. Stanton
> H. McDonald
> Witnesses."

And each of the other stakes are marked "San Juan Stake 2" and so on.

TUESDAY, DECEMBER 17. Cloudy all day with glimpses of sun.

Ready to start 7:30 A.M. but waited to take photos above camp. Completed and started at 8:20.

Stopped at 8:40 to take photos, the white sandstone formation spoken of
in my notes of June 29th and mountain slope, etc., described same date. At
this point high water shows 50 feet high. Along this stretch on right bank of
river is fine appearing vein of copper and silver located by one Wilson, a
prospector from Grand Junction.

At 10:10 A.M. stopped for photo up river. All around the point the cliffs
are from 100 to 200 feet high with the whole distance, except for about
500 feet, with a good bottom from 50 to 100 feet wide and the rock sloping
to the water. A very easy line to build. *But* it is a question for future service
whether a line cannot be gotten across this point at the low gap just above
where photo was taken thus cutting off 6 to 8 miles of distance.

Stopped at 11:20 at further end of bend where river turns to right. Took
photos. At this point is location of Jesse lode. Shows copper and silver. Made
July 29th '89 by Wm. P. Anderson and Scott Libby.

---

[10] For some fourteen miles below Hall's Crossing the Colorado ran over bedrock in places
and over frequent shallow shoals of gravel. In low water, as Stanton noted December 14–16,
1889, it was necessary to line and push and portage in a number of places.

Lunch 11:45. Restart at 12:30 and in a few moments pass our own campground, No. 29, of June 29 and 30.

At 1:20 P.M. stop at mouth of the Escalante Creek. Quite a volume of water coming out of its narrow canyon. So much so that it is impossible for us to go up it to locate the coal, which is some 18 or 20 miles up, as we intended. We give it [up]. One-half mile below Escalante we stop and take photos, mouth of creek. From the bend of river the slope is well described June 30 and the character of the slope and rock is just that shown in photo. So will not stop to photo it. See July 1st note.

All day today the sides of the canyon have been getting greener and greener, with grass, shrubs, willows, etc., etc., and we have seen quite a number of flowers in full bloom. And also find snipe on the sand bars (Gibson).

Stop and take photo as noted on July 1st. [Note] from July 1st did not take photo of this stretch to point as it is so much like so many we have, and the same general character continues as described July 1st and as it is late will not stop for photos till we reach the San Juan.

At 4 P.M. we turn bend to right and the Navajo Mountain comes in view covered with snow. Stop to look at placer bed.

At 4:30 P.M. go into camp at mouth of the San Juan River. Camp No. 47.

WEDNESDAY, DECEMBER 18. Clear in A.M. Cloudy P.M. Slight rain at 4:30 P.M.

At 7 A.M. go up on the bluff at mouth of San Juan River. The first bench is 175 feet above low water, and the second bench which is separate knoll is 525 feet above low water and is covered on top with 3 to 4 feet of hard grey *limestone*, the only limestone that shows for miles around. Left Nims on top to take photos from first bench up Colorado and from first bench up San Juan and mouth of San Juan and down Colorado.

Stake No. 1 is 6 feet east from large red sandstone boulder near cliff and marked + pointing to stake, and it also bears north 61°55′W to point on high cliff two miles up river and south 67°50′E to prominent point 1/2 mile down river on opposite side. No. 1 is about 2 miles up Colorado above mouth of San Juan River.

T. C. Henry	Robert B. Stanton
I. R. Burton	H. McDonald

11:30 A.M. returned to camp. Stopped for lunch. 12:30 started on the river again. Point ahead fully described July 1st. 1:00 P.M. took photo about 1000 feet up river. Went around point. Stopped and took photo of winter in the Navajo Mountain. Ran Rapid 94. See note of July 1st and Rapid No. 95.

Stopped and surveyed Reynold's "Denver Placer" and at 4:30 P.M. went into camp on island, just below Rapid 95 about 1 1/2 miles below the mouth

Fɪɢ. 24. Rest stop in Glen Canyon above the San Juan River. *F. A. Nims*. Miami University Library.

of Navajo Creek. Camp No. 48. Rapid 94 was easily run, the water being concentrated and not very rough.

The Denver placer notice on stake: Location Notice. Denver Placer Claim. Discovered December 18th 1889. Located December 18th 1889. Surveyed December 18th 1889. We claim 60 acres. E. A. Reynolds, Geo. D. Briggs, Jas. N. Hughes. Recorded in Kane County records.

Stake No. 1 bears north 8°56′W to prominent point of rock on cliff 1 1/2 miles up river, and north 29°40′E to mouth of Navajo Creek, and south 80°53′E to large chimney shaped rock on side of cliff on opposite side of river.[11]

[11] The San Juan placer claim was located on a high gravel bench on the right side of Glen Canyon about one mile above the mouth of the San Juan River. Several additional claims were staked at points below the San Juan during the next two days. They were duly recorded in the Utah counties of Kane and San Juan. Navajo Creek is probably identical with a Lake Powell tributary, Reflection Canyon.

THURSDAY, DECEMBER 19. Clear and windy. Clear all day.

Break camp at 7:30 A.M. Went about 1/2 mile or so round point and stop to examine Rapid No. 96 at 8:00 A.M. and take photos. Find this Rapid No. 96 (the split rapid, see note of July 1st) has today all the water in *one* channel.

Hogue discovers cliff dwellers' remains up side creek. We all go to examine them, and find the remains are either fortifications to protect the entrance to the side canyon or piers for a bridge around the cliff in high water in the side canyon. Photo shows these.[12]

Nine A.M., restart and run Rapid 96. All the water being in one channel this rapid is much more rapid and rough than it was last summer. It is nearly 1 mile long and the roughest we have had on this trip. Our boats run this rough water in grand style. Obey their helm easily; and although they dance over the heavy waves so as to almost dip their bows under water and the waves when struck right dash over the mens' head, yet they ride so steadily that I stood up in the bow of No. 1 all the way through this long run.

From 9:50 to 11 A.M. we stop to stake off the "Jean" and "Anna" placers.

> *The Jean Placer:* T. C. Henry; E. R. French; J. R. Burton; A. B. Coulson; G. S. Redfield; W. S. Stambaugh; G. M. McCampbell; Robert B. Stanton.
>
> *The Anna Placer:* S. O. Henry; J. O. Stanton; G. W. Gibson; I. H. Nelson; F. W. Blackford; G. W. Hurd; John Hislop; H. McDonald.

Each No. 1 stake has on it "The undersigned claim 160 acres for placer mining purposes as stated on this ground. Date of discovery December 19th, 1889," with list of names as above.

Photo shows fine placer bar not staked, about 80 acres. Do not stop to stake it, as it is so late. At any higher water it would only show sand flat. So think it safe till we determine what to do next year. *Later.* See stake at lower end of bar.

At 3:30 stop and stake off Reynolds Colorado placer claim.

---

[12] This is a first description of some presumably prehistoric ruins located under an overhanging cliff at the mouth of Aztec Creek. This stream drains the steep and highly-dissected southwestern slope of Navajo Mountain. A tributary stream in Bridge Canyon is spanned by the spectacular Rainbow Bridge. The stream was known to prehistoric peoples who camped at its mouth and it was possibly they who built the four enigmatic pillar-like structures so nicely portrayed in the Nims photograph. Writing later, Stanton thought of these ruins as the work of his "professional brethren, the prehistoric Civil Engineers." Dwight L. Smith, ed., *Down the Colorado* (1965) 106–107. Archaeologists investigating the site, which was one of the most frequently visited spots in Glen Canyon, suggested the possibility that the pillars may have been built in historic times. See W. Y. Adams, et al., "Survey and Excavations in Lower Glen Canyon, 1952–1958," Museum of Northern Arizona *Bulletin*, 36 (1961), 25–33. See C. Gregory Crampton, "Historical Sites in Glen Canyon Mouth of San Juan River to Lee's Ferry," University of Utah *Anthropological Papers*, 46 (June, 1960) for a review of the history of this and other sites in Glen Canyon below the San Juan River.

FIG. 25. This is the earliest photograph of the masonry columns at the mouth of Aztec Creek. The exact origin of this once well-known Glen Canyon landmark, now submerged beneath the waters of Lake Powell, is an unsolved mystery. Stanton thought the columns might be bridge piers built by prehistoric civil engineers! Except for the photographer the entire crew of the DCC&PRR survey decorates the site. *F. A. Nims.* Miami University Library.

Location stake is marked: Colorado Placer Mine. Discovered December 19th 1889. Located December 19th 1889. Surveyed December 19th 1889. Recorded in Kane County records.

> James N. Hughes; Ethan A. Reynolds; George W. Briggs; Harry McDonald.

We then sail down the long straight stretch running down to where river turns to the right. This is shown at its upper end by photo and the same kind of low perpendicular cliffs continue all through it and on to back of flat. We pass through Rapids 99 and 100 and at 5:30 P.M. go into camp on the bar where we camped the night of July 1st, No. 30. Camp No. 49. Made between 30 and 35 miles today.

At this camp we find Edward Mesken, an old trapper and prospector and his dog Sport. He was very glad to see us, as he was all alone. He owns a high bar on opposite side of river he calls "The Rotshilt" meaning "Rothchilds." Mesken was formerly, 1880, cook in Charprot's Hotel, Denver, and has been on this river for five years.

FRIDAY, DECEMBER 20. Clear. Cloudy 10 A.M.

Stop this A.M. to stake out the Henry placer and take photos on opposite side of river. Start at 9:30 and stop to stake Hislop's claim, the New York State. Our boat goes on to next bar to stake. Did not do it. This is all we will stake at this time. Our boat stops half way round next bend to wait for photos. We waited till 1:00 P.M. for Hislop. Ate lunch, took photos, and restarted at 2:00 P.M.

The Henry Placer:

> Robert B. Stanton; T. C. Henry; S. O. Henry; J. R. Burton; A. B. Coulson; G. S. Redfield; H. McDonald; John Hislop,
>
> > Locators.

Stopped at about 2:45 P.M. and took 2 photos. From end of flat to point beyond.

See special notes made today, under date July 2d.

4:30 P.M., camped on left bank of river. Camp No. 50. December 21st, stop 344 miles from Grand Junction, Colorado.[13]

---

[13] See Stanton's entry for July 1, 1889, Chapter II. Edward Mesken, colorful Glen Canyon figure, staked out his bar on September 18, 1889, during the interval between the first and second Stanton trips through Glen Canyon. Since known as Mesken Bar, the placer was on the right bank forty-five miles above Lee's Ferry. Stanton was busy these days staking claims and looking to the railroad survey. He refers frequently to the notes made on the first trip through Glen Canyon in late June and July. See Chapter II.

SATURDAY, DECEMBER 21. Clear and frosty. Cloudy P.M.

Waiting for photos. Start at 8 A.M. Stopped at 9 A.M. for photos. At 10:00 A.M. recommenced survey of railroad line, where Bush left off at Stanton 18112+44.[14]

From here to Station 18162+22 is same slope of debris steeper than 45°, and same continues 400 feet beyond to point of cliff as shown in photo.

Lunched and restarted at 12:15 P.M. At 12:40 stopped for photos. Start 1:05 P.M. On next stretch at 1:30 P.M. took photo. Took some time to change roll. See note July 2d. Restart 2:15 P.M.

Camped at 4 P.M. on left bank of river. Camp No. 51.

SUNDAY, DECEMBER 22. Clear. In camp resting. Much disappointed that we did not reach Lee's Ferry last night so as to get our mail. Camp No. 51.

MONDAY, DECEMBER 23. Little cloudy. Clear and awfully windy from 3 P.M. Heavy clouds in west.

Broke camp 7:30 A.M. Photos taken from bank about half way from bend below creek and further point where river turns to left. All around this point which has a long swing and easy turn, there is in most places a sufficient talus above high water and the cliff itself is rough and easy to handle. One-fourth mile beyond little creek coming in on left. Stopped at 8:30 and took photos. This is about 1/3 way into the bend turning to right. The talus continues all way to the end where river turns to left except for 800 feet just 1000 feet before getting to point then low cliff at bottom. Photos are taken on right bank opposite extreme point about 500 feet below mouth of creek on right.

10:30, commence survey and continued same on all the bend to right and stopped at point where river turns left. Photos taken.

Stopped our line 10 to 1200 feet from point of rock of July 2d. Quite a little rapid when the creek comes out. No talus. It commences again and is just as that for several miles back, earthly green slopes but very irregular. Took photos from 2/3 way down bend, showing point where river turns to left with creek coming in on right.

Wind blowing furiously. Fine gravel, low water, bars. Photos taken opposite Beauty Point. See note made today under date July 2d.

Wind blew so hard upstream that with swift current and hard rowing we could barely get along and at one time we actually lost ground. As the wind

---

[14] It will be recalled that the instrumental survey below Hite was left in the hands of Bush, Coe, Howard, Potter, and Sutherland (see Stanton's entry for June 26, 1889), who moved slowly along while Brown, Stanton, and the advance party went on to Lee's Ferry and Marble Canyon. At a point eighty-nine miles downstream, the party stopped at the mouth of a left-bank canyon, since known as Mystery Canyon, and now as Anasazi Canyon, and left their names, the initials of the company, and the date July 14, 1889, inscribed on the rock. Continuing on downstream the Bush group carried the survey to a point approximately 34.5 miles above Lee's Ferry, where Stanton picked it up on December 21.

was blowing so hard we quit work and pulled for Lee's Ferry at 3:30 P.M. The wind was terrific, upstream so that the waves, wind waves, were 4 to 5 feet high, breaking in white caps. The men pulled manfully against the wind 7 1/2 miles and reached Lee's Ferry, upper ferry, just above the creek's mouth at 5:30 P.M.

Camp No. 52. I went over to Johnson's to get the mail. Found 56 letters and a pile of papers. Ten letters for myself. Everyone went to reading their letters and the cook forgot to get supper. When he recovered himself he only had energy left to cook a pot of mush and coffee.

TUESDAY, DECEMBER 24. Morning beautiful clear sun. Sunshine all day.

FIG. 26. Christmas dinner in style at Lee's Ferry, 1889. Counting heads from left to right: Stanton (at head of the table), Nims, Edwards, Travers, Ballard, Gibson, Kane, Brown, Twining, Hogue, McDonald, Hislop. The rock building is the historic Lee's Ferry fort and tracking post built by the Mormons in 1874. *Al Huntington.* Miami University Library.

After the hard pull of last evening, I let the men sleep this morning. We had breakfast at 8:00 A.M. Went over to Johnson's to get some washing done and find some other supplies for Christmas dinner.

At ten-fifteen took two boats and went up river to complete our line. Reached point at 12 noon. Ate lunch and commenced work at 1:00 P.M. Ran 2 1/2 miles and then went to camp at 4 P.M. as tomorrow is Christmas. Camp No. 52 at the old Mormon fort just above Lee's Ferry.

WEDNESDAY, DECEMBER 25. Clear. Cloudy in P.M. *Christmas.* Spent the day writing letters and enjoying a Christmas dinner.

Menu

Soups
Oxtail, Tomato, Chicken

Fish
Colorado River Salmon

Meats
Roast Turkey, Roast Beef
Ox Heart, Braised Chicken
Game Pie

Vegetables
Mashed Potatoes, Stewed Onions
Tomatoes, Rice
Potato Salad
Wheat, Corn, and Graham Bread
Tea, Coffee, Chocolate Milk

Dessert
Plum Pudding Hard Sauce
Mince Pie, Apple Pie
Apple and Cherry Sauce
Chocolate Cake
Bents Crackers and Cheese (Utah)
Fruit
Arizona Apples, Peaches, Pears
Raisins and Nuts
Havana Cigars
Turkish Cigarettes

Our dinner was a complete success. Al. Huntington an old California '49er and Mr. and Mrs. Warren M. Johnson dined with us.

THURSDAY, DECEMBER 26. Clear and beautiful.

Resumed work on the line and completed it to the head of Marble Canyon. If we can get all things ready will start down the river tomorrow. And will write explanations of the last few days in my next book. Camp No. 52, Lee's Ferry, Arizona.[15]

[15] The classy Christmas dinner, one of the most sumptuous meals ever served at Lee's Ferry, was a surprise prepared by Stanton ahead of time. Unknown to the crews, the supplies were packed in the bottom of the boats. Fresh fruit, beef, and milk from the Johnson's Ranch completed the holiday spread. The table, decorated with wild flowers picked that day, was set in front of the "Old Mormon Fort," a stone structure built in 1874 to serve the combined purposes of defense against, and trade with, the Navajo Indians. See note 11, Chapter II for data on Lee's Ferry history, and W. L. Rusho and C. Gregory Crampton, *Desert River Crossing* (1981).

And so the day after Christmas, 1889, the instrumental railroad survey had been completed from Grand Junction, Colorado, to Lee's Ferry, Arizona, a distance of approximately 377 miles by river. The transit line over this distance was 355 miles. See Dwight L. Smith, ed., *Down the Colorado* (1965), 112, note 3.

During the course of the hearings in the "River Bed Case" (*U.S. vs. Utah*, Supreme Court of the United States, Number 14, October term, 1929), a suit to determine the navigability of portions of the Green, Colorado, and San Juan rivers in Utah, some of the Stanton crew members were called to testify about the operation of the DCC&PRR expeditions. Many pages of historically significant testimony were given by Franklin Nims, W. H. Edwards, Elmer Kane, and Harry McDonald.

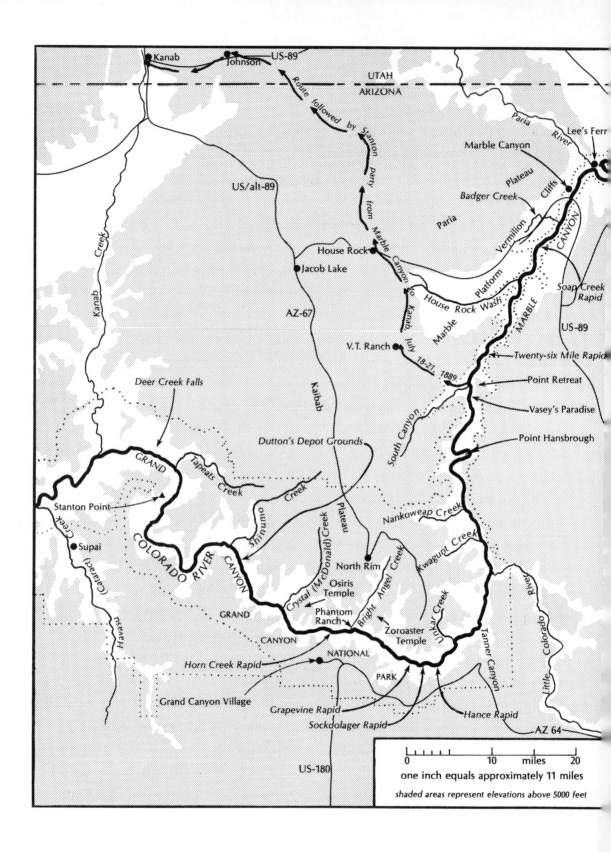

Kanab ● ●Johnson — US-89

UTAH
ARIZONA

Route followed by Stanton party from Marble Canyon to Kanab, July 18-21, 1889

Paria River

Lee's Ferry

Marble Canyon

Badger Creek

Paria Plateau

Vermilion Cliffs

MARBLE CANYON

US/alt-89

House Rock ●
●Jacob Lake

AZ-67

House Rock Wash

Marble Platform

Soap Creek Rapid

US-89

V.T. Ranch ●

South Canyon

┼ Twenty-six Mile Rapid

Point Retreat

Vasey's Paradise

Point Hansbrough

Deer Creek Falls

Dutton's Depot Grounds

GRAND

Tapeats Creek

Kaibab

Shinumo Creek

Plateau

Nankoweap Creek

Kwagunt Creek

Little Colorado River

Kanab Creek

Stanton Point

COLORADO RIVER CANYON

● Supai

Havasu (Cataract) Creek

Crystal (McDonald) Creek

North Rim

Osiris Temple

Bright Angel Creek

Unkar Creek

Tanner Canyon

GRAND

CANYON

Phantom Ranch

Zoroaster Temple

NATIONAL

Horn Creek Rapid ●

PARK

Grand Canyon Village

Grapevine Rapid

Sockdolager Rapid

Hance Rapid

AZ 64

US-180

0   10   miles   20

one inch equals approximately 11 miles

shaded areas represent elevations above 5000 feet

CHAPTER V

BAD LUCK IN MARBLE CANYON

Again Robert B. Stanton and company entered Marble Canyon only to be hit by bad luck on New Year's Day. Climbing for a better vantage point, photographer Frederick A. Nims fell and broke his leg. Carrying him out of the canyon was a very difficult and harrowing experience, and it delayed the progress of the railroad survey. Photography was now added to Stanton's responsibilities. Supplies and equipment lost in a rapid were replenished from the cache at Point Retreat. Farther downstream the party was faced with the grisly task of burying the remains of Peter Hansbrough, who had been claimed by the river on the first expedition. Finally, the company reached the Little Colorado River and the end of Marble Canyon.

LEE'S FERRY, ARIZONA, DECEMBER 27, 1889.[1] Cloudy. Rained during last night. Rain towards noon and hard till 2 P.M. Cloudy and some rain during afternoon.

Loading boats, preparing new supplies, etc. Ready for start tomorrow. We got from Johnson:

> Beef, 850 lbs.; Pork, 50 lbs.; Flour, 100 lbs.; Sugar, 150 lbs.; Rice, 50 lbs.; Beans, 50 lbs.; Baking Powder, 30 lbs.

and a number of little things to add to our stores so as to be sure to have enough to get us through without hurry. Mr. Johnson has been more than kind to us.

Camp 52.

LEE'S FERRY, ARIZONA, DECEMBER 28, 1889. Clear. Some clouds but beautiful day. Bright sunshine. Snow shows on Vermilion Cliffs.

I spent nearly all night, up to 4:00 A.M., in writing up my notes, completing accounts, and writing letters home and bidding good-by by letter to all my

---

[1] This chapter is taken from Stanton's Field Notes B, Part 2.

friends before starting down the Marble Canyon this morning. We were up at 5:30. Breakfast at 6:00 A.M.

It took us some time to pack up to get started as we had been in camp so long and everything was out of the boats. We were ready and started at 8:45. Landed directly to let photographer go on top to take photo. We then went ahead on shore and examined Rapid 101, Powell's "Long Rocky, Mad Rapid." We considered it safe and at 9:15 started on our downward trip. This rapid is between one and one and a quarter miles long, very crooked and full of rocks. We went in, all three in good line, and we danced over the waves in fine shape. Boat 3 did not steer off quite far enough, and struck lightly on one rock, but with no damage. I am very proud of the way our boats behave themselves. They are loaded with at least 3100 to 3200 lbs. and yet they danced as lightly over the waves as a bark canoe. I *stood up* in the bow of the boat all the way through for over a mile of this swift rapid. Our photographer is high up on the cliff and so we will have to wait.

Mr. Johnson and *all* his family including Al. Huntington and the teamster's family were out to see us go down the rapid. There were 32 in all; and as we were passing through the roughest part they gave us a hearty cheer. This certainly was a very successful run. I hope we may have nothing worse.

Started again at 10:45 A.M. Reached Rapid 102 at 11:00 A.M. Stopped for photos. Start 11:30. 12:00 stop for photo. We ran successfully Rapids 102, 103, and 104.

The whole line to the mouth of Soap Creek is very well described under date of July 9th so no use repeating it here, and to this is added the numerous photos we are taking.[2]

After lunch. We reached Rapid 105, at mouth of Badger Creek, at 2:00 P.M. Found it as impossible to run as ever on account of the huge boulders. Although the water is much lower and the waves are not more than 1/2 as high as last summer, still there is no clear channel. After examining it on left bank we crossed over and made, 2:30 P.M., portage of all supplies, except what are in the lockers and under the floor. About 1500 feet in distance. Mac, Hislop, Kane, and Ballard then let the boats down by swinging them into the current in some places and easing them along shore. All very successfully done. Completed portage and went into Camp No. 53 at 6:00 P.M. at mouth of Badger Creek 8 miles below Paria Creek, or Lee's Ferry.

---

[2] See Chapter III for Stanton's Field Notes made during the first run through Marble Canyon. In view of limited funds the engineer planned to survey instrumentally only the more difficult places in Grand Canyon. To complete the record, Stanton expected to make a "continuous photographic panorama of the entire route" through Grand Canyon, and to take complete notes. See Dwight L. Smith, ed., *Down the Colorado* (1965), 112.

The mileages given in the footnotes in this and the following chapters are derived from river maps published by the U.S. Geological Survey in 1924. Mileage runs from mile 0 at Lee's Ferry downstream to mile 355 at the head of Black Canyon, Arizona–Nevada.

SUNDAY, DECEMBER 29, 1889. Last night was the coldest night we have had since we reached the river. There was ice on the boats this morning. Bright and clear all day and in the sun very warm.

Hislop and I walked down the river about 3 1/2 miles to the point where Mr. Brown was drowned. What a change in the appearance of the place on account of the water being from 9 to 10 feet lower than it was last summer. While there is the same current on one side and the large eddy with the whirling water, and every now and then comes up a swirl as before, yet these are all so gentle that at a little distance it all looks like a quiet lake; and the movement is so smooth a light canoe would not be in danger.

Camp 53.

MONDAY, DECEMBER 30. Clear and sunshiny all day.

We were up early, 5:30, and had breakfast at six; but everything had to be loaded into the boats so we did not get started till 9:15 A.M.

At 9:20 reached Rapid 106. The water here is probably 9 feet lower than last July, so that this rapid has many rocks above water, and so the course through it is very crooked. The channel is very swift, and it only took 2 minutes to go the half mile and a little more. The run was made very successfully, but it was quick work dodging the rocks first one side and then the other. All hands behaved well and Twining came through in fine shape. Has very much improved in his steering.

Reached Rapid 107 at mouth of Soap Creek at 10 A.M. Immediately commenced portage of about 1/2 mile. We all worked till noon. Had lunch and then 5 of us went across river and commenced survey.

We stopped at 4 P.M. and went back to help down with the boats, to swing them down. All hands go to work. No. 1 got line caught in bad shape; but came out all right. Travers, Mac, and Hislop all three were thrown into the water near shore and got wet to their necks. Two good doses of whisky, a change of clothes, and a hot fire, brought them out all right. But remember this is the 30th of December.

We went into Camp No. 54 on the same spot of our old Camp No. 33 of last summer. This is the spot where we camped July 9th the last night Mr. Brown was with us, and where I divided my bed with him and made up his bed for him. Rather a sad place to camp in again.

Twining made a fool of himself today. After the boys had worked so well in getting the boats down, and three of them got wet, and Travers went through the water up to his neck to save one boat caught on the rock, Twining went up to the fire where Travers and Hislop were and said, "You boys seem to act just as if you were going in swimming. I'd see the boats in hell first before I'd get wet as you did." Hislop told me this, not as reporting to me, but to show what thanks they got for their hard work.

FIG. 27. Franklin A. Nims, expedition photographer, at Lee's Ferry. Miami University Library.

TUESDAY, DECEMBER 31, 1889. Some little rain during the night, and snow at 5 A.M. A little on the ground around our bed. Sun rose without a cloud. Clear all day.

Reloaded and ready to start 9 A.M. Our steering oar missing. Hunted and found it. Started 9:23. 9:25 enter Rapid 108, where President F. M. Brown was drowned July 10th. The water is 9 feet lower, and although the current is swift, the waves are not over 1/5 as high as then. We followed the exact course through it today as we did then and landed on the same sand beach where I landed, etc.

Taking up our line I note the point opposite Soap Creek is not nearly as difficult as noted July 9th. At that time the water was at least 8 or 9 feet higher and I only saw it from the opposite side at Camp No. 33. Yesterday and today we ran our line along this slope on left side and I find that by cutting the point at upper end of Rapid 107 and the point at lower end of same, as good a line can be located as on any of our "Mountain Slope."

Continuing past above point the slope is good to the crossing of the side canyon (see July 10). From here on to Rapid No. 115, [*blank*] miles from Soap Creek, the line would be located on the slope above the inner gorge. As full a description as necessary is given in notes of above dates [July 10 and 11]. I will not repeat. The river in narrow part above Rapid 115 is not over 125 to 150 feet, that is, the whole inner gorge.

After landing at sand bar at point where Mr. Brown lost his life, at 9:30 A.M., we resumed our survey and ran to point where river turns to left, by 12 noon. I considered this far enough to demonstrate our line and to comply with the law.

We lunched at 12 and at 12:45 started again downstream and our Boat No. 1 in turning out was drawn into the whirlpool exactly where poor Brown sank and although the water here is so much lower, 9 or 10 feet, it was whirled round more than once before the two powerful oarsmen and Mac steering could get her under control. And the whirls came up and roared along side our boat in a dull angry snarl, and as I stood in the bow they seemed to be lashing our sturdy boat eager for another victim. After turning round thus 2 or 3 times we succeeded in getting out of the whirlpool and started downstream for what is now the head of another Rapid No. 109.

This rapid is very crooked and is twice as bad as it was last summer when the water was higher; and this is the case with Rapids Nos. 110, 111, and 112. The reason for this is the nature of the rock. These rapids are not really formed as most are by boulders washed in by the shelving rock which dips upstream; and so at a lower stage of water the stream starts in smooth but drops over so suddenly that it makes awful waves at the bottom. Thus while these rapids look smooth from above they are simply terrific *after* the boat goes over the first pitch.

No. 110 being so crooked it took hard quick steering to make the two turns and to do this we had to go through the roughest waves. I stood up in the boat however all the way, and we pitched through at the rate of not less than 20 miles an hour. As the boats got into the worst part, they being so heavily loaded, pitched over one wave and right down into the next, the bow going entirely under the main part of the wave; and the whole wave, as I ducked my head to go through, it broke entirely over me and the bow oarsman just behind me. Boats No. 2 and 3 have the same experience. Our steersman says at one time he looked forward and we were both entirely out of sight covered over by the breaking waves.

Rapids No. 110 and 111 were straight and though heavy not so bad. But 112 was a terror. We stop and examine it, and find a clear but narrow V entrance next the left bank. This rapid drops down at least 5 feet and it was a great plunge when we went over it. The waves below were furious but free from rocks; and we plunge through at a fearful rate; and one boat dives under the waves as before; and I take an enormous wave right on my lap. Our boats however even so heavily loaded come up to the top as light as a feather.

Rapids 113 and 114 were very easy. At 1:30 P.M. we reach Rapid No. 115. (See note of narrow canyon and swirls on July 11th). At No. 115, we follow the same plan as detailed in July 11th, No. 1 first and then Nos. 3 and 2. I made three Detective [photos] of this Rapid 115 of huge boulders. Is as bad to run as before, though waves are only 1/2 as high. We portage all goods, swing around boats as before.

This part of the canyon is very narrow at the bottom of the inner gorge for some distance above Rapid No. 115. It is not over 125 feet to 150 feet and from point just below Rapid 110 to here as I remember to [*blank*] (see further on and fill in). The river fills it from wall to wall. Our line is above this inner gorge on a "mountain slope" or bench one to two hundred feet wide and rising on a slope just as that above Soap Creek. Our line rises on this from a point 1/2 mile above Soap Creek, where it is 40 feet above low water, to this point and a 1/2 mile beyond, to 265 feet high that is above the low water; but the river falls very rapidly in that distance. We will make a transit measurement of the height of this inner wall.

We finished our portage at 5 P.M. and went into Camp No. 55. When I got to camp I found Edwards in a sullen cranky mood. There was but little wood, and but few of the cooking things out. He wanted to know what I was going to do for bread, etc., etc., and was very impudent. I kept my temper, told Hogue to mix up some batter, and *I* baked cakes for the men. I have concluded I can not stand such work and shall ask Ballard to do this work. If he does not I will do it myself.

Camp No. 55. This is *New Year's Eve* and I am not in a very pleasant frame of mind, but think I shall work out somehow.

WEDNESDAY, JANUARY 1, 1890. Perfectly clear all night, and not a cloud to be seen this morning.

I got up this morning at 4:40, made the cook's fire, and went back to bed. At 5:00 got up again and waked Ballard. He says he will help me. He, Hogue, and I got breakfast. I cooked all the meat and at 6:00 called the men. Rather a good beginning for New Year's Day. My opinion of Edwards — he is a good cook, *but a perfect crank, impudent, and wasteful.*

We started from Camp No. 55 at 8:20 A.M. Ran down lower end of Rapid No. 115 in very rough water. At foot of this, river is narrowed in by fallen rock to two channels each about 30 feet wide. The water is piled up behind these so that it pitches down hill as it goes through, at a fearful rate, but perfectly smooth. The fall is about 4 feet. We shot by the rocks like a flash.

About 1000 feet below this we came to Rapid No. 116. (See description July 11th '89.) We stopped at upper end to take photo, and Nims, our photographer, with Hogue to help him, went up on rocks to take a photo. We were all out of sight except Hogue when we heard an awful scream from one of them and heard the other fall. It seems that they two had gone up on the side of the cliff; and Hogue wanted Nims to take the picture from a point about 17 feet up; but Nims wanted to get high enough to take the boats in the picture, and went up higher on a sloping shelf when his foot slipped; and he fell 22 feet.

Fig. 28. Camp at the mouth of House Rock Wash in Marble Canyon. At this point Robert Stanton took over the job as expedition photographer. This is his first exposure. *Robert B. Stanton.* Miami University Library.

He struck his foot on the shelf below where he was and turned back and fell on his back and head on the (rocks and ?) sand below. We got to him in a moment, found him bleeding at the nose and right ear, and on examination found his right leg broken just above his ankle. We have not been able to examine further but are doing all for him possible. This is a terrible blow for poor Nims and the expedition also. We will stay here today at Camp No. 56, 1/2 mile below our last camp.

Nims has been semiconscious all afternoon. Has thrown up several times with blotches of blood; but this has come from his right ear as he has been lying on his left side nearly all the time. He has passed urine several times without difficulty, and since we have put the splints on his ankle, he has simply gotten up on his knees to do it, and without any apparent pain. This seems to indicate no real injury anywhere except his ankle.

THURSDAY, JANUARY 2, 1890. Clear with a few clouds in P.M.

Nims was semiconscious all night. Sleeping most of the time. Two men sat up with him all night. This morning his color is good. The bleeding at ear and nose has stopped. His pulse seems good. His hands feel natural, and he has no fever. About noon he asked for a drink of water. He only complains of the bandages on his leg. I have concluded to move on at least to Rapid No. 118, which is formed by canyon coming on right and then consider what to do.

We put his leg in a box made by Mac, and bandaged it in the best way we can. We have made a stretcher of two oars and a canvas bed cover, and leveled down the load in No. 2 boat. We put Nims on stretcher by lifting his blankets and carry him to the boat. Without an extra groan from him we strap him in with the bed straps, and at 1:35 P.M. start.

We have smooth but swift water, 20 minutes, and then run Rapid No. 117 which is clear of rocks but quite brisk. Nims is asleep and does not know anything of it. We stop at 2 P.M. at Rapid No. 118. A portage is necessary as before. We put Nims under the ledge of rocks on dry warm sand where the sun has been shining nearly all day and make a big fire.

At Camp No. 57, old Camp No. 35. Have considered Nims's case carefully, and concluded that only the little bone of his leg is broken, that he has no other serious injury. That he received a severe shock by falling on the sand, and will soon recover. But that it would be dangerous for us to try to take him along, as in case of a boat being upset he could not help himself and might thus be drowned. Have therefore decided to take him out from this point to Lee's Ferry and leave him with the *Johnsons*. Mac, Hislop, and I will go up side canyon tomorrow and hunt a way out, and if we find one I shall go on to Lee's Ferry to get team while the other two men go back to camp and get ready to take Nims out the next day.

After portaging all supplies and carefully examining the rapid we conclude to run it with the empty boats. I do not go in the boats, as it is not necessary and there is no use my getting wet. No. 1 goes first with Mac, Gibson, and Kane. They go through in fine shape but in one plunge I can just see 1/2 the boat in the air and then 2/3 of it goes completely under water. Below this she climbs and dashes through the waves in beautiful shape.

No. 2 with Hislop, Travers, and Edwards goes next. Hislop misses the course a little and in the worst place goes over huge boulder under water. The bow goes out in the air; and as she drops the stern keel catches on the rock and grates off. This turns her on side, 45°, and she drops in the hole in this shape. Only an instant and she rights up like a feather and goes the rest of the way without striking bad waves.

No. 3 with Twining, Ballard, and Kane gets the right course; but going over the jump off, the bow drops quicker and the *whole* boat goes *literally* under the water of the rebounding wave and it covers them all. She bounds out light as a feather with no damage except the cockpit 1/4 full of water.

Measurement of inner gorge, January 2d, 213 feet, height of inner gorge above low water. Referring to my notes of July 11 '89, I think I then over-estimated the difficulty of a line on the slope above this inner gorge, although the alignment is more crooked than the river and the edge of this cliff shows a ragged profile. Yet it will be easy and cheap to blow the top of this off by big blasts into the river and get a solid rock roadbed.[3]

FRIDAY, JANUARY 3, 1890. Clear all day. Cloudy at night.

After breakfast this morning Mac, Hislop, and myself start 8:15 A.M. up side canyon to find way to take Nims out. We travel directly up the canyon for about four miles, over two or three bad places where the two boys help me up with a rope. We find all further progress cut off by perpendicular rise of over 100 feet in bed of canyon. We start back to look for place to get out on side. We soon find opening on left side of canyon and at 11:15 are out on top, 1700 feet up.

We eat a little lunch; and at 11:40 I start to head the canyon and go to Lee's Ferry and the two boys start back to camp on the river. I get across to the north side of this side canyon by going up it about 2 miles, and then climbing down where it is about 100 feet deep, and climb up on other side, through a crack in the rock, by putting my back on one side and knees on other side, and squeezing my way up. Got across at 1:20 P.M. Went right across the plain

---

[3] New Year's Day, 1890, brought some bad luck. Photographer Nims fell at a point below Sheer Wall Rapid at about Mile 15. Next day the expedition ran down to the foot of House Rock Rapid at the foot of House Rock Wash, running through Rider, or Ryder, Canyon, and there made preparation for the next move. Stanton never loses sight of the railroad. Here, opposite the mouth of Rider Canyon, with big blasts you could blow off the top of the cliff and get a solid rock roadbed!

to the wagon road along the Vermilion Cliffs. Reached the road at 2:30 P.M. very much worn out. Much to my surprise I found I was at least 7 or 8 miles above the Soap Creek Springs. Getting more tired all the time. I got to Soap Creek at 5 P.M. Ate some bread and meat and pushed on. I reached Lee's Ferry at 12:05 A.M. perfectly fagged out. Mr. Johnson was much surprised to see me, thinking some disaster as last summer had happened.

I was much rejoiced to find two letters from my wife here and this repays me for my 1700 feet climb and 35 mile walk to this place, if not the satisfaction of being able to get Nims out.

SATURDAY, JANUARY 4, 1890. Cloudy and blowing hard all day. Rain 6 P.M.

Lee's Ferry. Got up at 5:30 A.M. Mrs. Johnson put up plenty of provisions, and at 8:30 Mr. Johnson, his son, and I started back with team for the side canyon to get Nims. Heavy head wind all day. Team fagged out and we are obliged to camp 5 or 6 miles above where the men will be, about where I crossed the canyon. We traveled an hour after dark and only stop because the team can go no further. We are very sorry to stop here but it is impossible to go further with the team and I cannot go on myself as it is cloudy and snowing by fits; and it is impossible for me to cross the canyon where I did yesterday after dark, nor to head it.

If the men got up on top this afternoon, they are there without blankets, supper, or breakfast for tomorrow; and I am more worried for fear in getting Nims up someone else has slipped and been hurt.

SUNDAY, JANUARY 5, 1890. Clear with fleecy clouds.

Being so tired out we overslept ourselves. Got up at 6:30. Had some breakfast and at 7:30 started to head the canyon. Found it was going to take so long. I loaded my sack with bread and take can of milk for Nims. Cross the canyon and hurry for the point where the men were to come out. Found them, with Nims in good shape, at 9:15. They had slept out without blankets, supper, or breakfast, and were a pretty dilapidated looking set. Brown, Travers, and Gibson had gone to camp last night for food and came up soon after I arrived at 9:30 A.M.

I am much rejoiced to find that all went well yesterday and no one slipped or was hurt, and that Nims did not seem to suffer any by the trip, and must be better for he is cross and crabbed about little things.

Johnson with wagon reaches us at 2:15; and at 2:30 we lift poor Nims into the wagon on to a bed brought out by Mr. Johnson and cover him with extra blankets, and tie him in. We have put some cocoa, cornstarch, medicine, tobacco, etc., in Nims's sack, and have done everything in our power to make him comfortable. Johnson and his family are the kindest people in the world and have promised to take the best care of him possible, and know they will.

Nims knew Johnson perfectly when he came and put out his hand and shook hands with him. I told Johnson to do everything in his power for Nims. At 2:45 P.M. we bade Nims and Johnson good-by and all started down the side canyon for Camp No. 57 which we reached at 4:30.

Hislop gives me the following account of carrying Nims out of the canyon:

They left camp at 8:30 A.M. with Nims on stretcher made of two willow poles and the canvas from his bed. Eight men to carry: Hislop, McDonald, Travers, Gibson, Edwards, Brown, Ballard, and Twining. The lower part of the side canyon through which they went out is a very narrow gorge with perpendicular walls, with small rock benches near the bottom. They could carry him for some little distance in the bottom of the creek.

Then it was necessary to go along the little bench and in some places this was so sloping that a man could not stand on it alone. Two of these places they carried him by men going up, lying down on the slope catching on with toes and fingers and holding on to ropes attached to the stretcher, while the rest held to the stretcher and shoved him along; and in one instance the men holding the ropes could not stay on the sloping rocks without another man getting above in a better place and holding on to the lower man. Further on the creek drops over perpendicular benches 8 to 10 feet, and they drew him up over one of these with ropes also. This took them about 1 1/2 miles. Then for about 1 1/2 miles it was fairly good walking on the flat rock in bottom of creek.

Then came the climb of about 900 feet on the slope of loose rocks and earth at about 45°. At top of this for about 100 feet the way was out through a huge crack in the cliff, filled with immense sharp boulders. At one point they carried him through a hole under two of these and further up. Swung him over the top 15 feet high with ropes, and reached the top 1700 feet above the river at 3:30 P.M., having stopped 1/2 hour for lunch. Nims was strapped on to the stretcher, realized where he was going, and in one of the worst places raised up his head and looked over. Going down over the trail this P.M. I am perfectly astonished that they ever got him up at all, much less without injury to him or any of the men carrying him.[4]

[4] The rescue of Franklin Nims was a labor of the heaviest sort. He had to be lifted from the river bank up over the rim of Rider Canyon, a vertical distance of about 1500 feet; this within a horizontal distance of about four miles. Stanton's account of the adventure requires little elaboration. What good luck that the accident occurred where it did! Deeper down in the Grand Canyon, any attempt to carry out a stretcher-bound casualty might have been impossible. Nims eventually recovered enough to return to Denver without assistance. There the local press vigorously, and with some sensationalism, reported the accident, and the progress of the expedition. Denver *Times* January 28, 29, 1890; Denver *Rocky Mountain News*, January 29, 1890; Denver *Republican*, January 29, 30, February 5, 1890. Nims published two accounts, "Through the Colorado River," *Commonwealth*, III (Denver, August, 1890), 257–272, and "Through the Mysterious Cañons of the Colorado," *Overland Monthly*, second series, XIX (March 1892), 253–270. See Dwight L. Smith, "The Nims and Czar Incidents in the Denver Press," *Colorado Magazine*, 48 (Winter, 1971), 49–58. For a review

MONDAY, JANUARY 6, 1890. Rain for an hour last night. Misty snow in canyon since 8:30 A.M. Snowing hard on top. Snow stopped at 11:15 A.M. At 12 M. sun trying to shine. Clouded up and commenced to snow again at 2:30. Clear toward evening.

As we had hard work all day Sunday taking Nims out, I did not call the men till 8 o'clock. Breakfast, and then took it easy.

Packed up and start at 10:50. Run through Rapid No. 119, and stop at 10:55 to look at No. 120. This is much worse than at higher water as it is over a shelf of rock, and has a fall of 4 to 5 feet. We came through smoothly but went through waves that broke over my head. Rather severe to take such a bath, during a snowstorm. We run Nos. 121 and 122 easily. They are like 120, worse than in summer but not near so heavy as it. Stop at 11:15 at big rock to take photos. The chute by the big rock is not near so swift as last summer but the channels are narrowed to 40 and 20 feet.

We restart at 11:45 in the stretch of still water from the big rock on and reach Rapid 123 at 12:15 P.M. This rapid is as bad as last trip though the waves are not so high by half. It is full of boulders from side canyon and compels portage. The men immediately unload the boats while cook gets some hot lunch ready as many of us are wet.

The line on top the first bench continues at about the same distance above the river, 150 to 200 feet. Is somewhat more crooked than the river on account of numerous breaks in the upper stratum, but has a good easy slope. The lower strata are breaking up into benches, so if grade requires it we can soon come down from upper bench. The point on left side, opposite lower end of Rapid No. 123 is sharp and high, but can be cheaply thrown into the river.

After lunch, portage all stores and swing boats around 123. Reloaded and started at 4:45 P.M. After passing lower end of this rapid, No. 2 drifted hard against rock. We have still water for 3/4 mile; and we reach Rapid No. 124 at 5:00 P.M. and go into Camp No. 58, as this rapid is too bad to run.. (See notes of July 12th '89). We will portage in the morning our beds and light stuff and swing boats over loaded as we did before.

See note of July 12th '89 as to line and I add — There is but one proper way to construct along this *cliff* portion from Soap Creek to this (distance to be filled in hereafter), and that is by cutting down this first high cliff, throwing it into river, to whatever grade is required, by the line below this part.

TUESDAY, JANUARY 7. Cloudy and raw. Cloudy with fits of sun.

Up at 6:30. Breakfast ready. Men seemed to have had a bad night. At 8:00 A.M. commenced moving. Carried beds and other light stuff past

of Nims's contribution to the railroad project and the reliability of his published articles, see Dwight L. Smith, ed., *The Photographer and the River, 1889–1890* (Santa Fe, 1967).

rapid and at 8:15 swung No. 1 loaded over Rapid No. 124. All went through in good shape and we load bedding and start at 9:40 A.M.

At 9:45 we reach Rapid No. 125 at our old Camp No. 36, 1/2 to 3/4 mile below and stop to take photo. This rapid is not dangerous; but we are sure to get wet, so we shall drop boats with lines and not unload.

At this point the walls are all broken up and forming into benches, so that grade can be brought down to any level; but as the cliff is broken up and cut through by various water courses the work would be heavy in getting down. (See note of July 13th.)

We completed swinging round with loads and restarted at 11:08 and at 11:10 ran No. 126. Waves were high and I got a lap full of water. 11:27 we ran No. 127, easy. And at 11:34 stopped at No. 128. This is pretty wild and we shall drop boats over loaded. (See notes of July 13th '89.) I will take two photos here. As is easily seen by the photos, here and at Marble Pier, some 2 miles below the cliffs are broken and there is a fine sloping talus way above. High water mark is about 40 feet.

We lunch and start from foot of Rapid No. 128, at 1:47 P.M., and at 1:49 run No. 129 in 1/2 minute, and at 1:50 reach Rapid No. 130. Stop to examine, and conclude to drop boats over loaded. This we finish at 2:50 and at 3:10 start from this No. 130 which is our old Lone Cedar Rapid.

We have good quiet water for 10 minutes and then at 3:20 reach Rapid No. 131. This rapid we find is now a real *fall* of about 8 feet formed by a series of huge pieces of marble stretching all the way across the channel. On the right side there is a channel wide enough to drop the boats through. We cross over, and at once start to drop loaded boats over this fall. Nos. 1 and 2 go through easily and safely; but No. 3 gets a little crossways and is driven by the current on to one rock, and on examination we find has stove in her side breaking one of the ribs. Our *first accident.*

We run down 1/2 mile and camp at 4:00 P.M. at the Marble Pier. Camp No. 59, our old Sunday Camp No. 37.

All the rapids in Marble Canyon are much changed by from 6 to 9 feet lower water. Those formed over benches of rock, and such as No. 131 become *falls* with heavy but safe wave at foot. Those formed by simply *crowding* the water by falls of rock on one or two sides, like No. 116, are almost obliterated. Those formed by side canyons, and thus full of boulders, are either much harder on account of the boulders being exposed or little water over them, or are better by reason of there being one clear channel that can be seen and run. The waves in these are not more than 1/2 to 1/3 as high. In all cases so far the rapids are very much *shorter* and thus much more smooth water between them.[5]

[5] In Marble Canyon Stanton was finding out that rapids change with the stage of water, a bit of knowledge well understood by today's whitewater river runners. The high water

WEDNESDAY, JANUARY 8. Clear. Cloudy at noon. Heavy snow from 3 P.M. on to 6:00.

Stopped at this Camp No. 59 at the Marble Pier all day to repair boats and continue survey. Hauled up Boats No. 2 and 3. No. 2 had small leak and lower part of stern piece slightly broken. No. 3 is badly stove in on one side, two ribs broken, and one place chafed almost through where it was left while we took Nims out. This is blamable on Twining and Hislop. On Twining for not knowing how his boat was left and not putting it in a safe place, and on Hislop who says he knew it was on the rock and did not tell me.

Worked at boats till 3 P.M. when heavy snowstorm stopped us. The first *snowstorm* we have experienced this winter. It was certainly very dismal as the clouds gathered over the canyon and hung down almost to the river; and the narrow canyon became almost dark with the blinding snow blowing up the river.

Made my first effort at changing rolls in the roll holders. I think I have succeeded well. Hope so at least. As I have the photo work to do I have given Gibson some instruction in topography and shall have him do this work hereafter.

THURSDAY, JANUARY 9, 1890. Cloudy, all day. Camp 59. Worked on boats all day till 3 P.M. Shall not move till tomorrow. Party continued survey as far as they could go without the boats. Took two photos to try the rolls I put in yesterday. They seemed to work all right and reel off smoothly.[6]

FRIDAY, JANUARY 10, 1890. Fleecy clouds. Sun trying to shine.

Our boats were all repaired last evening and loaded as far as possible. We were up at 5:30 A.M. Breakfast 6:15. Ready to start at 8:15.

We swing, by line, our boats around point of Rapid No. 132. At the foot of this there is no place to land except among the rocks and the water is very rough, so as each boat is brought down it is manned and rowed down about

---

back in July created one kind of rapid; the low water of December–January, another. High water covering the rocks may make for an easier, safer run in some rapids. In others, where a clear channel can be seen threading the rocks, low water may be better. Modern boatmen have worked out a rating system for rapids on a scale of 1–10; ten being the most difficult to run. But in most cases ratings for the same rapid will vary with the amount of water coming down the stream.

[6] Here we see the engineer struggling with the intracacies of a view camera, a $6\frac{1}{2} \times 8\frac{1}{2}$ Scovil and Adams equipped with a roll holder. With Franklin Nims gone, Stanton assumed the job of photographer. That he knew nothing of photography at the outset, did not deter the young engineer. From House Rock to the end of the survey he exposed some 1600 negatives, ninety percent of which were clear and acceptable. Stanton wrote later that his success as a photographer was attributable to accident rather than skill on his part. See Dwight L. Smith, ed., *Down the Colorado* (1965), 116–117. A smaller camera, the Detective, was used along the way for informal snapshots.

1500 feet to head of Rapid No. 133 on sand bar. All came through safe except No. 3 which struck a rock in bounding over a wave and made a hole in her. This will be a lesson to us and we shall stop swinging the boats through such places loaded. We stop and repair No. 3, thus we have lost 2 1/2 days by broken boats and 4 days on account of Nims's accident. Rather a serious loss of time.

We lunch at 12 noon. At 1:00 P.M. after having portaged all our supplies past Rapid No. 133 we commenced to let down the boats past the rocks at the head of this rapid. McDonald, who has direct charge of the boats, adopted a new plan. By attaching a small line to bow of boat, and as Hislop and rest of men eased the boat down with long stern line, McDonald followed along shore and guided it with little line. Nos. 1 and 3 were put down thus very success-fully; but in putting down No. 2, McDonald made a mistake and drew in her bow when he should have let her out in main current; and before he could alter her course, she caught broadside on a rock and rolled half over with the water rushing full force in her cockpit. Being so strongly built she stood the strain well. I let McDonald and Hislop, whose boat it was, do all they thought best, till they gave up in despair of getting her off.

I then rigged a gin pole and could get best pull by direct line against and up the rock she was on. This easily raised her, but seemed about to break her in two; so I changed the direction of the line hoping to turn her over from the rock; but this we could not do as it was against the current. So I then changed back to first position determined to pull her off or break her in two in the attempt. After wriggling the pole and a few hard pulls she came over the rock with much less damage than I expected, at 5.P.M. We fixed her in safe place, loaded the other two boats, and moved down to sand beach at head of Rapid No. 134 and went into Camp No. 60.

The water, washing into the boat for nearly 3 hours, broke out the seats and bottom boards of floor thus releasing our cook stuff and cans under the floor. We lost:

> 1 tent; 1 boat cover; 1 tarpaulin; 1 ax; 1 rubber boot; 4 cans p. pudding; 18 cans milk; 6 cans syrup; 1 bake oven; 10 plates; 6 cups; 6 knives and forks; 4 large knives; 3 large spoons; 2 dippers; 1 dishpan; 1 bucket; 1 sauce kettle; 1 saucepan; 1 lunch bucket; 1 coffeepot; 1 camp kettle; 1 frying pan; 1 pot hook.

Camp No. 60.

SATURDAY, JANUARY 11, 1890. Clear, sunshine, but we are on the shady side, and get none all day.

All day in Camp No. 60. Repairing Boat No. 2. Completed work at 5 P.M. Went back with empty boat this A.M. and got No. 2. Bailed her out and rowed her down. On examination she is not as badly injured as we feared. Her keel is slightly cracked; and there are 4 small holes in her but no ribs broken; and she can be easily repaired and made good. McDonald and Travers will repair her.

Our camp here is at the same point where we stop for lunch July 15th '89, just after Hansbrough and Richards were drowned.

SUNDAY, JANUARY 12, 1890. Clear, and bright sunshine on top and in open parts of canyon, but we are on shady side and have no sun. Resting in Camp No. 60.

It was undoubtedly the coldest night, last night, that we have had since leaving Blake. The sun has been shining beautifully and bright all day on top and on the other side of the canyon; but where we have been the sun does not strike at all and is very cold. Yet all the snow of the last two storms that fell on the lower benches has melted off. Only a little shows in the shady nooks at top of canyon.

MONDAY, JANUARY 13, 1890. Clear and bright sunshine on top all day.

We are all up early this morning and start from our Camp No. 60 at 8:10 A.M. and at once run Rapid No. 134. It is quite a jump off with lively waves, and I get two of them in my lap.

We reach Rapid No. 135 at 8:15 A.M. I go over to right bank and take photos while the men make portage of *all* goods. We then ease the boats down with the lines. All being completed by 9:45 we load and start at 10:20. At lower side of Rapid No. 135 we found the old Indian dugout that we put in the river last summer at Rapid No. 107. We were going to put it in river again when some of the men said, let it stay. All our trouble last summer and this winter has come between the points where this was put in and here, so let her stay. I note that the Rapid No. 135 is 10 feet lower than last summer.

Starting at 10:20 we run Rapid 136 at 10:22, not bad but quite wavy, and run on smooth water for 1 1/2 miles and reach Rapid No. 137 at 10:35. We immediately made portage of all stuff in one hour, and lunch at 12 noon. The sun struck the beach where we were, the first sunshine we have been *in* since yesterday week.

Canyon above here is very narrow. Between the marble, walls are not over 200 to 250 feet apart, but on top of them is fine bench with regular mountain slope.

At 1:00 P.M. to 1:30 we *swing* our boats over Rapid 137 with great success. I photo last boat with instantaneous plate. This rapid is at head of Powell's 1 mile marble pavement on left.

We load and start at 2:05 P.M. It is a very difficult place to get out of with our loaded boats as the current dashes in towards the left shore and comes with great force against the rocks. No. 1 makes a dash and in very heavy waves goes out safely. No. 2 fails and is driven ashore. Strikes against a sharp [rock] and cuts a small hole in her side. No. 3 starts well out at first, but is thrown in and shaves an icy rock, but with no damage. We lose 10 minutes waiting for "No. 2" and then sail 1 mile along marble pavement and reach in smooth still water Rapid No. 138 at 2:35. Stop to examine and fix "No. 2." Start at 3:15. Run Rapid No. 138. I get one wave in my lap.

At 3:50 we run Rapid No. 139 along the right wall of cliff and run No. 140 at 3:55 without stopping. We reach Rapid No. 141 at 4:03. Stop and examine and then run it at 4:13. At 4:15 stop and examine No. 142 and at 4:22 run it and in one minute more run No. 143. Have a beautiful sail for 1 1/2 miles and at 4:40 reach our old Camp No. 40 opposite Point Retreat, the scene of our turning back last summer.

Camp No. 61.

As soon as we landed we went to look at the cave where we cached our supplies and blankets last July. We found everything there in perfectly good condition and dry. The only damage was by the rats to one sack of flour. We get 4 pairs blankets, enough cooking utensils, plates, cups, etc., to make good our recent loss, and enough good supplies to make up our loss by Nims's accident and delay. We get

> 100 lbs. flour; 30 lbs. rice; 20 lbs. sugar; 20 lbs. coffee; 2 gallons sorghum; 6 lbs. baking powder.

All very acceptable. We also take the old photographic instruments, my revolver, and a couple lbs. tobacco.

This has been our best day's run since we have been in Marble Canyon. Everyone and everything worked smoothly and together. We have made between 10 and 12 miles. Two portages of all our stuff, one in one, and one in one and a half hours. Very quick work.

I note remarkable changes in some of the rapids since last summer. Nos. 132 and 133 are made by a complete line of huge boulders across the river, and at this stage of water these make a sudden fall and then a very short rapid below. Whereas with 10 feet more water, the fall at the rocks would be less, but the whole rapid would be, as it was, much worse to run. While No. 134 being formed by two falls of debris crowding the channel into a narrow space penning the water up above, and now at this low stage this rapid is quite smooth. All the rapids from No. 137 to Point Retreat are of this last formation and hence we find them this trip vastly better than last summer. No. 144 at mouth of side canyon opposite Point Retreat, which last summer was a roaring torrent with main current dashing against and along the base of wall of Point Retreat, has absolutely disappeared and left nothing but smooth water in its place.

TUESDAY, JANUARY 14. Clear sunshine, for 6 hours on our camp.

In Camp No. 61. Repairing boats. Rearranging stores and preparing for the new country below. Party making survey around Point Retreat. Took two photos from bench 450 feet above river.[7]

WEDNESDAY, JANUARY 15, '90. Clear and bright sunshine.

Very cold this morning and we are obliged to go easily. We pack up and start at 10:40 A.M. Stop at 10:43 to examine Rapid No. 145, and at 10:50 we run it. It is very crooked but not bad. 10:52 stop 3 minutes to examine No. 146 and are through it at 10:56. Here we stop to continue survey and take photos at Station 93+. At 11:04 start again and in one minute are through Rapid No. 147. No. 1 grazes her stern post on a rock but no damage. No. 3 grazes same rock and springs a leak. Stop 1/2 mile below to continue survey.

Lunch at 12:45 P.M. in beautiful sunshine, and at 1:57 P.M. we start again. At 2:06 we stop to examine Rapid No. 148 and at 2:08 we run it. A side wave wets my legs and feet, and turns to ice over my shoes. This is a long 1/2 mile gravel rapid. The water for a mile is smooth and in some places quite swift.

Beautiful turreted cliffs on right with numerous cave and windows high up to the top and across one side wash. A natural marble bridge, under which the sky makes a fine effect. At foot of this cliff are little springs 10 to 12 feet above river. Running out of perpendicular wall and below them clinging to the wall large bunch of maidenhair fern, with icicles among them. Ferns bright green. I take Detective pictures of these.

2:25 run Rapid No. 149, without stopping. 2:27 run Rapid 150, without stopping. This last is the narrowest channel of the river we have seen not over 50 or 60 feet wide.

We travel on smooth water till 2:32 and stop to take photos. This is the narrowest and grandest part of Marble Canyon we have seen. The walls are perpendicular on both sides, for from 300 to 400 feet high cut through by quite a number of side streams which only cut down short distance, leaving about 100 feet of clear marble at bottom, giving wonderful turreted appearance to top. Canyon 250 to 300 feet wide.

We start from taking photos, after warming at fire of driftwood at 3:00 P.M. on a beautiful sheet of still water and reach head of Rapid No. 151 at 3:15. This is quite heavy and full of rocks and requires a portage. So we begin at once and cook. Go to getting supper as we shall stop here all night,

---

[7] Now in camp again at the mouth of South Canyon, opposite Point Retreat, the stores cached when Stanton left the river on July 18, were a welcome addition after the losses sustained on January 9 when McDonald pinned a boat to a rock in 26 Mile Rapid (RBS 133).

and I go to writing up my notes. We have done good work today and have come about 7 1/2 or 8 miles. Camp No. 62.

Portage made and boats dropped by 5:10 P.M. Our journey today has been our first over *new* water. Our last summer's trip ended at Point Retreat, old Camp No. 40, and our last night's Camp No. 61.

My notes must be brief as I have so many things to attend to. Noting line from Point Retreat on I find that from Station 144+93 a lower bench of marble with some talus is beginning to form which indicates some change in canyon beyond.

Our journey today *up to* Rapid No. 151 has been smooth. All the rapids have been comparatively good. They would be much worse at high water.

Fig. 29. The Colorado River in Marble Canyon, flowing from right to left, loops around Point Hansbrough. The Kaibab Plateau on the skyline. Stanton planned to swing the railroad line around the bend on top of the talus slope at the base of the cliffs (1967 Photo). *John M. Kitchen.* C. Gregory Crampton.

From Point Retreat to Rapid No. 151 I estimate there would be some 12 small "overhead" drains.

THURSDAY, JANUARY 16, 1890. Clear and beautiful sunshine.

Everyone overslept themselves last night, and being very cold this morning we had breakfast late, 7:00 A.M. Loaded up and start below Rapid No. 151 at 9:50 A.M. No. 151 falls 6 to 8 feet. While the boats were loading I took photos. I hope [one of them in particular] will turn out well as it has the most beautiful reflection of the rising sun and cliffs in the still water that I have ever seen.

From Rapid No. 151 to where river turns again to left, S-course, the marble is broken down to 250 to 300 feet. One halfway between these points, one cliff of marble rises straight up 700 to 800 feet high.

Reach Rapid No. 152, 10:02. Stop to examine. This is made by side canyon on right, 100 foot span. Marble much broken up at this point but rises up bold beyond to where river turns again to right, 600 feet high. 10:06 run Rapid No. 152. I got an immense wave all over me. At point where turns to right, marble is broken back on point side up river; but at the extreme point it is perpendicular 6 to 700 feet high but very much broken on lower side of point. This would make short tunnel and come out on lower marble on each side, *if high line*.

10:16 we reach and run Rapid No. 153 made by canyon on left, 200 foot span. Rapid easy at this stage of water. This is 1/2 mile way from 152 to point where river turns sharp to right. At this point at higher stage of water would be bad rapid with huge marble rock in center of river. Run it at 10:20.

At 10:24 reach Rapid No. 154. Stop to examine and take photos. Rapid formed by side wash on left. Start 10:53 and run Rapid No. 154, a 5 foot drop but easy water below. Lost 10 inches [of boat] No. 3.

Marble beyond Rapid 154 shelves off towards river down to where river turns to left with side wash coming in on right. This is only an amphitheater 100'×150' washed out by very small stream from top. Line would be back of it. *If line was on top*, span quite a number of small water courses high up and on top marble requiring small 6 foot to 8 foot openings.

At extreme point of turn to left side, canyon comes in from right span and forms Rapid 155. Stop to examine at 11:13 A.M. and take photos. The side wash at Rapid 155 is rather a small one on top of marble but has cut out a cavern 100'×200' almost arched over. Locate line back and make small opening. Here we find large mesquite and ferns. We start at 11:40 and at once run Rapid 155 and I get three waves over my head and my legs and feet are completely wet.

Water from last rapid to point where river turns to right beautifully smooth. The marble on right stands almost perpendicular, 350 to 400 feet high. Our line would have to be quite high and cut top of this cliff and throw it into river in order to retain my first idea of crossing river at Point Retreat high up and coming down river on top of the marble. This I see today will be impossible. All through today's run line must be on talus at foot of cliff. Will take this up in general remark later.

At 11:52 we reach and run Rapid 156. Side wash on left, at 1/4 mile from where river turns sharp to right. High water mark is only about 25 feet, about 5 feet lower than at Vasey's Paradise. The high 350 to 400 foot cliffs on right continue all around this bend to where river commences to turn again to left, then it breaks up lower down and in ragged points at top. At this point, just at turn to left, is side canyon, 200 foot span.

12:06 we reach this Rapid 157 and run it. Easy light waves.

About 1/2 mile beyond is another side canyon on right which we reach at 12:10 and stop for lunch at head of Rapid No. 158. After lunch we measure height of perpendicular marble cliff and I change photo rolls before starting.

Restart, 2:02 and run No. 158. Long, 1500 feet. Crooked and bad rapid and come at once into smooth water. A very fine high 100 to 150 foot talus on right giving a beautiful line all round this curve to the left. Same on left side with fine growth of mesquite. The sheer wall above talus continues to point where river turns sharp to right. The talus grows larger. The water is beautifully smooth and still, 1 1/2 to 2 miles to 1/2 mile past where river turns to right.

We stop at 2:30 P.M. on bar made by side canyon on left and take photos. These show the talus and wall above. This bar is at head of Rapid No. 159 and is 1/4 mile past extreme point of sharp turn to right noted above. The point is quite sharp and I first thought would require two tunnels, but on going further round I think line can be located on this heavy talus without tunnels by filling in in center and cutting pretty close to points. Perhaps however the second point may yet require short tunnel.

Start at 2:57 and in one minute ran Rapid 159. Straight and easy. Good waves but none went over boat. Great many water courses come in on left but few on right.

At 3:03 we reach head of Rapid No. 160 which compels a portage on account of huge rock in center. So we go to work at once and will camp here tonight. Camp No. 63.

The railroad line from Marble Pier to this point, which I call Hansbrough's Point, is the most important part of the whole route thus far surveyed. After fixing the line from Lee's Ferry to Marble Pier, as described in previous notes, I thought to follow the same plan below: that is, continue on the talus below Marble Pier till the marble cliffs became perpendicular, as they do, and then follow on top of marble on slope above it to Point Retreat, being just above Point Retreat about 200 feet above river; tunnel Point Retreat; cross the river on bridge about 200 feet above low water; tunnel the opposite point and get again on the slope above the marble; and then gradually get down, as I thought the marble dipped down river below the crossing.

This I find to be a mistake. The top of the marble seems to be generally about level and the river is cutting down deeper and deeper in it, so that while at Point Retreat the perpendicular marble cliff, as measured, is about 300 feet high. It is 700 feet at this Point Hansbrough, as measured a little way above here yesterday. This necessitates an entire change of my plan of location.

A fine talus has formed from Rapid No. 151 to this place, and our high water mark is only about 25 feet up and nearly all the way is over 100 feet high. Taking this into consideration one of the following plans will have to be adopted. Which one, depends on cost to be shown by a locating survey.

A. Follow same line as before *to* Point Retreat. Tunnel this point not over 150 feet high. Cross at same place as before. Land in small tunnel, at extreme point on right bank. Half tunnel around lower side of point and get down to about 50 feet above low water as soon as possible. From half tunnel for about 3 or 4 miles on this line before reaching Rapid No. 151, the line would have to be built entirely in the river as the walls are perpendicular for 600+ feet up, though they are ragged and honeycombed towards top. This 3 to 5 miles would be very expensive work. Having passed Rapid No. 151 the line would then be on the talus, to Point Hansbrough.

B. Follow same line as above to about Rapid No. 157 or beyond. Then work down so as to be about 70 feet up at Point Retreat. Follow around Point Retreat on line built in river. Cross on bridge say 70 [feet] high near Vasey's Paradise. Support line on talus, it is good, from Vasey's Paradise to point where river turns to right, Station 140 of January 15, and build line in river from there to Rapid No. 151 as in A.

This line would have expensive work around Point Retreat, but would save time tunneling that point. It would also have a longer expensive line in river to Rapid 151 but would save tunnel and half tunnel at point on right bank beyond Point Retreat.

The bridge crossing on line B would be perhaps 50 feet longer than on A, but would be lower. The crossing as measured on line A is 350 feet but with bridge seats, etc., might reach 400 feet, a single span.

One thing however is settled: our line must be down on talus or stolen river line at Rapid No. 151.

FRIDAY, JANUARY 17, 1890. Clear and bright sunshine. Cloudy at noon but cleared up later.

Up at 5:45. Breakfast at 6:15.

7:30 A.M., after breakfast this morning we took the remains of P. M. Hansbrough and buried them in a mesquite grove under the marble cliff on left side of canyon just below where side canyon comes in, directly opposite Rapid No. 160. I offered a short prayer, not for our poor Peter but a petition that we might be spared his fate; but if called upon to meet the same death, that we might each be prepared to go. We covered his grave with marble slabs, and Gibson cut on the cliff beside it "P.M.H. 1889." Standing over the grave is a marble wall 700 feet high.[8]

Our boats are hauled out on the beach being repaired, so we will be late starting. The boats are repaired. We load and start at 10:33 A.M.

The river is still falling. It fell 6 inches last night.

Stop 10:35 at head of Rapid No. 161 to examine. It is clear and easy. 10:42, we run it.

Around Point Hansbrough continues a fine talus for 1 mile to the extreme turn to right, where cliff is somewhat broken at bottom and juts out into river. This can be easily cut and make good line around it. This talus continues beyond the point, but just as it turns on west course, new bench of sandstone (see note January 20th) comes up and broad talus is on top (see note, January 18th 1890). This starts as nothing at head of Rapid No. 162 just at point and rises to about 40 feet high at end of this west course, about 1 1/2 to 2 miles.

At 10:48 reach Rapid No. 162. Stop to examine and take photo. Restart at 11:03 and run Rapid No. 162 full of rock, huge waves, and crooked channel. Go through in very fine shape but all three boats just touch on rock at lower end. Beautiful still water for 1 1/4 miles ahead. At 11:25 reach head of Rapid No. 163. At 11:32 we run Rapid No. 163. It was not as bad as it looked from shore. Beautiful still water below this rapid which is formed by [wash?] from left side.

Along this stretch to where river turns to left are about 10 small water openings required, but they can be small as very little debris shows as coming down from the high cliffs above. Just at turn to left are two immense caverns

[8] On January 16 the Stanton surveying expedition went into camp at the foot of President Harding Rapid (Stanton 160, camp 63). This was at the head of a four-mile hairpin bend in the Colorado. This loop and other complexities of the canyon architecture, obliged Stanton to make some involved calculations to find a line for the railroad. He concluded that the best bet would be to bridge the Colorado at Point Retreat and bring the line down the right side; thus the first railroad bridge across the river would be located 248 miles below the confluence of the Green and Colorado rivers.

During the day Stanton was so taken up with these ideas and plans — "Cut top of this cliff & throw into river," tunnels, bridges and alignments — that he neglected to note that the skeleton of Peter M. Hansbrough, lost to the river in July, was found near camp. A pair of peculiar shoes, still on his feet, made identification positive. Burial was at the base of the canyon's towering left well. Langdon Gibson carved the inscription. To the spectacular peninsula, or core, of rock on the inside of the bend, Stanton gave the name "Point Hansbrough." In 1923, the U.S. Geological Survey river mapping party spent the day of President Harding's funeral at this same camp site. Later, the rapid was named for the president. Lewis R. Freeman, reporting the government survey, recalled the Stanton camp here, "Surveying the Grand Canyon of the Colorado," *National Geographic Magazine*, XLV (May, 1924), 514–515.

washed out by streams coming over top of the marble. They are not wide through lower bench, 50 feet and 50 foot spans, and would be perfectly clear as the caverns back catch all the wash.

Timbered plateaus show on top at end of this west course.

At 11:48 A.M. we stop at side canyon to take photos and are much surprised not to find any rapid formed by this side canyon. I go up the hill to take photos and find wild flowers in bloom, green grass 3 inches high, and birds singing in the mesquite bushes; and as I show the flowers to the men below, they strike up the familiar air from the Mikado.

Beyond this side canyon, 80 foot span, this lower bench our line is following keeps rising, and about 1 1/2 miles below is about 100 feet high. A second talus begins to form at the side canyon. In this stretch to point where river turns to right are 2 waterways, 30 foot spans.

We stop after photos are taken at 12 noon and lunch and restart at 1:00 P.M. At 1:18 we reach long gravel Rapid No. 164 and run it. It is over a half mile long. We run it in 3 1/2 minutes. At 1:22 we land at head of Rapid No. 165. Stop to examine. Full of rocks. A narrow channel. We run it at 1:29 P.M., safely. This last Rapid 165 is at point river turns right.

The stretch beyond is 1 1/2 miles, and about center of this we land on left bank at 1:35 and take photos. In the half of this stretch above is one waterway 30 foot span, and in lower 1/2 are two immense amphitheaters washed by streams coming from high over the marble. Each would require about 60 foot spans.

Start at 1:58 P.M., and reach head of Rapid No. 166 at 2:02 P.M., and stop to examine. This is formed by first side wash on right. Start and run No. 166 at 2:08 P.M.

The lower talus along this stretch is growing larger and higher. First bench is growing higher but is broken and ragged and material is easily gotten to make first class roadbed on lower talus. The *alignment* ever since Rapid No. 159 is most beautiful.

We run very small Rapid No. 167 formed by wash on left. At 2:11 P.M. and at 2:14 stop and look at head of No. 168 formed by the second wash on right. And just before we land we discover our old Boat No. 5 of last summer's trip, from which Hansbrough and Richards were drowned on July 15th. We stop to get some iron from the boat and at 2:27 start and run Rapid No. 168, a very shallow gravel rapid. We touched our keel on the gravel.

This part of the canyon surprises me. High water is between 20 and 25 feet up; the canyon is 1000 to 1500 feet wide; broad flats at the mouths of the side washes; high sloping talus on both sides covered with green grass and bushes, mostly mesquite; while the main marble walls rise 1000 feet above the river. It must be a beautiful spot in summer, the whole of the way of to-day's run.

At 2:35 P.M. we turn again to right. At this point the talus is smaller but the first bench is much broken up so it will make beautiful line. Beyond this the talus is much better with plenty of ragged marble to fill up with.

No waterways on right of any importance over a mile. We stop at 2:50 to take photos from middle of bend and restart at 3:18 P.M. Opposite where took above photos are two high washes with large basins back, 2-20 foot spans.

At 3:30 P.M. we stop to examine rapid about 1/2 mile above the mouth of the Nankoweap canyon. And at 3:50 P.M. we run this Rapid No. 169.

At 3:55 we stop to examine long, gravelly, shallow rapid just below the mouth of the Nankoweap. It looks bad because very shallow. At 4:10 we start and run it, No. 170, and are surprised to find plenty of water. We go through safely. Do not touch a rock. This rapid is 1/2 mile long.

We go into Camp No. 64, at 4:20 P.M. We are by river about one mile below mouth of Nankoweap. Will stop tomorrow to photograph this section and will then describe it.

This has been one of the most successful days we have had on the river. This portion of the canyon through which we have sailed today is wonderfully beautiful.

It as widened out somewhat but still for some distance the marble cliffs stand perpendicular for 600 to 800 feet above the talus and at some points from the water itself. This marble as noted before is of various beautiful colors but I find that what I supposed last summer was red and scarlet marble towards the tops of the cliffs is only the grey and other marbles colored by the wash from the iron stained sandstone above it. It is as beautiful as before in the canyon, but would not be so when quarried.

Groves of mesquite, large bottoms covered with grass, beautiful portion of canyon from Point Hansbrough down side canyons, 6 to 800 feet high and some only 60 feet wide.[9]

SATURDAY, JANUARY 18, 1890. Clear and warmer. Very windy all day.

At Camp No. 64 one mile below mouth of the Nankoweap.

This crossing of the Nankoweap is the most extensive waterway our line has crossed on the whole river. The stream itself is not over 30 to 40 feet wide,

[9] On January 17, the Stanton survey crew ran ten miles and camped at the foot of the Nankoweap Creek Rapid, having traveled through an extravagantly beautiful section of Marble Canyon. The charm of the landscape was not lost on our engineer-diarist who uses the word "beautiful" more times in this day's notes than in those of all of the preceding days combined. During the day as he caught glimpses of the snow-covered, forested crest of the Kaibab Plateau towering above him on the west, Stanton noted the change in climate and plant life. Below Point Hansbrough the course of the river is southward. Thus the warming rays of the winter sun penetrate the canyon depths and create one of those miniclimates so characteristic of Grand Canyon. The crew basked in the warmth of the place and, upon sight of the freshly-picked flowers, opened with "The Flowers that Bloom in the Spring," from Gilbert and Sullivan's operetta, *The Mikado*, a first for G and S in Grand Canyon.

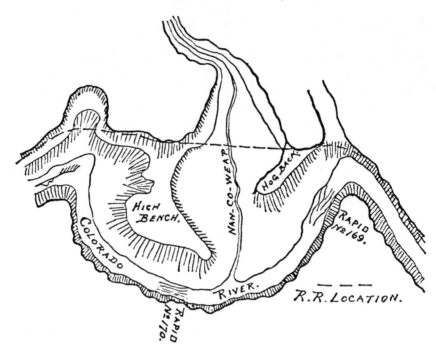

FIG. 30. Sketch map of the mouth of the Nan-co-weap. Miami University Library.

but the *wash* from slope to slope is about 800 feet. Grade would be say 40 to 60 feet above low water. Cut the two hogbacks and I think [it] would be best to cross this wash by a trestle with about an 80 foot span over main channel. Of course, it is impossible to fix such points definitely at this time. They must be carefully studied after a *location* survey.[10]

Return from survey and start at 11:13 from Camp No. 64 one mile below the Nankoweap. Just after passing the Nankoweap and just before getting to point is large washed out cavern but small stream 20 or 30 foot span.

[10] Nankoweap Creek is a short, steep gradient drainage heading on the eastern face of the Kaibab Plateau. From Point Imperial on the North Rim of Grand Canyon, one may look directly into Nankoweap Canyon, the waters of which drop 6000 feet in about seven miles. The Nankoweap has long been an access route from the rim lands to the canyon floor. The lower valley was populated by prehistoric Pueblo peoples, the Anasazi, who for a hundred years after about A.D. 1050, lived here in some numbers and built the cliff-side structures, probably granaries, visible from the river and much visited by modern voyagers. Always interested in the canyon's prehistoric life, Stanton was the first to describe and photograph this ruin. His notes about the site on January 18, scattered among crude sketches, are interpreted as follows: The ruin consisted of four "entire" rooms and four rooms with "half walls." Doors were 18″ by 12″ and the "upper" room had a "thin stone slab cut exactly to fit the door, with two staples made with willow and cross bar to put on the outside." Sticks and small stones plastered with mud formed the "arch" of the doors. Nankoweap Creek and Kwagunt Creek, reached on January 19, are names given by the Powell Survey.

From the above wash down to where river turns to right are *six* small streams coming over the top 5-10 foot and 1-30 foot spans. The talus all along this stretch is very much larger than any we have found in this canyon running up in places 300 to 400 feet. The material is good, easily handled, and the alignment is first class.

Stop at 11:17 to examine Rapid No. 171. Start and run it at 11:30. It is a regular snorter [S-curved] shape and 1/2 mile long. Through it at 11:32 and right into No. 172. Through it at 11:34 and stop to examine No. 173. Start at 11:43 and run it. The most dangerous one we have run. Full of huge rock; but we come through safely.

The wind is blowing great guns up the river and the sand is simply blinding. The water is good. No rapids for 2 1/2 miles, but on account of the wind it is a very hard [to] pull through regular wind waves.

Rapid 170 is just below, say 500 feet, [of] the mouth of the Nankoweap. Camp No. 64 one mile below mouth. Rapid 171 is 1/2 mile below camp and [Rapid] 172 [is] 1/2 mile below that. [Rapid] 173 [is] 1/4 mile below 172.

We had great difficulty in landing as wind was blowing off shore, in gusts, sometimes whipping the water up into foam. Stop at 12:30 P.M. for lunch. Rest some time. Wait for a lull in the wind and take photos.

Start again at 2:15 P.M. and run at 2:16 Rapid No. 174. Not at all bad. This is just *above* side canyon opposite our noon rest.

At 2:21 we stop to examine No. 175 formed by the side canyon on right. We find it very bad at lower end and conclude not to run it. We ease the boat down loaded, which is a slow and tedious job but safe. We are through and start at 4:02 P.M.

At 4:07 we stop to examine Rapids 176 and 177 while I take photo from flat looking up the *Kwagunt*. The Kwagunt is a side canyon almost as large as the Nankoweap. In formation it is the same and the wash below is almost identical except that there are almost no hogbacks as at the Nankoweap. The bend of the river is the same caused by the wash and the rapids are in almost the same position. Kwagunt will take 600 feet of trestle with large span for waterway. At 4:35 we row across to left bank and look again at Rapid No. 176. It is very bad, full of huge boulders, and very crooked channel. At 4:50 we start and run it safely by the various currents *helping* us to steer by the rocks. At 4:52 we are through and into No. 177 which is 1/2 mile long and shallow. Our boat strikes once on rock under water and makes small cut on her right side; but she does not leak fast.

At 4:55 we run Rapid No. 178. It is easy. At 5:05 stop to examine No. 179 and at 5:09 run it. Very crooked and steep but we go through safely by 5:10, and at 5:11 stop to look at No. 180. At 5:15 run it and at 5:17 stop again to look at No. 181. At 5:20 we run this and at 5:30 P.M. we go into camp on right bank about 2 miles below the Kwagunt.

Camp No. 65.

Hasty note: From Kwagunt to point where river turns to left, 1 side wash 100 foot span. Note wash at Camp No. 65 and smaller openings.

Sunday, January 19, 1890. In Camp No. 65 *resting*. This camp is about 4 miles above the mouth of the *Little* Colorado River, which is in sight. We hoped to get to that point last night but it was impossible on account of the high wind.

The storm that seemed to be coming up so strong died down towards night. Yesterday about 9:00 P.M. it commenced to rain, and rained gently till about 3 or 4 this morning. It turned cold and clear and today has been a most beautiful sunshiny day.

Monday, January 20. We repair the slight damage to Boat No. 1, pack up, and start 9:00 A.M. Sail through a beautiful bay of still water for 3/4 mile and stop at head of Rapid No. 182, to examine and take two photos at 9:05. At 9:11 we ran it. It was very shallow; and we struck bottom three times but only once I think with any damage at all and that very little. This rapid was very crooked, a regular letter S in shape and long. A huge rock at its head by which we had to cut very close in order not to be drawn against shore at the sharp turn below. This was done very successfully by all boats but it took very hard and quick steering to make the two sharp turns at about 15 miles per hour. It was shallow in places but the waves did not indicate any special rocks below; but it seemed to be full and on three of these we touched.

From side wash where we camped are seven small side washes with 10 to 30 foot openings, to point where river turns to right, above Little Colorado River.

We stop about 1/3 way between last camp and the right turn as above at 9:20 and take photos. Restart at 9:42 A.M.

Just beyond last rapid shows a new foundation of hard *sandstone* in thin strata coming up from river. This is very hard in thin 1 to 2 foot horizontal layers and is very coarse formed sand like conglomerate, yet all of the same kind of sand from the size of a pea down.

As noted on the 17th, the first new formation. Since we entered the marble began to show just below Rapid No. 162. It *seems* to be a mixture of sandstone, limestone, veins of mineralized matter, and several veins 3 to 4 feet of apparently good iron ore. These veins are small at first but increase as the stratum grows higher. At the Nankoweap the veins of iron are quite large, 4 to 6 feet. This stratum is yellow, grey, and whitish color in layers, all horizontal or dipping slightly up river.

As the strata of conglomerate sandstone comes up, this mineralized formation rises up and back on top of it and under the marble and seems to be growing thinner, and the marble benches back above it still further from the river.

The last *wash* is the last of the seven noted on previous page, our last photos were taken 3/4 mile back on left bank. This wash is the last but one before reaching the Little Colorado River, this one being just about right point above Little Colorado River. At 9:52 we reach Rapid 183 formed by this wash and run it without stopping, and at 9:54 stop to examine Nos. 184 and 185. At 10:14 we run them both and are through at 10:16.

This was probably the most difficult two rapids we have run. In starting it was necessary to shave close to rock and then steer hard off and yet keep in channel. This brought us in direct line against which the whole force of the current was breaking in center of stream. To do this we turned sharp into eddy above and pulled down eddy to get new start for No. 185. The difficulty in this one was that the whole force of the current beat against and back of, against shore, rock. To avoid this it was necessary to cut across the current at the head. There was plenty of room, but as our bow struck the eddy and the current our stern, we whirled round like a shot.

At 10:25 we reach and run Rapid No. 186 without stopping. Safe.

At 10:27 stop to take photos about one mile above Little Colorado on left bank.

We start again at 10:47 and at 10:49 run Rapid No. 187. And at 11:00 A.M. we land at mouth of the Little Colorado River, which comes in on the left. The stream is small, about 1/4 that of the main river at this stage of water; but the canyon is nearly as wide as the main canyon except at bottom. On right bank is very pretty bottom extending up for a mile. The canyon is identical in form and appearance as the main canyon.

As we have come down the river from the Nankoweap the canyon has had more of the *appearance* of the walls of Cataract Canyon. The slope of debris or talus extending from the river up 200 to 300 feet like a regular mountain slope to the foot of the marble which is receding as the other formations are rising from below.

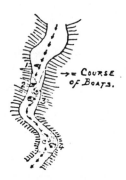

Fig. 31. Sketch map of Rapids 184 and 185. Miami University Library.

The marble above Rapid No. 162, where the first change from marble shows, is about 800 feet high and in many places rises in sheer walls from the water's edge. From Point Retreat, about 300 feet high, the marble rises rapidly; but the whole inner gorge is formed of it till we reach Rapid No. 162, when the new formation comes in at bottom and the marble widens out, making a much more open canyon as described above.

After the difficult stretch of line, for railroad purposes, from above Point Retreat to Point Hansbrough as described under date of January 16th, the location of a road is a very simple matter to the *end* of *Marble Canyon*. It can be put on the slope at any elevation desired and with not very heavy grading work, except at some few points which would be cut heavily to make better alignment. The alignment, however, is generally very good not to exceed 6° and with some very good long tangents.

The waterways and crossings of side canyons would be the most expensive items. I have noted these each day but of course do not think these notes absolutely correct. This is a very important matter and would have to have long and detailed study; but from my observations and study of the case I do not think it will be such an expensive item as at first thought.

1. At the large side canyons such as the Nankoweap and the Kwagunt, the canyons are so long and large that a very sudden and great rise can hardly be looked for that would bring down this far such boulders and debris as are now at the mouths of these creeks. These would be crossed by iron trestles with good waterway, spans in center.

2. Another class of side washes are incipient canyons 1'/4 to 1/2 mile long, etc., etc.

3. Washed out canyons.

4. Small draws with ditches.

5. Overhead draws.

Hasty note: Marble Canyon generally good railroad line with only expensive work [from] Point Retreat on, as noted, [in] general remarks. The new strata noted January 17th is not sandstone but stratified limestone and quartzite with mineral matter between and large veins of iron ore showing plainly at the Nankoweap.

11:30 A.M. photos up Colorado River from south bank of *Little* Colorado [and] from same point up Little Colorado. We all walk up Little Colorado for a mile or two, but see nothing of great interest.

Lunch at noon.

At 1 P.M. make survey on right bank of Colorado. 1:30 P.M. take photo of mouth of Little Colorado and of the Head of the *Grand Canyon*.[11]

---

[11] Without incident, though they had a tricky ride through 60 Mile Rapid (RBS 184, 185), the surveyors reached the mouth of this Little Colorado River. Coming down from Point Retreat, Stanton noted the appearance of new strata coming up below the Redwall,

and the changing and widening profile of the canyon. Before reaching the Little Colorado, the party had passed through the Tonto Group of Cambrian rocks: Muav Limestone, Bright Angel Shale, Tapeats Sandstone. The first two strata were full of color — gray, green, brown — suggesting the possibility of mineral development. But to Stanton's engineering eye, the steps and ledges resulting from the differential erosion of these formations, was most encouraging. For example, the lowest member of the group, the Tapeats (Stanton's "Conglomerate Sandstone"), hard, resistant to weathering, was left as a platform (the Tonto Platform) after the soft, weak Bright Angel Shale was stripped away. Through this section the engineer wrote that the location of the railroad would be a "very simple matter."

The Little Colorado (Powell used the Spanish term *Colorado Chiquito*), marking the end of Marble Canyon, is a major tributary of the Colorado in Grand Canyon. Even though it drains much of northeastern Arizona, and parts of New Mexico, the Little Colorado *is little* excepting times when it is in flood, a phenomenon common during the summer months when cloudburst storms up country send water rushing down stream. Through a narrow and sinuous canyon, whose walls tower over 3000 feet at the mouth, the Little Colorado enters the Big Colorado 61.5 miles below Lee's Ferry.

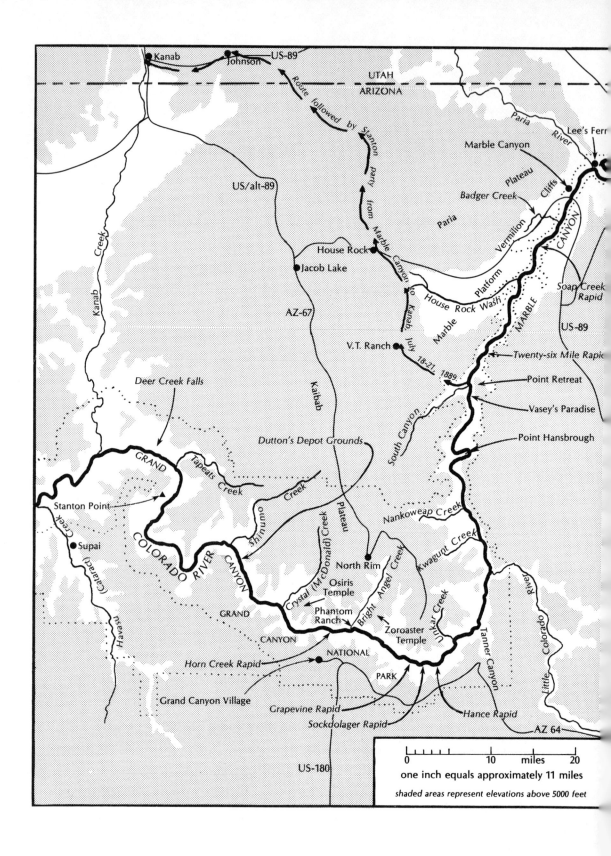

Kanab
Johnson
US-89
UTAH
ARIZONA
Route followed by Stanton party from Marble Canyon to Kanab
Lee's Ferr
Marble Canyon
Paria River
Plateau
Cliffs
Badger Creek
Vermilion
MARBLE
US/alt-89
Paria
House Rock
Jacob Lake
House Rock Wash
Platform
Soap Creek Rapid
AZ-67
Marble
US-89
V.T. Ranch
July 18-21, 1889
Twenty-six Mile Rapic
Point Retreat
Kaibab
Vasey's Paradise
Deer Creek Falls
Point Hansbrough
South Canyon
Dutton's Depot Grounds
GRAND
Tapeats Creek
Nankoweap Creek
Stanton Point
Plateau
Kwagunt Creek
COLORADO RIVER CANYON
Shinumo Creek
Crystal (McDonald) Creek
North Rim
Unkar Creek
Creek
Supai
Osiris Temple
Colorado River
GRAND
Phantom Ranch
Zoroaster Temple
Tanner Canyon
Little Colorado
Havasu Creek (Cataract)
CANYON
Horn Creek Rapid
NATIONAL
PARK
Grand Canyon Village
Grapevine Rapid
Sockdolager Rapid
Hance Rapid
AZ 64
US-180

0   10   miles   20
one inch equals approximately 11 miles
shaded areas represent elevations above 5000 feet

CHAPTER VI

PASSAGE TO BRIGHT ANGEL

From the Little Colorado to Bright Angel Creek, a distance of twenty-six miles, the Stanton railroad surveyors entered an area shaped by the Grand Canyon's oldest rocks. The kaleidoscopic formations of the Younger Precambrian period appeared to offer prospects for mineral development, verified by Felix Lantier, a prospector met along the way. Entering the narrow V-shaped Granite Gorge of the Older Precambrian, the party encountered some of the roughest white water on the Colorado, and one boat was severely damaged, causing a long delay. Throughout this section of Grand Canyon, Robert Stanton found few serious obstacles to railroad construction.

MONDAY, JANUARY 20 [continued].

At 2:30 P.M. we make our first start down the *Grand Canyon* of the Colorado, "The Great Unknown," "The Grandest Gorge on Earth," etc., etc.[1] Will enlarge on this when I have more time.

At 2:33 P.M. we run Rapid No. 188, the first in the Grand Canyon. It is about 1/2 mile long and we are through it by 2:35. Stop 2:47 at first side canyon about 2 miles below mouth of Little Colorado River and take photos. Restart at 3:20.

Stop at 3:24 to examine Rapid No. 189. It is a double rapid, one fall at top, with very crooked curve to right in rapid below and then sharp turn to left over another fall between huge rocks on both sides. The falls are 4 to 5 feet high.

We start to run this at 2:35. Run the first 1/2 and turn into eddy on right. In doing this my boat is carried by current too far and in getting into eddy is turned round and comes within a few feet of going over the second fall stern foremost. But by extra exertions of the oarsmen and the steersman, Mac, stand-

---

[1] Stanton's notes here are taken from his Field Notebook B, Part II.

For J. W. Powell, *Exploration of the Colorado River of the West* (1875), 80, the Grand Canyon — the "Great Unknown" — began at the mouth of the Little Colorado. Stanton follows the same usage.

ing up and rowing with his long sweep, we got into eddy safely. Nos. 2 and 3 came through better.

We then run second part. No. 1 and 2 go through, all right. No. 3 goes over the fall finely, but by a mistake of the steersman in the lower part of the rapid is dashed against a rock in center of stream and crushes a great hole in her side. Are through at 3:45. We all pull down across the bay we are in and at 3:50 P.M. go into Camp No. 66 on right bank for night and repairs, 3 miles below Colorado Chiquito.

The Grand Canyon of the Colorado.

The stratified sandstone that was noted this morning as coming up under the more soft mineralized strata increases in height as it runs down the canyon, till at first side canyon about 2 miles down it is about 100 feet high. Above canyon it is broken back in strata making an easy line on most any grade. In this distance there are 2–10 foot openings and 2–30 foot openings. The side canyon will take an 80 foot span. Perpendicular side walls.

Beyond the side canyon this stratum forms into a perpendicular wall, very ragged at *top* and easily broken down. There is a small talus under it. The two sharp points at side canyon would be cut heavy, and build line beyond under the cliff on what talus there is, and supply rest from top of ragged top of cliff. From this side canyon to point where river turns to right are 6 small openings, which could be made "overhead" drains, with great ease.

[This] describes about first 3 miles of the *Grand* Canyon.

TUESDAY, JANUARY 21, 1890. Clear and cold.

In Camp No. 66 repairing Boat No. 3 after her accident of yesterday. This camp is about 3 miles below the mouth of the Colorado Chiquito River and at head of Rapid No. 190.

We lunch at 12:30 P.M. after repairs are completed on Boat No. 3, and after lunch pack up and start at 1:45 P.M. We row upstream and around an island in river so as to go down left hand side of this Rapid No. 190 which at this stage of water is split into two channels by this gravel rapid. Run No. 190 at 1:50.

Our camp last night was 1/2+ mile above extreme point to right. Side wash at camp, 20 foot span, with 3 small overhead drains to point. Talus on this stretch much heavier than above.

At 1:58 stop at head of Rapid No. 191 to take photos just beyond this point to show talus.

Just below the first side canyon below Colorado Chiquito, noted yesterday, comes up a new formation of a purplish *shaly* rock which seems to be soft and parts in very thin layers, inclined upstream; and the hard conglomerate rises up on top of it.[2]

Restart at 2:15 and run Rapid No. 191. Just beyond the above point is side wash, large overhead, 20 feet. The talus increases in size on the shaly sandstone. One 20 foot and 10 foot spans, between here and side canyon which we reach at 2:27 P.M. A 60 foot span. At 2:27 we stop to examine Rapid No. 192 at mouth of this.

At 2:35 we start. From here to where river turns to right, 2 small openings, 10 feet. Just before getting to point, side wash, 50 foot span.

At 2:41 we reach and run Rapid No. 193 without stopping. Good drop, swift but clear of rocks.

At 2:45 stop at head of Rapid No. 194. At 3 P.M. we run it and at 3:03 P.M. go into Camp 67 on left bank in order to wait till morning to take some important photographs.

After landing at camp, Hislop, Kane, and I go across river and take three photos, showing supposed volcanic dike of Powell, the side canyon to the mountains, down river. Taken 3:30 P.M. from point just below side canyon about 5 miles below Little Colorado.

One point puzzles me here. Powell's description of his trip in '69 notes volcanic dike at this point through which river cuts forming gateway to more open country below, with *fall* below dike and very bad rapid compelling portage, etc. We find here the dike a rapid without fall, only about 3 feet in whole rapid; and the rapid is not formed by the dike but by the wash from two side canyons coming on opposite sides. We ran it with the greatest ease though of course it is filled with boulders. If this is not the rapid referred to we shall come to it tomorrow and I will correct this.[3]

[2] Stanton notes here a formation not seen before coming up under the Tapeats Sandstone. This was first strata of the Younger Precambrian series of formations visible from the river for nearly sixteen miles below the Little Colorado. The series — tilted, faulted, full of color, shot through here and there with igneous matter — make up the roots of a mountain system worn down to a rolling plain millions of years (the Great Unconformity) before the Tapeats was laid down. That these strata are rather soft and easily eroded accounts for the wide valley through most of this section of the canyon. Writing later about this section, Stanton said it had the appearance of having been "upturned, tumbled over and mixed up in every imaginable shape, and form, showing most gorgeous colorings of mineralized matter, from dark purple and green to bright red and yellow." Dwight L. Smith, ed., *Down the Colorado* (1965), 144.

[3] Stanton's Camp 67 was probably above Lava Canyon, possibly near the mouth of Carbon Creek at mile 64.7. In his *Exploration of the Colorado River of the West* (1875), 80–81, Powell probably refers to Tanner Rapid at mile 68.5, seven miles below the Little Colorado. Stanton appears here to have overestimated the mileage from the Little Colorado. Anyone working with the Stanton field notes may have some difficulty in pin-pointing the engineer's day-to-day progress through the canyons. Except for a few streams, nomenclature of canyon tributaries was non-existent. Stanton's mileages, when given, are helpful and generally quite accurate. He does count rapids, and he counts everything from shoals and riffles to major

WEDNESDAY, JANUARY 22, 1890. Clear and warm when sun comes out from behind the cliffs.

Sail at 8:30 A.M. Take instantaneous picture of fleet. I land and remain with cook to take photos.

The boats stop at 8:40 to examine Rapid No. 195 and at 9:00 A.M. they begin portage. This rapid is very long, 1/2 mile. Upper part is shallow and boulders, and lower part falls over ledge of rocks dipping heavy upstream, about 6 foot fall. The supplies are all portaged and the boat swung down by the lines by 10:30.

They load up and start. The cook and I walk down the beach to the next large wash coming in on left and take photos showing railroad slope on opposite side. The boats load and start at 11:17 and run Rapid No. 196 at 11:19 while I take instantaneous picture of them in Rapid No. 196 from the shore.

Make note of wonderful break up of country, immense deposits of iron and other minerals, and look it up in Dutton. The country from the volcanic dike referred to above is all broken up and washed away showing strata running in every direction. Of course there is a better description in Dutton so I shall confine my notes to the shape of the country for railroad purposes.[4]

From the dike down: just beyond dike on right side a canyon comes in from way up in the mountains, 100 foot span. For 1 1/2 miles the rock in soft strata, is sloped back at less than 40° and cut up in contour by small washes. These 5 in number would require say 10 foot *openings* and one 20 foot directly opposite side wash on left.

From this point down, side wash on left bank, 1 1/2 miles, the banks stand up more boldly but not high, and are of soft and hard strata easily worked. Two 10 foot and 1-20 foot openings.

The boat stops at 11:20 for me and at 11:26 we start again all aboard. We stop at 11:32 at head of Rapid No. 197 and at 11:43 run it, long and steep but free of rocks. Heavy waves at foot. Mac makes splendid steer and we do not get a drop of water. 11:50 we stop at hogback just above next side

---

rapids — but most of these can be identified only with difficulty and many of them not at all. Rapids do change, of course, seasonally and physically.

[4] John Wesley Powell's two voyages of discovery on the Colorado in 1869 and 1871–72 constituted the first work undertaken by the "Powell Survey," which was first under the direction of the Smithsonian Institution. Later it was transferred to the Department of the Interior and named officially the United States Geographical and Geological Survey of the Rocky Mountain Region. This and the Wheeler, King, and Hayden Surveys were consolidated in 1879 to form the U.S. Geological Survey. Before the consolidation, Powell assembled a roster of brilliant men who mapped and studied much of the Colorado Plateau and published books of primary importance. Among the most capable of these students was Clarence E. Dutton, whose works on Utah's High Plateaus (1880) and on the "Tertiary History of the Grand Cañon District," *Monographs* of the U.S. Geological Survey, II (Washington, Government Printing Office, 1882) are classics in geological literature. Stanton refers here to the latter work which contains tables of mileages in Grand Canyon, p. 240, but nothing on mining potential of the canyon.

canyon on left and take photos. We lunch at 12:25 and changed the photo rolls.

We start again at 1:21 P.M. and enter Rapid No. 198 at 1:24. Part the way down No. 1 strikes bottom on round boulders, and runs up on top of two, and sticks. This rapid is very shallow and wide. No. 2 goes by us and through with hitting only slightly. No. 3 could have done the same but Twining made his usual mistake; and in going by us turned his boat sideways and went down broadside, bumped over the rocks and got through, but came within an ace of going overboard. He spun around with both legs and arms in the air, but he fell in the boat, but he and Brown both lost an oar, but got both. We being stuck, we threw a line to the men on shore and they gave us one pull; and we swung off the rock without damage, at 1:42 P.M. We start off as soon as the line is coiled up.

At point to right, [as] noted above, we stop at 2:00 P.M. to wait for Brown who left his coat. One 10 foot opening on point, easy 6° curve.

From this point along the next sweep of the river the walls are quite steep but of easy material to handle and make good bank; but it would have to be very secure as the river runs in close on this side.

We start again at 2:10 and at 2:20 stop at head of No. 199. Hogue and I go up on the hogback at mouth of canyon to take photos. At 2:43 the boats start through Rapid No. 199. They go through in pretty good shape, but No. 1 sticks for a few moments in shallow place.

2:45 photos from hogback, just *below* side canyon.

We start at foot at 3:10 P.M. and stop at 3:17 P.M. to look at Rapid No. 200. At 3:25 we start and run No. 200. It is a long 1/2 mile gravel rapid, steep and swift, but plenty of water. These rapids in this wide section of the river are made by gravel and small boulders, all round, and not dangerous but very worrying.

The same character of walls continue to sharp point, turns to right with 2-20 foot openings. Rounding the cliff is broken very low and can be cut to any grade desired. Around this point the same character of low cliffs broken in points.

At 3:30 P.M. we camp at foot of Rapid No. 200 in Camp No. 68.

After camping we go across the river to look at the mineral country. Coming back we met Felix Lantier, an old miner from Flagstaff.

This book [Field Notes, Book B] will be sent out to Flagstaff, Arizona, by him.

THURSDAY, JANUARY 23, 1890. Grand Canyon of the Colorado River, Camp No. 68, about 8 miles below the mouth of the Colorado Chiquito.[5] Fleecy clouds and sunshine.

[5] Stanton's notes through the remainder of this chapter are taken from his Field Notebook C.

We were much surprised and pleased last evening to meet Mr. Felix Lantier, an old miner, prospecting in this country. He is going in a few days to Flagstaff and will take out mail, photos, etc. Hence we have stopped in this Camp No. 68 to write letters and fix up notes to send by him. McDonald and Travers are doing some little repairs on the boats.

After lunch I conclude to move down a few miles and camp and then finish my notes, and Lantier will come to our camp tonight to get them. We take photos at 11:00 A.M. from hogback below side canyon.

We start at 1:30 P.M., and at 1:37 we reach and run Rapid No. 201 without stopping, a long gravel rapid with deep channel on right.

We stop at 1:42 at head of Rapid No. 202 to examine it. We stop at 1:55 and in one minute are all stuck at the head of the rapid on the gravel as we expected to be. The water is spread over thin so that for about a boat's length it is only one foot deep. We work over it with rubber boots and get all through at 2:20 and start and run the rest of the rapid by 2:22, and stop to examine the next one, No. 203.

Taking up our line from the bend opposite the large side canyon that comes in on left, after passing the immense iron dike the formation is thin layers of sandstone in broken ridges but low. These ridges extend to side canyon that comes in on right. In this sandstone 3-10 foot openings and 80 foot span at side canyon. Beyond the waterway of this side canyon the point of gravel and sand rock comes out very far. This point must be cut heavy so as to get good alignment to strike the slope on the next stretch.

From this cut for over a mile to point where river turns sharp to the right the alignment is a tangent along a slope and low bluffs of the same thin stratified standstone, with five 10 foot openings.

At 2:30 we run No. 203 with ease. Plenty of water.

At 2:33 we reach and run No. 204, a long shallow gravel rapid which at higher water would be simply good swift running; and at 2:36 we are through it, 3/4 of a mile below, and go into Camp No. 69 to complete my notes to send out by Lantier.

Camp No. 69. The cook and I go up on hill to photograph. 3:00 P.M. photo showing red sandstone cliff of thin strata around the point. 3:15 P.M. photo showing the marble castle in the distance. 4:15 photo showing the Grand Canyon above the narrow gorge showing the entrance to the narrow gorge on the left. 4:15 [photo of] old Indian fort on this point.[6]

---

[6] Camp 68 must have been on the right bank at about mile 69.5, at the foot of Tanner Rapid (RBS 200); Camp 69 was in the vicinity of mile 70.3, left bank. Among the photographs made on January 23 was one of the "old Indian fort" perched on a hill overlooking the mouth of Unkar Creek across the river. According to archaeologists, the structure was in use by Anasazi Pueblos for about fifty years during the twelfth century. The open valley of the Colorado, between the Little Colorado and Unkar Creek, was well known to the prehistoric Pueblos who left behind more structures here than elsewhere in Grand Canyon.

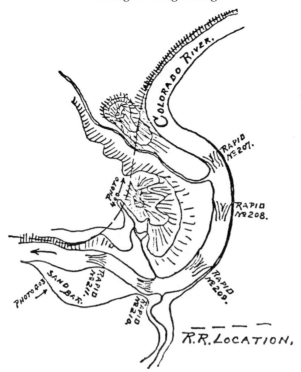

Fig. 32. Sketch map "in first 14 miles of Grand Canyon." *Robert B. Stanton.* Miami University Library.

FRIDAY, JANUARY 24, 1890. Mr. Felix Lantier, the miner who has taken out our mail, spent last evening with us. He told me a great deal about this mineral country we are now in. He has located many claims, one near Powell's volcanic dike which he says is 150 feet wide of gold, silver, and copper. Samples of this he gave me.

The immense iron dike opposite the big side canyon he says assays $5 in silver, $2 in gold, and from 12 to 18% iron. This deposit covers nearly the largest part of this basin. I have samples.

He says on the east side of this basin there is an immense blanket vein 10 to 12 feet thick of lead carbonate ore. It is cut through at various places by the washes, and his assays show 15 to 25 oz. silver and 30 to 40% of lead. He has promised to send me a large sample of this. He also says there is a similar deposit some 6 or 8 miles down the river on the same side of the river on which he has a location.

D. D. Fowler, R. C. Euler, and C. S. Fowler, "John Wesley Powell and the Anthropology of the Canyon Country," U.S. Geological Survey *Professional Paper* 670 (Washington, Government Printing Office, 1969), 8–20.

One mile up side canyon on right side of river he has found a basin of blue roofing slate and will send me samples. About 60 miles up Little Colorado is large deposit of coal, veins 12 feet thick. Supposed to be the extension of the Trinidad deposit, a very fine coking coal. He also says that the west side of the river has been but little prospected.

His address is Flagstaff, Arizona.[7]

Clear all day with a few fleecy clouds.

The point last referred to in yesterday's notes is an easy curve 4° to 5°, and then to a gravel hill; in all about a mile, at end of which is side wash, 40 foot span; beyond this 1/4 mile of low bluff 10 to 40 feet high.

Then the same stratified red sandstone, 100 to 150 foot bluffs, with good flat bench of rock at bottom to make bank upon. Continues to point where river makes curve to left, caused by large wash coming in on right. In this stretch there would be 2-40 foot and 1-10 [foot] openings. Our line would not follow river around this *left* bend but would cross flat and hogback formed by the side wash on right.

We break camp and start at 8:10 A.M. At 8:20 we reach and run Rapid No. 205 without stopping. Quite high waves and I get one all over me. Rather a cool bath so early in the morning.

At 8:27 we reach and run without stopping Rapid No. 206. And at 8:30 stop at head of Rapid No. 207 on left bank, and spend 3/4 hour examining it and No. 208, 3/4 mile further on. No. 207 is formed by shelves of sandstone dipping up and across stream and making a complete fall with square blocks of stone at foot of fall. No. 208 is formed by round boulders come out from the wash on the right. It is very rough in waves and full 3/4 mile long, but I think [it] has plenty of water. At 9:15 we row across stream to right bank and unload for a portage of No. 207.

10:30 A.M. photos from hill in center of bend.

[7] Prospecting in Grand Canyon, dating back at least to 1871, was intensified during the 1880s as the canyon became better known. Powell's *Exploration of the Colorado River of the West* (1875) defined the geography of the canyon, and hard rock prospectors must have been intrigued by his mention of the colorful formations, crystalline rocks, and granite in the Precambrian Series. Prospectors entered the great canyon by a number of routes. In fact, nearly all of the trails reaching the river from the rim areas were built by, or named after, early prospectors. One of them was Seth B. Tanner. Among the first to prospect the eastern part of Grand Canyon, Tanner improved an old Indian trail from the South Rim which reached the river at the mouth of Tanner Canyon. It was near the canyon's mouth that the Stanton party met Felix Lantier, prospector and miner. Stanton was much interested in prospects along the way, especially in Glen Canyon, where claims were staked on the second expedition. Lower Marble Canyon seemed to hold some posibilities for mineral development, and the prospects between Lava Canyon and Tanner Canyon, noted by Stanton and praised by Lantier, were bright indeed. In addition to Lantier's prospects, one George McCormick operated the so-called Tanner mine in this area (Mile 66.2 LB) from about 1880 to 1907. See G. H. Billingsley, "Mining in Grand Canyon," (Flagstaff, 1974) and C. Gregory Crampton, *Land of Living Rock* (New York, 1972), 149–155, 189–192, for an overview of Grand Canyon mining.

The cook and I go up on the hill to take photos. McDonald, Hislop, Gibson, and Ballard drop the boats down while the rest of the men portage the supplies. All are at the lower end at 11:05 and we reload. All loaded at 11:30 and we stop for lunch.

Start at 1:00 P.M. Run Nos. 208 and 209 and stop at 1:07 at No. 210. This is a sudden drop of about 8 feet over a reef of boulders and compels a portage, only short 200 feet.

1:45 P.M. we go ahead about 1/2 mile and take photos of narrow gorge up river [and] gateway to the "Narrow Gorge." Portage is made and boats loaded and we start at 3:18 P.M. At 3:19 we run Rapid No. 211 and at 3:23 we enter the Great "Narrow Gorge" of the Grand Canyon.

The side wash is a large one and should have at least a 100 foot span, if not more on careful examination.

This carries our line notes to point where the river enters the narrow gorge, that is to the *"Narrow Gorge."*

There is about 1/4 mile of the gorge to point where river turns square to right. There is good slope with sandstone above much broken up. No difficulty in this portion, nothing more than rough hillside work. Smooth water for 1 1/2 to two miles. Stop to take photos.

Start again at 3:45 P.M. 3:55 stop to examine Rapid No. 212. 4:06 start and run it. Good water but very quick time. Smooth water for one mile.

Stop at 4:13 to examine Rapid No. 213. Find it very long, shallow, but very steep, hence very swift and full of rocks. A good channel seems to be through it by dodging the rocks; but there are so many of them that I conclude not to venture but to portage it, ease the boats through with lines. We are all worn out by our two portages of today. And at 4:30 P.M. we go into Camp No. 70.

One mile down from last point noted two side washes come in on right. The sandstone is very much broken up, 40 foot and 30 foot spans. The work is simply rough hillside work. River then turns slightly to left, and at this point we stop and take at 3:30, photos one mile in the "Narrow Gorge" and start 3:45.

The next stretch of nearly a mile has broad talus slope with high water only 20 feet. In this stretch one 30 foot span. Rapid No. 212 formed by side wash, 40 foot span. Beyond this sandstone stands up in one point 150 feet high. It juts into river and is easily cut. This stretch to where river turns sharp to left is not at all bad work. Slopes at foot of cliff, points easy to cut. Work will compare in general to Clear Creek Canyon.

Some willows at this camp that have never been touched by frost.

SATURDAY, JANUARY 25, 1890. Misty clouds but sun coming through. Heavy wind late in evening.

Begin portage at 7:00 A.M. At 8:15 A.M. I take photos from lower side of "creek." Portage of stuff was done at 9:00 A.M.

McDonald sick.

We eased boats down by lines through this long rapid over 1/2 mile by 12:30 P.M. and went to lunch.

1:30 P.M. take photos from left side of point turning to right. Around this point is an easy curve. Talus below high water, but bench easily cut for material.

We load and start at 2:05 P.M. and at 2:08 run a small Rapid No. 214. And at 2:10 P.M. turn point to right and sail down through a beautiful bay of quiet water for 1 1/2 to 2 miles and stop at 2:20 on left bank to examine Rapid No. 215. We find it an immense and long rapid full of huge boulders both above and under water, and impossible to run at this stage of water as it is so broad there is no distinct channel (at *Red Canyon*).

We unload all boats. Drop No. 2 boat through the rapid with lines, two men in to keep it off rocks along shore. It goes down very well by lifting over some shallow places and worming around between the rocks, while men above keep a tight line on it all the time. It takes however a long time; and being all tired out with the long portage this morning, we cover up our supplies for a storm is coming up; and at 5:00 P.M. go into Camp No. 71 just above the creek on left bank that forms this rapid.

Beyond this point good talus and sloping sides with high perpendicular cliff above, and rough points of the granite jutting out into the river, easily to make bank from talus to talus or from point to point. Two waterways, 1-20 feet and 1-30 feet in first 1/2 mile [or] more. Next 1/2 [or] more mile, talus 60 to 80 feet high, broad, high water 20 feet to where creek comes in on left through deposit of red colored earth. Fine slope on left bank beyond creek 600 feet high. The side canyon on left that forms Rapid No. 215 is very beautiful, pinnacled and buttressed and timbered far up at its head among the snow.

SUNDAY, JANUARY 26, 1890. It blew great guns all night last night. Today has been cloudy with occasional showers.

Camp No. 71. I walked down river about a mile and high up on the ledge and had my first look down the *Great Granite Gorge* which commences about 1 mile below here. It was the most wonderful and grand sight I have ever looked upon. Will try to get to the same point tomorrow and photograph it.

Oppressively warm. Flies, millers, and moths flying about.[8]

---

[8] Lining down past the steep rapids at Unkar Creek (RBS 207) and Nevills Rapid (RBS 213), the survey party went into camp on January 25 at the head of Hance Rapid (RBS 215) at the mouth of Red Canyon (as Stanton observes in a note added in May 1917). The engineer found much to admire here in the Grand Canyon landscape: the view up Red Canyon to the snow-covered South Rim; the "grand sight" downstream into the Upper Granite Gorge. About a mile below Red Canyon, the Colorado crosses another great

MONDAY, JANUARY 27, 1890. Cloudy, clear by noon. Spring April showers and sun in P.M.

Commenced at 7:00 A.M. to make long portage by Rapid No. 215, and swing boats, easing down by lines. Long and tedious. Completed by 11:30 A.M. Lunch. Load and start, 1:15 P.M.

11:30 A.M. photos from just below side canyon on left at Rapid No. 215, Camp No. 71, showing first glimpse of the Black Granite Gorge.

After rowing across river we stop at head of Rapid No. 216, which is about 1/2 mile from head of No. 215. This is a very heavy fall on left bank with shallow boulders on right bank. We drop the loaded boats down part way on right side, portage supplies, and ease boats empty through center part. Load up and at 4:50 P.M. run the lower half of this rapid which at its lowest end just enters between the two black granite walls of the Great Granite Gorge. Photo shows mouth of gorge from Rapid No. 216.

We stop at 4:55 P.M. at head of Rapid No. 217 and take photos in the Granite. At 5:05 we start and run Rapid No. 217. Pass through a smooth bay of water, and at 5:10 P.M. run Rapid No. 218 without stopping, then through about 1/2 mile of smooth water and camp at head of Rapid No. 219, at 5:25. Camp No. 72.

After coming round the point above Rapid No. 215 on broad slope of thin stratified sandstone, then line would fill in heavy at head of rapid where it has cut out and blast channel in boulders to keep river from washing against bank too heavy. From this point one mile on good talus slope to head of *Black Granite*, 2-20 foot waterways.

From commencement of the Granite to Rapid No. 219, the walls of the canyon are pinnacled and buttressed with points jutting into the river, but *no* perpendicular walls. The general slope is say 30° from perpendicular, although the points are more abrupt. The work is *much easier* than the average work in the Black Canyon of the Gunnison.

Our Camp No. 72 is on a little sand bar 2 or 300 yards above the head of Rapid No. 219. We got into camp late, and at once all hands climbed up between the crags and gathered wood. Two or three good sized mesquite bushes gave us sufficient for a campfire and cook a good supper and have

---

unconformity, a time gap of millions of years separating the Younger from the Older Precambrian formations. In sharp contrast to the stratified sedimentary formations of the Younger Precambrian, the older formations are metamorphic, hard, dark, somber, forbidding. A complex of crystalline formations — predominantly schists and granitic rocks — nearly two billion years old form the basement rocks of Grand Canyon. They erode typically to form a ragged, steep-walled, V-shaped gorge in which the river is severely constricted. Indeed, in Grand Canyon the Colorado is at its narrowest here. The water is fast and the rapids are among the heaviest in the canyon. This is the Granite Gorge of which there are three segments: Upper, Middle, and Lower. The Upper Gorge, starting just below Hance Rapid, is forty miles long.

plenty for breakfast. The weather is very warm which is a great comfort and saves wood. The bar we are on would all be covered by 10 feet more water.

TUESDAY, JANUARY 28. Showery during night. Clear sunshine this morning with a few flying clouds.

Canyon at Camp 72 not over 150 feet wide at bottom. High water 50 feet up.

Break camp at 8:45 and at 8:50 stop at head of Rapid No. 219. This rapid is formed by boulders from creek on left, and as the gorge is so narrow, it has had no chance to form bar; but the river has washed the boulders down the canyon, forming a bad rocky rapid 1/2 mile long. With 3 or 4 feet more water it would be easily run but at this stage the rocks are too near surface, and so we conclude to let boats down loaded. Boulders at mouth of creek and along shore offer footing, part way, while men climb over crags to little bays where are more boulders and catch the boats below. Two men go in boats to keep them off the rocks. At 9:45 take photos from crag just below Hance Creek.

While bringing down the boats one of the men found at the mouth of the creek one leg of a pair of woman's embroidered drawers, and they all gave it a cheer. I have picked some real spring flowers just come up and saw one *mosquito*.

The work of getting down the boats has been very tedious and hard on the men.

We ate lunch at 11:30 A.M. after passing 1/3 of the rapid, and after lunch, 1 P.M., let boats down to about the middle of the rapid, 3:10, and then ran the rest. All boats struck once or twice but without damage. "Captain" Twining backed out from running his boat through so Hislop steered it for him and he rowed.

All were tired out and at 3:30 we went into Camp No. 73, about one mile below our camp last night.

This Rapid No. 219 is I think the one Powell went through August 14, 1869, "with 39 or 40 foot fall and 3 dams." We find the creek, the first and third dam, and the 30 or 40 foot fall perhaps, but the middle dam has changed. This rapid stops and a new rapid begins below our camp. At a higher stage of water these two would be one and the present one below here would make the "third dam." [9]

[9] Hance Rapid (RBS 215, 216) is bad and dangerous at all stages of water. Lining and portaging of supplies was probably easier during the low water of January, 1890. Owing to the low water, a few beaches appear in the narrow gorge (Camp 72, January 27) which are otherwise covered. And the steep walls offer practically no talus for campsites. Rapid 219, at the mouth of Hance Creek (RBS note May 1917) is another bad rapid — the Sockdolager, a word meaning (among other things) something unusually large or exceptional. Powell's men referred to the Colorado River as the "Sockdolager of the world," and it was probably

Photos from Camp No. 73.

The granite walls continue beyond the point where photos were taken, the same as above, as far as I can see, about 2 miles. The granite stands up, if there is any strata to it, vertical or rather inclined upstream a little. It is craggy and in points, but broken back in rough, irregular benches, which in many places are covered with earth and grass. The drainage down these cliffs does not show very large water ways. Probably 2-20 foot openings in each 1/2 mile would be sufficient. Except at creeks, but none have come in on right side so far. There is not a perpendicular cliff of granite so far nor for the two miles I can see ahead.

WEDNESDAY, JANUARY 29, 1890. Clear.

Breakfast at 6:00 A.M. but did not start early as all were worn out by yesterday's hard work.

Loaded and set sail at 8:20 A.M. Run Rapid No. 220 at 8:21 and Rapid No. 220, second part, immediately after a *fall* of 10 feet, the sharpest drop we have gone over at any on our trip. A sure *fall* as much as the volume of water can be.

We stop at 8:25, 1/2 mile down at head of Rapid No. 221 to examine it. Huge rocks but apparent clear chute in center. At 8:43 we run it. There is a very sudden drop of 8 or 10 feet and huge waves. We go through safely but pitch and tumble in great shape. One wave is cut through by boat and as it breaks slaps me with great force on the right cheek, knocking me flat back on my seat. I was standing holding on to bow line.

Stop 8:45 to take photos at left bend of river, 1 mile below Camp No. 73.

We also examine Rapid No. 222 and at 9:20 run it. We plunge through the waves and I get 3 immense ones all over me so that I am drenched to the skin.

At 9:25 we run No. 223 without stopping. Light waves but very swift. We then enter quiet water which forbodes a great fall below. At 9:30 we stop to take photos about 1 mile below last at bend of river to right.

For the first mile from our last night's camp the canyon walls are more craggy and buttressed than above. The points jut out into the river further and the washes between them are deeper and wider. The points form benches above so they are easily cut. Many of them are only 20 to 30 feet above high water, and the whole slope of the canyon is as before, about 30° from perpendicular. There would be 2 or 3-30 to 60 foot spans; but most of the washes, or rather crumbles, for they show no evidence of water as they are covered with grass and greasewood, would be filled.

they who labeled the rapid during the second expedition in 1872. Hance Rapids, Creek, and Trail (from the South Rim, reaching the river at the mouth of Red Canyon) were named after John Hance, early Grand Canyon prospector, hotelier, guide, and story-teller.

Start at 9:45 A.M. We restart after taking photos on a beautiful quiet stream. At 10:00 A.M. we stop on left bank opposite creek on right and take photos.

After taking photos Mac, Hislop, and I climbed up the granite slope up little wash to top of granite and found a beautiful cove. Wonderful place for sheep and goats.

Along this stretch for 1 to 1 1/2 miles commencing at point where photos were taken, past the long bend to right, the right shore is broken down so that it has a regular slide *slope* broken by little points of rock. Can locate line at any elevation.

Beyond this the crags are broken into sharp points, but sloping back from river, with waterways between them. Cheapest in these places to put in spans, 30 to 50 feet.

This takes us to next bend to right. From this point to next bend to right same crags continue but jut further out into the river. At this bend, slight curve, to right there is a little stream coming in on right, 50 foot span, but no rapid.

One-fourth mile beyond, stream comes in on left and makes Rapid No. 224. Slope to this rapid. Crags not so prominent. General slope more even.

On our trip up [the granite slope] we found and sampled a very large vein of quartz which seems to be filled with fine ore. I have some samples. This whole section is cut up by a large number of fine veins of quartz, generally vertical but pitching in various directions and cut through by the river and side streams for 200 to 300 feet deep. To me it looks like a wonderful mineral field, entirely unexplored.

We lunch at 11:30 A.M. and at 12:35 set sail again. At 12:40 we stop about 1/4 mile down at head of Rapid No. 224, Sockdolager. This rapid is formed the same as No. 219, from side wash, and the boulders are all across the canyon and washed down for 1/2 mile. The rocks are so close to the surface that it is impossible to run it. But at this stage of water there is a good shore of boulders and broken granite on right side, making it comparatively easy to let the boats loaded down by lines. At a higher stage of water this would be impossible as there would be no foothold.

One thing I note today on all these granite walls: being broken up into crags and little valleys between, the valleys are full of grass, greasewood, cacti, and mesquite bushes. So that, while the rocks are black and sombre, the whole picture is enlivened by the green colors. And where one can get a glimpse of the red, grey, and bright-colored sandstones above, the contrast is most beautiful. Of course, the bright colors of the canyons above — Cataract, Glen, and Marble — are wanting in the Granite, but the vegetation gives an appearance of usefulness, as in contrast to the utter barrenness of *some* portions of the sandstone country.

At 1:30 P.M. take photos from head of Rapid No. 224, 1/4 mile below last pictures. On either side, except on the sloping cliff where one could not stand and hold a line with any power, and with 6 or 8 feet more water, the waves would be at least 10 feet higher. We think this is Powell's "75 or 80 foot fall." It is a regular *incline* and no fall.[10]

About 1/2 way down Boat No. 1 swung out in current, dipped her nose under water, and *filled*, and just then swung into shore, where the cook and I were far ahead of the rest of the men on a gravel beach. We both at the same moment jumped into the river and caught her and held her till the other men came. We bailed her out. Will see what damage is done at camp tonight. No. 2 and 3 came through this portion all safe. No damage to goods in Boat No. 1.

The next stretch from the gravel beach on for 200 feet was very difficult. The current very swift and large rocks close to shore. In letting down Boat No. 3, Hislop who had the front line, made a mistake(?) and pulled her in the wrong chute. The men above could not hold her stern in, as Mac had not put out the extra 50 foot stern line as I had directed him to do; and the current caught her and swung her around crossways of the rocks, with her bow over the little fall we were trying to get by. She turned 1/4 way over and filled at once. We at once went to unloading her. With a rope around his waist, Travers went out into the boat and passed out the beds, bags, etc., till he was so cold he could not stand. When he came in and, in the same way, Ballard took his place. The current was rushing over the boat and it is a wonder that all the bags were not swept away. They were hauled in from the boat by attaching the grapnel to each as the men lifted them out.

Camp No. 74.

Several bags escaped and were caught by Gibson below with boat hook. We lost the cook's warsack, Nos. 18 and 20 of provision bags with 100 lbs. flour and some little stuff, 1 shovel, 1 bucket. We worked till 6 P.M. to get No. 3 out, but to no avail; and we had to give up for the night.

About 8:00 P.M. we heard her move and found that the river was rising and the boat had moved off the rocks ahead into the hole below. We worked at her for about an hour but could do no good and gave up again till morning, not expecting to see a piece of her there next day.

We drew Nos. 1 and 2 upon the gravel beach in the little cove above, and prepared for the night. Our condition was not the pleasantest. All the blankets of No. 3's crew soaked, all of No. 1's partially so, hardly enough wood to cook coffee with, and nothing but a huge pile of rocks to sleep among. However we made the best of it. Everyone was in a hopeful and good natured frame of mind.

[10] In a note, probably added later, Stanton labels his 224 the Sockdolager, but it is the famous, or rather, infamous, Grapevine Rapid, so-called, the story goes, because the many big rocks exposed in low water appear to resemble so many grapes on a vine.

We gathered some little driftwood sticks and a few bushes from up on the cliffs; had coffee and flapjacks for supper, and several pipes of tobacco; divided our dry blankets among all the men and lay down among and around the rocks to sleep. It was a beautiful moonlight night; and by various turnings so as to make our bones fit the depressions in the rocks or by changing the pressure of a rock from the middle of the back to the middle of the stomach, we managed to get some sleep and quite an amount of rest.

THURSDAY, JANUARY 30. Clear.

The river raised about 2 feet last night and pushed the boat down off the rocks where she was caught, into the hole below. After about two hours work, we succeeded in getting her out, badly smashed on one side. We hauled her up upon the rocks. She is not beyond repair and McDonald, Travers, and Edwards immediately start to work. Have concluded to cut her down to 18'2", in length. Work at boat all day, while rest of men sort over supplies and dry out all goods, etc. I find we have good 60 days' supplies.

Camp No. 74.

FRIDAY, JANUARY 31, 1890. Cloudy. Clear by 10 o'clock.

Camp No. 74. Hard at work on Boat No. 3.

Being obliged to stay here till our boat is done, the matter of wood to cook with is a very serious item. We have gathered all the wood in reach, and today moved our cook and his outfit a quarter mile down river on another pile of rocks where there is a little more wood. To do this we have to climb to our meals up over a high cliff in one place holding on a rope. Below this is some more driftwood and the men carry it up a little at a time, for climbing along these granite walls is no easy or very safe matter. It is a good thing it has turned so much warmer as we can have no fire to sit by.

SATURDAY, FEBRUARY 1, 1890. Camp No. 74. Misty clouds all day.

This morning I take two photos from high point on cliff from center of Rapid No. 224.

About ten o'clock, as our boat repairs are progressing so well, we let No. 2 boat down past where we had the disaster; and from that point at 11:00 A.M. Hislop, Kane, and Gibson ran the lower half of this rapid with the empty boat, and moored her in a cove 1/2 mile below. This was so successfully done that after lunch we led No. 1 boat down to the same point, and loaded her with nearly all our heavy loads, etc.; and the same crew ran her down to the same cove. The rest of the heavy goods will go down in the same way in No. 3 when she is done. And we will carry our beds and small things to the cove where the boats are; for although this is in the granite of the Grand Canyon, it is even possible to walk along the sides by going up and down over the crags.

SUNDAY, FEBRUARY 2, 1890. Clear. Camp No. 74.

The river rose nearly a foot again last night, making in all from 2 1/2 to 3 feet rise since last Wednesday. This endangers our boats in the cove below; and as we are almost on the last stick of wood to cook with, I consider it a necessity to push on the work on Boat No. 3 this Sunday. So we all go to work, determined to get away from here as quick as possible. It being proper, in my opinion to work today under the present circumstances.

MONDAY, FEBRUARY 3, 1890. Clear, all day.

We are hard at work again on Boat No. 3. She is drawing towards completion; and I had hoped we would get off by noon but find it will be impossible. The work on the boat is completed at 5:00 P.M., and a very satisfactory job it is. I think also it is *quick* work. Four men, 38 hours work to cut this boat in two, take out 3'10", put her together with nothing but the old stuff, caulk her, and complete her ready for the water.

FIG. 33. There are few good stopping places in the Granite Gorge. A rest stop at the foot of Grapevine Rapid. Stanton at left. *James Hogue.* Miami University Library.

The place where the work was done was on a pile of broken granite rocks of every shape and form so that one side of the boat was as high as a man's head above where one could stand and the other was resting on a rock. No place to stand evenly upon, and it was climb up and down, over and in and out of the boat to do the work. McDonald and Travers deserve a great deal of credit for the work they did while others and myself did some effective help.[11]

Tuesday, February 4, 1890. Clear all day.

At 9:00 a.m. Boat No. 3 is finally completed and loaded; and her own crew start with her and run very successfully the lower half of Rapid No. 224, and come to anchor in the cove 1/2 mile below where the other two boats have been since Saturday. I think it quite a triumph of our boat building skill in the canyon to find our new boat is almost without a leak and rides the waves like a duck. She is easier to steer as she is only about 18 feet long and has 4'10" beam.

We take considerable time to load as we have to portage our stuff from the cook camp across a very rough cliff and load the boats while they are swinging in the cove, where they were tied several days since. We start at 10:55 and are whisked around pretty lively in the whirls and eddies at the foot of this rapid, as the water dashes from one side to the other of the narrow canyon. At 11:00 a.m. run Rapid No. 225 without stopping, in one minute, and at once stop at head of No. 226 to examine and photo.

We start again at 11:20 and run No. 226, the heaviest rapid, the highest waves, we have ever run with loaded boats. We were struck first one side and then the other, and turned us first one way and then the other, like a straw in the wind. Through the heaviest waves we went head on in good shape but one high fellow went all over the whole boat and struck me so hard in the stomach as to give real pain. But we all came through safely and at 11:25 ran Rapid No. 227 without stopping.

At 11:30 we stop at head of No. 228 for photos. This point is at mouth of little creek on left about 2 miles above *large side canyon on right.*

We start *after lunch* at 12:45 and at once run No. 228. At 12:47 we run No. 229, and at 12:50 we run No. 230, and at 12:53 stop at head of No. 231 which compels a portage, creek [to] right. This is a fall of from 8 to 10 feet but the V extends about 100 feet. Just at end of this is a huge hole and wave curling and breaking beyond it. Beyond this point the waves are very low and easy. All the fury is concentrated in *100 feet and one wave.*

[11] Lining down Grapevine on the right side, the surveyors quickly ran into trouble. Boat No. 1, the *Bonnie Jean,* was nearly lost in the upper part of the rapid. In a bad place further down, Boat No. 3, the *Sweet Marie,* tipped, filled with water, and jammed between two rocks. Most of the cargo was saved, but the boat was badly damaged, though reparable. Camped on the rough granite at the river's edge, and with the constant roar of the rapid in their ears, the crews labored for five days, performing ingenious major surgery on the hull.

From Rapid No. 224 to point where we take lunch at mouth of little creek coming in on left, the walls of the canyon are of the same nature as above, craggy and broken, and have considerable slope with benches.

This whole granite formation thus far is a very simple problem for construction. It simply means cutting these crags and *side hill* granite slopes with small fills between. Some of the points will have to be cut heavy and some of the fills will be high, on account of filling in the river and getting above high water, 40 to 50 feet above low water, but these banks will be perfectly secure as they will be of solid granite.

The nearest approach to a perpendicular granite wall is opposite where we lunched. It is not perpendicular but broken in little benches, and through the middle is a wash which breaks it up. Nowhere yet has there been a wall 200 feet long and *perpendicular* 50 feet above high water. When I see this from further on and not opposite, it is not near so perpendicular as I thought it.

From the lunch point to Rapid No. 231 the sides of the canyon are much more broken and sloping than above, and the points come out further into the river. Two small streams come in on right requiring 50 to 100 foot spans, according to where, how high up, line is located.

We immediately go to work and portage all our stuff, about 150 feet and *swing* the boats around head of the rapid very successfully by 2:00 P.M. There being a very small and bad eddy to load in, we had to load one boat at a time and run her down to make room for the others. My boat the second to start. Got off at 3:40 P.M. and at 3:45 stopped about 1/2 mile below to wait for other boats and take photos 100 feet above river. Less than 1/2 mile above the side canyon ahead. Rapid No. 231 is I think Powell's bad fall of August 14th. The water through here is full of whirlpools, eddies, cross currents, etc., and fully justifies Powell's description at a higher stage of water. On leaving No. 231 we were whirled out of our course, and driven against the cliff, but without damage.

From Rapid 231, about 1/2 mile to where photos are taken, the granite is much more broken up than any part we have passed, and sloping more back. The rock seems to be stratified standing *on end* in sharp jagged points. Easily cut and handled. The work would be *cut* and *fill*, and plenty of room to *fill* without interfering with the river. The banks would be short but high. High water is about 40 feet.

From this point 1/4 mile or less ahead to where side canyon comes in on right — don't know what it is — the granite looks like thick layers of slate standing on edge. Along the river is a broad, 100 foot, flat ragged bench, with good easy slope going back from it. This section for a mile to 1 1/2 miles above and 1/2 mile below seems to be a "secondary upheaval" and entirely out of place with the dark granite above and the red granite below.

We were ready to start at 3:30; but as we have had a bad week of it with little fire and less comfort, I concluded to camp here where there is plenty of mesquite wood. McDonald and I start to explore the side canyon. It is a beautiful clear stream of running water, about 6 feet wide in a black and dark canyon of granite about 10 to 20 feet wide at bottom and sloping back to grey and darker sandstone above. On south side of main canyon we get glimpse of the red *flaming* sandstone cliff above spoken of by Powell; but I have been much surprised that we can see so little of these upper cliffs. Only a very few points are then visible since we entered the Granite down to this place.

Taking this whole section from the commencement of the Granite to this side canyon, the canyon is in two distinct parts: the inner granite gorge which is from 100 to 250 feet wide at bottom, and sloping back in rough craggy slope to a height in the neighborhood of 1000 feet; and the second part above. (See Dutton). Have been much surprised that we can see so little of this second upper part from the river, etc. This is true to the Bright Angel Creek. This whole breakup seems to be full of quartz veins. We have some rich specimens of silver ore; but the veins seem much broken up and are in blotches through the granite.

WEDNESDAY, FEBRUARY 5. Clear all day.

We had a good rest and sleep last night by quiet running water, quite a relief from the roar of No. 224 where we were obliged to sleep so long. Our camp was on a large sand beach with plenty of mesquite wood.[12]

We were up at 5:15 and breakfast at 6:30, but it is hard to get started as we have such a trifling worthless fellow for a cook that we have to wait on him almost every time we move. We start at 7:50 A.M. and in 2 minutes run Rapid No. 232, a small one at the mouth of the *side canyon*, and stop to take photos on left bank opposite the mouth.

We start again at 8:18 A.M. and at 8:19 A.M. run Rapid No. 233. And we land on left bank at 8:21 A.M. at head of Rapid No. 234, about a 6 foot fall over a dam of boulders. This is a short rapid formed by boulders washed down from the side canyon we have just passed. There is not enough water over the boulders to run it, except on right side, and there the water pours over a sharp point of granite and makes it impossible there. So we conclude to *ease* our boats loaded along this side among the boulders. We drop our boats through very successfully and are ready to start at 9:47 A.M.

At 9:51 A.M. we land again at head of Rapid No. 235. We find this is formed by a side canyon on right which comes in about 200 feet before the

[12] Lining around 83-mile Rapid (RBS 231), the Stanton party went into camp at the mouth of Clear Creek on the right at Mile 84.1. After the long stay, perched on the rocks at Camp 74, a good night's sleep on a sandy beach beside the quiet waters of the creek must have been pure luxury. Stanton refers here to C. E. Dutton's "Tertiary History" (1882).

change of formation noted above. This rapid has very large boulders and heavy waves for 100 feet at its head. The lower part has a great fall and sharp waves but seems to be clear of rocks. We make portage of stuff past head of rapid and ease boat down this side chute between.

The same bench and broken slope of slaty material continues for 1/2 mile below the side canyon when the formation changes to a more compact red granite also blue. Rapid No. 235 is just at the change of formation from the black slate appearing granite on edge to the more massive *red* granite below. This red granite has less slope than the black above but for 1/2 mile ahead has a flat slope at bottom running into river between the coves, with plenty of rough slope to get material from. And from here, head of Rapid 235, shows a high sloping *talus* for a short distance at extreme end where river turns to right, about 3/4 to 1 mile.

Fɪɢ. 34. In the Granite Gorge nearing Bright Angel Creek. *Robert B. Stanton.* Miami University Library.

I notice that below this point high water mark does not appear so high, perhaps 30 feet. We find this is formed by a side canyon on right which comes in about 200 feet before the change of formation noted above. This rapid has very large boulders and heavy waves for 100 feet at its head. The lower part has a great fall and sharp waves, but seems to be clear of rocks. We make portage of stuff past head of rapid, and ease boat down through side chute between the rocks to a cove in the cliff. We take instantaneous picture of portage.

At 11:35 A.M. all boats are in the cove ready to start. We pull out in order and strike the current just below the heaviest waves and go down like a shot

FIG. 35. Bright Angel Creek (center) flows into the Colorado River. This is the busiest corner on the floor of Grand Canyon. Mule-riding tourists and hikers from both rims can reach the river here and cross it on the suspension bridge, and there are accommodations at Phantom Ranch (not shown) a short distance up the creek (1963 Photo). *A. E. Turner.* Bureau of Reclamation.

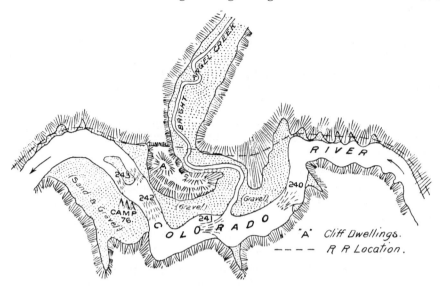

FIG. 36. Sketch map of the mouth of Bright Angel Creek. *Robert B. Stanton.* Miami University Library.

through the remainder of the rapid. The current beats against the right cliff and we are almost carried against the cliff. The rebounding waves keep us off and we get in good line for the heavy waves at lower end. We strike them head on and go clear through the heaviest; and wave after wave breaks completely over our heads. We are through in 1 1/2 minutes; and at 11:40 A.M. we land on the slide rock talus noted above drenched through, make a big fire, and have lunch.

We restart at 1:10 P.M. and drop our loaded boats by No. 236 which [is] about 1000 feet below our lunch stop. This rapid is of recent formation and made by several huge pieces of the cliff fallen from the left side, one immense piece filling the center of the river, just above the level of low water.

We are through this and again set sail at 1:53 P.M. and land about 800 feet below on left bank to take photos at 1:55 showing slide talus above noted.

From the talus for 1/2 mile down, while not being perpendicular are very smooth and little slope and have concave side to river. Bank would be by cutting point of next turn to right and hauling up and from talus above. As we go by this part of the river and look back at the walls, and not across at them, they are not so perpendicular as they looked but are considerably benched, but higher up than above.

We restart at 2:15 P.M. and at 2:19 stop to examine Rapid 237 formed by side wash coming in from the left. At 2:23 we run it. I get one wave in my lap but the rapid is free of rocks. At 2:26 we run Rapid 238 without stopping and have a *couple of miles* of smooth water below.

At 2:31 we stop to take photos. Restart at 3:17 P.M.

The quiet water continues for 1 mile ahead. That is as far as we can see.

At 3:27 we run Rapid No. 239, a small one from side canyon on left. And at 3:33 stop on right bank and take photo about 1'/2 mile above mouth of the *Bright Angel.*

From the last point noted above as difficult, the right wall for 3'/4 to 1 mile ahead is much more broken and better slopes, ragged and stepped back, not at all difficult for such class of work, with occasionally a very steep cove that would have to be filled in the river. The same broken slope continues 1'/2 to 3/4 mile beyond to where river turns to left.

Around this bend to left the granite is very much more broken and the slope much flatter. Several waterways, 40 foot spans. This work around this bend is *easy hillside* rock work. One side wash, 80 foot span. The narrow black gorge seems to end as this bend to left commences and the canyon become wider, and both sides break up considerably. I am much surprised at this, and on examination find we have taken the last photos at point about 1/2 mile above the mouth of the Bright Angel Creek.

We find the large tree where Powell camped August 15th, the houses, mealing stone, pottery, etc.

After taking photo we start again at 4:12 P.M. and at 4:14 run Rapid No. 240 and in quick succession, 4:16 and 4:17, run Nos. 241 and 242. And at 4:18 P.M. stop on left bank on large gravel bar covered with driftwood for Camp No. 76, about 1/2 mile below mouth of the Bright Angel Creek. This last mile run was very quick. Three rapids with hardly any distance between them, and it took some lively steering to follow their crooked course.

After landing at camp I take my boat, cross the river, and Kane and I climb two hundred and fifty to 300 feet on top of ridge which runs out on lower side of Bright Angel Creek for photos. We climbed up on river side of ridge. First view of Bright Angel. Beautiful stream, clear water winding through green meadow bottom, etc. Canyon of black granite with slopes covered with green bushes, etc., with distant cliffs above of grey and red sandstone.

Climb to pinnacle of ridge. Find ruins of cliff dwellings; 4 or 5 on very top; mealing stone, pottery, etc. View up river gorgeous in color and grand in outline. Shivas Temple on the left 5000 feet above the river of white and grey sandstone. Set on top of bright red ledge, which in the setting sun seemed as if in a blaze of fire. Whole surrounding country above brilliant with color and grand in form.

Photos 4:45 P.M. looking up Bright Angel, [and] showing Shivas Temple. 5:30 P.M. view of Shivas Temple from Camp No. 76, sunset.

All these Rapids Nos. 240–244 are formed by the boulders and gravel washed from the Bright Angel Creek.

Taking up the railroad line: From point 1/2 mile above Bright Angel the line would not follow river around left bend past mouth of creek, but would cut across, bridge the creek 150 feet, and tunnel point. This is the first and only tunnel so far in the Grand Canyon. Call it "A."

This whole breakup is full of *mineral*. We passed yesterday evening the great vein that Jack Sumner and Powell have said so much about. It is about 3/4 mile above Bright Angel on right side. I did not stop and test it for various reasons best known to myself, but located it for future use. From the general appearance I think this a very rich mineral section.

The Bright Angel Creek is certainly a beautiful stream, etc. *Dark* canyon from beginning of granite to within one mile of the Bright Angel, etc.

Have spoken of Shivas Temple in several places. Do not know this is correct but it is a very beautiful and prominent point.[13]

[13] On February 5, 1890, the surveyors went into camp on the left bank just below the mouth of Bright Angel Creek. They had come eighty-eight miles from Lee's Ferry, twenty-six from the Little Colorado, the last eleven through the Granite Gorge. Stanton found that construction of the line everywhere below the Little Colorado would be feasible even across the hard rocks of the Older Precambrian. A "very simple matter," he wrote. Cut away the slopes to suit and the roadbed would rest on "solid granite." A tunnel and a long bridge would be necessary, though, at Bright Angel! The engineer took note of the changing character of the formations in the gorge and of the possibilities for mineral development.

Named by Powell in contrast to the muddy Dirty Devil at the head of Glen Canyon, Bright Angel Creek, a fine stream of clear water, heads on the lofty southern side of the Kaibab Plateau. Improved trails from both the North and South rims, a suspension bridge over the river, and overnight accommodations at Phantom Ranch facilitate tourist travel to Bright Angel, today the most visited place in inner Grand Canyon.

Powell, in his *Exploration of the Colorado River of the West* (1875), 86–88, reported prehistoric ruins near the mouth of the creek, the same ones seen by Stanton. These, located near the river's edge and immediatly adjacent to the Kaibab Trail, a short distance downstream from the Kaibab suspension bridge, have been examined in detail by archaeologists, who find that the site was occupied by prehistoric Pueblos briefly in the eleventh century, and again in the twelfth century. For a book length study, see D. W. Schwartz and others, *Archaeology of the Grand Canyon: The Bright Angel Site* (Santa Fe, 1979). On the hill near his proposed tunnel location, Stanton found ruins not seen by Powell.

Many of the prominent features of the Grand Canyon are burdened with oriental names, a practice apparently begun by C. E. Dutton of the Powell Survey and carried on by others. Stanton's Shivas Temple was probably Zoroaster Temple, a magnificent butte north and east of the mouth of Bright Angel Creek and standing 4700 feet above it.

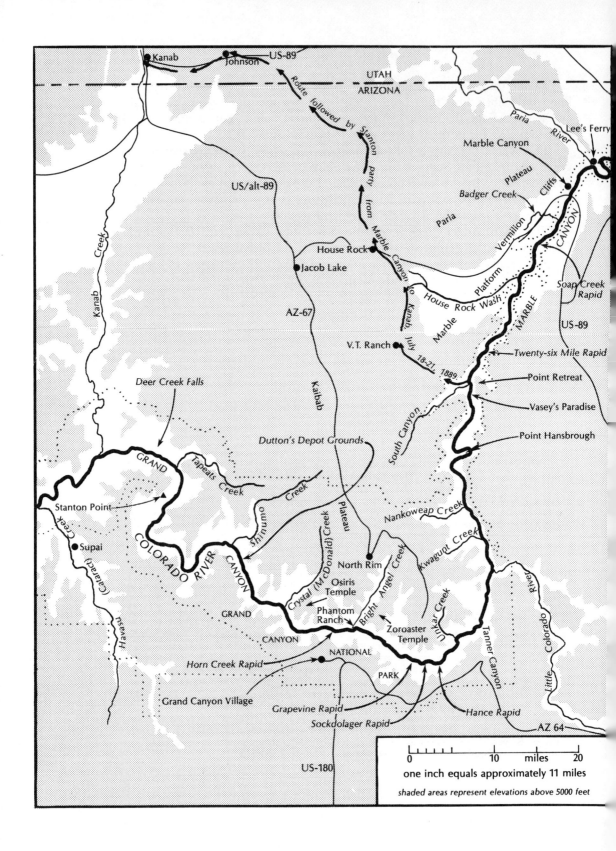

one inch equals approximately 11 miles

shaded areas represent elevations above 5000 feet

CHAPTER VII
AVENUE OF MAGNIFICENT VISTAS

There was more rough water below Bright Angel. A boat was smashed and lost in Horn Creek Rapid, but after that the explorers were somewhat more careful and managed to get through the rest of the Upper Granite Gorge without serious mishap. Harry McDonald left the expedition at Crystal Creek and there, taking a respite from the gloomy gorge, Stanton and two others, on an overnight hike, climbed out to the top of Osiris Temple to view the splendors of the canyon. After more laborious days on the river, conditions improved. At Bass Rapid Stanton even found a place suitable for a depot and switching yard. Below this point the shallowing Precambrian rocks permitted extensive views of the towering cliffs of the outer canyon. These grand vistas were not lost on the engineer who wrote about them as well as about railroad alignments and bridges. Arriving at Kanab Creek, the expedition was half way through the Grand Canyon.

THURSDAY, FEBRUARY 6, 1890. Clear. Windy from southwest. Up at 5:30. Breakfast at 6:00 A.M.

Shivas [Zoroaster?] Temple bears N 40° E magnetic from mouth of Bright Angel Creek.

7:30 A.M. flat above Camp No. 76, photos.

We load and start at 7:55 A.M., and at 7:57 run Rapid No. 243, and at 7:58 run Rapid No. 244; and at 8:00 A.M. land at head of No. 245 and take photos: 1/2 mile below Rapid No. 244, one-half mile further down right side at side canyon, side canyon on left, and sandstone cliffs beyond.

At 8:35 we set sail again and at once run Rapid No. 245, and at 8:39 land 1/4 mile below at head of No. 246, on left bank. This being full of rocks at lower end, we drop boats through with lines.

Directly opposite last photo, just below side canyon on left, take photo.

The rest of the men let the boats over Rapid No. 246 with lines by walking along the bench of the cliff 30 to 40 feet above the water with the line, while two men stay in boat, Hislop and Travers, and keep it off the cliff; and as they get by point of cliff, the men with the line come down on sand bar and let boat down over shallow gravel part of the rapid, while the two men get out into the water and lift boat over the higher rocks. All are down by 10:15 A.M. and the men warm and dry out by big fire.

After passing the tunnel just below the Bright Angel, for 1/4 mile the line has a smooth hillside slope past Rapid No. 243. From this point, to where river turns sharp, to left line along broken cliff of granite as above. This is sharp turn of cliff to left and then to right. Line would tunnel 300 to 400 feet of point [and then] along rough granite slope with crags and benches.

We are ready and start at 10:33, and at 10:34 run Rapid No. 247, and at 10:35 run Rapid No. 248, and stop 1/2 mile below on left bank to take photos at 10:40. Last view of Shivas Temple.

We restart at 11:00 A.M. and at 11:08 stop on right bank 1/2 to 3'/4 mile below last stop at head of Rapid No. 249 to examine it. It is the most powerful rapid we have met on the trip. It falls about 16 to 18 feet over huge pieces of angular and square boulders of rock fallen from the cliff and filled in by smaller boulders from small side creek on left. The fall itself is not over 250 feet long but as the water drops over the rocks it makes holes behind them 6 or 8 feet deep and dashes up rebounding waves 10 feet high. Two instantaneous pictures.

This section from one mile above Bright Angel to 1 1/2 miles below is very much broken up and seems to be of a softer kind of granite, more stratified and slaty and standing on edge like that of the canyon 10 miles upriver. All the

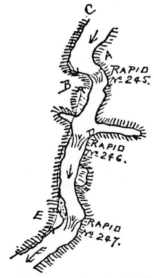

FIG. 37. Sketch map of section of the river just below Bright Angel Creek. *Robert B. Stanton.* Miami University Library.

rough slopes are filled with soil and covered with grass and bushes, making a very pretty contrast of green with the black and grey granite rocks. This seems to be much more fertile than the granite canyons of Colorado.

The inner gorge is also so much broken down that the beautiful white, grey, red, and flaming scarlet sandstone cliffs of the upper strata are plainly in view from the river, making a gorgeous and wonderful panorama. Especially was what we suppose to be Shivas Temple, brilliant on its flame colored base last night at sunset.

From last side canyon on left for 1 1/2 miles to sharp turn to right ahead of where photos are taken, the canyon walls are rough steep slopes, with points as above Bright Angel. Along here it is more broken and rough on left than on right. The same character of line continues for 3/4 mile further to Rapid 249, formed by small creek on left, and for 1 to 1 1/2 miles beyond where river turns to left. On this last stretch there is a good deal of talus running out in points into the river and well above high water.

At 11:30 A.M. we take photos from head of Rapid No. 249 at little creek on left. Photo shows the talus above referred to, and extends about one mile down river just to point where bend commences.

We at once unload everything and commence portage of stuff. Take from 12 noon to 1:00 P.M. for lunch, and complete portage by 1:30 P.M. On examination we conclude the right side is best to swing boats down, and so cross over again.

At 1:45 P.M. the line is strung ahead and No. 1 boat is swung out into the stream. She rides the huge waves with ease and goes the full length without injury. The men and line work well and play out smoothly, but when she reaches the foot of the fall she seems like a young colt eager for a play. She turns her nose out towards the current, and, as it strikes her, she starts like a shot for the other side of the river. The men hold to her manfully, and, after crossing the current, she turns and comes back into the eddy, and for a few moments stands still just as a young colt ready for another prance. Soon she turns her nose slowly to the current again, and the men put their wills into arms and hold her once more. She does not cross the current; but on reaching the center, dips her bow under, as if trying her strength, comes up at once, rises on a wave, and then as if for a final effort to gain her liberty dives her head under, fills with water, and goes completely out of sight. In a very few moments she rises, her whole deck above the surface, and, as it were, slowly and leisurely floats sideways across the eddy towards shore and quietly stops alongside a shelving rock, seemingly well satisfied with her frolic and ready for a rest. Kane ran ahead and caught her. She was bailed out and none the worse for the prance.

This difficulty made me decide to adopt Powell's plan, now that we had one boat below, and turn the boats loose at head of rapid and catch them below.   At 2:45 all being ready, the boat below waved.   No. 3 boat was pushed off.   She entered the rapid in good shape just in the line No. 1 followed.   One-fourth way through, a wave struck her stern sideways and turned her under the worst fall in the rapid.   She dove under but came up all right, was forced up-stream by the rebounding wave and then driven back by the fall.   This time she went clear of the rebounding wave, but in leaving it a shot up of the edge of the wave turned her over.   She rolled once and came up 1/2 full of water.   Being thus heavy she floated with the current and sideways to the cliff where the full strength of the current was beating.   When she struck it she rolled over face to the cliff and struck; and the force of the water tore her to pieces in a few minutes.   Thus our first real disaster and second mishap to No. 3.

Besides the boat, we only lose 5 pieces of bacon in her stern locker.   While this is a great disaster a greater one would be to lose another boat.   Hence we cross to this side, No. 1 below and No. 2 above the rapid.   No. 1 is brought up to near where our stuff has been portaged at lower end of rapid, and we go to work to prepare to *portage Boat No. 2* in order to be perfectly safe.

This is the first time we have been obliged to *portage* a boat.   We fix skids over the rocks, ease her down the first chute, and take her out and slide her on her keel on the skids for a couple of hundred feet.   This is done by 5:30; and we leave her there for the night, ready to put into the water below the dangerous part of the rapid.   And go into Camp No. 77.

Very little is said tonight but I notice McDonald is very glum.[1]

FRIDAY, FEBRUARY 7.   Clear.

We have breakfast this morning about the usual time, 6:15 A.M.   After breakfast I told everyone that it would be necessary for everyone to throw away all useless stuff they had to make our loads lighter.   McDonald spoke up in an angry manner and said he would not throw any of his private stuff to save the company's property; that with all the men, 5 in one boat and 6 in the other, we would have to throw away so much provisions that we could never get to Peach Springs, and would have to go out soon anyway; and for his part he would just as leave start out now from here.   I simply answered it was the privilege of everyone to leave whenever they thought best.   And the conversation ended.   I was much surprised to see Mac show the white feather so soon, and only sorry because of its effect upon the other men.

---

[1] Stanton's No. 249 was Horn Creek Rapid, a savage stretch of white water highly respected by modern river runners.   The *Bonnie Jean* behaved like a bronco when it was lined through the rapid, so Stanton decided to use the "Powell Plan": Turn the next boat loose at the head of the rapid and catch it below.   The result was predictable.   The *Sweet Marie*, so recently remodeled, was reduced to a mass of floating splinters.   To be on the safe side the *Water Lily* was portaged, not lined, around Horn Creek.   Frederick S. Dellenbaugh, who rode with Powell on his second trip through Grand Canyon, wrote that Powell never used such a "harum-scarum" method of running rapids.   See F. S. Dellenbaugh, *The Romance of the Colorado River* (New York and London, 1902), 363.

Hislop says he has come to stay, the same as he did last year. And with him I shall fight it out if it takes all summer. I certainly wish Mac would carry out his threat and walk out, the sooner the better for all concerned. I learn that Mac opened his kit sack and threw away about 1/2 of what he had!!

I repack most of our provision bags and find we have 17, some of them only half full; with the two photo sacks gives one boat 10 sacks and the other 9, and 4 grip sacks each. Nothing more is said about loads. Everything is put in the boats that is necessary and no provisions left.

Our greatest difficulty is to carry the men. We take Ballard in our boat to ride on the load in the center. Hislop has Hogue and Brown on center load and Twining in bow.

We get loaded at last and start at 9:45 A.M. McDonald in a bad humor, and everyone except Hislop and Hogue imitating him because they seem to think the world will not move unless Mac starts it. We are at last off and no one seems to put much force in their work; and the waves of the lower end of the rapid drive our boat against the cliff. Kane and I ward it off, and we get by safely. Hislop gets out all right.

We stop 1/4 mile past this side wash on left side to take photos at 9:55 A.M., about 500 feet above side canyon on right which forms small Rapid No. 250.

We restart at 10:10 A.M. and at 10:11 run Rapid No. 250. One-half mile further on we stop 10 minutes to get the bacon out of the airtight locker of No. 3 which we find floating in an eddy. We get six pieces.

On the 1 1/2 mile stretch from head of Rapid No. 249 the wall is much broken up in large points and deeper ravines than before. The talus before noted coming from these ravines. In this stretch are 6 spans from 20 to 40 feet. This stretch extends to side canyon coming in on right at commencement of bend to left. This side canyon or big washout has no rapid, 50 foot span. Beyond this as river turns to left the walls are very much broken up into sharp pinnacles and points of stratified rock, granite, standing on edge.

Opposite photo point 1/4 mile on from last side wash is side canyon, 80 foot span. This same class of formation continues around this long turn to left, for *one* mile or so to point where river turns to right. One-third [to] half way down is small side stream 50 foot span.

At 10:26 we stop on right to look at Rapid No. 251, and at 10:36 run it by cutting across the current and whirling completely round in the eddy. This is done to keep from following the current which drives with great force upon a low point of rocks that jut out into the river on right side, and would be utter destruction if we followed it and struck the point.

At 10:42 we stop on left side at mouth of side canyon on left, no rapid, 3/4 way to *point to right*.

We restart at 11:17 A.M.

We stop at head of Rapid No. 252 (1'/4 mile past point side stream comes in on left and forms Rapid No. 252) at 11:22 to examine and take photos.

We pass point referred to above as turn to right at 11:20. The walls are very much broken and very sloping.

We restart at and run Rapid No. 252 at 11:43 A.M. in fine shape with all our crews.

At 12 noon we stop *one* mile from last rapid at head of No. 253, formed by large side canyon large on left, and small one on right, and lunch.

From point just below side canyon I take photo 1:15 P.M., Rapid No. 253, supposed point *Sublime* at the top.

Rapid No. 253 compels a portage. It is made of immense boulders from this side canyon, is about 300 feet long of the fall, and a drop of 12 to 15 feet. We commence unloading at 1:15 P.M.

The whole canyon has changed since passing the first side canyon, on right, as noted this morning. The granite is coming down lower, and the canyon is widening out. The walls are very much more broken up. The rock is apparently stratified and standing on edge. This makes the points sharp and short. The whole slope is much flatter, about 40° from vertical, and benched back in broken benches, making construction very simple and easy. The material will be easy to handle, and hence cheaper than the stretch of solid rock above. The side canyons and washes are more frequent, requiring a large number of bridges. I have only attempted to note those from 20 feet up. Opposite Rapid 253 is side wash on right opposite large side canyon on left, 60 to 80 foot span. At 2:15 take photo down river to point to right from bench at lower end of Rapid No. 253.

At 3:50 the portage is made, the boats let down by lines and loaded, and we start once more. At 3:51 we run Rapid No. 254, a long 1/2 mile crooked rapid with many whirls and boils.

We stop at 4:00 P.M. on left side opposite big side canyon and take photos.

We start at 4:15 and at once run Rapid No. 255, and enter a beautiful bay of water, run about 1'/2 mile, and land at head of Rapid No. 256 at 4:25 P.M. and go into Camp No. 78. Rapid formed by side canyon on left.

From Rapid No. 253 to point where river turns sharp to right, the right wall is almost all *slide* slopes, with ridges of rock between. The distance is 1 to 1 1/2 miles. In that distance, 2-20 foot to 30 foot spans.

Just before turning to right are side *canyons* which form Rapid No. 255 coming in on both sides, 100 foot span. After leaving these two side canyons the river bends sharp to right, and the right side of the canyon cannot be called a wall. It is a *slope*, in most places 30° to 40° from horizontal. Slides covered in blotches with earth and grass and small bushes, with small ridges of broken up and loose granite rising between. This continues 1/2 mile to Rapid No. 256, and for 1'/2 mile beyond to right bend. These are the most astonishing canyon walls, easy mountain slopes, cheap and easy of construction.

The canyon is growing more and more picturesque and beautiful the further we proceed. The granite has lost its awful and threatening look and slopes back in beautiful hillsides of variegated brown, grey, and green. Above this close to the river is a stratum: 200 feet of dark sandstone in sharp horizontal strata, standing in perpendicular walls, jutting out in points to the edge of the granite, and beaded all over with small points of the strata standing out in the air; and the top edge cut into small points and crevasses, through which the light shines, giving a rough saw-toothed appearance. At the side canyons and from the bends of the river the upper portions of the whole canyon are brought into view, showing the sandstone cliffs, benched back from 3 to 6 miles, and over a mile high.

As we sail along the smooth stretches between the rapids each turn brings some wonderful picture more beautiful than the last. As miles away down the river with the placid water between its walls of *brown* and green for a foreground, there rises above the dark sandstone bench, tier upon tier, bench upon bench, and terrace upon terrace, stepping back further and further and higher and higher, and in their immensity of height and proportions, seeming to tower almost over our heads. First above the darker sandstone rises sheer walls of red sandstone a thousand feet or more, with sloping mesas above covered with bushes and grass, and above these a dozen or more smaller terraces of scarlet and flame color stone, stained on many points with black and the little slopes between them, relieved by the bright green of the greasewood and bunch grass. Above these rise for perhaps 2000 feet terrace upon terrace of the lighter grey, yellow, and white sandstone ledges. Capped by pinnacles and spire turrets and domes in every imaginable shape, size, and proportion. With all the little slopes covered with pine, cedar, and piñon trees, their bright green standing out in bold relief against the light colored sandstone walls. For shapes, etc., see notes ahead and compare Dutton.

SATURDAY, FEBRUARY 8, 1890. Cloudy. Clear by 10 *o'clock*. I slept really cold last night the first time this winter.

Photos from Camp No. 78 at side canyon.

We commenced to unload the boats and portage the stuff at 8:00 A.M. and *swing* the boats down by lines, all being ready to reload by 9:30. We commence to reload but find that Boat No. 1 has sprung a leak in coming down so we have to pull her out on the rocks and repair her. This takes 1 1/2 hours and we at last get started at 11:00 A.M. Below the rapid is a beautiful sheet of still water which does not speak well for a long run without a bad rapid.

We stop 11:12 on left bank 1 1/2 to 2 miles below last pictures and take photos.

We start again at 11:25 A.M. And at 11:35 stop at head of very long rocky Rapid No. 257. We look at this and find it requires a portage at lower end, but we think we can let the loaded boats down by lines 2/3 of the way. At 12 noon we lunch. At 1:00 P.M. commence to drop boats down. All down easily and safely and stuff portaged. We are loaded and start at 2:30 P.M. From the point to right, as noted yesterday and which we pass at 11:03, the side of the canyon is rougher and badly split up into heavy points with washes between, but not difficult work, 3-30 foot spans, as the waste from these points can be thrown into the river.

We have come about 1 1/2 miles around this right bend or nearly 2 miles from the side canyon, and the character of the slope is the same. About 1/2 mile ahead is a side canyon on left, which undoubtedly forms a bad rapid. The cliffs are the same as these for that distance to side canyon left and seem to continue the same for 2 1/2 miles ahead to where river turns to *left*. This is the straight almost north course commencing 3 miles or so from McDonald's Creek at point just above this Rapid No. 257, and is almost straight for 2 1/2 miles or so. The sharp abrupt points continue down this stretch, 2:45 P.M.

This is not at all difficult work for rock work though it will be expensive, except to waste a great deal in the river. All the material on this straight stretch is the kind referred to before, strata standing on edge and split up *like* coarse slate. About every 1/4 mile must be an opening of 20 feet to 30 feet. The same character of wall continues on to the large creek. In that neighborhood the whole country is broken and upset and washed out as at the Bright Angel. This large creek is quite a large side canyon, not so big as Bright Angel, and the sides are very sloping.

Directly opposite this is also a side canyon, apparently not running back so far, or it turns abruptly a short distance from the river. These two form Rapid No. 258. Not less than 80 foot span for this large creek. Rapid No. 258 is a long, 1/2 mile, shallow rapid formed by the boulders from these two creeks. The river here is quite wide, 400 or more feet. So we shall portage everything and can easily let empty boats down with lines.

At 1:30 P.M. take photos from side canyon 5 miles above Shinumo Creek on left. This is a most beautiful stretch of water, hardly a ripple for 2 1/2 to 3 miles.

We stop at 3:00 P.M. at the mouth of *a large creek* and as we wish to climb to Point Sublime on Monday, we go into Camp No. 79 on the beach just above the mouth of the creek and at head of Rapid No. 258. Photos from knoll at mouth of creek. This large creek right side of river.[2]

---

[2] Even though the boats were overloaded and mutiny threatened, a remarkable run was made by the Stanton expedition on February 7 and 8, 1890. Granite, Hermit, and Boucher

SUNDAY, FEBRUARY 9. Clear. Sunshine.

Camp No. 79.

We had breakfast at 9:00 A.M. and after breakfast I went down to where McDonald was sewing and had a talk with him. I commenced by saying, "Mac, I want to ask you a question. Have I ever asked you do do anything unreasonable?" He answered, "No." "Well then what has been the matter with you for some days? You have been in such an unpleasant humor?" He answered with an oath, "I am tired of having two or three of us do all the work, while Twining and Brown stand around doing nothing."

I said, "Mac, I know that but how can I help it? You know I would have discharged them both long ago if it had been possible. I know how hard it is but that is no reason why you should vent your spite against me and the boats." "I have nothing against you, Mr. Stanton, and I often say things I am sorry for afterwards."

"But, Mac, it makes it very bad for you to be always threatening to leave and walk out." He raised his head as quick as flash and said, "By God, I'd a good deal rather go out right here, and would have gone out above, but I've agreed to go through."

Not believing that it was the agreement that was troubling him but the money he would lose, I thought I'd test him, and said, "Well, Mac, if you feel that you want to go, I shall not hold you to your contract; and if you leave from here I will give you a check for all I owe you tomorrow."

He bit at it as quick as a trout snaps a fly and said, "Then I'll go out from here," and then added more quietly, "I believe it will be best for the whole party for me to go, as long as these two men are here." I concluded by saying, "You understand I am not asking you to go, but if you want to go you shall have the check and we part good friends." "Oh, yes, I understand that, and I'll go," was his reply.

I must add my own impressions: Two things enter into McDonald's determination to go out. [First,] I know that the work is hard and that a great deal fell on Mac to do, but I am paying him *extra* wages for the work he is doing. I am also aware of the utter worthlessness of the two men he mentions. But McDonald has been for years a hunter and trapper and prospector, going and working by fits and starts, as he saw fit; and this regular work day after day,

---

(RBS Nos. 253, 256, 257) rapids were all lined without incident. Camp 79 was at the head of Crystal Rapid at the mouth of Crystal Creek, named by Stanton, McDonald Creek. The engineer was becoming more and more appreciative of the beauties of Grand Canyon. The Upper Granite Gorge widens somewhat below Bright Angel Creek, affording viws of the colorful terraces and buttes standing high above the Precambrian rocks. At Crystal, Point Sublime, four miles distant to the north, rises 5000 feet above the level of the Colorado River. Stanton refers to Shinumo Creek, upstream from Crystal Creek. The stream by that name today is ten miles down river.

week after week, for several months, is too much for him and he is dissatisfied and makes Brown and Twining an excuse.

Second, the rich quartz veins we have passed are tempting him back, for he says he will only go out far enough to get a horse and outfit and come in to prospect, so that his consideration for his contract was all bosh and he would have left before but for the money he would lose.

I do not know what the future has in store for the expedition but as I see it now, I am glad McDonald is going to leave.

Photos 11:45 A.M. mouth of McDonald Creek, side canyon opposite McDonald, ruins of Indian village, and cook; 12:00 noon, down from 1/4 mile below McDonald.

Mac told me today that at one time he asked Twining to go in water to help off boat and he put his thumb up to his nose and wagged his hand at him in derision.

Soon after having the conversation with Mac, I related it to Hislop. He was much surprised. I find this evening that Mac has not told anyone he is going to leave but only that he is going hunting.

MONDAY, FEBRUARY 10, 1890. Heavy wind. Storm all day.

This morning McDonald told the men that he was going to leave. Of course all are sorry. Hislop says we shall miss him in our work, that he is sorry he is going; *but* that we will get along without him.

Twining came to me very much disgruntled. Asked what were my intentions, was he to go out at Peach Spring, etc. I said, "Yes." And then he wanted to know why I had not let him know Mac was going from here, so he could go with him. I told him for the reason that I considered it almost impossible for him to walk out from here and I wished to take him to Diamond Creek where he could walk out. He was very gruff and very sour and talked and acted like a fool.

Grand Canyon of the Colorado River
February 10th 1890.

Received of Robert B. Stanton check on State National Bank of Denver, for one hundred and ninety-seven ($197.00) dollars in full settlement of all claims of whatsoever nature against the said Robert B. Stanton or the Denver, Colorado Canyon & Pacific Railroad.

[signed] H. McDonald.

I paid Mac off and bade him good-by in a pleasant manner; but while I am glad he is going, *under all existing* circumstances I feel he has violated all the pledges he has made me and broken all the faith and honor a man could break by deserting me and the party in this place and at this time, and that his conduct for the last week or two has been most shameful and dishonorable in the extreme.[3]

Hislop, Kane, and I start on our climb up the canyon to see the top. We start from camp 7:50.

Climb to top of granite and first bench of sandstone, 1025 feet, and take views. Follow up slope, get on bench of marble, and go long distance to right towards river. Climb along bench. Hislop climbs to backbone. Can't get up. Go back, far to left hand point. Climb along ledge then up and over a narrow divide. Up through a crack. Very difficult. Then around left side of point.

Start up a crack. Hislop and Kane help me. Come to place, they can't help me. Swing myself around point, whole body in air, small toe and finger holds. Straight down below 800 to 1000 feet. Start up another crack, boulder in crack. Hislop gets up. Kane stoops [and] I stand on his back. Hislop takes my left hand. I steady with my right, and he lifts me bodily in air over boulder. Afraid to trust heavy loose rock that had held both Hislop and me when in air.

Go further up. Come to place on backbone, 2 feet wide, long 300 feet down on each side. Crawl over, pushing off loose rocks. Wind blows. Climb third crack inside boulder and out through hole to top. Reach top of this. Walk around and camp. Plenty good cedar wood. No water.

TUESDAY, FEBRUARY 11. Pretty good rest. No water. Climb up higher. Take photos.

Start down. Must go down marble at head of creek. Very steep, little points to step and hold on. Get near bottom. Last jump. Hislop down. Kane lets me down with strap in mid-air. After 30 hours find water, coffee, etc. Reach camp 6 P.M.[4]

---

[3] McDonald was one of that restless breed who trapped, hunted, and prospected most of his life. Undoubtedly the mineral prospects in Grand Canyon intrigued him, and he may have had misgivings about the future of the railroad project. Leaving the Stanton party he must have had a rough hike up Crystal to the snowy, wintry heights of the Kaibab Plateau. But in 1891, he was back as a member of a prospecting venture known as the "Colorado, Grand Canyon, Mining & Improvement Company," of which J. D. Best was in charge. The party from Green River, Utah, traveled through Cataract Canyon and Glen Canyon, but the boats were abandoned at Lee's Ferry. Four of the group went on by horseback to prospect the Kaibab and Bright Angel Creek, but they found little more than fine hunting on the Kaibab Plateau and "scenes of wild enchantment" along the canyon reaches of Bright Angel Creek. C. Gregory Crampton, *Land of Living Rock* (New York, 1972), 189–191.

Among the photos Stanton took on Sunday, February 9, was one of James S. Hogue seated on the walls of an Indian ruin. This ruin, dating from the first half of the twelfth century, had also been seen by Powell in 1869. D. D. Fowler, R. C. Euler, and C. S. Fowler, "John Wesley Powell and the Anthropology of the Canyon Country," U.S. Geological Survey *Professional Paper* 670 (1969), 14–17.

[4] These cryptic notes refer to a climb out of the canyon to the top of Osiris Temple east and north of the mouth of Crystal Creek. After so much time spent in the dark Granite Gorge, Stanton wanted to reach the snow line along the rim of the canyon visible in places from the inner gorge. With John Hislop and Elmer Kane, he made the overnight hike, and later,

Fig. 38. John Hislop, C.E., McGill University, 1884. Stanton wrote that he owed the most to Hislop, his first assistant, for the final success of the railroad survey. Miami University Library.

WEDNESDAY, FEBRUARY 12, 1890. Clear.

I understand that "Captain" Twining has been venting his grievances while we have been gone. He is very much aggrieved that he was not allowed to go out with McDonald. Says he is very little inclined with the expedition since McDonald has gone, for he has no confidence in anyone else. And in a very mysterious way says, "Wait till I get back to Denver." A threat that means all sorts of vengeance, I suppose. For what, I don't know.

The men who stayed in camp Monday and Tuesday portaged all our supplies to the foot of Rapid No. 258 fully 1/2 mile from its head. This morning

with these notes at hand, he wrote a description of the "Birth of a Canyon Day" seen from Osiris, which is one of the better pieces in the body of descriptive literature of the Grand Canyon. See Dwight L. Smith, ed., *Down the Colorado* (1965), 165–172.

at 7:00 A.M. we begin to pack. Carry beds and cook outfit down, and let the boats down by lines, 2 men in. The boats are all down at 9:45 and we load up. We are loaded, going quietly and carefully to work, and start at 10:30 A.M.[5]

At 10:40 we stop at head of Rapid No. 259, a bad rocky rapid formed by side wash on right, 1 1/2 miles below McDonald Creek, a worse rapid than

[5] Stanton's notes on February 8 and 12 on No. 258, Crystal Rapid, give us a good description of the "old" Crystal as it was in 1890. The "new" Crystal was created in December 1966, when a heavy storm dumped several inches of rain on the southern end of the Kaibab Plateau. An enormous flash-flood full of rocks and gravel and logs roared down Crystal Creek and pushed tons of debris into the Colorado. Instantly Crystal was transformed from a mild rapid, which Stanton had lined easily, to one rated as tops in difficulty by modern river runners. R. O. Collins and R. Nash, *The Big Drops* (San Francisco, 1978), 158–178, size up the new Crystal.

FIG. 39. Elmer Kane, Stanton's strong righthand man and companion on hikes away from the river. Photo at Lee's Ferry Christmas, 1889. *F. A. Nims.* Miami University Library.

last. This requires a portage and we at once commence to unload on left bank. 11:45 take photos opposite first side canyon below McDonald Creek. We take an hour for lunch, 12 to 1, and at 1:45 P.M. both boats are both down, 2 men in, and ready to load.

The walls of the inner canyon from creek at Camp No. 79 to next side canyon on right, a distance of 1 1/2 miles, are benched and broken as before. Side canyon, 50 foot span. From this side canyon to next on right for 1'/2 mile, same formation except that slope is flatter, regular hillside rock work. From this point to point where river turns sharp to right 2 1'/4 miles below Camp No. 79, Rapid 262, the walls are more abrupt in the points that jut out into the river. The formation is of two kinds, the massive red granite and the black slaty kind. The red stands in bold points while the slaty material crumbles and washes away. These coves can be easily filled with the material from the points. Two-20 foot spans. This same formation continues to point where river turns right 4 miles below McDonald Creek. The latter half mile has broad and high sloping talus of large pieces of granite well above high water.

We are loaded and start at 2:15 P.M. and row across the current and land on left bank at head of Rapid No. 260. This rapid is very steep and rocky at foot and a long curve to left, bringing current close to cliff on right at foot. We examine it and at 2:35 let our loaded boats down by line which is completed by 3:35 P.M.

Hislop, Travers, and myself climb over a high point of the cliff and down for 1/2 mile and examine the next two Rapids No. 261 and 262. We concluded we could run both of them at one time as there was no water to stop in between them. The situation was this, Rapid No. 261 was simply very heavy waves clear of rocks. No. 262 has 3 large rocks under water which formed the separation of the draw into the two channels around the immense rock nearly in center of river, 50'×50', and 20 feet high downstream and sloping into the water upstream. There were also 2 or 3 large rocks above water in left channel.

It was my opinion that the proper course was through the left channel; but on account of the rocks, Hislop feared we might be dashed against them as we would be going so fast in that part of the rapid and he felt satisfied we could cut across to right channel, which had much lighter waves, after we passed No. 261. My fear was that we could not make this offing in time and we would be drawn on to the rocks under water.

We started at 4 P.M. from the cove and into No. 261. These were the largest and strongest waves we had ever encountered. Our Boat No. 1 dove over the first wave and fairly went out into the air and dropped flat bottomed on the next wave, which was lower, with a crash as if she had fallen upon a rock, the noise was so great. She then dove through the next wave in the breaker which went over our heads; and then her bow being so low, she dove completely under the solid part of the next *wave*, the boat out of sight, and the water poured over and into us in one solid mass; but the boat goes through so fast *she* only takes in small amount of water. Just here Hislop who was steering made his first fatal mistake. Having such a rough passage ourselves, he forgot our boat to see how No. 2 got through. In *a moment* we started to make the offing for the right channel but we were too late. The current caught our stern and we went broadside over the worst waves and rocks. Our keel stuck on the first rock, and for a moment I expected our boat to turn completely over with us underneath; but the next moment we went over the rock, and as our noble boat dropped behind it she righted up and started with almost good head on.

Every man jumped to his work and we went by the rock at [the] point in good shape; but just then Hislop made his second mistake; he turned again to look at Boat No. 2, and we lost our course; he turned in a moment and shouted lookout ahead. In about 2 seconds our boat struck with full force on her nose against the right cliff but thanks to the strength of the boat she did not so much as spring a leak; but the load shot forward breaking stays, straps, and fastenings. Boat No. 2 came through No. 261 in good shape. Tried to follow No. 1 but got further to left side. Missed the rocks but was carried broadside on to [another] rock. The rebounding wave kept her from striking hard but she stuck on the rock. The crew got out on the rock, and although she filled with water, they got her off and around in eddy back of rock and bailed her out. It was only 2 minutes from the time we started at head of No. 261 till Boat No. 2 was on the rock.

In the meantime we attempted to get back to the rock as soon as we knew *something* had happened to Boat 2. Failing, we landed on left bank, and ran up. Saw the men all safe, but could not tell what would become of the boat. We ran to our boat again and by hard pulling reached the eddy behind rock, but by that [time] the boat was off.

After bailing out No. 2 we rowed down at 4:55 about 1/2 mile and went into Camp No. 80 at 5:00 P.M. Damages: all blankets and photo instruments wet. I hope my pictures on top are not spoilt.

The canyon has become much more narrow from a point 1 1/2 miles below Camp No. 79 at McDonald Creek. The course of the river is very crooked and the "outlook ahead is only a few hundred feet"; but as this crooked course of the river is caused by these jutting cliffs, it will not cause a bad railroad alignment. These points must be cut, 20 feet to 50 feet through, a few longer, and a very good alignment will be the result.

THURSDAY, FEBRUARY 13, 1890. Clear. Very windy and clouding up from southwest at 11 A.M. Small shower 3:45 P.M. Snow on mountains and cold wind 5 P.M.

We were so tired after the work and excitement of yesterday that none of us woke up early this morning. I woke at 6:45 A.M.

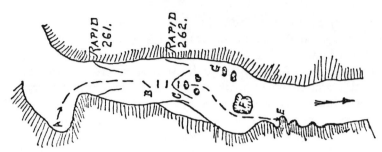

Fɪɢ. 40. Sketch map of Rapids 261 and 262. *Robert B. Stanton.* Miami University Library.

We had breakfast at 8:00 A.M.

In the wreck yesterday the photo instruments, rolls, etc., all went under water. I laid them all out last night, and it took me some time to straighten them out this morning. The instrument or lenses are not hurt. One roll, *no pictures* on it, was wet. The gelatine roll on which was the pictures I took on top Monday and Tuesday was only damp on the one exposed negative. The pictures on top and yesterday's work I believe safe. I cut them off and shall make special effort to save them.

Packing up and starting was slow. Everyone was tired out. We start at 10:42 and at 10:44 ran Rapid No. 263, with high waves, 2 in my lap, and at 10:45 cut into eddy and land on left bank just below head of Rapid No. 263 and take photos.

We start again at 11:05 A.M.; and our boat is caught in the whirlpools and turned round and round, and drifts down in every shape, unmanageable till we get into quiet water below when we right up our course and row to the head of Rapid No. 264, where we land at 11:10. This rapid could be easily run except that the whole force of the current dashes against the foot [of the] cliff which overhangs some 8 or 10 feet, whole cliff 50 feet, in separate ledges. So we unload, portage the stuff about 150 feet, drop the empty boats past head of rapid on right side, load and drop them 200 or 300 feet further in eddy to a sand beach, and then take an hour from 12:20 to 1:20 P.M. for *lunch*.

A storm is brewing and blowing from the southwest, so we wait a while. At 1:15 take photos, head of Rapid 264. Thirty foot span over wash which forms No. 264. High water from 40 to 45 feet.

The walls from last point described down to deep side canyon on left at Rapid No. 265 are the same form but almost entirely of the solid massive red granite. This juts out into the river in points 50 to 100 feet high and sloping back with large slides of broken rock between them and in other places bays of still water. These points are not perpendicular even at the water's edge except in short distances 50 feet to 100 feet and then only vertical for 10-20-30 and 50 feet up.

We start at 1:33 P.M. and stop 1 mile below on left bank at 1:41 and take photo.

We restart at 1:58 and row 1/4 mile and across to right side in swift current and land on sand beach at head of Rapid No. 265, formed by side canyon on left. We at once begin to unload as this rapid is a terror and full of rocks. The portage is over a granite slide of immense pieces of rock and is the very worst portage we have had to make on the whole river, though not the longest. We let down Boat No. 1 by line without a scratch. Boat No. 2 did not get so good a start at the head of the rapid. She turned a little and a wave filled her 1/4 full. She was then so heavy that she stuck on a rock, midships, and filled full. With line on stern pulling down and line on bow up we got her out in a few minutes and bailed her out, and then got her down successfully, at 4:20 P.M.

At 3:00 P.M. we take photos from right bank at head of Rapid 265.

Boat No. 2 sprang a leak on the rock but not a bad one. We shall be obliged to load and move on as we are among the rocks, so that we can neither leave the boats to rest here, nor get them out to repair them. We load and start at 5:00 P.M. and land one mile below at 5:10 at head of Rapid No. 266 and go in Camp No. 81 on right bank.

This has been a most wearing day on me. Perhaps it is because I slept in wet clothes last night.

The granite around this last section is hard, red, and massive. This seems to have turned the river out of its general course and driven it in many courses. This is one of the most difficult and expensive points for a line on account of the massiveness of the rock; but there is no engineering difficulty at all, only the matter of expense. All through this section most wonderful alignment, long tangents and easy curves. Few drains around the point and all easily handled, and many can be made "overhead" when hillside cut is made in granite.

This here is the only evidence I can see of Powell's overhanging cliff. Small points that really do *overhang* 5 to 10 feet and are 10 to 50 feet long, generally *slabs sticking out*. See note at end of February 14th.

FRIDAY, FEBRUARY 14, 1890. Clear.

Spent all morning in Camp No. 81 repairing Boat No. 2, drying beds, reassorting and packing provisions. Lunch at 12 noon.

At 12:45 P.M. we begin to pack up, but takes some time as everything was unloaded. At 1:45 P.M. we begin and drop boats 500 feet to head of Rapid No. 266. This rapid is very rough and rocky one, and at this stage of water cannot be run. A drop of 10 feet to 12 feet in 300 foot walls from 50 to 100 feet high. At the head of it, on right for 200 feet, there is no footing for portage, and for 600 feet on left, so must let the boats down loaded.

We take the right side. Hislop climbs over cliff 500 to 600 feet up with small line attached to heavy line, and drops it over the cliff. He gets down to the river and draws heavy line over, attaching it to boulder. We draw it taut and fasten to boulder above. Our boat is then manned and with short line around this and line to slide along so as to keep her stern from being caught by current and swept out, and long line held by men upstream as the first boat is let over the rocks below, by 2:45 p.m. This is repeated with second boat leaving one man, Kane, above to hold long line above. He then loosens hand line, and it is pulled in, and he, being with Hislop the best climber, goes up over the cliff and gets down safely. Second boat over at 3:15. The climb down on lower side was very difficult. I took two pictures as they came down. The boats are then unloaded and we portage the stuff to an eddy below, and the boats let around by lines by 4:30 p.m.

We start at 4:55 and at 5:00 p.m. land at head of Rapid No. 267 and at 5:05 we run it easily, and at 5:10 land on left bank at foot of rapid on sand bar with plenty of wood, and go into Camp No. 82.

Rapid No. 267 is formed by side wash on left with small wash on right, 20 feet overhead. After passing around the southwest corner of Point Sublime, the character of the canyon walls changes very rapidly. The massive red granite gives way to a more broken mixture of red and black and slaty granite much broken up; and for the 2 1/2 to 3 mile north stretch has in most of the distance a fine talus and sloping hillside form near the river while the higher portions are more abrupt. For the last mile of this stretch the formation is mostly of the "slaty" rock and the slopes continue up to the sandstone. Two or 3 small streams come over the higher portions of the cliff which I think can be handled by 20 foot overheads.

We have only made 1 1/2 miles today.

Our camp tonight is just past the southwest corner of Point Sublime, 1 1/2 miles below Rapid No. 266. This Rapid No. 266 is the worst one we have had to get over and around. The rocks all over it are large and the force of the waves irresistible. After getting over its head as above described, we got into our boats in the to me most dismal and uncertain place we have ever set sail.

The canyon is narrow. The walls come nearer being perpendicular than at any point we have passed. It is getting dusk, and the sharp curve in the river to the right prevents seeing but a short distance ahead. The walls at the water's edge for 20 to 50 feet are vertical and cut and polished in vertical seams. No wood, no landing place in sight. The roar of the rapid in our ears, and the huge waves of its lower half dashing in every direction forming whirls, eddies, and back currents. Out into these we pull in anything but a pleasant frame of mind.

We get out of the rough water, after being twisted and turned and dashed about in the whirls and eddies, and row through about one mile of good water, when we hear the roar and see the dashing waves of a rapid below. Hislop, Travers, and I land and walk up on the broken granite just beyond the massive red; and as we get up high enough, we can see around a left turn in the river; and what a view opens to our sight: a wide open canyon for five miles, almost straight with green glassy slopes at an angle of about 45° coming down to the very water's edge, the river almost like a placid lake with only a slight ripple at intervals of a mile or two, indicating easy rapids. The whole picture charming in the extreme, but to cap it all, at our feet a short easy rapid and just below it a dry sand beach covered with drift wood. What joy, what joy, and what a change of feelings since leaving our last hard portage. We fairly run to our boats, jump in, and dash through the rapid and into the eddy on the left and in a few moments are landed on the beach. The whole party as if overcome by the happiness of·the prospect of a comfortable night, fairly scamper out of the boats and make one rush in a friendly scramble for places on the dry sand to sleep, like so many school boys let out at recess. And we soon have a hot supper, and are sitting around the most cheerful campfire we have had for a fortnight.

The massive *red* granite which forms the base of Powell's Plateau is the cause, I suppose, of the river making the sharp south course around this point. This, wherever we have met it, stands up in more bold and sheer walls than the black, grey, or slaty kinds. The southern part and especially the southwest point, is the most difficult piece of railroad line we have passed in the Grand Canyon. Difficult only in point of expense.

N.B., *February 23d.* In these notes of Friday and Saturday reference is made to *Powell's Plateau.* This is not correct. The point I supposed to be Powell's Plateau was not it but a prominent point above *Shinumo Creek* and is Point Sublime.

SATURDAY, FEBRUARY 15, 1890. Clear.

Kane and I climb the cliff on left bank about 1/2 mile and 250 feet above river to take photos at 7:30 A.M. Show granite point extreme southwest point of Point Sublime, as difficult a piece of work with one exception as we have found in the Granite to Rapid 266.

We get back to camp and find boats loaded, ready to start. We sail at 8:10 A.M. and in 3 minutes stop on right bank to take photos showing north rim on west side of Point Sublime from 1/4 mile below Camp No. 82 which is shown.

We start again at 8:33 on a stretch of two miles of clear water and at 8:45 land on right bank at head of Rapid No. 268, which is a very sudden drop of 10 to 12 feet and requires portage of all stuff and short portage of boats at the very head of the fall. The men commence to unload at 9:00 A.M. and I take photos from head of Rapid No. 268. Portage is made and boats portaged overhead and let down by lines rest of way and we are loaded and start at foot of rapid at 10:50 A.M.

From this point Rapid No. 268 magnificent views of the upper canyon are opened to right both up and down the river. Up the river the left side is much broken into points coming far out towards the river, with their variegated colors, rising from the dark and bush covered green granite the beveled ledge of dark brown sandstone, the sloping mesas and then the yellowish grey limestone much broken, with the massive red marble above it standing in sheer walls of 500 to 800 feet. Covered by the dozen little steps of flame colored sandstone, with the little benches between covered with scrub trees of green capped with the high points of grey, yellow, and white sandstone fringed with the thick growth of cedar and pine. Down the river to the northwest seems one massive wall a mile high stretched across the canyon as the river turns to the right, as we get a broad side view of the same class of country described above.

We pass the small canyon noted without a rapid, but 1 1/2 miles beyond land at 11:00 A.M. at head of Rapid No. 269. This rapid though heavy could be run but for two heavy rocks at foot. [It] is formed by two side canyons, the *larger* on left. Begin to unload at 11:15 and swing boats down with 2 men in them in 25 *minutes*, and in 15 minutes more the whole stuff is portaged, a distance of 450 feet. Lunch 11:50 A.M.

We begin to load at 12:50 P.M. At 1:00 P.M. take photos from center of Rapid No. 269.

From Rapid No. 268 for 1/2 to 3/4 mile to a side canyon on right, 50 foot span, is broad talus and very sloping banks. Hardly looks like a canyon at all — that is, the main Colorado Canyon. This same character of wall continues for 2 1/2 miles further to head of Rapid No. 269, with 3 side washes on right for 60 foot spans.

The slopes from here on for [blank] miles are laughably easy [compared to] the granite walls [as portrayed, opposite page 86] in [*Exploration of the Colorado River of the West* by] Major Powell. There are almost no walls but hillside slopes from water's edge to top of granite, 600 to 800 feet, on point at angle of about 40° from horizontal. High water mark, which at south end of Powell's Plateau was 50 feet, in this opener part of the canyon is not over 30 feet. A few points of *Point Sublime* are seen from the river on our right.

We start at 1:15 P.M. and run one mile and land on right bank at 1:20 P.M. at head of Rapid No. 270 which could be easily run if it had 4 or 5 feet more water, but as it is, it is too rocky. We portage all our stuff, beginning at 1:20 and shoot the boats, over head of rapid with 2 lines and are all safely down at 2:45. This rapid has at least a 10 foot drop so we ought to have nearly two miles of good water along here.

At 3:00 P.M. we are loaded and tow the boats through the strong bank current of the eddy for 300 feet and then set sail on smooth water at 3:10. At 3:20 we run a small Rapid No. 271 and at 3:25 stop at head of Rapid No. 272 and go into Camp No. 83 for Sunday.

Adjust distances run today about [*blank*] miles in all. Can enlarge on the beautiful river. Dancing rapids and lakes of still water between and green grassy slopes down to the water's edge.

SUNDAY, FEBRUARY 16, 1890. Cloudy all day with south wind.

In Camp No. 83, resting on left bank at mouth of small side canyon.

Most beautiful views from this camp both up and down for several miles each way. The long easy slopes of the inner gorge [are] covered with grass and greasewood bushes in their bright green spring coloring mingled with the shiny polished black granite running down to the water's edge, with two or three rapids in sight and glassy lakes of still water between. The whole picture hemmed in at either end with mountains of flaming red, capped with towering pinnacles of grey and yellow, and the green fringe of the mountain pine and cedar interspersed with glimpses of snow "J.H." [John Hislop?]

2:00 P.M. take photos from center of Rapid No. 272.

And to the west of our camp, a most gorgeous and wonderful amphitheater; wonderful in the greatness of its dimensions and grandeur of its architectural proportions; beautiful in the curious detail of its finish, and the blended colors of its frescoed alcoves and galleries. (Hunt up architectural description.)

MONDAY, FEBRUARY 17, 1890. Cloudy. South wind. Cloudy all day. A few sprinkles.

We begin to break camp at 7:30 A.M.; and by 8:30 everything is gathered up from our Sunday rest and portaged to lower end of Rapid No. 272 which is not so very bad except that at this stage of water the rocks are so near the surface it would be utter destruction to attempt it. So we let boats down along shore with lines, and skid them over one hard place. First boat goes down in 30 minutes and second, No. 1, in 15 minutes.

At 9:30 take photo [of] amphitheater up little side canyon west of Camp No. 83.

It takes some extra time to load as we had all the lockers open. We are loaded and set sail at 9:53 A.M.; and at 9:55 run Rapid No. 273, a long but not difficult one and are through it in 2 minutes, 1/2 mile distance. I got one huge wave completely over me.

At 10:10 we stop 1/2 mile beyond where river first turns to left and take photos. One-half mile further on, we walk, take photos at head of Rapid No. 274 [at] 10:45. These pictures show Dutton's Depot Grounds. These grounds have perpendicular granite walls next to river, so no room is lost. [They] are semicircular in shape from 2 to 2 1/2 miles long. The washes through them are very narrow, with almost perpendicular granite walls, so [they can] be cheaply bridged for side track purposes. This is a most beautiful piece of land for depot and *shop* purposes.

One mile from our last night's camp river turns to right. To that point, canyon walls same as those above, long sloping broken rock slides and points jutting up above the general slope and into the river.

For two miles or further, about N 20° E, the first part is more abrupt but very much broken up into points; and then the whole side of the canyon is broken back away from the river at point where river turns to left with long sweep, forming a flat, on top of the granite 50 to 60 feet above low water and at just about what grade ought to be, well above high water mark, from 200 to 300 feet wide and from 1 1/2 to 2 miles in length of almost perfectly level country. This is caused by the breaking away of the granite and washing off of the lime and sandstone above it, and can be graded to 400 feet wide with but little expense. High water only 25 feet.

After photos and looking over the depot grounds we set sail again at 11:08 and at 11:10 land on left bank at head of Rapid 274, nearly one mile beyond where river first turns to left. This is a very short but rocky rapid but seemingly good channel to let boats down loaded on left side. We begin this work, one man in boat, at 11:20 A.M.

The boats are both down at 11:40 A.M. and we set sail again at 11:45 A.M. After passing Rapid 273 the river has been smooth and beautiful, though the current is swift. A delightful change to have several miles of good water without bad rapid instead of several bad rapids to a mile.

Rapid No. 274 is formed by creek on right 1/2 mile below the general breakup of the granite as noted above. From this locate its position.

[About] 1/2 mile or so below Rapid No. 274 river turns sharp to left and narrow channel, on right at turn. At the turn to left the country is much more broken up than at any point we have passed. The granite slopes entirely out at the river, but rises again 1/2 mile beyond pretty abruptly to 150 feet high on right, but with good easy line around it. From this point on for 3/4 mile river runs about west course. This 3/4 mile takes line to mouth of *Shinumo Creek*. We start at 11:45 and at 11:55 after making turn to left land for lunch. Water again like a lake from No. 274 to and for 1/2 mile beyond. Lunch [at] noon. Photo from lunch point 3/4 mile above Shinumo Creek, 60 to 70 feet above low water. And from the same place but 300 feet above river.

We start at 1:45 P.M. and at 1:51 land on right bank at mouth of *Shinumo Creek*. Cross over and at 2:05 P.M. commence to let loaded boats down with lines over Rapid No. 275. All down at 2:30 P.M. At 2:15 take photos.

At our lunch point, on the flat above river, 60 to 70 feet, are the remains of a large village of supposed cliff dwellers. The walls of dozens of square houses laid dry. One house [with] smooth inside walls. Remnants of pottery, arrowheads, etc. And further up on the slope numerous remains of houses under overhanging rocks and cliffs, one under rock with partition walls laid in mortar not more than 2 to 1 1/2 feet high. The whole hillside seems to be covered with these cave houses.

We start at center of Rapid No. 275, run the lower end at 3:00 P.M., and at 3:02 run No. 276, which is very lively. Two large waves go over me, one hitting me square in the face and drenching me to the skin.

At 3:04 we stop on right bank to examine rapids ahead. Find long rapid or very swift water extending from about 1 1/2 miles below *Shinumo* Creek for 1 1/2 miles down. We start again at 3:22 and at 3:23 enter this long Rapid No. 277, run one half mile of it, stop in eddy on right and go into Camp No. 84, 1 1/2 miles below Shinumo Creek.

After turning around the point beyond Shinumo Creek there is about 600 to 800 feet of limestone along the river's edge as it turns again to the left.

The railroad coming along the beautiful flat above Shinumo Creek would, in order to save distance, [have] some bad work at points beyond creek, and to make much better alignment would tunnel both points at the creek, and perhaps have to cut the bed of the creek lower at the crossing in order to get waterway sufficient. High water between 25 and 30 feet.

4:00 P.M. take photo 1 1/2 mile below Shinumo Creek.

Beyond the limestone point noted the granite rises again in bold cliffs but not perpendicular. See tomorrow's notes.

Just above our Camp No. 84 in the limestone cliffs are a great number of cliff dwelling ruins, with cemented granaries as at the Nankoweap.[6]

---

[6] Leaving Crystal Creek on February 12, the Stanton party spent five laborious days on the river traveling twelve miles! Camp 84 on the right bank was approximately at mile 110, one and one-half miles below the mouth of Shinumo Creek. After a scary ride through two rapids (RBS 261, 262) just below Tuna Rapid, the explorers entered a long stretch of the Upper Granite Gorge where the river was tightly confined. Portaging and lining in the absence of banks and beaches was difficult and hazardous. February 13, Rapid 265 (probably Sapphire Rapid) was "the very worst portage we have had to make." But there were some bright spots — a grand campsite on the 14th, and the beautiful vistas of the walls, cliffs, terraces, amphitheaters, and plateau rimlands of the outer canyon made possible by the lowering walls of the Granite Gorge.

Throughout this section Stanton found that the rail alignment would be "wonderful." No "engineering difficulty at all," although construction in the massive rock in places would be expensive. Indeed, just above the mouth of Shinumo Creek (mile 108.6) Stanton found a place suitable for a depot and switching yard, which he named after Clarence E. Dutton of the Powell Survey. In Denver in 1889 the two men had discussed the railroad project and Dutton had asked, "what will you do for side track room and depot grounds along the walls of the Grand Canyon?" A mile-long bench or terrace, centering at a point about opposite the mouth of Bass Canyon and at the head of Bass Rapid (RBS 274), seemed to be such a place, whereupon the engineer named it after the geologist, "Dutton's Depot Grounds." Had the railroad been built, Dutton's Depot might well have become a busy place. Already by 1890, William Wallace Bass had established a tourist camp on the South Rim near Havasupai Point. Not long after Stanton came along with the survey, Bass opened a trans-canyon tourist trail which crossed the river at Bass Rapid and passed right through "Dutton's Depot Grounds." One can picture the arrival of the trains, the dudes alighting from the steam train to take the mule train to either the South Rim or the North Rim!

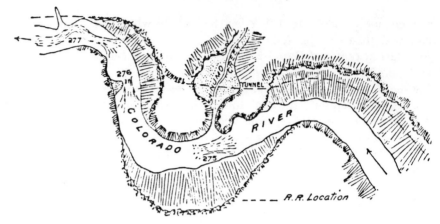

Fig. 41. Sketch map of the mouth of Shinumo Creek. *Robert B. Stanton.* Miami University Library.

Tuesday, February 18. Cloudy. Shower at 9:30 a.m. and all a.m. Snow on top. Sprinkling late in evening.

We load and start on the remainder of Rapid No. 277 at 7:58 a.m. In about 2 minutes we make 1/2 mile and in coming around a very sharp turn in the rapid to the right, No. 1 boat kept a little too far to right to avoid slide rock of boulders on left. Our bow was caught in small whirl and we were carried towards right bank. All this time we were going downstream very fast. Our steersman Hislop seeing two large rocks ahead downstream just under water with large wave breaking over and below them shouted, "Pull hard for the shore"; but it was too late. In a moment our bow about 3 feet back was drifted on the first rock and keeled over downstream. I caught the life line on upper side and raised my left foot out ready to jump clear of the boat if she upset; but the stern swung downstream and fell in the hole behind the rock, and in doing so threw Hislop overboard clear of the boat. At the same time the boat drifted loose and down the rapid, stern first. Hislop was about 10 feet ahead of us, held way up out of the water by his life preservers. In a moment we had caught up with him and pulled him in to the boat. Just then No. 2 passed us, and threw Hislop an oar to steer with as he had lost his. All hands pulled their hardest to get out of the rapid and in a very *short time*, before we had gone 1000 feet from where we struck, we were safely landed in an eddy on right bank. Boat No. 2 came down safely but in trying to get into eddy run

---

Prehistoric man came this way also. The ruins found by Stanton (also seen by Powell) on the depot grounds were built and occupied by the Anasazi Pueblos during the first half of the twelfth century. D. D. Fowler, R. C. Euler, C. S. Fowler, "John Wesley Powell and the Anthropology of the Canyon Country," (1969), 16–18. Stanton mentions a number of ruins above their camp No. 84. This was on the right bank at about mile 110.1, one and one-half miles below the mouth of Shinumo Creek.

the top of her nose full force against a high rock. The only real danger was in being carried over the next Rapid No. 278 which was about 1000 feet below where we landed and very swift water to the head of it. The mistake was that when the boat got into its first position, instead of trying to pull into the big eddy, he should have packed water and turned her head downstream. *He* says it was *his* fault.

8:30 A.M. photos show long Rapid 277 where Hislop was washed overboard [and] Rapid No. 278.

The general character of canyon walls for 1 1/2 miles after leaving the short patch of limestone — granite, standing in bold cliffs, much broken into points, and buttresses with large slides of debris between, forming high talus slopes. Good alignment and easy line by cutting these points and filling *on the slopes* between.

We haul out Boat No. 1 and find one small hole near her bow where she first struck; easy to repair. We portage stuff by head of Rapid No. 278, while this is being done. And at [*blank*] let boats down the first short drop of No. 278, about 6 feet and *very rocky*. No. 2 is floated down and let over the head of Rapid No. 278. At 10:30 No. 1 is repaired and she is lowered successfully at 11:00 A.M.

We load and start at foot of No. 278 at 11:20 and at 11:25 land one mile below on left bank and take photo. And at 11:40 we restart, and at 11:40 1/2 run Rapid No. 279, and at 11:42 run Rapid No. 280; both of them small and easy.

Lunch at 11:46 A.M., 3 1/2 miles below our last night's camp.

1:20 P.M. photos down 2 1/2 mile stretch [and] up river from opposite lunch stand.

From last point noted to lunch point, the granite is of the slaty kind with the slope of the strata towards the river, which makes a smooth, somewhat broken wall at angle of from 20 to 30° from perpendicular. The river is plainly seen for 2 1/2 miles ahead. The river has for the last 2 miles a due west course and then bends to left. The walls are the slaty granite with the general slope about 45°. Easy of construction and splendid alignment. There are one side wash on right, 60 foot span, and one 38 foot span. The high marble and sandstone cliffs down river and on right are one solid mass of flame colors, some black ledges; one highest point on right is the light sandstone with same nature of granite with green bushes below, with the same beaded sandstone between. In photo the high are at same flame color with black stains and snow showing in timber in notch to right.

We start down again at 1:45 and in 3 minutes make 1/2 mile to head of Rapid No. 281. We stop to examine and conclude to drop loaded boats down by lines. The boats are down safely and we start once more at 3:15 P.M. This rapid formed from side wash on right is not as bad as some we have run but has very high waves and the lower end beats furiously against the cliff on right bank, with large rock nearly at end of current which turns it off from cliff. It is a question whether if we attempted to run it we could keep off this rock so we decide as above.

We sailed two miles on beautifully quiet water and at 3:33 landed on right bank at small side canyon which forms Rapid No. 282. We stop and take photo showing beautiful *butte*, which is very familiar to me in some of Powell's or Dutton's works.

We row across river and go into Camp No. 85 at 4:00 P.M. opposite the side canyon.

It has been showering in the canyon all day and snowing on the Kaibabs [Kaibab Plateau]. The most beautiful picture of snow we have seen this winter came in view east of us as we came down this last stretch of river this afternoon. The whole tops of the plateau down to the red sandstone was completely covered, and the green trees stood out in bold relief against it.

Note February 19th: I believe we camped last night opposite a very large side canyon. Correct notes of 18th as to camp and of the 19th as to position of photos, etc., that refer [to] this camp. Remember to make special note and description of the granite rocks *in* river at our Camp No. 85 as shown in photo.

WEDNESDAY, FEBRUARY 19, 1890. Cloudy. Partially cleared up by noon. Sunny in P.M.

8:15 A.M. photo across river. High cliffs in notch, red below, grey tinged with white. Timber on upper benches. Lower strata same as before. 8:30 A.M. photo from same point *down*. The high cliff in center has yellow limestone at bottom. All above flaming red. No trees.

The first mile below this Camp *No. 85* is a hard one to navigate. Rapid No. 282 is formed by two side canyons on opposite sides of the river. These have washed in an immense quantity of boulders that have been washed down the river for a mile and formed two rapids. This first one, No. 282, is very steep and full of rocks to the surface.

After packing up, we start to work at it at 8:30 A.M. We portage the stuff to foot of rapid on a small gravel bench. Let the boats down by lines over the first 200 feet and then skid them over a bad place out of the water, next to shore. Photos from point 1/4 mile below last pictures.

The portage is made and the boats let down to the gravel beach by 10:30. We load up, and at 10:55 A.M. start and run and in 5 minutes land, after running No. 283, at head of No. 284 on left bank. This is formed by side wash on right, 80 foot span, very rocky at low water, and cannot be run at its head. This rapid No. 284 is fully 1/2 mile long. We at once go to work to let boats down loaded, 2 men in boats, past the first 500 feet.

This is done and we start at 12:00 noon and in 2 minutes we land 1/2 mile below on right bank for *lunch*. This point is 2 to 2 1/2 miles below where we camped last night. High water mark about 50 feet.

From point where river turns to left, above Camp 85 and at end of 2 mile stretch described yesterday, the granite cliff for 1/4 mile is quite smooth, the strata of the slaty material being parallel with stream. This goes to side wash, 50 foot span. From this on for a mile the wall is a broken up mixture of hard red strata, soft slaty black, and loose rock slides, sloping on an average about 30° to 40° from perpendicular. The granite is getting much lower and the sandstone coming down rapidly. This same character of wall to point where river turns to left, with some very bold granite points. Beyond this the canyon must be very narrow, as the high water mark is between 50 and 60 feet.

12:30 P.M. photo 1 1/2 miles below Camp No. 85.

At 1:30 P.M. we cross and land 500 feet below at head of Rapid No. 285. We let boats past head of rapid by 1:45. We row across eddy and look at rest of rapid at 1:50 P.M. At 1:55 P.M. we started and drifted and then had a narrow shave on the rock, but pushed off with oars — the force of the current is all on the right side of rock in center of river — and then pulled out into the lower end of the rapid and were through it in 2 minutes.

We stopped for Boat No. 2, and at 2:05 ran Rapid No. 286, and in 5 minutes landed to take photo at point where river turns to left. Course of river from big rock to photo point S 23° W magnetic, and from here on for at least 2 miles, from same setup, to center of river at end of stretch course is S 5° E magnetic.

From our lunch point, the walls are almost the same as those just past except the rock is almost all grey granite standing in bold points with large broken slides of immense pieces of angular granite. This same formation continues for 3 miles further to point where we take photos at 2:45 P.M. Two side canyons, 60 foot span. General slope of granite 35 to 45° from perpendicular.

Note wonderful view of the heavily snow covered Kaibabs [Kaibab Plateau] to the northeast from above point of photos while it is warm and spring-like where we are.

We restart at 2:50 P.M. on a smooth stretch of swift water that extends for 2 to 3 miles or more. Beautiful views up and down the river, with long line of high marble and sandstone cliff on right quite near the river.

At 3:08, still in quiet water we land on right bank for photos. These are taken about 1 mile below where river makes this bend all in swift but quiet water.

On this south stretch of 2 to 3 miles the granite lays at an angle of about 45° with some broken rock forming flatter low water talus. The granite is much broken up but the strata or broken lines are parallel with the river and hence not many *deep* gullies. I note 8 or 10 waterways for 20 foot spans, and one 50 foot span. Some may be handled by overheads. The granite is getting lower and lower.

The long stretch of river from the bend to left below the big rock, to the bend to right just before entering on the due west course, is wonderfully *beautiful, grand,* and *picturesque.* The regular form of the inner granite gorge, capped with the "beaded" sandstone. The beautiful stretch of smooth but swift water. The rich green coloring of the grass, bushes, and the flowers among the granite breaks, and the shiny sparkling black granite. The marble cliffs on left coming close to river in great frowning buttresses. On the right, the marble cliffs running almost parallel with river; broken into smaller buttresses of every imaginable shape, capped with several benches of the upper red sandstone, all a *flaming red.* To the northeast this range rising higher and higher to the grey and yellow benches covered with timber. To the south the turn of river to right is cut off by the same *red* granite and sand cliffs *seemingly* a straight wall cutting off any further progress.

We start again at 3:36 P.M. on the same smooth swift water, and at 3:45 pass side wash on left without more than a little ripple. This is on turn to right and we land at 3:49 on left side 500 feet above side canyon on left which forms Rapid No. 287. We take photo from commencement of due west course showing bench of granite below sandstone cliff.

Start at 4:06 and at 4:07 run Rapid No. 287, a long one and complete letter S. We turn in second eddy and lose a few minutes and get under way again. At 4:12 we run a small chute not worthy of a number, and at 4:15 land on left bank for Camp No. 86.

4:20 photo from 3/5 way down due west course.

4:40 P.M. granite on right about 100 feet high. High water 35 feet. Granite rises quite sheer for 50 to 60 feet and then slopes back.

Around this bend to right the granite is 50+ feet high and forms a beautiful railroad bench, with easy curve, between the river and the first beaded sandstone cliff.

We pass Rapid No. 287 and are practically out of the granite, though there are *patches* ahead on the right, and left also.

The "beaded" sandstone has come down to the water. High water here only 20 to 25 feet.

Below the point where the granite drops under the sandstone is talus above high water mark, but not high enough for line. This can easily be made from the sandstone bluffs above. On right of this west course the marble stands in two immense sheer buttresses out near the river, with the slope formed by the crumbled yellow lime about 400 feet wide, from top of "beaded" stratum back to foot of marble. On *left* the remainder of the granite and the lower limestone have crumbled into an even sloping talus 50 to 100 feet high, running from water's edge up to marble which on this side is quite broken up and benched up to the top. The beaded sandstone has entirely disappeared on this side since the side canyon which forms Rapid No. 287. On this west course are 4 water-ways, 10 to 20 feet.

THURSDAY, FEBRUARY 20, 1890. Cloudy [and] rain.

At 8:00 A.M. take photo. We take it easy this morning; wait for light for photos.

We start on quiet but swift water at 8:15 A.M. At 8:20 we run small Rapid No. 288 and at 8:26 land on left bank, at side canyon which forms Rapid No. 289. 8:30 A.M. we take photos 1 to 1 1/4 miles below last.

The same broken nature of the marble and high talus continues on left side to Rapid No. 289. We start at 8:50, row across, and examine Rapid No. 289; and at 9:02 run it in first class shape though it is heavy and rocky but straight chute between the rocks in center. We go only a few feet from them on each side.

We stop at 9:06 at head of Rapid No. 290 and examine it. It is easy with only one rock in center. We also look at No. 291, 1/4 mile ahead formed by larger wash on left. We start at 9:18 and run No. 290 without a drop of splash, by keeping to right of high waves.

9:24 stop for photos to next turn to left, and to where the granite seems to entirely disappear, with the "beaded" sandstone down to the water. Course N 20° E magnetic, *1/2 mile*.

From our Camp No. 86 to point where river turns sharp to right the granite on right side forms a bench from 20 feet to 50 feet above low water, with the "beaded" sandstone above and from 75 to 100 feet back from edge of granite. This makes splendid railroad bench around this turn and on low parts plenty of material to work from in the sandstone above.

Around the right curve beautiful line for railroad. Granite not over 10 feet high at water's edge but large sandstone talus above high water.

This same low bench of granite continues around and through N 20° E magnetic course to where river turns to left. Sandstone there comes down to water. Line would come round on easy curve just under the "beaded" sandstone to left turn and then jump on top of sandstone bench. Above the sandstone the slope up to the limestone below the marble, 500 to 800 feet wide and at an angle of 20° to 25° from *horizontal*.

From the side canyon on the left at Rapid No. 289, line can be located on the limestone slope or at foot of beaded sandstone on talus made sufficient by breaking down this sandstone.

We restart after photos at 9:52 A.M. on beautiful stream of placid water. At 9:56 A.M. we pass entirely out of view. Take detective photo.

10:05 stop to examine and at 10:08 run No. 291, long gravel. At 10:15 stop and look at Rapid No. 292 and at 10:20 we run it and stop on right bank for photos at 10:23 at Rapid No. 293. Take them 1000 feet beyond.

At 11:18 A.M. we start again and run Rapid No. 293, a long crooked *gravel* rapid but easily run, and at 11:30 A.M. we stop for lunch and to change the photo rolls. This latter takes some time. 1:15 P.M. take photos.

We start again at 1:35 P.M. and at 1:38 we run Rapid No. 294 and are through it in just 2 minutes. It is a regular letter S, very swift and rough, but free from rocks. Below this is a stretch of a mile of very swift water, then a smooth bay all the way to where first side canyon comes in on left.

Through this stretch of west and northwest course from our lunch point the "beaded" sandstone rises right from the water's edge in rough perpendicular cliffs for about 40 to 60 feet. This can easily be cut to any grade throwing the waste in the river, for above it is the long easy slope of the limestone.

The "beaded" sandstone is gradually coming down to the water; and at point where first large side canyon comes in on left runs out at water's edge, but is broken back in benches from the water.

We reach first side canyon on left at 2:00 P.M. and land at head of Rapid No. 295. At 2:07 we run No. 295 in fine style. High waves but we cut through on left and miss them all. *What* beautiful rapids all day today. "Dancing," "prancing," etc., etc.

At 2:10 we land at foot and stop for photos at first side wash. We start again at 2:30 and at 2:35 land at Rapid No. 296, a very shallow gravel rapid. We go through at 2:40 and touch once on bottom. Stop 5 minutes and start 2:45. At 2:50 we land at head of No. 297, another shallow gravel rapid. At 2:55 we run it and land at 3:00 P.M. at *second* side canyon and Rapid No. 298.

We start at 3:15 and run No. 298 in 2 minutes. Very high waves caused by water dropping over ledges of the "beaded' sandstone ledge as it goes down.

At 3:20 we stop and go into camp No. 87. Our sugar is entirely gone.

3:45 P.M. photo at mouth of second side wash.

On right side between first and second canyons on foot is side wash, 60 foot span. Beyond this around the right turn the slopes are very high and cut by the water showing a face of *conglomerate* nearly fifty feet high at the point, this more a mass of debris on either side but a mass of cemented stone and gravel in middle at point.

[Note:] Enlarge on beautiful railroad line — few washes, grassy slopes, easy curves, and grade.

FRIDAY, FEBRUARY 21, 1890. Rained steady all night. Clouds breaking away 8 A.M. Soon commenced to rain. Rained hard all A.M. *Raining almost all day.* The clouds this morning hung down 3/5 of the way from the top and formed a varied picture among the peaks and buttresses along the river. Looking up river on right the line of cliffs at top and clouds down between each pair made them look immensely higher, while in one direction the clouds hung low and the top of one very prominent buttress shown out above in the clear, giving it the appearance of an immense mountain hanging *over* the river. Sun breaks through the clouds, lights up the outer points, and the clouds *skulk* away into the recesses.

High water mark little over 20 feet.

The colors of the long stretch above our camp are very regular.

First at bottom the "beaded" sandstone brown and dark, grassy slopes above.

Second, the limestone strata of 5 to 20 feet, dark brown, grey, yellow, dark green, and above higher ones of yellow and grey tinged with red.

Third, the red colored marble.

Fourth, the flame colored sandstone.

Start from camp in a gentle rain at 9:20 A.M. and at once run Rapid No. 299 and stop at 9:26 at head of No. 300. At 9:29 we run it, easy and small. At 9:32 stop to look at Rapid No. 301, about 1 1/2 miles below camp. We start at 9:45 and run No. 301. It is about 1/2 mile long, very high and *twisting* waves. I get wave after wave over me; and in making an exclamation one wave catches my mouth open and I swallow *nearly* the whole of it, so that I am wet from head to foot both inside and out. At 9:50 we run Rapid No. 302 without stopping, and at 9:53 stop in a lull of the rain to attempt a photo.

We start at 10:10 and at 10:15 stop on left bank at mouth of very *large side canyon* at head of Rapid No. 303. It is raining *hard* and we all go up the wash a short distance under a shelving cliff and wait for the rain and *lunch*.

Opposite this large side canyon the river is forced out by wash from canyon but line can cut both points as the slope is very wide.

On right there is a beautiful talus slope overlying the remnant of the "beaded" sandstone and the lower portions of the limestone strata. The slopes on right, and left also, get higher and higher. They are here 200 feet high running back to the upper benches of the limestone and in many places broad and flat.

The rain continues and in a little while small streams begin to pour over the top of the marble cliffs in every one of the *recesses* at the top and drop 600 to [blank] feet through the air to the limestone slopes below, and in a time run through the gullies and over the sandstone into the river. The fall is so far from top of marble that the streams break into spray before they strike. A wonderfully beautiful picture: the streams, the clouds playing back and forth in and out of the *alcoves* and up and down the buttresses and pinnacles on both sides of the river.

At 12:30 as we are sitting, resting after lunch, we heard a roar up the side canyon and looking up saw a stream of red water rushing down. Grab everything and run. Get across before it reaches us.

These flats and slopes cut by gullies the same as those in Cataract Canyon. Many little streams come over the marble in rain. These must be provided for in case several can be taken through one opening. All have good basins behind to catch in, which will save much work.

At 12:30 take photos from point lower side of large side canyon. Rapid No. 303 is formed by the large side canyon coming in on left. It has washed out great quantities of boulders, and formed this rapid which is fully one mile in length.

Start at 12:45 p.m. and run half of it. Land in eddy on right and examine. Start again at 1:01 and land at foot at 1:04 p.m. The "beaded" sandstone is rising and high water mark is up as much as 50 feet. We must be approaching the narrow granite gorge again.

We start at 1:30 and at 1:35 stop to look at Rapid No. 304. At 1:45 we run No. 304 and I again get drenched to the skin. We stop at 1:52 to look at No. 305. To save time while I take photos, the crews run Rapid No. 305 and wait for me below. These photos are taken at bend in river to left. 2:00 p.m. rain. Photos taken under an overhanging cliff 30 feet high. Project 10 feet to keep out of rain.

Start at 2:07 and run No. 305 and at 2:10 land to wait for sketch. We start again at 2:23 and at 2:25 see a good camping place, dry sand under shelving rock and plenty of wood. It is raining hard, and as we see the *granite* coming in again about a mile below we stop and go into Camp No. 88. Dry sand, a good shelter, and plenty of wood. But all our smoking tobacco is gone!!! [7]

The "beaded" sandstone which has now begun to rise so rapidly, has in fact never disappeared since the granite went out. It has gotten very low, showing only for some time only about 10 feet, though it may have been higher as it was covered with the debris of the limestone and marble above. To this point, Camp 88, the limestone or the marble has in fact never come down to the river

[7] During the four days February 18–21, the Stanton expedition negotiated eighteen miles of the Colorado flowing through a canyon of broad, sweeping meanders. The beauty of the grand geological spectacle of cliffs upon cliffs running from the river up to the snow-covered rimlands was not lost on the engineer who wrote about his feelings along with data on road-beds and bridges. The canyon profile had changed dramatically. Nine miles below Shinumo Creek the hard metamorphics of the Precambrian had gone under, revealing at close range the familiar horizontal sedimentary formations seen in lower Marble Canyon. Below the Granite Gorge the rapids were less troublesome and even exhilarating.

Swinging around the great bend below Conquistador Aisle, the explorers would have seen to their left a sharp, southward projection of Great Thumb Mesa (opposite Powell Plateau on the right) standing out on the skyline 4200 feet above the river. This bold peninsula of rock now bears the name Stanton Point, honoring the first man after John Wesley Powell to run the full length of the Grand Canyon. After dodging a flash-flood in Fossil Canyon, the surveyors went into Camp 88 at about mile 126, just at the head of the Middle Granite Gorge. It was a good and comfortable camp. Two essentials were missing, though. The sugar and tobacco were all gone!

at all. If it is really the granite coming in again below here, where are Powell's marble walls rising vertically from the water's edge? If I find it comes later on I will acknowledge [such].

High water 40 to 50 feet as the "beaded" sandstone gets higher and narrower. About 200 feet between the sandstone cliffs. They are 50 to 70 feet high.

SATURDAY, FEBRUARY 22, 1890.
Photos 1 mile above lower granite gorge, 7:45. The perpendicular cliff *is 30 feet high.*

We start at 8:12 A.M. and at 8:14 run Rapid No. 306. Quite easy. At 8:16 we land at head of Rapid No. 307. The bad part of this is short but very rocky, 5 or 6 foot drop. This rapid is formed by a large side canyon on right. Large through the marble but small in the "beaded" sandstone. Fifty to 80 foot span on *examination.* In the 1/2 mile above this are two 30 foot openings. At this side canyon the black glazed granite rises suddenly up and continues to rise as far as I can see.

At 8:25 we begin to let boats over Rapid No. 307 by lines. At 8:38 both boats are down and we start again at 8:43 A.M. At 8:45 we run Rapid No. 308, a small one. At 8:49 we run Rapid No. 309, a small one. Water along this north stretch is quite smooth after Rapid 307, but swift; and we are making beautiful time.

At 8:55 we land on left bank at right turn for photos: garden on top granite, [and] showing mountain with snow in distance.

We start again at 9:27. The water is smooth but swift. We stop at 9:33 at large side canyon on right which forms very bad rocky Rapid No. 310, 8 to 10 foot fall. Around this we *portage* all our stuff and *swing* our boat down with lines.

From point some miles back where "beaded" sandstone begins to rise, railroad line would be on top of this stratum until it rises too high for grade then cut it into river to make road bed on low water talus *now* under it. This would be the line till it reaches the granite. This then would serve as the low water talus and bank still [would] be made from sandstone above. Side was on right, 40 foot span. At this side wash, granite 60 to 70 feet high, forming a beautiful bench for line. High water about 30 to 40 feet.

From right turn, the granite rises rapidly, is of the slate kind. Stands with the strata dipping *into* the river from the right. The line would be rough but easily handled. The "beaded" sandstone is on top as before. Some of its points would perhaps have to be cut to give good alignment. This is the character to and for a short distance beyond side canyon, 80 foot span. At side canyon noted take photos.

The boats are down at 10:25. We load and start at 10:50. At 11:00 A.M. we land about 1 mile below on left side at head of Rapid No. 311 formed by side wash on left. It has 8 to 10 foot fall and is very very rocky. Boats are down by lines loaded by 11:30 and we stop for lunch.

We start at 12:30 and sail through a beautiful sheet of water on curve to left, till 12:50 when we land at head of Rapid No. 312 formed by side canyon on right, 60 foot span. While cook and I go up to take photos the boats at 12:55 P.M. [run Rapid No. 312] in about 3 minutes cross side canyon, 60 foot span, fine bench on lower side. There the granite is smashed to flinders as far as I can see to sharp turn to left.

1:00 P.M. photos from upper side of canyon. Shows the nearest approach to perpendicular granite walls we have seen in the Grand Canyon granite.

From the right side canyon just left for one mile, the right wall is much broken and the points stand up pretty straight, as the strata are much more vertical, 10° to 15° from vertical; but these points are easily cut. The tops of the highest are only 40 to 50 feet above railroad grade. On left side of canyon the slope is flatter.

From lunch point, side canyon on left, granite is very bold in points, but considerably broken up requiring simply to cut the points heavy, one or two 50 to 70 feet up. These however are only *points* 50 to 60 feet through and easily cut and thrown into river.

At 1:20 P.M. photos from point on lower side of canyon 1000 feet below last.

We start at 1:42 P.M. and at 1:47 stop at Rapid 313, and take photos. The rapid is easy, so to save time the boats at 1:55 run it, while we take the pictures, in one minute.

We start at 2:06 from foot of Rapid No. 313. At 2:19 we stop at head of No. 314, formed by large side canyon right. It is 1/2 mile long, immensely rocky, has about a 20 foot fall, and requires a portage. We start to work at 2:30 P.M. Portage the stuff and lower boats by lines, 2 men in, from rock to rock. The portage is made and boats lowered by. We load and start at 4:50 P.M.[8]

The granite from the last side canyon right to and around the turn to left is smashed all up and looks in shape and stands in forms like the Idaho lava. The slopes of the slopes are in general from 40° to 45° from perpendicular, are (1 side wash 50 foot span) generally regular and smooth and covered with

---

[8] Stanton's Rapid 314, probably Dubendorff Rapid (mile 131.6) between Galloway Canyon and Stone Creek, commemorates a 1909 river run from Green River, Wyoming, to Needles, California, organized by Julius F. Stone, who had been associated with Stanton in a Glen Canyon mining venture, 1897–1901. Nathaniel Galloway was guide and head boatman. Seymour S. Dubendorff, boatman, flipped a boat in this rapid, but he came out of it with no more damage than a bloodied head. In his account of the voyage, *Canyon Country* (1932), 94–95, Stone referred to "Dubie" as "gritty as a flapjack rolled in sand."

grass and greasewood. One 30 foot span. The general curve to left makes a beautiful line anywhere up the slope you wish. High water not over 20 feet up.

This takes us to side canyon on right, 80 foot span, forming Rapid No. 314. About 2000 feet below this is much larger side canyon, 100 foot span. This has not formed a rapid but comes into lower end of No. 314 without affecting it.

The rain of the past few days has been snow on top, for we see the distant high peaks covered with fresh snow, making a beautiful picture with the green trees shining out against the snow. 2:30 P.M. photos. Through this portion of the canyon the coloring below is not so bright as it was above where we entered the granite this time.

There came in at point noted where granite is smashed to flinders, a to me curious change. I must see Dutton's work. The granite dipped down very low to water and as it rose again on top of it was a layer of yellow and grey *limestone under* the beaded sandstone that has always heretofore been directly over the granite. This layer of limestone has increased in thickness, from a thin edge to about 100 feet, and lays between the granite and the beaded sandstone.

Fig. 42. Sunday camp at Tapeats Creek. *Robert B. Stanton*. Engineering Societies Library.

The slope above the sandstone runs up quite flat to the broken up portions at bottom of marble.

From the side canyon Rapid No. 314 the slopes for 3/4 mile down, past the next side canyon, 100 foot span, are the same as those above resembling the Idaho lava, and are quite flat and easy. This extends to the small side canyon about 1 1/4 miles above Tapeats Creek. At this point the wall on right changes altogether. It is composed of the same "lava" rock, and it stands at an angle of about 10° from vertical, and is from 50 to 80 feet high.

Above this cliff are good slopes, but, except at the point where it is only 50 feet high, are too far up for use. Line to be located here to cut and waste top of cliff and thrown into river to make bench. The whole is about 1 1/2 miles in length. On left side of this bend the slopes are very flat formed of debris from the upper cliffs.

At 4:55 run Rapid No. 315 without stopping. At 5:05 we stop on left bank and look for a campground. At 5:10 we run Rapid No. 316 easy and go into *Camp No. 89* at 5:12 P.M. at foot of Rapid No. *316* and about 3/4 mile *above Tapeats Creek*.

SUNDAY, FEBRUARY 23, 1890. *Cloudy, sprinkling*, occasionally all day.

I have been much puzzled for the last 3 or 4 days as to our position on the river, since our Camp No. 85. When McDonald left us we supposed we were at the mouth of *Shinumo* Creek; and taking our work from there on and the supposed distances we ran each day and the courses of the river, I thought we had passed the southern point of Powell's Plateau the evening of February 14th; and therefore I began to look for Kanab Wash on the evening of the 18th, and on the 19th supposed we were running the south and southwest courses from Kanab Wash. But I find this was not at all correct; and while all my notes in this book are correct *in detail* and description of the canyon and country, the position of our camps and photos are a long way out. We are today *camped* [at] No. 89 *about 1/2 mile* above Tapeats Creek. My notes as to position, etc., must therefore be all corrected for a long distance back. This can easily be done when I get to run my regular maps, as the notes are made by courses from one bend to the other noting right and left as they come. I have today changed the principle items in these notes.

3:00 P.M. photos one mile above Tapeats Creek, according to *corrected* distances. The palisades shown here commence 1/4 mile above at side canyon.

From our camp we can see two high clear rock peaks just beyond the Tapeats Creek on right of river. They are the first absolutely *barren* points I have noticed on the river. I think they are marble. The snow makes a beautiful appearance on the sides of the canyon making the *slopes* between the perpendicular cliff of marble and upper red sandstone quite white; and the higher ledges and the plateaus are heavily covered; and as the sun comes out, the whole picture lights up with a wonderful effect.

MONDAY, FEBRUARY 24, 1890. Bright sun. Cloudy by 8:30 A.M. Clear P.M. Heavy snow on top last night. This A.M. snow shows lower on the sides of the canyon than at any time this winter. The cook called me at 5:30 A.M. saying the river had risen 3 feet last night and all our goods on the bank were under water. But little damage to anything. No loss. Certainly a sudden rise.

We load up slowly as usual after a Sunday camp but got started at 7:40 A.M. At 7:48 we land on left bank opposite mouth of Tapeats Creek at Rapid No. 317. At 8:05 let loaded boats past head of rapid. The boats are down at 8:40 A.M.

8:00 A.M. photos, mouth of Tapeats Creek [and] down from mouth of Tapeats Creek.

The slopes on left bank are much flatter but would not give so good an alignment as on right.

We start at 8:47 and run the foot of the rapid and land on left bank at 8:52 at head of Rapid No. 318, about 1/8 mile below Tapeats Creek. This rapid is in two parts. We start at 9:06 run No. 318, and land in eddy at 9:08 A.M. 9:15 photo down from side canyon on each side about 1/4 mile below Tapeats Creek. We stop a while for Hislop to warm as he fell overboard in pushing boat by Rapid No. 317.

We start again at 9:36 and run No. 319 in three minutes and land in eddy left side. Rapid No. 319 is formed by wash on left and has some huge rocks in it. We go through safely with hardly a wave.

We walk ahead on left bank to look at Rapid No. 320. This is a regular ripsnorter. The current beats against the first rock so hard as to pile up 5 feet high and turn both ways in such force that nothing could live in it. We must go across let down by lines, and then we can run the rest. To save time I go ahead 1/2 mile and take photos at head of granite, and climb down the granite wall 50 to 60 feet into the boats. At 10:10 the crews row across, and at 10:45 have let down; and they run lower end at 10:52 A.M.

10:30 A.M. photos showing west side snow of Powell's Plateau head of granite 1 1/2 miles below Tapeats Creek, narrow granite gorge about 1 1/2 miles long.

Boats stop for us and we sail again at 11:00 A.M. At 11:15 we run small Rapid No. 321 and at 11:18 land on left bank at head of Rapid No. 322, and at end of granite. 11:30 photos showing lower end of granite patch, down river, [and] bridle fall at end of granite patch.[9]

Hislop is very wet so we stop for lunch.

[9] Both Tapeats Creek, a name employed by the Powell Survey, and Deer Creek Falls, so briefly described here as "Bridle Fall," are among the most popular stops on tourists runs of today. Powell's excellent description of these two places in his *Exploration of the Colorado River of the West* (1875), 92–93, apparently did not tempt the engineer to further exploration.

Fig. 43. Downstream at the mouth of Kanab Creek. *Robert B. Stanton.* Miami University Library.

A little way above Tapeats Creek and for the 1/4 mile below, a second lower bench formed. Saving some of the heavy cutting noted Saturday. Tapeats Creek, 150 foot span. At point beyond creek, 1/4 mile, all the granite and "*lava*" rock suddenly drops down and out, at this side wash, 50 foot span. Beyond this the slope is about 45°, is possibly limestone underneath, but is covered with sandstone debris from the beaded cliff above. This does not continue more than 1/2 mile where the granite suddenly rises up again. The granite rises very rapidly, and in 1/4 mile from first bend to right below Tapeats Creek is 80 feet high; and then the wall benches back to the sandstone.

These granite points are practically perpendicular but would cut a very small figure in a railroad line. Since high water is 35 feet and up, grade would be here at least 25 feet more and so would leave but little to cut down. Even with these I have not yet found a cliff 200 feet long and perpendicular, 50 feet above high water. The most prominent point does overhang 15 feet in points 50 feet long, which makes overhanging *points* but not *walls*.

Going through this piece of granite the walls are very ragged and broken into points which stand up very bold. Grade must be high and through these into river. No real difficulty for line. Below the granite on long right turn of river the slope is a great mountain slide of debris from above, undoubtedly overlying the "beaded" sandstone, which at end of granite has dropped out of sight. High water mark has again dropped to about 25 feet.

We lunch and then start at 12:55 and run Rapid 322 over 1/2 mile. In 3 miles both boats did beautiful steering among the rocks and waves. We go right on in smooth but swift water. We see cliff dwellings on left side.[10]

We stop at 1:05 to look at Rapid No. 323. It is clear of rocks but very high waves, a drop of 8 to 10 feet. Exciting river. Run it. Light at 1:15. Several waves all over the boats and at 1:17 land for photos from center of left curve.

We start at 1:40 and at 1:48 stop at Rapid No. 324. Not bad except close to cliff. At 1:55 run No. 324 very successfully without shipping any water. At 2:02 P.M. we run No. 325 without stopping. Strikes hard against left wall but we cut out very successfully. We stop at 2:08 to examine Rapid No. 326. One immense wave in it. Photos from second large side canyon above Kanab Wash.

At right turn of river the "beaded" sandstone jumps in a rough perpendicular wall 60 to 80 feet high, broken through occasionally by breaks, though of small washes, making large slopes up to marble above. This sandstone has a talus almost everywhere, a good part of which is above high water, so it will not be hard to make good alignment. This character continues around long swing of river to left. Two 50 foot spans on this swing to its center. At center, at Rapid No. 323 on right, beaded sandstone 100 feet high for a distance of 75 feet overhangs 20 to 30 feet.

We continue on long left turn, 1-50 foot span.

The "beaded" sandstone has sunk out entirely and there are immense mountain slopes running up to the marble, that is, the sandstone is covered up by the debris. This slope continues as far as we can see ahead.

---

[10] At about mile 138.4 the thirteen-mile-long Middle Granite Gorge ends. And here on the left side, several prehistoric granaries, noted by Stanton, are reported to be still visible. As the Precambrian rocks and the resistant Tapeats Sandstone capping them drop below the river level, the canyon profile changes again. Below Fishtail Rapid (RBS Rapid 326), mile 139, the canyon becomes narrow and steep-walled and the river fast. Sailing right along, the Stanton party went into camp at the mouth of Kanab Creek.

Rapid No. 326 [has an] immense wave curling over. Travers volunteers to run it first though Hislop was ready. He makes a most successful trip. Hislop follows in as good style. Not the most dangerous but the highest waves of any rapid yet run. At 2:50 Boat No. 2 ran No. 326, and at 2:55 Boat No. 1 ran No. 326, both very successfully.

Start 3:00 P.M. Stop 3:06 to examine No. 327. At 3:10 we run all [of] it, very swift but not high waves.

3:15 stop at No. 328 and at 3:20 run it. Get turned round at head and go down broadside, and then past some ugly rocks on left. We go stern foremost but turn easily below.

From Rapid No. 326 for four miles to Kanab Wash.

The water is very swift; the whole river moving as one but filled with great whirls and boils, but very small eddies. We came through this run in great style, though our boat was twisted and turned in every direction. Such good swift water, even with the whirls and cross currents was a great relief after the hard rapids of the day. At 3:33 run No. 329 without stopping.

3:45 stop on right bank and take photo showing regular talus mountain slope, taken just before river turns to right about 1/2 mile above *Kanab Wash*.

At 4:00 P.M. we start again, and at 4:12 P.M. we reach *Kanab Wash*. We cross Kanab and go into Camp No. 90 in willows on flat in Kanab Wash, 50 foot span on right.

Slope increasing on right side, not so high on left. This slope and 1 second [one] continues around bend to right to the side canyon on right, which proves to be Kanab Wash. The last 1/2 mile is about 60 to 70 feet with more broken points of marble above it before coming to the main marble cliffs. In the convex side as river turns to left, is side canyon which on reaching it we find to be *Kanab Wash*.[11]

5:00 P.M. photos from bank just above Kanab Wash.

---

[11] Kanab Creek, heading north on the high Paunsaugunt Plateau in Utah, is a major tributary of the Colorado River in Grand Canyon. Below Kanab in Utah and Fredonia in Arizona, the stream drops down through a narrow, meandering inner canyon which at river level reaches a depth of 1300 feet. Owing to its easy gradient, Kanab Canyon offers a ready access to the floor of Grand Canyon. John Wesley Powell ended his second river expedition here early in September 1872, and went out to Kanab, leaving his two boats behind. One can imagine how much Stanton hoped to find these boats to relieve the crowding in his own fleet. But before 1890, as Dellenbaugh, *A Canyon Voyage* (1902), 244, tells us, both boats had fallen victim to man and floods. Measured from Lee's Ferry, at Kanab Creek, the Stanton expedition had traveled just over half the distance through Grand Canyon.

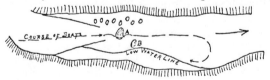

FIG. 44. Sketch map of Rapid 326. *Robert B. Stanton.* Miami University Library.

CHAPTER VIII

FAST RUN TO DIAMOND CREEK

It was a record run — 82 miles in five days. From Kanab Creek to Diamond Creek the Colorado was kind to the voyagers. During the first two days the fast water on the rising river was alarming, but there were few big rapids. Lava Falls was easily lined. As the surveyors moved along, Stanton noted the changing aspects of the canyon: the steep, precipitous walls above Lava Falls; the dramatic expression of volcanism below the falls; the widening canyon at Granite Park. Before reaching Diamond Creek, the explorers had entered the Lower Granite Gorge. As the expedition moved along, Stanton was kept very busy with notebook and camera. Always the optimist, he found good alignments all along the way and few serious obstacles to railroad building.

TUESDAY, FEBRUARY 25. *Clear.* Very cloudy and sprinkling since 10 A.M. all day.

River raised again last night. It must now be 5 to *6 feet* higher than Sunday A.M.[1]

We stop this A.M. to make survey at mouth of Kanab Canyon which makes us late in starting.

At Kanab Wash is Rapid No. 330, fully 1 1/2 miles long formed by boulders and waste from Kanab moved down canyon. Not high wave but very swift. I stood up all way down No. 330.

---

[1] During the two days, February 25–26, 1890, the Stanton expedition made a fast run down to Lava Falls, a distance below Kanab Creek of 35.5 miles. The rapids were few, and they were all run, including Upset Rapid, mile 149.7 (probably RBS 355), though some were run "light," i.e., without extra passengers. Throughout this section the inner canyon was dominated by precipitous walls, many of them nearly vertical, and Stanton was put to it in places to find a location for the railroad. He was kept busy keeping up with the photographs and notes. The rain and rising water on the 25th, and the great waves breaking upstream, made it "a most trying and worrying day" for the engineer. The waves, so graphically described by Stanton, appear to have been similar to the "sand waves" commonly seen at flood stage on the San Juan River in Utah before the construction of Glen Canyon Dam.

We start 8:35 and at 8:37 entered the rapid and make the first mile by 8:43 when we stop to look. At 8:50 we go again and make 1/2 mile in about 3 minutes including starting and stop.

We land 1000 feet above Rapid No. 331 made by side canyon on right, 50 foot span and though it is not difficult at Hislop's request we run this "light." At 9:10 ran No. 331 and landed in eddy in 3 minutes for photos between 1 1/2 and 2 miles below Kanab, 3/4 mile above bend to right, first below Kanab.

We start 9:30 and stop at 9:34 at No. 332. *Canyon* left. It is rough but clear. Start 9:40 and run No. 332 and stop at 9:45 to wait for No. 2 caught in whirl. Wait 2 minutes.

Just before entering Rapid 332, No. 2 caught in immense whirlpool on left side, is turned and turned round, no power to get her out. Gets in vortex and one side of boat is drawn down so water pours over gunwale, by no effort of men; but the whirl shoots them up and out. As we go over No. 332 we see them go into whirl. The water is so piled up, back current between us, that we can only see their heads over *hill* of water. In coming down *we* got broadside in rapid, then turn, stern down, and then round. Boat entirely out of control.

From Kanab down the talus is much lower but the top is still above high water and the bottom bench of marble is easily broken down for material.

Note 2 miles below Kanab. The talus has almost disappeared, entirely so above high water. But the first bench of marble is lower and the limestone below has some bench. And about 1 mile ahead a big talus shows up. From Kanab to that point the line will be *expensive* to cut the marble bench to make roadbed.

The river is still rising. The current is very swift and getting more so. The whole distance is like one low continuous chute and the ride is very exciting. I stand in bow of No. 1 and look out ahead for rapids and rocks. We get sometimes caught in whirls and boils and thrown first one way and then the other, and sometimes round and round, from one side of the river to the other. This is in the 4.75 feet per mile fall so this is all caused by this sudden rise of ten or more feet which was noted above, and of course here where it is narrower *much more*.

Stop at 10:00 A.M. for photos 1/2 mile above sharp turn to right.

Start at 10:20 and at 10:22 run Rapid 333 and at 10:24 run Rapid 334. Not very heavy but swift on account of high water.

Around long right bend the cliffs are much broken and will give a much easier line than the first part described from Kanab down. At center of this bend, canyon on right, 60 foot span.

We turn sharp bend to right at 10:25. All round this sharp right bend cliff is much broken, and the points are high. They are easily cut. *Around* the *point* is a fine bench on top the fossiliferous limestone the right height, the lower edge

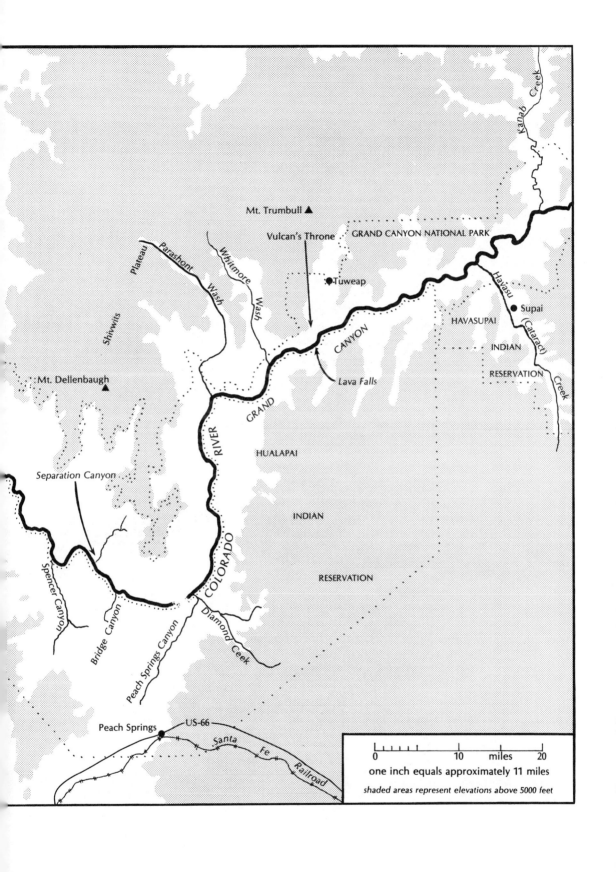

Mt. Trumbull ▲

Vulcan's Throne

GRAND CANYON NATIONAL PARK

Plateau

Parashont Wash

Whitmore Wash

Shivwits

●Tuweap

Havasu

● Supai
(Cataract)

HAVASUPAI

INDIAN

RESERVATION

Creek

Kanab Creek

CANYON

Lava Falls

●Mt. Dellenbaugh ▲

GRAND

RIVER

HUALAPAI

Separation Canyon

COLORADO

INDIAN

Spencer Canyon

Bridge Canyon

Peach Springs Canyon

Diamond Creek

RESERVATION

Peach Springs ● ——US-66——

Santa

Fe

Railroad

0		10	miles	20	

one inch equals approximately 11 miles

shaded areas represent elevations above 5000 feet

Fig. 45. Lunch stop. The steep, precipitous walls of the inner canyon below Kanab Creek. Where do you build a railroad here? *Robert B. Stanton.* Miami University Library.

being above high water, and a fine slope on top; and the curve is regular and little work as far as I can see ahead.

Stop at head of Rapid No. 335 about center of turn to left 10:35 A.M. *Quick stop* necessary. Very quick run, only few hundred feet from head of rapid. Not difficult but very rough on account of rise of river. Enlarge stop and shelving rock, jump, etc.

River must be still rising. Heavy rains above. Heavy clouds over us now and cold damp wind.

This section around this quick curve to left is very simple. The bench is entirely above high water. The slope is rock, the stratified limestone only covered with debris.

At center of turn to right, side canyon 60 to 80 foot span. This is long turn to left after sharp right turn. The walls of the marble above slope are as nearly perpendicular as they are made, *but* the fine bench and slope make a railroad independent of these perpendicular walls.

At 10:54 start and run No. 335. No. 1 misses the high waves but No. 2 goes over them all. Through it in 2 minutes. Stop in eddy below. At 11:15 we start and run in same swift current till at 11:30 stop for photos and conclude to lunch. Photos from point just above *sharp* turn to left at end of long turn to left.

All around the left turn beyond side canyon on right the line improves. The stratified fossiliferous limestone is getting higher and the marble is much broken on its lower benches.

Grandeur of this section from Kanab down, all marble except lower strata of fossiliferous limestone. Colors not so bright as above. General impression of *perpendicular* walls, etc. Wonderful ride all morning. Exciting and somewhat dangerous. Sharp turns. Going so fast cannot tell what is ahead. Sharp lookout. [It was a] quick and exciting stop at head of No. 335.

After lunch we start at 12:45 P.M. As we turn on south course beautiful peak with this top comes in view covered with snow. Just after lunch we turn the sharp left bend and get on the south course. All round and on this south course walls same as last cross section and *photos* taken at lunch. Drainage all along to be provided for small streams from top of cliff. This same character of wall and line continue around next swing to right, as above. Some places the limestone is higher and at others lower. The line to be located high up and so cut the points not so badly.

We stop at 12:56 to look ahead. Start at 1:07 and run Rapid No. 336. At 1:09 we get in whirls and eddies and waltz around at great rate for a few minutes. At 1:13 land at head of No. 337 and at Hislop's request run it light. At 1:22 stop in eddy. At 1:24 and at 1:27 start again and at 1:38 land to look ahead.

Very hard to land. Current more swift. Walls vertical and overhanging points for 50 feet up from water. Land at last on few rocks. Hislop and Kane climb up cliff and go ahead. Huge rock in center of river; clear channel right side. At 2:05 start; whole current draws toward rock and we are *nearly drawn on i·* but go through without a scratch. Marble rock very sharp. Total destruction to strike it.

We stop at 2:10 to take photos. A most trying and worrying day to me; the rapid water, rising, raining, attempting to take notes, etc., etc.

We start at 2:25 and run Rapid No. 338, and at 2:30 to look ahead, thinking we saw a rapid. We start at 2:38 and again stop at 2:40 to see great rapid
ahead, and when we get to it find it only rolling waves. When we stopped to
look ahead at 2:30 P.M. we thought we saw a bad rapid ahead on left side.
When we got ahead a little on shore there was nothing in sight but swift smooth
water. We started again and ran 5 minutes when all three of us, Hislop,
Travers, and myself, saw again a heavy rapid with breaking waves ahead. We
land with great difficulty and walk down the talus, but there is no rapid. We
walk ahead 1/2 mile to where the waves are breaking, and after studying them
for some time, find that it is an immense body of water moving down the river
from what we suppose to be a great cloud burst above. We watch them carefully and the waves rise up gradually as they move down the river to 12 to
15 feet high and the whole width of the river, 150 to 200 feet, and they break
upstream just as a huge breaker at sea.

A half dozen of these rise and roll and break with a great roar and then
they subside and the water settles down. The same movement is repeated a
little distance down, and then further and further. Now they begin again
opposite us and the whole operation is gone through with again. This occurs
at regular intervals; and as these waves are of such force, the bends in the river
so sharp, and the current so swift on account of the rise, it is difficult to land
and difficult to see the rapids ahead. I fear we may be drawn into one of these
swells just as we approach a rapid, and unable to get out of it be carried over
the rapid *with it*. This I believe would be utter destruction to the boats and to
the men's lives. Hence I conclude to stop where we are till morning believing
this "tidal wave" will subside, and not thinking it right to run such a risk without more thought.

It is hard to imagine the force and grandeur of the phenomenon: the greatness of the stream, the height and width of the waves, the narrow canyon, the
towering walls, our perfect helplessness on the water, our boats like little chips
tossed from one side to the other, turned round and round and perfectly unmanageable; and it is something, something to inspire awe and caution.

We go into Camp No. 91 on right bank, [*blank*] miles below Kanab Wash.
Worrying day. Lovely evening. Find sack of tobacco. *Watch boats*, build up
bed, and sleep well at last. Rocky Camp No. 91.

Note from back. In Rapid No. 335 No. 2 boat badly taken over the high
waves. One rowlock washed out and are carried far below before they can
land. We carry their two extra men down to them, and have a hard pull to get
there out of eddy and whirls. We have actually to pull up on a *mound* of
water. My *paddle* comes in fine play.

After the river makes the *sharp* turn to left, with side canyon right, 80 foot
span, and enters on the general southwest course, it makes 4 large swings first
right then left, etc. We are camped about center of the first of these to right.

WEDNESDAY, FEBRUARY 26, 1890. Still cloudy. Drizzling rain at times all day. The river *fell* last night about one foot.

Almost everyone gruff and grim this morning because we had bread, mush, bacon, and coffee for breakfast. I did not let the cook bake hot biscuits last night; and this morning because knowing how low our stores are I wanted in this way to cut down on the amount of consumption with putting the party on half rations, which I am afraid will have to be done before we reach Diamond Creek.

We pack up and start at 7:45 A.M. Rapid No. 339 at 7:52. Rapid No. 340 at 8:00. [Neither] not large but immensely swift, by high water. Stop at 8:07 for photos on next right bend from Camp 91.

At point of Camp No. 91, the first bench of marble is about 100 feet high; but as the canyon here is narrow and waste would raise the water very rapidly, our line must be located quite high.

After photos taken we start at 8:20 and at 8:25 run Rapid No. 341. At 8:30 A.M. we ran Rapid No. 342 with very swift current at foot of it, and but a short distance from it to next Rapid No. 343. Between these, we encounter a great *swell* such as described yesterday. We are carried through this swell and are turned *quartering* and as our boat rises and falls over these waves 10 feet high, we are certainly rocked in the cradle of the deep. We are approaching the rapid below and attempt to pull out of current, but in a moment find it impossible. Then by great effort of Hislop at stern and I with paddle at bow, we turn boat head on and go into the rapid. With the swell and the rapid at same time we get an awful shaking up and a wetting from head to foot; but our good boat rides it safely at 8:35 A.M.

Notes before 9:00 A.M. kept on piece of paper on account of rain.

In Rapid No. 343 our boat after starting in at head "bow to," was caught between two waves and in an instant whisked round; and we went down through the greater part of the rapid in a regular waltz and finally stern first, a dangerous and exciting ride, the boat entirely unmanageable, and at the mercy of the whirls and eddies. This just at beginning of right turn. In this last rapid I *got wet wet and I am almost frozen.*

One very important item must be remembered on all this fine bench. Besides the *spans* here noted *drainage* must be provided for a great number of small streams that come down from the very top of the marble at every little *crevice.* I think this is much helped by the fact that most of them have basins washed out into which they first drop. *This is very important* to study.

The same fine bench continues around this *right* turn, about the same distance above river. At the *point* of turn the marble above is quite rough and requires some heavy cutting.

At 8:49 we run Rapid No. 344 on the northwest course and at 9:50 No. 345 at beginning of short left turn. Stop at 8:55 at head of Rapid No. 346, at side canyon on right nearly opposite point of left sharp turn. Land on left side and take photos at 9:00 A.M.

This rapid is a very dangerous one. The whole current beats against the left wall, no talus, and rolls out in one great boil 6 to 8 feet high which would be utter destruction to get into. By starting up high and getting good speed at start we believe it is safe. To be sure, all extra men are landed on right bank and it is run light in good shape. Around this sharp bend to left, the splendid first bench continues even more smooth than before, and being on outside of curve makes beautiful alignment. [End of pre-9:00 A.M. notes kept separately.]

Same general formation of canyon on this southwest course as we had all yesterday afternoon. At and around right bend just below Camp No. 91 the points that rise above the general level of the railroad bench are very abrupt and high. The cutting would be very heavy but easily handled. Around left bend same good bench as before. This continues around next right turn and down stretch to next left turn. But it is noticeable that the bench on left wall is smoother than on right.

9:00 A.M. photos opposite side canyon on sharp turn to left, after northwest course. Side canyon, 60 foot span.

Start 9:32 and run Rapid No. 346 in 2 minutes, light, and wait for men. Start again at 9:42 and at 9:47 run small Rapid No. 347. Stop at 10:00 at head of Rapid No. 348, large side canyon on left. Start and run No. 348 at 10:13, quite long and rough at bottom.

Stop at 10:20 for photos a little above where river first, 1 mile, turns to left after canyon on right. [One] shows Mt. Emma in the distance.

We start at 10:33. 10:35 run small Rapid No. 349. Stop at 10:43. Stop at head of No. 350. Side canyon on right, 100 foot span. Run this rapid light at 10:55 and at 11:00 A.M. we stop for *lunch* at end of second short northwest course at large side canyon on right.

After lunch we start at 12:27 P.M. At 12:45 stop and take photo about 2 miles above *Cataract Creek*. We start again at 12:48 and at 1:00 P.M. run Rapid No. 351.

The 2 miles above Cataract Creek is a most wonderful and beautiful view. The wide canyon, after the narrow above lunch, broad river, high talus slopes covered with green above high water mark, variegated colored walls mostly red with *bright* red in distance and the wonderful shapes of the *benched* walls!!!

All round this sharp turn to left a beautiful bench, lowest part 30 feet above high water, more regular than some further back, and being on outside curve is *good* alignment.

We begin now to turn to right again. The canyon is *widening out* on the stretch beyond the first right turn, the bench *same* as before. Notable fact, this bench keeps right with the *grade* of *the river*. High water mark all through

Fig. 46. Profile sketches of the canyon looking upstream and downstream a short distance above Rapid 350. *Robert B. Stanton.* Miami University Library.

here 25 feet. The same bench continues in same general form to and around the left turn past our lunch point at end of second northwest course. From lunch point on the first bench that we have had all day seems to be getting higher, and as the canyon gets wider a high talus slope is forming at bottom under the marble.

One-fourth mile below lunch point the talus increases at a 45° slope to from 75 to 100 feet high, and it is underlaid by solid rock slope of the horizontally stratified limestone; and it will be easy to come down from the fine railroad bench we have had all yesterday and today to this fine talus slope just after crossing the side canyon at our lunch point. Two 30 foot *overheads* here.

At 1:05 P.M. the stratified limestone is rising and a stratum of grey lime shows above the water on both sides.

At 1:15 P.M. we run long shallow Rapid No. 352 formed by large side canyon on right. At 1:17 land at foot 1/4 mile above Cataract Creek on left. 1:30 P.M. photo from Cataract Creek up. Start at 1:40 and at 1:44 run Rapid No. 353 formed by Cataract Creek.[2] Stop in eddy to pick up photos at 1:47. Start again and at 1:49 P.M. and at 1:52 run Rapid No. 354.

[2] Cataract Creek, a name first appearing on the map issued in 1861 by the government survey under J. C. Ives, is now Havasu Creek. Together with the Little Colorado and Diamond Creek, it is one of the largest left bank tributaries in the Grand Canyon region. Fed by numerous tributaries and springs, the stream heads south and east on the Coconimo Plateau and flows through a winding canyon well over thirty-five miles long.

About seven miles from the river where the canyon widens a bit, the Havasupai Indians have lived for some centuries. Below their village at Supai, the turquoise-blue waters of the creek drop down over five dramatic waterfalls before entering the Colorado through a narrow gorge 2,200 feet deep.

After turning to left the 2 miles above Cataract Creek opens up, beautiful; talus slope all the way to large canyon on right, 150 foot span. Under strata rising up and marble receeding and canyon getting *wider*.

Opposite Cataract Creek the talus on right side is washed out by the river being forced over by the wash from Cataract Creek. Below this, however, the talus is much larger than even above the creek. The canyon is gradually widening out and as it does the benches of the marble get more frequent up the sides of the canyon. The stretch to and around left turn below Cataract Creek, the talus is getting higher and broader and the benches of marble are getting more frequent and closer together. Half way down this stretch side canyon on right, 50 foot span.

At 2:00 P.M. we stop 7 minutes for Hislop to shoot a duck. But he misses it. At 2:18 we run Rapid No. 355, and at 2:28 stop at large side canyon on right, 80 foot span. Start at 2:43 and at 2:44 run this long letter S Rapid No. 356, 3/4 mile in 4 minutes. This would have been very shallow and rocky but for the rise in river.

At 2:50 we run Rapid No. 357, and stop at 2:53 for photos from center of southwest course.

We start again at 3:10 P.M. and at 3:12 run Rapid No. 358. At 3:16 run Rapid No. 359. At 3:19 run Rapid No. 360.

General character of these rapids that we run right along without stopping — a sharp drop at head, swift water; two currents, one from each side meeting high waves; high water now; dashed one side and then other; but clear of rocks; and boats that so far can ride anything.

At 3:25 we run Rapid No. 361. At 3:30 we run Rapid No. 362. At 3:32 we run Rapid No. 363.

Just at turn to right into a general west course, and at 3:35 pass the 1st lava monument *in* river spoken of by Powell.

On this southwest course shown in photos there is a magnificent talus slope high and broad at one point. The whole side of the canyon is broken in one slope to the very top. The walls lower down are one series of benches, some wider than others and all covered with green grass and greasewood bushes.

The lower part of this southwest course the strata of limestone are rising and slopes getting higher and higher, the canyon widening out; and at foot of slope formed on the stratified limestone has a 10 to 20 foot cliff at foot of it, and another talus forming below it.

Land at 3:40 P.M. to take photos 1/4 mile past turn to west course. Beautiful view down river, wonderful change, etc.

Black lava in two immense cliffs. Hills in distant barren rock, cone shaped. Cinder cones on left. Beautiful slopes at bottom, winding quiet river, and perfect stillness. Green bushes and flowers. Grass, etc., at foot, all commingled. Make beautiful grand and awe inspiring picture. Extinct volcano, etc., etc.

FIG. 47. Some of the dramatic expressions of volcanism between Lava Falls and Whitmore Wash. Stanton wrote that the scenery was beautiful through this section and railroad construction would be cheap (1965 Photo). *Parker Hamilton.* C. Gregory Crampton.

Hasty note: Canyon divides into sections. Close granite widens out. Fine slopes. Closes again to Bridal Falls [Deer Creek Falls]. Widens out with fine talus to Kanab Wash. From Kanab to nearby lunch point of February 26, close again. This widens out *to* lava, etc., etc.

We start at 4:02 in quiet water and soon hear the great roar so familiar, and at 4:20 P.M. stop at head of the great cataract formed by the lava dike and go into Camp No. 92 on left bank. This lava cataract is No. 364.

Hasty Note: Wonderful ride all day Tuesday and till lunch on Wednesday 26t'. Stand in bow, look round corners. Swift current swells, small eddies, hard stops. Jump and hold on to line. Whirlpools. Look at rapids ahead. Don't stop by waves, try to stop, can't. Exciting, awful, and dangerous but no other way. Walls on each side for 50 to 80 feet, perpendicular, etc., etc.

THURSDAY, FEBRUARY 27, 1890. Clear all day. River fell 2 feet last night. Cleared off last night and turned terribly cold. I suffered more from cold this morning than any day this winter.

Everyone frozen. Have to go into the water so we wait till sun comes over cliff. We Hislop, Travers, and myself, walk down and look at rapid. Conclude to skid boats on left side, of this great cataract Rapid No. 364. We also look at No. 365, the second fall about 1/4 mile below. Think we can run it well.

Hislop sets fire to grass in swamp formed by the great springs on left bank. Commence portage at 9:00 A.M., made; and boats skidded down over rocks on left side at 11:00 A.M. and packed up in 15 minutes. They wait for me, for photos, made necessary by the smoke from Hislop's big fire. We then eat lunch to save another stop. Photos taken at mouth of fissure on left bank opposite volcano.

Note the fissure, springs, swamp. Great wash of boulders from fissure, cut through later 50 to 60 feet deep and also by river. The fault on left side, etc., etc.

We start after lunch from foot of Rapid (cataract) No. 364 at 1:05 P.M. and at 1:10 land on opposite side to take photos. At 1:16 boats run No. 365 with ease, light, and land 1:18. New rolls. 1:15 P.M. photo, 1/2 mile below volcano opposite fault.

The same magnificent talus continues past the right turn that enters on the general west course and to the volcano. Along the lava the talus is not as heavy but it is continuous and can be made permanent notwithstanding the cataract by dropping huge blocks of lava for base of bank. The lava is not perpendicular but is benched back considerably. The fall of this cataract No. 364 is about 15–18 feet in 200, and rapid below.[3]

From the volcano the line would be on good slopes, but not even as they come out in great banks, making more work. One 30 foot span. Some lava *slide* on top. Think it is solid underneath.

We start at 1:35. Run No. 466 [366] at 1:37. Run No. 467 [367] at 1:38. Run No. 468 [368] at 1:42. Run No. 469 [369] at 1:56. Easy rapids, 2 to 4 foot fall.

---

[3] Less than a mile past the "lava monument in the river" (Vulcan's Anvil and other names), the Stanton party went into camp on the left bank at the head of Lava Falls (RBS 364). Named by the Powell Survey, Lava Falls Rapid is the big one in Grand Canyon; the one most feared. On a scale of one to ten, Lava rates a ten in nearly everyone's book. Given the lore that built up about the rapid as one of the worst drops in the West, Stanton's approach to it was anticlimatic. As head of only the second party of definite record to float the Colorado at this point, Stanton lined the rapid on the left side as Powell had done. He skidded the boats over the rocks and portaged the baggage; all through in two hours flat. Stanton's estimate of the rapid's fall is about right. Lava drops thirty-seven feet and twenty feet of that occurs within the first hundred yards. See Chapter Ten, "Lava Falls" in R. O. Collins and R. Nash, *The Big Drops* (1978), for an analysis of the rapid and its place in white water lore.

General explanation of their character: rapids not difficult but high waves, twisting and curling, so as to toss boat badly and the bow dives under and ships water.

Opposite third lava pile, we stop at 2:00 P.M. on left bank just below beginning of big turn to right for photos.

Start again at 2:20 P.M. At 2:21 run Rapid No. 470 [370]. At 2:24 run Rapid No. 471 [371] at right turn. At 2:27 run Rapid No. 372. At 2:30 run Rapid No. 373. At 2:33 run Rapid No. 374, long, takes till 2:36. At 2:37 run No. 375, quite sharp.

At the lower volcanic pile just above last turn to left before big turn to right, the lava and beyond it, the marble stands up very bold. Marble 500 feet long, 100 to 110 feet high, but has talus in patches under it, 1:55 P.M. Just beyond this as river turns to right, the talus grows very large, with abrupt points breaking through talus. One 30 foot span at the extreme turn to right.

Lava comes out bold in a point; 800 foot tunnel through it brings on to good talus. The lava has run down river and shows on side cooled in fantastic shapes. Fans, screens, etc., etc. At 2:45 we stop for photo up river after long left swing just before river turns to right again. Lava all through here, run down the canyon, filling the breaks, etc., and washed out again. Hot time then!!! [4]

Start again at 3:00 P.M. At 3:01 P.M. run Rapid No. 376, [and] at 3:04 P.M. run Rapid No. 377. All along here patches of lava, mostly on right side of canyon. From tunnel point around the left swing beyond, the wall stands vertical at 80 to 100 feet. At its base is a talus all the way. The first 1 1/2 miles this talus is small but this can easily be supplied from slope above. River broad, plenty of room. The talus increases rapidly as we go down till at end of the left swing it is 75 feet at 45° slope. High water 25 feet, photo.

And at commencement of next right turn the slope is a regular mountain. Just before stretch before turn, to right, side canyon, 80 foot span. All round this stretch and the right turn and along the stretch before river turns to left same great talus with occasional points of lava jutting out and smaller talus under them. No trouble to line. All *under* cliffs.

---

[4] One of the striking features of the western section of Grand Canyon below Lava Falls is the boldly manifest evidence of recent volcanism in the form of intracanyon flows, lava cascades from the rims, dikes, and cinder cones. Volcanic displays are notably prominent between Lava Falls and Whitmore Wash, but volcanic features are visible from the river for over eighty miles below Lava Falls. Powell viewed the lava cascades and Vulcan's Throne (Stanton's "Volcano"), perched on the canyon rim, both in the immediate vicinity of Lava Falls, as remarkable geological phenomena. Stanton saw these and other features down the canyon as interesting aspects of nature, but primarily as obstacles to railroad building. For the engineer there was always a feasible way for the railroad. Across the lava cascades he would have to drop "huge blocks of lava" for the base of the roadbed, and downstream at about mile 183 an 800-foot tunnel would have to be built through a prominent lava point. Stanton is still holding to the right of the canyon where he has maintained the survey since crossing the river at Point Retreat in Marble Canyon.

At 3:23 we come to turn to left. Stop at 3:23 for photo up river 1/2 mile, up S 70° or so, west course from turn to left course. Shows lava and benched form of marble.

Start at 3:33 and at 3:35 run Rapid No. 378, huge rocks in center. We go left of it and shoot by, not an oar length off.

Stop at 3:43 above *large* side *canyon* on right course, N 45° W. Start 3:54 and run No. 379 at 3:55. Long rough curling waves. And No. 380 at 4:00 P.M.

Stop at 4:06 for photos 3/4 mile above sharp turn to right below large side canyon.

Immense slopes between the jutting points all along this afternoon's run.

The general character of the canyon, from the volcano to our Camp No. 93 is that of a line railroad on good easy mountain slopes with the points of lava and sometimes marble jutting out close to the river; and this has caused the river to wash away the talus; but the points are not high, not over 80 feet, and as the river is wide and not very heavy fall, a permanent line can be built under these cliffs cheaply.

Some special points are noted as we passed them.

From large side canyon, 100 foot span. To this last right turn where we camp tonight, there is one of these lava cliffs and then broad high slopes. The alignment could not be more beautiful. Only the one little short tunnel through the lava point.

Start at 4:20 P.M. Run long shallow rapid at 4:23, No. 381. At 4:25 see flock of mountain sheep on left bank 150 feet up. Stop and two men go after them, but failed to get any.

We go into Camp No. 93 opposite next sharp turn to right, about 1 mile below the side canyon on right passed above. All our meat is gone. We have plenty of good rice, flour, oatmeal, corn meal, peaches, and coffee.

The general character of canyon from volcano not so grand as that above. Volcanic action *very interesting*. Lava must have filled up the canyon, largely deposits in crevices high up. *Hunt this up.*

General scenery not so grand as above but wonderful. Colors are dull. Shapes and forms beautiful. Generally rounded as if more worn by some action, and generally much lower. *Hunt this up.* Some beautiful scenery at points, as we turn bends of high points and curious profiles.[5]

FRIDAY, FEBRUARY 28, 1890. Clear, all day.

At the sharp point to right at Camp No. 93 the red granite comes up to about 25 feet high with the same "beaded" sandstone on top, and over it at

---

[5] Passing the mouth of Whitmore Wash and Rapid (RBS 379), Stanton took note of the "very interesting" aspects of volcanism through this section, and of the "beautiful" align-

the point. Quite a pile of lava, on right side of river. On left side where camp is another pile of lava all broken into basaltic shapes, as is the case at many places above here.

Start at 7:53. Run Rapid 382 at 7:55. We started into this rapid this A.M., early for the thermometer to be only +29°; and it took us in good earnest, wave after wave, 3 in so quick time that I could not breathe between them. Went all over me so that I was drenched to my skin. More water went over me and into the boat than at any one rapid we have run yet. My clothes froze on the outside, ice all over the boat; and when we stopped to make fire and photo we had to thaw out the instruments before we could work!!!

Stop at 8:05 for photos, spoiled.

While we take photos at 8:18 boats run Rapid No. 383. Shallow gravel, light and easy. Stop for us at 8:22.

Start 9:18 after getting warm at fire. Run Rapid No. 384 at 9:20. Run Rapid No. 385 at 9:23. Run Rapid No. 386 at 9:33. Run Rapid No. 387 at 9:40, [all] shallow gravel rapids. In many places the lava shows where it ran over gravel banks now 10 feet below high water mark, showing river was as low as now when lava ran. One place at level of present low water, at *bottom* of this, very large basal forms.

Stop at 9:42 for photos at large side canyon on left. Side canyon nearly north and south.

The granite drops out 1 mile below. Fine bench on granite all the way. The sand and limestone drop again forming 100 to 150 foot talus, 1-30 foot waterway, around right turn and down stretch. River then turns left, and in short distance turns sharp to right. On this stretch the lava on right. Lava stands up vertical 30 to 40 feet with great slope on top. Line on top of lava. High water, 20 feet.

Canyon widening. Around this right turn runs back 1000 to 1500 feet in irregular benches. This continues all round point to next stretch.

We start again at 10:05 and run Rapid 388 at 10:08. Run Rapid 389 at 10:11. Run Rapid 390 at 10:15. Stop at 10:23 at large side canyon left. Run No. 391 from side canyon on left, large, at 10:28.

Stop at 10:30 for photo down from large side canyon on left, stretch 1 mile below northwest. Opposite this point the lava has run on gravel bed on top of granite and since then river has cut through lava and 20 feet into the granite.

I am almost frozen.

At next turn of river to left after the large side canyon on left, all round left bend marble low, broken back in low slope to top. Good talus below, 1-60 foot span [and] 1-20 foot span.

---

ments for the railroad. Camp 93 was on the left bank at about mile 189.7. In this general area mountain sheep are frequently seen by modern voyagers.

At turn to right, same lava bank rises with great slope on top. Easy to throw off the lava at the points and get line as low as wished. After this turn the next small left and right turn and down the northwest stretch, the marble slopes back with many breaks and benches and a general flat slope with *great* talus at foot. Simple and easy.

We start at 10:53 and at 10:55 run Rapid No. 392, shallow gravel. 11:00 run Rapid No. 393, shallow gravel. 11:04 run Rapid No. 394, shallow gravel. 11:08 run Rapid No. 395, shallow gravel. 11:10 run Rapid No. 396, shallow gravel. 11:20 run Rapid No. 397, shallow gravel.

The canyon from the volcano to northwest course, just before lunch, has been "all broke up." It seems to me (see Dutton) to have been upheaved in many places by the volcanic action, and to have been vastly more washed out than the districts above. The marble does not stand in vertical cliffs on its benches as above but is split up in all manner of forms and shapes as if stratified both vertically and horizontally though the most of the breaks are vertical (see Dutton). There were some more solid forms just after lunch but did not last long.

Very *remarkable the distance* the lava has run down canyon.

One 30 foot, 4-20 foot, 1-50 foot, 1-10 foot, [and] 1-60 foot spans on the northwest course and around left turn to right point. These are the large openings. No account is taken of *small* waterways.

At point turn to right marble comes out bold, canyon narrows, 2-20 foot spans. Talus in patches all round point. Very easy to make bank. River is wide. High water not over 15 feet. After point, granite higher but large talus.

We land at 11:30 A.M. on right bank around this left turn at large side canyon on right where river turns to general S 10° W course.

12:30 P.M. photos at large side canyon on right.

Start after lunch at 1:10 P.M. and at 1:12 run No. 398, shallow. 1:14 run No. 399, heavy rocks. 1:15 run No. 400, heavy rocks. 1:18 run No. 401, light. All formed by the wash from large side canyon where we lunched. I walked because I was cold and wet.

Stop at 1:17 and start again at 1:25 P.M. Since northwest course the canyon is getting grander. The walls are rising and the walls are growing like those above volcano, though much *more* benched as river begins again to turn to left lava cliff 30 foot above talus, 600 to 800 feet long. Easy to handle good line. Two 20 foot spans.

Good talus below lava bench all around left turn, 1-40 foot span [and] 1-10 [foot] span. This brings to large side canyon on right. Course of side canyon about N 45° W, 100 foot span.

Beyond this to general right turn of river, the fine large talus continues 1 1/2 miles.

Three 20 foot, 1-50 foot, 1-20 foot, 1-20 foot, 1-20 foot, 1-20 foot, [and] 1-30 foot waterways to right turn at Rapid 304. These are the openings down N 20° W stretch.

At 1:27 run Rapid No. 402, brisk. At 1:30 run Rapid No. 403, light.

Run Rapid No. 404 at 1:43 P.M., long gravel by side wash on right. At 1:50 run Rapid No. 405, gravel.

At 1:53 stop for photos at end of S 20° W course where river *begins* to make turn for its *Southeast* course.

This 50 to 60 foot talus is formed mostly of large broken rock. In places the 30 foot wall is gone and the bottom slope extends up to the top of second slope. The alignment is so good that the 30 foot wall need not be cut except

FIG. 48. Rest stop at Granite Park. *Robert B. Stanton.* Miami University Library.

if wished for material. At extreme of this stretch the wall is of lava, and one point juts out in river and stands vertical, 70 feet. River very wide and this can be thrown into river chiefly, and make clear alignment.

We start at 2:30 P.M. At 2:30 run Rapid No. 406, long shoal.

From last photo point, the canyon gets wider and wider and the hills break up in sections.

At point of photos, wash through lava, 30 foot span. Beyond this the lava juts out same as above in one point, on around this left turn immense slopes covered with green, 1-20 foot span. All these great slopes are underlaid by solid rock slopes as shown by washes, though some may be *deep debris*.

One to 1 1/2 miles below another lava on top my "beaded" sandstone, easy to throw it in river, wide, if need be to straighten line.

At this turn we enter our southeast course, 1-20 foot span. At 2:50 stop on left bank for photos opposite very large side canyon on right.

Start at 3:08. Large side canyon on right, 80 foot span.

This large side canyon on left, about one mile below the last large one on right, has forced out its boulders so far as to drive the river against the right bank and wash out all the talus and lower soft strata; but the wall left is of much broken up marble at an angle of about 25° from vertical and can easily be handled even though it is necessary to widen river by using some nitroglycerin on the boulders at mouth of canyon. High water about 15 feet.

At 3:10 run Rapid No. 407. 3:16 run Rapid 408.

We stop at 3:20 P.M. at very large side canyon on left, which forms the first bad rapid we have had since the volcano. This is full of immense boulders. We start at 3:30 and let down by [line] to nearly the end when some ugly boulders require a portage. Portage all made and boats skidded down by 4:30 P.M., Rapid 409.

At this point there is a fine spring of pure water and plenty of wood, and being tired we go into Camp No. 94. One duck for supper.

River still falling and today in places shows the fall of the last rise to be 6 feet. This in this *wide* portion of the canyon indicates that we had in the narrow part of the canyon, where we were at its height, fully a 30 foot rise.

SATURDAY, MARCH 1, 1890. Clear.

Up this morning early. Breakfast at 6:00 A.M. Everyone anxious to get to Diamond Creek as soon as possible.

At [blank] take photos from Camp No. 94 at large side canyon on left, 1 or more miles below last *large* side canyon on right.

We pack up and start at 7:30 A.M. and at 7:35 run Rapid No. 410; and at 7:40 run Rapid No. 411, a long 1/2 mile, incline falling 12 to 15 feet and very swift.

At 7:45 stop for photos on *right bank* at mouth of next side canyon.

We start at 8:11 A.M. and at 8:16 run Rapid No. 412. At 8:18 run Rapid No. 413. At 8:20 run Rapid No. 414. Long gravel chutes.

Stop at 8:30 A.M. for photos on granite point, 1/2 mile above right turn 18 miles above Diamond Creek.

From Camp No. 94 turning to right, the slope runs up 400 to 500 feet with flattening out next to river. To side canyon on right 30 feet, to 20 foot span at this side, and for some distance each side, the beaded sandstone rises making for the distance of 1/2 mile a *level* broad bench for railroad. Beyond this to and around left turn same flat slope 500 feet back. Beautiful *flat grassy hill-sides*. This portion of canyon looks more like a *broad river valley* and one expects at every turn to see it open up into farms. This same character continues down stretch and around right turn at point. This lava continues round point of sharp turn to right, easy slope below it.

We start at 8:45 A.M. and at 8:46 run Rapid No. 415. Stop at 8:50 to examine Rapid 416. The several side canyons that come in at this point have brought down great quantities of small boulders. Down canyon [they] form succession of rapids. Just at turn large side canyon on right, 100 foot span.

Start at 9:05 A.M. Stop at 9:10 for photos *in* first bend to right. Left side down stretch and round left turn, 1-20 foot span. High talus slope underlaid by stratified limestone and my beaded sandstone continues to point of right turn. Three 10 foot openings to point. (Turn point at 9:45.)

Start at lower half of No. 416 at 9:32 and run No. 417 at 9:34. At 9:37 run No. 418. At 9:41 run No. 419. At 9:51 run No. 420. All long inclines with rapid fall but light waves. And stop at 9:53 for photos [of] the Cathedral in convex of second turn [and] opposite center of Cathedral from mouth of side canyon [on] right.

After turning down the bends beyond the point noted at 18 miles above Diamond Creek the walls of canyon are more solid and are formed just the same as those near Kanab Wash. This only lasts for a few miles and then the whole country breaks back again in very fantastic shapes.

The great Cathedral was wonderful to me. Can enlarge on this in general. Colors all dull except green.

Around right bend and down next stretch to side canyon on right, 60 foot span, same high talus. Limestone. Beaded sandstone on top rising higher. Just below the side canyon the "beaded" stone is up 80 feet and granite comes up 30 feet. Limestone between. Granite drops out in 400 to 500 feet. Sixty foot span.

Start at 10:18 and at 10:20 run Rapid No. 421. Stop 10:24 to examine No. 422 and at 10:29 start and run it, a sudden drop, regular fall of 5 feet.

The same mountain slope continues from last side canyon around light bend to right down stretch and around bend to left. (The bend before the two *short* ones turned us on our S course, 10:35 A.M. — Check this.) At this bend lava on left. One 30 foot span.

At 10:35 run small Rapid No. 422 down next stretch also, then another short turn to left and quick to right at this point. Sandstone cliffs rise from water 10–20 feet high. High water 25 feet. Lava side on right. This sandstone continues and soon gets above high water with sloping bench on top to large side canyon on right, 50 foot span. Stop here 10:53.

From this side canyon, on around left bend, same sandstone bench with mountain slope above it. This continues down stretch and part way round turn to right where granite again comes up, only 100 feet.

Start at 11:05 and at 11:08 run No. 423. Stop at 11:20 for photos at lower end of southeast course, up on slope. This last stretch comes down, has a southeast course.

Start at 11:45 and at 11:52 run Rapid No. 424 and at 11:57 stop on right bank for *lunch*. 12 noon photo about 1 mile below last on level with river.

After turning right bend at end of southeast stretch the point is covered with lava but very broad talus below it. From there on the beaded sandstone rises to about 75 feet but is not sheer. Has slope of about 35° from vertical. At places it stands more vertical and has talus below it. This continues down stretch and around left turn to point of right turn.

We start at 1:00 P.M., after lunch. At 1:01 run Rapid No. 425. At lunch point, 2-20 foot spans. After lunch granite all along in spots 10 to 15 feet high.

What a beautiful stretch of river: the hills broken back far off and then coming close to, 20 foot opening, the river in all kinds of fantastic shapes, gravel terraces, rounded domes, spires, and peaks. No perpendicular walls of any height, but more beautiful and wonderful on that account.

At 1:15 P.M. we stop at head of Rapid No. 426, formed with two others below it by the wash from large side canyon on left. This has forced out river and washed away bank on right in the usual way, just at turn to right above side canyon the solid granite walls begin. Photos while boats run No. 426 to save time at 1:27. On top the granite is my same beaded sandstone, and an easy bench under it on the granite, 2-30 foot spans.[6]

---

[6] On February 28, 1890, the Stanton expedition made a good run of sixteen miles from the camp below Whitmore Wash to Camp 94 at the foot of 205 Mile Rapid (RBS 409). The party nooned at the mouth of Parashant Wash (RBS Rapids 398–401) where the river begins a long loop to the south separating the Shivwits Plateau on the north and the Hualapai Plateau (location of the Hualapai Indian Reservation) on the south.

Running down from Parashant, the explorers soon found themselves in an ever-widening canyon taking on the appearance at Granite Park of a "broad river valley." Here, three large tributary canyons (one unnamed and Granite Park on the left side, and 209 Mile on the right) open out on the Colorado. In this section one is treated to a variety of majestic views unlike those of any other part of Grand Canyon. The rimlands high on the horizon, but standing back from the river four or five miles, are occasionally visible over successive strata piled up in huge, widely-separated steps. Just below Granite Park a mid-channel gravel bar produced a long riffle (RBS Rapids 416–420) giving the men a choppy ride. At mile 210 on

Boats stop at 1:31 and we all start at 1:37 and at 1:39 run No. 427. At 1:42 run No. 428. All of them very heavy. Boat goes clear through the waves and ships lots of water, in 427 turned twice round.

The granite walls are very ragged jutting out in points, the same as way above. The granite is very much shattered, cracked in every direction, and easily handled. In slopes from the water to the beaded sandstone at about 35° from vertical, 1-50 foot span. High water 25 feet, granite about 75 feet. Sandstone on top 25 to 30 feet.

Stop at 2:00 P.M. at head of Rapid No. 429 from side wash on right, 60 foot span, to take photos.

At this side canyon on right the regular form of inner gorge as section above stops, at and beyond granite, much broken up. See later.

Start at 2:27. Run Rapid No. 429 at 2:28. The largest, *highest* boils I have seen, in short distance, but awful 3 and 4 feet. Beyond side canyon at photos granite same for 1/4 mile to large side canyon on right.

At 2:35 run Rapid No. 430. At this point, granite same as before. [Good track?] on top but the granite has a slope of about 45°, as easy as any hillside.

Stop at 2:41 to look at Rapid No. 431, a long shallow one. Start at 2:47 and run it and run No. 432 at 2:55, both heavy, and stop at 2:57 for photo up from point at end of southeast course.

Start at 3:13 P.M.

All round the right bend after above noted point granite slopes continue just the same till end of southeast course. There it is much more broken up, 1-30 foot span, and slopes back very flat to foot of high marble, and sandstone broken back too.

We run Rapid No. 433 at 3:18 and at 3:26 stop 1 mile above Diamond Creek for photos. From turn to south course the general character is same as past to the Diamond Creek on left side.

Start at 3:42 and at 3:44 run Rapid No. 434. At 3:46 run Rapid No. 435. At 3:50 run Rapid No. 436. [These are] brisk but easy.

Land at 3:55 at mouth of what is put on government map as Diamond Creek. I start up creek to examine. I can find no trace of wagon road or evidences of anyone being there. I go back disappointed. Will go to next creek and look.

Start [at] 4:25. Run No. 436a which proves although clear of rocks one of the heaviest we have run fully loaded but we dash through it with a rush as we are running for our mail. Land at 4:40 . Photo half way on west course.

---

the left, Stanton photographed a prominent pointed dome which he named "The Cathedral." At this point the party was about sixteen miles above Diamond Creek. By the time they reached 217 Mile Rapid (RBS 426) the explorers had entered the Lower Granite Gorge through which the Colorado flows for approximately forty-seven miles.

We start at 4:50 P.M. All the way from Rapid 436 as far as we can see on this west course, about 1 1/2 miles, the water is as smooth as a lake. Just past Rapid No. 436 the granite rises to its usual high almost abruptly.

From the large creek on left down west turn and stretch the granite walls are the same as those in upper granite gorge, but much broken up and general slope 40° from vertical.

The breaking up is in fine pieces, making very easy and cheap line to construct, 1-30 foot span, 1-40 foot span.

At 5:00 P.M. we run *small* Rapid No. 437 and at 5:05 we land on sand bar to examine the next rapid. As soon as we get to shore I jump out. Am surprised to find so large a creek. In a few feet I see RMS written in large letters on the sand. I call out to men and they all run up in wild excitement, and give a cheer and toss their hats on the ground and into the air, for it is Diamond Creek in fact. We soon discover a more convincing proof, a trail and a woman's footprint. All are happy and we go into camp at once, Camp No. 95. At last we have reached Diamond Creek!! The much sought for.[7]

[7] The Stanton expedition had traveled a long 225.5 miles from Lee's Ferry to reach Diamond Creek, the historic gateway to the western section of Grand Canyon. Access was by way of a Diamond tributary, Peach Springs Canyon, of fairly steep gradient but open and passable to pack animals and wagons. In his important exploration of the Colorado River, Army Lieutenant J. C. Ives reached the river here by mule train in 1858. See his *Report Upon the Colorado River of the West* (Washington, 1861). When Stanton writes of the "Gov. Map," which led him to confuse 224 Mile Canyon with Diamond Creek, he may be referring to the map accompanying the Ives *Report*. Stanton is agonizingly silent about the published maps he was using for reference on the railroad survey. However, when it came to reliable maps showing the course of the river, he had little choice. In 1871, Army Captain George M. Wheeler ended his incredible upriver trip from Fort Mojave at Diamond Creek. A detailed map of the trip, incorporating much of the Ives data, was issued in 1878, and included in Wheeler's *Report upon United States Geographical Surveys West of the One Hundredth Meridian. Vol. I, Geographical Report* (Washington, Government Printing Office, 1889). Maps issued by the Powell Survey — U.S. Geographical and Geological Survey of the Rocky Mountain Region — were available. Powell's own *Report on the Lands of the Arid Region of the United States*, first issued in 1878, second edition 1879, new edition edited by Wallace Stegner (Cambridge, Harvard University Press, 1962) includes a map of Utah incorporating much of the data gathered by Powell on the river trips, and by his land parties operating in the adjacent canyon country. The *Atlases* accompanying C. E. Dutton's *Report on the Geology of the High Plateaus of Utah*, and his *Tertiary History of the Grand Cañon District* (Washington, Government Printing Office, 1880, 1882) also reflected the results of the survey's explorations in the canyon country of the Colorado River. When Major John Wesley Powell became director of the U.S. Geological Survey in 1881, he began the production of a standard series of topographic maps. Some of these "Reconnaissance Maps" covering the Colorado River, had been published before 1889 and may have been used by Stanton during the railroad survey.

With the completion of the Santa Fe Railroad in 1883 (then the Atlantic and Pacific), hardy tourists bent on seeing the Grand Canyon from the river's edge traveled the twenty miles down from Peach Springs Station afoot or horseback, or jolted along in wagons, or even stages, over a primitive trail. Low on food, and so long out of touch with the world, the Stanton explorers at Diamond Creek jumped ashore with a cheer. They were at the foot of the trail that would lead them out of their canyon prison. The letters in the sand, and the imprint of the woman's shoe, told them that.

CHAPTER IX

OUT IN THE OPEN

After the break in the journey at Diamond Creek and Peach Springs, where three men left the survey, Stanton and his seven companions pressed on with the work. In the Lower Granite Gorge they ran both Separation and Lava Cliff Rapids which Powell had described in dramatic detail. Near the end of the canyon Stanton wrote that he now had a good idea of the greatness of the Grand Canyon as a whole, and he had found nothing to prevent the construction of a railroad all the way through it. Passing through the "Southern Gateway to the Grand Canyon" the explorers found themselves out in open country. Passing two ferry locations they finally reached Rioville at the mouth of the Rio Virgin where another ferry was being operated by the noted pioneer, Daniel Bonelli.

SUNDAY, MARCH 2, 1890.[1] Camp No. 95 at mouth of Diamond Creek.

Elmer Kane and I started from camp at 8:45 A.M. to go to Peach Springs, to telegraph our safe arrival and get mail. Stopped some little while at Farlee's house at forks of creek and reached Peach Springs at 3:15 P.M. Having stopped on the road one hour, and traveled 24 1/4 miles, in 5 1/2 hours and climbed up 3000 feet.

I telegraphed to [my wife] J. O. S. [Jean Oliver Moore Stanton], to C. F. Martin and T. C. Henry. Found great quantities of mail and everyone well except Gibson's father who died February 20th.

Peach Springs, small railroad station, about 200, one *good* store by J. N. Cohenour and wife.[2]

---

[1] This chapter is taken from Robert B. Stanton's Field Notebook D.

[2] To capitalize on the numbers of Grand Canyon visitors stopping off at the Santa Fe's Peach Springs Station, J. H. Farlee established a stage line and a small tourist hotel at the confluence of Peach Springs Canyon and Diamond Creek about a mile from the Colorado. For Stanton, Peach Springs was the first accessible mail and supply point since the expedition had entered Grand Canyon. J. N. Cohenour, storekeeper, was also postmaster.

Owing to its accessibility, Diamond Creek is much used today as the take-out point for numbers of recreational river runners.

MONDAY, MARCH 3. Peach Springs, Arizona.

Have met quite a number of kind railroad men here: J. P. Green, Master Mechanic; A. M. Beal, Division Superintendent, Needles, California; I. L. Bailey, Agent.

Have found no photo rolls from New York. Telegraph to Scovill & Adams Co. tonight.

TUESDAY, MARCH 4. Received answer from Scovill & Adams Co. Goods just shipped today. This will cause me much delay and large expense.

WEDNESDAY, MARCH 5. Judge C. M. Funston of *Kingman, Arizona,* came up here and we spent a very pleasant evening together. He is quite interested in our road; promises to give me much information as to the mining interests in this section. He is editor of the *Mohave County Miner.*[3]

THURSDAY, MARCH 6, 1890. Twining, Hogue, and Brown came up from camp. I settled up with them and discharged them. All passed off pleasantly. Hogue started east on the evening train. Brown and Twining will go tomorrow morning.[4]

FRIDAY, MARCH 7. Working all day on the photograph notes of the pictures taken in the Grand Canyon.

I was greatly pleased to get telegram from W. H. Jackson & Co., Denver, saying my "negatives all right." [5]

SATURDAY, MARCH 8, 1890. Rained all morning in Peach Springs. Cloudy and windy all P.M.

SUNDAY, MARCH 9, 1890. No church. Everything goes on same as any other day except the men put on their weekly clean shirt.

---

[3] Reports of the expedition's progress to the mouth of Diamond Creek appeared in several newspapers as a result of Stanton's contacts at Peach Springs: Denver *Rocky Mountain News,* March 4, 1890; San Francisco *Examiner,* March 4, 1890; Salt Lake *Tribune,* March 4, 1890; Kingman, AZ, *Mohave County Miner,* March 8, 1890.

[4] With the departure of Twining, Hogue, and Brown, expedition personnel consisted of Robert B. Stanton, John Hislop, Reginald Travers, Langdon Gibson, W. H. Edwards, Elmer Kane, and H. G. Ballard. A new cook, George Melick, was engaged at Peach Springs to replace James Hogue. All of these men completed the railroad survey from Diamond Creek to the Gulf of California.

[5] Back in Marble Canyon where he replaced F. A. Nims as expedition photographer, Stanton had had no experience in photography. His first films taken out by Felix Lantier were sent to the photographic studio in Denver. This was headed by W. J. Jackson, already well known for his western photographs, many of them made in connection with railroad construction. The telegram from Jackson was good news. As we can see from the photos reproduced in this book, Stanton's negatives were indeed "all right."

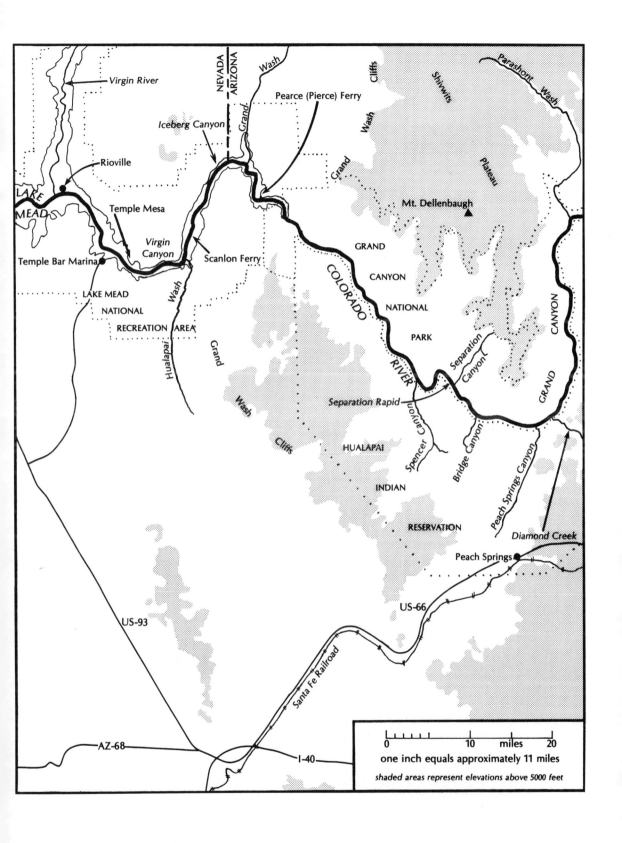

Virgin River

NEVADA
ARIZONA

Wash

Cliffs

Shivwits

Parashont Wash

Pearce (Pierce) Ferry

Iceberg Canyon

Wash

Grand

Grand

Plateau

Rioville

Mt. Dellenbaugh

LAKE
MEAD

Temple Mesa

Virgin
Canyon

GRAND

Temple Bar Marina

Scanlon Ferry

CANYON

COLORADO

NATIONAL

LAKE MEAD

Wash

NATIONAL

PARK

Separation

Canyon

GRAND

RECREATION AREA

Hualapai

Grand

RIVER

CANYON

Separation Rapid

Wash

Cliffs

Spencer Canyon

Bridge Canyon

Peach Springs Canyon

HUALAPAI

INDIAN

RESERVATION

Diamond Creek

Peach Springs

US-66

US-93

Santa Fe Railroad

			miles	
0		10		20

AZ-68

I-40

one inch equals approximately 11 miles

shaded areas represent elevations above 5000 feet

MONDAY, MARCH 10, 1890. Much disappointed that the photo rolls did not come today. This waiting is geting *terrible*.

TUESDAY, MARCH 11, 1890. My photo rolls arrived last night. So we will be off this morning.

Started from Peach Spring Station at 9:30 A.M. and reached mouth of Diamond Creek at 2:00 P.M. J. H. Farlee took us in buckboard, myself and our new cook, George Melick. Find it will be so late before we can get ready to start that I have concluded not to go till tomorrow morning.

Photos: from point just above Diamond Creek; showing mouth of Diamond Creek; Castles on the Rhine up Diamond Creek; 3/4 mile above Diamond Creek, 800 feet above river, showing Aubrey Cliffs in the distance.

As noted in my last book the granite gorge begins about 1 1/2 to 2 miles above Diamond Creek where large canyon comes in on left. The granite walls are quite rotten and broken up with points of harder rock sticking up above the general slope which, except on these points, varies from 35° to 50° from vertical.

A splendid roadbed can be gotten by cutting and wasting rock in river.

The river has risen about 2 feet since Saturday's rain.

WEDNESDAY, MARCH 12, 1890. Clear. River up 6 to 8 inches more last night.

We are up early this morning but of course it takes a long time to get started as it always does when we have been in camp more than overnight. We are camped No. 95 at mouth of Diamond Creek, at head of Rapid No. 438, which is very heavy.

We are packed up and start at 8:15 A.M. and at once run Rapid No. 438 as far as sand bar on right. We cut several waves and ship quite a little water. We land at 8:18 on right bank and take photos from 1/2 mile below Diamond Creek.

The canyon wall below Diamond Creek for 1/2 mile is identical with that above. At photo point, side wash on right has washed out very wide, requiring an embankment, unless line can be so located as to tunnel next point where river turns sharp to right. This I think is the line. After looking further I guess not. See topography of survey, 30 foot span.

In coming through this last rapid, No. 2 shipped an oarlock and turned and ran in shore. Struck her bow hard against a rock; so we have to stop, haul her out, and repair. Quite an initiation for our new cook in the bow seat of No. 2. He was thrown clear out on the bow deck and clung on to the life lines with one leg hanging over the side.

The repairs are made at 11:30 A.M. and we reload No. 2 and start at 11:55, and run Rapid No. 439. Very bad on left, behind big rock. Immense boils on left, after passing first drop drove us off in fine style, though beautifully, and run No. 440 1/4 mile long at 11:58.

From stopping point for repairs, down for 1/2 mile to where river turns to right and starts northward, the wall has the granite very much broken back. Slope is very irregular but *easy construction*. High water about 40 feet. The same nature of walls continues to point. The point is abrupt and the work here would be heavy but simple.

Stop at 12:02 P.M. for lunch. Photo up river from about 2 miles and below Diamond.

We start at 1:36 after lunch and at 1:38 run Rapid 441. At 1:40 run Rapid 442. At 1:43 run Rapid 443. Quite heavy with waves in first all over us and very powerful whirls at bottom in which we are caught and No. 2 passes us.

At 1:48 we stop on left bank for photos about 1/2 mile above where river makes sharp turn to northwest. Start at 2:25 P.M. and at 2:25 run Rapid No. 444, and at 2:28 run Rapid No. 445 and at 2:34 land on left bank at head of Rapid No. 446 and take photos just 1/4 mile around sharp point where river runs northwest. The point referred to on last page is very abrupt, and practically perpendicular for about 100 feet, is cut right in two by a wash, 50 foot span and has sharp point of rocks beyond. Would make some pretty heavy work but nothing more than a little heavy expense. Cut hard through into river, which is big and wide.

Beyond this point the wall is the same sloping granite.

3:10 P.M. photo grotto [and] grotto inside.

We start at 3:40 P.M. and run Rapid 446 at 3:42, and stop at foot at 3:44 to look ahead. Start at 3:54 and at 3:57 stop at end of northwest course where river turns more northwest for 1/2 mile and then turns to left. At this point at 4:00 P.M. take photos.

We start at 4:20 and at 4:20 run Rapid 447. At 4:22 run Rapid 448. At 4:27 run Rapid 449. Very, very wet, all over me to the skin. One 30 foot span. One 50 foot span. And at 4:30 land on left bank, at head of Rapid No. 450 and fine wood and so go into Camp No. 96.

The same character of granite. Broken up into a general slope, though the slope is not so flat as above, with points of harder rock standing up over the general slope. These must be cut very heavy in order to give a good line. But it will make a magnificent roadway.

At 4:45 take photos.

The granite since leaving the bold point at Grotto Canyon stands up more boldly and higher. The slopes are rougher and more in little benches. Make a good line, but heavy work. General appearance more like Colorado granite canyons.

Perhaps from Diamond this far should be noted, *12-10 foot openings*.

THURSDAY, MARCH 13, 1890. Clear. River rose more last night.

Canyon on right at Rapid No. 450, 100 foot span. We pack up and start at 7:42 A.M. and at once enter Rapid No. 450.

It is very heavy on account of high water and at lower end a huge rock on right around which the water draws, and one in center to avoid. We go so close to rock that the stern grazes it and plunges into a hole that, before we plunge, looks 10 feet deep; but just as we go over the brink, thanks to a kind Providence, the waves roll in and fill the hole, so we go over with a terrible shake but safely. This at 7:45 and go into swift water full of immense boils and suck holes. Are turned once.

At 7:45 stop for photos.

From photo point on the granite is in heavy points jutting out and above the granite slope. This makes heavy and expensive work. The line is simple and alignment good if the points are cut heavy. This is only a matter of powder and extra cost.

We start again at 8:15 A.M. and at 8:17 run Rapid 451. Not heavy but crooked and full of boils. We stop 8:25 on right bank at head of Rapid No. 452, formed by large side canyon on right and small one on left, about 1 mile above where river makes sharp turn to north. 8:30 A.M. photo. Start and run Rapid 452, *light*, at 8:45. Stop at 8:48.

Restart at 9:00 A.M. and at 9:05 run small Rapid No. 453 and at 9:09 land on right bank just where river begins to turn to right or its north course. 9:15 photo.

For about 1 mile above here, the slope of the granite is more flat and even.

Around point to right as far as I can see the wall is much broken but quite bold. Same heavy work as above. One 50 foot span. Another one 50 foot span.

We start at 9:23 and at once run small Rapid No. 454, and at 9:28 stop to examine Rapid No. 455 formed by side canyon on left, at first point of right turn. Very heavy rapid. Start at 9:35 and in 2 minutes run No. 455. Very heavy with curling waves so that boat rocks fearfully from one side to the other, 10 to 12 foot drop. Am completely wet. At 9:43 run Rapid No. 456 with very heavy boils and sucks at bottom. Turn extreme southwest point and stop 1/4 mile beyond to take photos at 9:45 A.M.

Around this point to right where river turns to northwest and then north, the granite is again of the broken up slaty nature but has bold hard points sticking out and above general slope. High water is between 40 and 50 feet and to get first class line locate 75 to 80 feet up, boldly through points in river and get solid roadbed. This same character continues for 1/2 mile ahead as seen in photo. One-50 foot span this end of first point *back*.

We start at 10:15 on smooth but swift water, and stop at 10:25 at large side canyon on left at head of Rapid No. 457. And at this point take photos. On this northwest course 1-50 foot and 1-30 foot span. Granite well broken up but very bold at point.

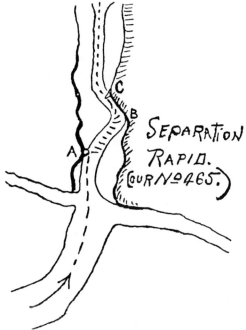

FIG. 49. Stanton's sketch of the historic rapid. The first fall is at "A." Then the current rushes to "B" and thence along the cliff to "C" where there is a sharp projecting rock. Miami University Library.

Start at 11:00 and at once run Rapid No. 457. Clear of rocks, but with immense waves, not as high above level of river as some, but decided by all to be the *longest* and largest and deepest waves of any rapid we have run; but being long we rode them beautifully and shipped little water. Boats when they dove into the trough went entirely out of sight.

At 11:05 ran Rapid No. 458, and at 11:10 landed at head of Rapid No. 459 for lunch. At 12:30 take photos.

The granite seems to be getting lower beyond, 1-80 foot span. The same general character. Slopes, with bold points.

We start at 12:38 and at once run Rapid No. 459. It has 3 large rocks, 2 on left and one on right. We miss all, but in passing by third one, left, the wave from it strikes boat broadside and fairly lifts it sideways drenching Gibson from head to foot. *Terrible* hole to look into going at such a speed behind the rocks.

At 12:44 run small Rapid No. 460 and at 12:48 land on left bank at point where river turns to left for photos. Opposite this point is a real *perpendicular* cliff, 200 feet on railroad line, 100 feet above railroad line, and 100 feet below to water; but this can be easily handled by dropping off top. Same general granite walls as above.

We start at 1:26 and at once run Rapid No. 461; heavy waves and the worst *boils* and *swirls* we have met yet. And at 1:30 stop to look at No. 462 which has heavy waves which we run at 1:34. And at 1:40 run smaller one, No. 463. And at 1:43 stop for photos, at end of *west* course where river turns to right. Along this west course the granite is very bold and very hard, in large points coming out into river, *like clear creek*.

We start again at 2:10 on swift water and at 2:15 run Rapid No. 464 without stopping. Stop at 2:24, 2/3 way down north course for photos.

The granite stands up very bold and sheer but not perpendicular. The work would be heavy but could on this north course come down nearer high water as there is quite a good bench. All of this work is only a matter of a little extra expense.[6]

We start at 2:45 and at 2:50 stop to examine Rapid No. 465. This rapid is formed by two large side canyons coming in directly opposite each other, the larger one on right side. We stop some distance above on right bank, climb over the broken up cliff above the side canyon and down across it, 100 foot span, and on to the high cliff below.

The cliffs are vertical on both sides on left for 300 to 400 feet, perhaps more, and on right side 80 to 100 feet. The water fills the whole channel. A portage of boats or dropping by lines is impossible. The current draws in at head of rapid over huge rocks on both sides and drops very suddenly over first fall. It is driven against left cliff just as it goes over second fall, and the rebounding waters from the cliff, the rushing water from the right, and the fall make a torrent of *slashing, curling, jumping* waves broken into one mass of yellow dirty foam such as our boats never went into before. After the current leaves this point it *all* rushes on to the cliff, and along the cliff is one immense *boil*; and then the current turns sharp around the point at which is a sharp projecting rock.

After examining carefully we conclude this rapid must be run; there is no other way. There is no hesitancy on the part of anyone.[7] We start into the

---

[6] At Diamond Creek the Stanton party had already entered the V-shaped Lower Granite Gorge where, through its upper section, the river raced along narrowly confined between the dark, brooding walls of the Older Precambrian metamorphics. For fourteen miles down to Separation Canyon, the river was full of rapids, half a dozen of which are rated from light to heavy by today's river runners. With some help from a "kind Providence" Stanton ran them all. One boat was slightly damaged in Diamond Creek Rapid (RBS 438) and there were some close calls and repeated drenchings as the high waves broke over the boats. Rapid 457, at the mouth of Bridge Canyon, is the site of the proposed controversial Bridge Canyon Dam.

Between rapids the engineer found time to photograph important points along the way and to keep up on his notes. The roadbed would be "easy" to build in some places. Elsewhere heavy work would be required, but then that was "only a matter of powder & extra cost," he wrote.

[7] Stanton's 465, mile 239.5, Separation Rapid. For Stanton and his crew this was a big one and there was no way to line it. No one hesitated; they would run it. At the same

rapid in good spirits and good shape at 3:07 P.M. Our boat goes over the first fall, over and through great waves that break over us. As we approach the

---

place on August 27, 1869, Major J. W. Powell had reached the same conclusion. But three of his men balked and backed out. They'd had enough of the river. Tensions and antagonisms within the party may have contributed to their decision. Rather than go on, the brothers O. G. and Seneca Howland, and William Dunn, decided to walk out to the Mormon settlements along the Virgin River. Topping out on the Shivwits Plateau, the three men were killed by Indians. Powell describes the "separation" and his running of the rapid in the *Exploration of the Colorado River of the West* (1875), 96–102.

Some fifteen years after the railroad survey, Stanton began writing a history entitled, "The River and the Canyon, the Colorado River of the West and the Exploration, Navigation and Survey of its Canyons, from the Standpoint of an Engineer." Before he finished the work, which he revised almost up to the time of his death in 1922, the manuscript ran to over one thousand folio pages. The work was never published in its entirety and none of it during his lifetime. Stanton's account of his railroad survey took up eleven chapters in the work. These have been edited by Dwight L. Smith and published under the title, *Down the Colorado* (1965), cited frequently in this work.

During his writing Stanton spent much research time on the controversial James White who claimed to have floated through Grand Canyon on a raft in 1867, two years before Powell's voyage. To his own satisfaction the engineer discredited White's story and thus saved for Powell the honor of being first. Then, in six chapters totalling over a hundred pages, Stanton offered up an extended literal critique of Powell's narrative in the *Exploration* which in places he found flawed enough to conclude that it was not very good history. One such place was Powell's account of the affair at Separation Rapid. Powell doesn't mention it but Stanton learned (from Jack Sumner and William Hawkins, both of the 1869 party, reminiscing some forty years after the event) that lingering frictions between Powell and some of the crew had something to do with the separation.

There the matter might have rested, but in 1918 a monument commemorating the Powell voyages was dedicated on the South Rim west of Grand Canyon Village. The bronze plaque listed the crews of the 1869 and 1872 Powell voyages through Grand Canyon. Conspicuously absent from the 1869 roster were the names of the Howland brothers and William Dunn. The omission was approved by Frederick S. Dellenbaugh, who had traveled with Powell on the second voyage, and who wrote of the three as deserters undeserving of honorable mention. See his *The Romance of the Colorado River* (New York and London, G. P. Putnam's Sons, 1902), 228, and his *A Canyon Voyage* (New Haven, Yale University Press, 1926), xxiv–xxv.

Robert Stanton thought that the plaque on the Powell Monument should be replaced with one including the full roster of the 1869 trip. Enter now Julius F. Stone, industrialist, who had been associated with Stanton in the Glen Canyon mining venture, 1897–1902. Stone had run the Green-Colorado in 1909; his diary account of the trip, *Canyon Country*, appeared in 1932. Stone believed that history had been falsified by the omission of the names from the Powell Memorial plaque. Anxious to set the record straight, he arranged for the editing and publication of Stanton's chapters on James White and the affair at Separation Rapid. These appeared under the title *Colorado River Controversies*, by Robert Brewster Stanton, edited by James M. Chalfant (New York, Dodd, Mead & Co., 1932). Stone supplied a foreword. To compensate for the omission of the names on the Powell Memorial, Julius F. Stone placed a bronze plaque on the canyon wall at Separation Rapid which reads in part, "Here on August 28, 1869, Seneca Howland, O. G. Howland and William H. Dunn separated from the Original Powell Party . . . For Further Information See 'Colorado River Controversies' Obtainable from University Libraries . . ." A new edition of the Stanton book, with commentaries by Otis R. Marston and Martin J. Anderson, has been published by Westwater Books, Boulder City, Nevada, 1982. Stanton's research on White and Powell forms the basis, the starting point, for continuing investigations on both matters which continue unabated to this day. O. R. Marston has compiled a history of the famous rapid, "Separation Marks," *Journal of Arizona History*, 17 (Spring, 1976), 1–20.

second fall it seems to me our time has come; for to look down into that seething, roaring, slashing abyss I cannot see how our boat can live to go through it. It is but a moment and we are in it. How we came through I cannot tell for the foaming waves lash over our boat from every side completely blinding us.

In a moment more we are out of it, and we have time to breathe. Our boat is right side up. I turned to see if any of the men are washed out. They are all in their places and working hard, for as I turn again forward, I see our boat has turned broadside and thus goes down over the high waves. I expect every moment we shall dash into the cliff and our good boat be smashed to flinders; but just as we seem ready to strike, Hislop does his best with his steering oar and turns the boat a little, and a huge boil comes up and strikes our right bow and turns us from cliff to left. I shout to the men, "That's good, that's good, we are passed it." The words are hardly out of my mouth when our boat strikes with a crash on the projecting rock. We stop. I am thrown against the bow of boat, Kane against me, and Hislop over on Gibson. We straighten up, the bow of the boat sinks over the rock but does not move. A great wave comes over the whole boat and dashes me out into the whirlpool below the rock. I sink, and as I go down it seems as if I am going to the bottom of the river drawn down by the suck. I come to the top, Kane says 50 feet away, and catch my breath just in time to go under another great wave. After that my life preserver keeps me well up so that I bob over the waves without any difficulty and am carried down the current into quieter water. No. 2 boat fares better, does not get turned sideways, but only misses our boat in passing a few feet, but is turned round and is coming stern foremost. They row down hard, catch up with me, and Edwards and Melick draw me into the boat.

Being so trained in timing everything I involuntary take out my watch which is still going and find that it is just 5 minutes since we entered the rapid. Judging from the time it takes to *run* such water, I must have been in the river about 4 minutes. In the meantime, Hislop who had lost his steering oar jumped to shore to look after me. A rebounding wave lifted off our boat and Kane and Gibson brought her down though *full* of water. She was perfectly safe from sinking by the 10 airtight compartments.

We all land 1/2 to 3/4 mile below. Haul out our boat with blocks and fall on the rocks and find a hole 18″ × 10″ in her side. A copper patch is put over it. We are loaded and start again at 4:10 P.M. At 4:14 we run Rapid No. 466, almost as bad as last. The water rushing against cliff on left and then against huge rock extending half across the river on right. We *shave* both of them but go through safely, row down a mile, and at 4:22 go into Camp No. 97 on right bank at head of Rapid No. 467, pretty well tired out with the day's work.

The railroad line from the two side canyons at Rapid 465 down this stretch of about 2 miles will be heavy. The perpendicular cliff at upper end has good flat broken top, say 80 feet above river, but the whole distance is a succession of bold points with good slopes between. It is only a matter of a high line and some heavy cutting at these points.

The waterways are not many and none difficult, say 2-30 foot, 2-20 foot, 5-10 foot openings.[8]

FRIDAY, MARCH 14, 1890. Clear.

8:30 A.M. photo from point 200 feet above river and 1/2 mile above first turn to left, towards the south course. One 50 foot span just above this. From this point just above our Camp No. 97, the granite walls seem to get softer and assume the regular slope of the easy granite far up river. A slope of about 40° from vertical. Can see from here to left turn where river runs south about 1 1/4 miles.

We pack up and start at 9:48 A.M. and in two minutes run into Rapid No. 467. Very heavy waves but we miss the most of them and land on left bank at 9:52 1'/3 mile below camp, for photo showing big rock and *to* Rapid No. 465. Am sorry I did not take photo from point above Rapid 465 before we started yesterday but did not think of it at the time and I was too cold when I got out of the water.

We start again at 10:10 A.M. and at 10:12 run Rapid No. 468 and at 10:18 reach *left* bend and stop for photos. One 30 foot span at bend and 2-20 foot [spans] before, at first 90° turn as shown on map. The granite on this left bend is much broken back, with some jutting points, but makes good easy line.

Start at 10:40 and run Rapid No. 469, light, and stop 10:47 at head of No. 470, light, which is at second left turn. Around this bend the granite is more broken back into flatter grassy slopes. A very easy line around it with some bold jutting points. We start again at 10:53 and at once run Rapid No. 470, and at 10:55 run No. 471, a long letter S with gravel bars. This seems to indicate better water. At 10:58 stop about half way down south course on left for photos. Two 50 foot spans. Granite on this S course is much broken up, one or two gulches washed out far back, some heavy bank for good line and one, in center, bold point out to river.

Start at 11:21 A.M. and at 11:23 run Rapid No. 472, light, and at 11:25 run Rapid No. 473. This channel only 75 to 80 feet wide; and water boils all

---

[8] On the running of Separation Rapid, this record will not show a more precise account. Who but this engineer would have recorded the time from the start through the rapid to the rescue? And note that the rapid had been run, the boat repaired, and camp pitched in just over an hour!

Separation is no longer a hazard. The waters of Lake Mead now cover it. Indeed, one may say that the rapid is the point of separation between the free-flowing river and the river condemned to make its way through a series of reservoirs throughout most of the rest of its course to the Gulf of California.

through rapid with great force; and at 11:28 run Rapid No. 474; and at 11:38 run Rapid 475; and at 11:40 stop on left bank in center of right turn for photos.

All round this right bend at end of S course the slope is quite flat, full 60° from vertical. Easy line and good curve to extreme point, then cliff is bold, but bench at right grade for line helps it. Sharp cut at further point.

Start at 11:56 and at 11:58 run No. 476. And at 12:05 land on left bank at head of Rapid No. 477. This to me is the most dreadful rapid we have met. It does *look* like destruction to attempt to run it and it is two days' work to get round it any other way. Will cross river and look at it after *lunch*.

1:00 P.M. take photos at large creek coming in on left at beginning of northwest course. Show Rapid No. 477. Good line all round this right turn as far as can see. On left opposite rapid is real perpendicular cliff 1000 feet high but on right side good sloping granite, same at yesterday's No. 465. On right high up on granite is a pile of basalt. Where did it come from?

After lunch we pulled across river and looked at rapid from that side. It seems almost impossible to let boats down as I thought on right side. We come to conclusion that the best and safest plan is to let down by lines overhead of rapid, which can be done at mouth of creek on left bank, and run from there. There will be one huge rock on left center of river to miss and to keep off wall. But I think it can be done well. Shall keep my photos on this side, and as I can with my one arm be of no service to the men I will stay also and lighten the load.

The basalt point opposite the creek that makes this Rapid 477 extends out on top of granite far into the river and at least 50 feet above grade, 150 to 200 feet wide. This of course will make heavy cut but material can easily be disposed of.

From this creek, Rapid 477, for 1 1/2 miles and more down this northwest course the right wall has the granite broken back into a good slope nearly to the top. These granite steps are solid grey granite.

At point where river turns due north, the granite juts out very bold. Will look at it when we get there.

At 3:00 P.M. the men begin to let the boats down by lines past head of rapid and at 3:30 one boat is safely in eddy past the first drop; and at 3:40 the second boat is safely down to the same place. The first boatmen then take time and carefully get ready and at 3:52 No. 1 starts to run the remainder of the rapid. This they do very successfully going inside both the *small* and large rock but skimming along close to the cliff at a fearful speed. After passing the large rock they come out away from the wall into the clear current and land a short distance below. At 3:56 No. 2 starts. She got through safely outside of small rock, gets into the swiftest water and is unable to stop. They pick up the photos and, after losing 3 minutes, start again at 4:04 P.M.[9]

[9] Stanton's 477, Lava Cliff Rapid, at the mouth of Spencer Canyon, the last big rapid on the Colorado, was drowned by the encroaching waters of Lake Mead. On the right side

Stop at 4:14 on left bank at beginning of *north* course.

The point referred to back was not so bad. Granite broken up into rough hard points only requires powder, 1-50 foot span. Same nature continues on the north course to turn to left.

Start again at 4:35, and run No. 478 at 4:38, and run No. 479 at 4:41. Both small.

Seems to me at this time that very difficult work ended at sharp left turn just after starting this A.M. and that work from then on is between that and the easy granite slopes.

Stop after left bend just before river turns to right and take photos, 4:45 P.M.

Start at 5:00 P.M. and at once run Rapid No. 480.

Opposite point where we took the last photos is a *real* perpendicular wall on the railroad side about 400 feet long and 300 feet high. This is the most difficult point we have encountered for a railroad line in the *Grand Canyon*!! The canyon is very narrow, the wall vertical, on a slight curve to right, is very compact and solid granite, and can only be handled in one of two ways: first by tunneling the whole bend which would be very long and expensive, and second by rounding this cliff with a *half tunnel* which would not be over 400 feet long. As this is the only point on the whole river where such a piece of work would be necessary it is anything but an insurmountable difficulty. Beyond this, still in the part creek cuts through the granite with vertical walls, 60 to 80 foot span, and beyond this a bold point easily handled. After that the granite goes back in a very good slope.

At 5:07 we stop to look ahead and at 5:10 we start again and at 5:13 run Rapid No. 481. And at 5:18 P.M. land on left bank and go into Camp No. 98.

[Note:] Since running the last north course we have made one long bend to left, then long bend to right where the high vertical wall is, and then another long one to left, and we are camped at sharp turn to left, just before *sharp* turn to right.

SATURDAY, MARCH 15, 1890. Clear. The river fell 4 to 6 inches last night.

At Camp No. 98. 8:15 A.M. take photos. Last picture shows very sharp turn to right. From the heavy work at right turn noted yesterday, the line is good

---

of the rapid a nearly vertical cliff of the Precambrian, surmounted by the remnant of an ancient lava flow, rose about 150 feet from the river's edge and about "50 ft. above grade," as the engineer notes. Since Stanton still plans to bring the line down the right side, the lava block would make for some "heavy" cutting. Easy to dispose of the waste, though. Dump it in the river.

Stanton was handicapped by a withered left arm, and this kept him from some of the heaviest labor. Anyone who reads these field notes will agree that the handicap restrained his activity very slightly otherwise.

granite slope around right and left bends to this sharp right turn ahead. This is simply bold points and heavy work.

Start from camp at 8:30 and at 8:34 A.M. run light Rapid No. 482. At 8:38 A.M. run light Rapid 483, and at 8:42 stop on right bank after turning the left at camp, turn a right and, next left turn to take photos.

After leaving camp the point spoken of above is quite sharp and bold. A creek, 60 foot span, cuts through it. The upstream side can be tunneled, 200 feet. Then on to bridge. From this on to good bench shown at end of photo.

This stratified benching granite continues all the way around this long left swing to where river turns to right again.

Work is heavy but simple by keeping the line high as the benches are of solid grey granite.

We start at 9:07 A.M. and at 9:09 run light Rapid No. 484, and at 9:12 run light Rapid No. 485, and stop at 9:20 on left bank just at beginning of next right turn. For the last 1/2 mile before reaching this point, the granite walls are perpendicular next to water and for 50 to 100 feet up, and then bench back in good easy benches. Good line high up.

9:30 A.M. photo. Around point of turn to right is quite bold but easily worked on upper slope.

We start again on smooth but swift water at 9:52 and at 9:54 run light Rapid No. 486. And at 10:00 A.M. stop on left bank, at mouth of large side canyon on left at point where river turns due north. Around this right turn cliff very bold but benched back. Good line can be located, but heavy and expensive work. Beyond this up north course granite benched back same as above to next small left turn. This stretch has slopes like the easy slopes above Diamond Creek, though *flatter*.

We start at 10:20 A.M. and at once run Rapid No. 487, heavy and crooked but safe. 10:26 run Rapid 488, just at left turn. Side wash, 20 foot span. Rapid, clear, beautiful view, high waves. Wet and stop at 10:35 at center of next right turn. Small wash on left.

From the beginning of this general north course the whole character of the walls and of the rock change. The granite seems more rotten, is rapidly getting lower, and slopes back in regular slopes nearing 45°.

10:45 A.M. photo. Directly opposite is lava pile. High water mark is coming lower also.

We start at 10:52 and at 10:54 run light Rapid No. 489. Rapid No. 490 at 10:56. Rapid No. 491 at 10:58. This last had high waves and we took in a big one all over me.

We stop at 11:08 A.M. at end of north course where river turns sharp to left and creek comes in from due north. Take photos. Say to here, 3-20 foot spans and 10-10 foot spans.

The character of wall described above continues to sharp left turn with side canyon on right from north. After looking at this from lower side I see the point runs up so that line can be built with open cut or very short tunnel.

We start at 11:25 and at once run heavy Rapid No. 492. Immense rock at left at top and current beats on great rock projecting from right bank below, clear channel between but great twisting waves. Taking a good deal of water over my legs. Stop at 11:42 for lunch. Photos on left bank 3/4 mile below head of rapid.

The same character of sloping granite as far as can be seen around this left turn.

We start after lunch at 12:58 and turn left bend to very low broken side wash on right. There at 1:06 P.M. we run sharp little Rapid No. 493 with powerful whirls at bottom and land 1 1/2 mile below where river turns sharp to right for photos. Magnificent views from here, high marble cliffs above with rather red coloring. Lower cliffs mostly black and brown. Last few miles finer than any in this lower granite. Line has good slope all round here as far as can see right, 4-20 foot and 2-30 foot spans to this right turn.

Start at 1:30 P.M. in very swift water but no rapid; but at 1:32 enter Rapid No. 494, light. 1:36 enter Rapid 495. Around right bend 2-20 foot and 2-10 foot spans. At 1:42 P.M. turn sharp to left northwest course, 1-30 foot span.

Granite slopes on, continues all round this turn and down northwest stretch. Side washes, 2-20 foot spans. Run down this long 2 mile course, and land at end where river turns to left with side canyon on right, 100 foot span, and large side canyon on left 3/4 mile further on with river then turning to right. Land for photos at 1:55 P.M.

Beyond this point of granite is not very high but juts out to river. This point is immense — 1500 feet long and 800 high — of lime sediment from lime springs. At lower end great springs run into river, one making most beautiful *white* fall of about 50 feet. High water drops very suddenly on this last stretch and is only 20 feet at this point.

We start at 2:18 and at once run long Rapid No. 496. Run long Rapid No. 497 at 2:23. Run short heavy Rapid No. 498 at 2:26, and land at foot of it on left side at 2:28 for photos. The point we have [covered?] is very bold, but as river is wide and high water low we can afford to pitch it in river.

Start at 2:45 P.M. and at 2:47 run crooked Rapid No. 499, and at 2:54 run sharp Rapid 500. Just before the right turn above 3-10 foot and 2-20 foot spans to this right turn. The granite is getting lower and lower, now about 75 feet, and the Potsdam sandstone is coming down with it. River broad.

We turn right bend and at 3:00 P.M. run Rapid No. 501, quite brisk. We stop 1 1/2 mile below point of right turn for photos. Looking down northwest stretch, the granite disappears where river makes vent, small right bend 1 1/2 miles ahead.

All this stretch from some distance back is very simple hillside slope, but to get *best* alignment would require some heavy side hill cuts on points. One-half mile from point line would be on the sandstone above granite, 3-10 foot spans [and] 1-30 foot span.

Opposite this, lava on left. Where from?

We start at 3:25 P.M. and at 3:28 run light Rapid No. 502 from side canyon on left. We turn right turn at 3:35 P.M. and go down stretch to where river turns sharp to left. Granite and the Potsdam sandstone entirely run out where river turns sharp to left on west course, first turn above, main turn to west.

At 3:41 we begin left turn by running Rapid No. 503. Stop at 3:45 at first west course, before big west course. At this left bend there are 3 wide washes, 3-50 foot spans, perhaps larger. Granite and sandstone disappear at first one on right and opposite third one on left. Slopes on right bank great flat wash banks of gravel and pieces of marble covered with grass and bushes. Magnificent and grand views. High marble mountains *near* river but no bright colors. Beyond third wash limestone and marble slopes, wind down to water's edge with their flat slopes running high up to the marble cliffs.

Start at 4:05 and at once run Rapid No. 504 which is very long and crooked and running close to cliff, 1/2 mile long, a moment's breath. 4:12 run No. 505, more crooked and heavy than last. Two waves lap over boat and fill it over floor, and completely drench Kane and myself. 4:23 run small Rapid 506.

At 4:27 stop at beginning of main west course for photos at side canyon on right, 60 foot span.

Beyond here around left turn to next right turn broken and rough limestone and marble cliffs come to river. These are all deposits from springs. At point of next right turn, limestone bold and high. See note farther on.

We start at 4:46 P.M. and at 4:48 run long letter S, Rapid No. 506. At 4:52 run light Rapid No. 507. At 4:54 run light Rapid No. 508. At 4:58 run light Rapid No. 509.

All this lime cliff noted above is deposit from mineral springs, 100 to 150 feet high above river. This can be easily handled as river is wide; and simply have to blow these high points off for between them are beautiful slopes of the limestone ledges, stratified quartzite, etc., etc.

We turn right turn then left, and right turn ahead has high points of same material. This only requires a little more powder to make good line.

Just before this point, at 5:05 we run long Rapid No. 510, quite sharp and crooked, and at 5:10 run Rapid No. 511, sharp and full of whirls. At 5:17 land on left bank, about 2 miles below last photos and take [others].

The lime *deposit* on right continues to this point. Stratified lime and quartzite slopes beyond.

We start at 5:33 and at 5:37 run long Rapid No. 512 and at 5:40 run long Rapid No. 513. Side canyon on right, 50 foot span.

The same fine slopes, grassy hillsides formed by the horizontal stratified limestone under marble, continue far ahead.

At 5:50 we run long light Rapid No. 514. At 5:52 we run long light Rapid No. 515. At 5:55 we run long light Rapid No. 516. Three 20 foot spans, 1-50 foot span.

FIG. 50. Travertine deposits (right) at Camp 99, the last in Grand Canyon. *Robert B. Stanton.* Engineering Societies Library.

We continue down this stretch; and the hillside slopes formed of the horizontally stratified limestone, quartzite, and mineralized matter, the same that first showed above the Nankoweap, continue all through. At turn to right, these slopes are very flat formed by the wash from two side canyons, 2-30 foot spans, and are cut through by the washes. Beyond this the same good hillside slope continues as above the point.

The river here is broad but a number of turns make an easy but rather crooked line, not over 4° curves, however. The marble is close to the river, the slopes running up to its foot, and quite a number of little washes coming in, say 2-20 foot spans and 8-10 foot spans. 6:02 and 6:04 light gravel Rapids No. 517 and No. 518.

We then turn left into a short 1/2 to 3/4 mile nearly west northwest course. Shown in photos taken at noon [March] 16th at our Sunday Camp No. 99.

And at 6:10 P.M. go into Camp No. 99.

[Note:] Impressions of the lower granite canyon: Granite higher. More vertical walls, more bold projecting points, and difficult work. A real canyon. River more powerful, the *bad* rapids worse, and the good rapids bad. Whirls, boils, and cross currents, far stronger and more powerful than anywhere else. Rapids that could not be portaged, and must be run, etc., etc. Peculiar deposit of lime from great mineral springs on both sides, run down over slopes, carrying pieces of rock and embedding them, forming a rough conglomerate. This cut through by streams and polished.

SUNDAY, MARCH 16, 1890. Clear. The river rose about 6 inches last night, and has risen 6 inches more today. Beautiful bright day.

And a glorious rest. My bed will be dry tonight for the first time since leaving Diamond Creek. Camp No. 99.

Hasty note: From granite down the views become more grand. The marble mountains come near the river and rise towering over it. The cliffs are not so vertical as in upper canyon. The marble seems to be more rotten as it approaches the end of the canyon. The bright colors are entirely wanting, but the nearness of the peaks to the river give one a more correct idea of the greatness of the *whole canyon*.[10]

[10] Once through Lava Cliff Rapid, the worst was over, and the Stanton Survey moved along rapidly. There were more rapids, of course, but they were easily run, though the men were often soaked by high waves. After four days on the river, the party went into camp at about mile 274.5, some thirty-five miles below Separation Rapid and about four miles from the mouth of Grand Canyon. As the flotilla moved along through this section, Stanton noted the changing face of the canyon. As the walls of the gloomy Lower Granite Gorge dropped down and finally went under (Stanton has found a name for his "beaded" sandstone — the Tapeats, capping the Precambrian — which he now calls the Postsdam Sandstone), the great cliffs, breached by the several side canyons, stood high above the river in massive, tiered promontories. The engineer wondered about the origin of the remnants of ancient intra-canyon lava flows, and he described the extensive travertine formations deposited by "mineral

MONDAY, MARCH 17. Slightly cloudy. River fell last [night] 6 inches.

On the northwest stretch where we camped Sunday, the slope made by the lower limestone ledges is regular and smooth, covered by debris from the marble above, and occasionally has points of mineral lime run down from above over the slope. High water about 20 feet. An easy line, 2-20 foot spans, to point where river turns to right.

We slept a little late this morning. Dry blankets were a comfort.

Got loaded and start at 8:15 A.M. At 8:20 A.M. we run long shallow Rapid No. 519, just at right turn. This point on right turn is formed by lime deposit from springs, small springs with ferns all round it. One 30 foot span. Can cut to any line wanted. At 8:26 run light Rapid No. 520. On the northwest stretch past point the slope is at first flat, 50 feet high, of gravel, 1-30 foot span. One-fourth way down this stretch stop at 8:29 on left bank and take photo.

We start again at 8:39 A.M.

River *begins* to turn to left, and on right side is high 150 foot bluff of *lime deposit,* nearly *vertical* from the water. This extends about 1/4 mile beyond this, the same deposit extends for 1/4 mile further but is not over 50 to 75 feet high. On left the Potsdam sandstone rises up again.

As we proceed I see that the real walls of Potsdam stone are under this deposit, showing in places, simply covered by this deposit.

At 8:45 stop 2/3 way down stretch on left bank, for photos about 1/3 way down 75 foot deposit.

We start at 8:58 A.M. Smooth water all down this stretch, no rapids beyond. All along this great lime deposit are little springs near the water's edge and the rocks covered with ferns. Say 2-10 foot waterways in this.

Beyond as river turns to west, is a patch of granite 20 feet high with the Potsdam stone on top. High water about 15 feet. One 20 foot opening.

Beautiful railroad bench on granite under the sandstone all around this left turn, 1-40 foot opening, 1-10 foot opening, or if the grade will suit, a beautiful line on flat on top of the sandstone.

We turn left bend at 9:10 A.M. and get our first real view out of the Grand Canyon. At 9:15 we land on left bank and take photos, at end of granite and Potsdam stone, showing last close view of canyon and the Grand Wash Cliffs, [and] showing out of Grand Canyon and the rocks at the gateway.[11]

---

springs" noted in many places in the lower canyon. Having come this far and seen all of these things, Robert B. Stanton had developed an appreciation for the "greatness of the whole canyon." There was nothing in the landscape to prevent the building of the line: At one point about three miles below Lava Cliff Rapid, the engineer found the most difficult place in Grand Canyon for railroad construction, but even this was "anything but an insurmountable difficulty," he noted.

[11] At this point the Stanton expedition had reached the mouth of Grand Canyon, the "Southern gateway" — 278 miles below Lee's Ferry. The canyon ends abruptly and dra-

We start again at the mouth or southern gateway to the Grand Canyon at 9:45 A.M. At this point, the granite which is about 60 feet high with the Potsdam stone on top, chops square off on both sides. The banks on either side are formed of *wash* gravel, pieces of broken stone, and sand in some places cemented together. The banks are from 50 to 60 feet high, sloping to the water's edge, cut by a number of small washes, small waterways.

One mile down some little bluffs of red sandstone 20 to 30 feet high, on right. The river spreads out broad large gravel bars and islands and a swift current among them. High water mark is only 10 to 12 feet.

Will now number the light gravel rapids, as on Series "B." At 10:03 Rapid No. 1, Series B.

At 10:05 land on right bank at Pierce's Ferry, abandoned. Gravel banks are higher, 100 feet. At 10:15 take photos from top of bluff at Pierce's Ferry showing southern gateway to the Grand Canyon, [and] Pierce's Ferry. The washes that come in on right are small to here, 5-10 foot openings.[12]

Start again at 10:33 and at 10:35 run long gravel Rapid No. 2, winding among gravel islands, 4 minutes through it. Just beyond Pierce's Ferry large wash on right, perhaps 50 foot span. Banks washed away. Railroad will have to build bank across this. Beyond the gravel bluffs get lower 50 to 75 feet, flat slopes to the river, and long sweeping curves.

---

matically as the river flows through the Grand Wash Cliffs, towering over two thousand feet above the water. Geologists explain that the radical change is accounted for by the downthrow of the familiar horizontal strata of Grand Canyon along the north-south trending Grand Wash Fault, which in this area marks the transition zone between the Colorado Plateau and the Basin and Range geographical provinces. In all of the distance from Grand Junction to this point, the survey for the DCC & PRR had been confined to the canyon lands, a predominant feature of the plateau. Henceforth the survey would be run through open country with only an occasional short, rough-sided canyon to slow its progress.

[12] Having reached the open country, Stanton has nothing to say here of the exhilaration he felt upon leaving behind the great canyon that had held him confined so long. But he wrote about it in an article, "Through the Grand Cañon of the Colorado," *Scribner's Magazine*, VIII (November, 1890), 591–613, and again, along with an appreciation of the canyon's beauty, in his long work on the Colorado River. See Dwight L. Smith, ed., *Down the Colorado* (1965), 220. Compare this passage with J. W. Powell's often quoted remarks in his *Exploration of the Colorado River of the West* (1875), 102–103.

Beyond the Grand Wash Cliffs for some seventy miles the Colorado River follows a westward course, and thus it formed a barrier to pioneer traffic moving along north-south lines. Prospectors drifting back and forth between mining fields in Nevada, Utah, and Arizona, and Mormon colonization in northern Arizona, accounted for most of this traffic which was heavy enough to prompt the establishment of several ferries. One of these, a mile downstream from the mouth of Grand Canyon, operated by Harrison Pearce, 1876–1883, was opened to provide a crossing for Mormons moving to Arizona from Utah. The ferry saw little use after 1883; when Stanton arrived in 1890 it was abandoned. The name (altered in most of the records to Pierce) is preserved in the Pierce Ferry boat landing on Lake Mead.

After counting 520 rapids in the long run through the canyons, Stanton now began a new numbered series for the comparatively light rapids below Grand Canyon.

At 10:46 run Rapid No. 3. At 10:49 run Rapid No. 4, quite brisk and rocky. The bluffs are flatter and more broken. Beautiful sweeping bend to left. Cheap easy line on gravel slopes, but quite a number of openings for waterways.

At 10:58 run Rapid No. 5, with brisk waves and strong whirls. Splashed and am wet once more.

4-10 foot spans	1-30 foot span
5-20 foot spans	1-50 foot span

on this stretch and round left bend *to* right turn.

As [it] turns to right, it cuts through high dike of limestone and marble with the strata dipping sharp to the south, making bold bluff at point of turn 150 feet high. Heavy work but not difficult.

This continues with more slope towards river down short north stretch with 2-30 foot spans and continues around left turn. Around this the walls are almost perpendicular at lower part; at end of this bluff break back into low bluffs as before. Whole distance of this heavy work 3/4 to 1 mile. It ends at the Grand Wash which comes in from north, 150 foot span.[13]

Just here at 11:15 we enter Rapid No. 6, heavy, and at 11:18 Rapid No. 7, heavy and wet. We stop 1/2 mile below and take photos at 11:26 A.M., showing mouth of Grand Wash. Slopes between photo and wash covered with lava.

We start at 11:54. The bluffs on right are low and broken up. Points of limestone coming out bold 20 to 40 feet high, and the flat slopes above covered with gravel and lime conglomerate. All the rock in this section is set on edge with incline slope approaching 45°, dipping south and east.

At 12:04 run Rapid No. 8, and at 12:10 P.M. land on right bank where river begins to turn left, for lunch. [At] this right bend, before lunch, the slopes run way back so that line would not follow river but cut way back on edge of bluffs. Up to this lunch point, 4-10 foot spans [and] 2-20 foot spans.

From this point on, river turns to left. The right bank is upheaved, limestone sloping away from river. Good line but all solid rock.

We start at 1:38. Around this bend, several waterways, 2-10 foot openings, several smaller.

At point where river makes sharper left turn we run Rapid No. 9, 1:48 P.M., 3/4 mile long.

Made side wash from right. The right wall from this sharp left turn is of the same upheaved limestone sloping from the river. At point of photos debris makes good talus slope.

---

[13] Grand Wash, coming in on the right, now forms a large bay at the upper end of Lake Mead.

Stop at 1:54 one mile from sharp left turn for photos. Last shows most beautiful stretch of river we have seen.

We start at 2:10 P.M. Four 10 foot openings to this point ahead, 2 miles, where river turns to right, and 4 more 10 foot openings, 1-20 foot opening. After leaving the photo point this same character of wall continues for 2 miles to turn to right. First 1/2 mile good slope, then second 1/2 mile good bench, then third 1/2 mile. *Later* this is cut in two by wash, making 2 points; and as there is nearly 1/2 mile ahead of low flat slope, line might be located further back and thus only make two heavy cuts.

Beyond this flat slope as river turns to right, rough points, small but easy rock work line.

At 2:23 run Rapid No. 10, formed by side wash on right, 1-30 foot span. At 2:31 run sharp Rapid No. 11. Side wash right, 50 foot span. Beyond this side wash, low rock bluffs. These are cut through by many little washes.

Two miles ahead river turns sharp to right. Same low bluffs all the way to that point requires 6-10 foot openings, 4-20 foot openings, 1-30 foot opening.

At 2:45 run Rapid No. 12, [and] at 2:55 run Rapid No. 13, [both with] long shallow gravel.

At 3:00 P.M. land at extreme end of this long southwest course where river turns right for photos.

Start again at 3:21 P.M. After rounding this point to right as river begins turn to left the bluffs are very low and flat next to river, though high further back, 3-10 foot openings, 1-40 foot opening. Around this left bend the whole country is broken away. Bluffs on right 20 to 30 feet high, on left 10 to 12. River very broad and good current. Seven 10 foot openings on right to point where river turns to right.

At 3:43 run light Rapid No. 14. Stop at 3:55 P.M. for photos.

We start at 4:30 P.M. and at 4:33 run light Rapid No. 15. And at 4:45 land on left bank at *Scanlon's Ferry* and go into Camp No. 100. W. L. Haskin & Son.

The whole line since the long southwest course has been on what is simply broad bottom land with low bluffs back, so that it need not follow close to river but can cut off bends. Here at Scanlon's Ferry, it is open and flat. Scanlon has fine irrigated garden.[14]

---

[14] Below Grand Wash the Stanton party passed through the short Iceberg Canyon to emerge once again in open country. Nine miles below the Pearce facility Scanlon's Ferry was started by one Mike Scanlon, prospector, about 1883. The ferry was later sold to Tom Gregg. A summary of the history of the Colorado River crossings between the mouth of Grand Canyon and Fort Mojave will be found in Melvin T. Smith, "The Colorado River: Its History in the Lower Canyons Area" (Ph.D. Dissertation, 1972). The names of Scanlon and Gregg are preserved in a number of geographical features in the Lake Mead National Recreation Area.

Tuesday, March 18, 1890. Cloudy all day.

8:00 A.M. photos from Scanlon's Ferry.

We start at 8:17 A.M. Four 10 foot spans, 1-50 foot span. A line can be located straight across the big wash opposite Scanlon's Ferry coming from and to the low bluffs at the hills on either side. Low bluffs continue to right bend of river. Except where otherwise noted these low bluffs are earth, gravel, and rock mixture. As river turns to right, line can keep way back till reaches rock bluffs on next left turn.

Fig. 51. Out in the open. Bonelli's Ferry at the mouth of the Virgin River. *Robert B. Stanton.* Engineering Societies Library.

9:50 pass mouth of Hualapai Wash. Heavy rapid 6 to 8 foot fall. Rapid No. 16. On right wash also 50 foot span. Under small canyon turning to right, 2-20 foot spans. This little canyon has granite walls sloping from water and much broken. The right turn is rather sharp and perhaps would require a short 200 foot tunnel. Beyond the granite slopes are flatter and more broken.

One 30 foot span at 9:00 A.M. and light Rapid No. 17, as river turns again to left. The granite slopes are rough and shattered up, making good easy line and fine alignment.

We stop at 9:12 A.M. for photos in Hualapai Canyon.

Start again at 9:25 A.M. All through this Hualapai Canyon the granite slopes are of the easiest kind, granite broken and shattered slopes about 40° to 45°, and good alignment like the easiest slopes in the upper granite canyons. Two 20 foot spans, 3-10 foot spans, 1-30 foot span. We stop at 9:52 A.M. on left bank for photos at mouth of side canyon on left.

We start at 10:26, *light* Rapid No. 18, 2-10 foot spans. This Hualapai Canyon ends about 1/4 mile below photo point, and line runs on to sloping hillsides of conglomerate sand rock covered with wash of earth and gravel, 1-10 foot opening.[15]

At 10:35 run good Rapid No. 19. At 10:40 run light Rapid No. 20. These slopes are about 50° from vertical and make the very cheapest kind of hillside construction. The alignment around this long right swing is beautiful. One 50 foot span, 2-10 foot spans.

10:45 sharp little Rapid No. 21, 2-10 foot spans.

Slopes continue with many *small* washes but no large ones. Many of these small washes can be turned together, say 6-10 foot openings to point.

We stop at 11:00 A.M. on left bank at point of right swing about 3/4 mile above where river turns sharp to left [for photos].

We start at 11:28 A.M. Three-fourths mile down sandstone bluff for 1/4 mile to this bluff, 2-10 foot openings, 1-20 foot opening, 1-30 foot opening. This bluff easily handled by cutting low bluff under the Citadel,[16] and making roadbed in river. River very wide, no trouble. 11:40 run light Rapid No. 22.

After passing this Citadel river turns left with long swing beyond to right. The bluffs are exceedingly low. Line will not follow river but cut straight for [*blank*] on this stretch, 1-40 foot span, 1-20 foot span, 2-10 foot spans.

We land at end of this cut off line at 12 noon for lunch [and] photos.

Start again after lunch at 1:15 P.M. At 1:23 run long shallow Rapid No. 23. At 1:27 run long deep Rapid No. 24. From lunch point line would run

---

[15] Hualapai, or Hualpai, after the Indian tribe. Stanton applies this name to the short canyon now called Virgin Canyon. Hualpai Wash emptied into the river at the head of the canyon.

[16] Stanton's name for the imposing formation now known as The Temple, or Temple Mesa, towering about 300 feet above the waters of Lake Mead on the shore opposite the Temple Bar Marina.

straight across the big bend to bluffs on the northwest course. Perhaps 2-20 foot and 1-30 foot openings. After cutting across the big bend the bluffs beyond are very regular and even in alignment, first a low bench 30 to 50 feet up sloping with easy slopes to river, then higher bluffs back.

From look ahead, I think line would be on face of these *lower* bluffs, but perhaps on top; *further on not on top.* They are cut through by many *small* washes — many can be turned into one opening — and some larger ones; but it is a beautiful cheap line all through. Or perhaps line best on bottom below bluffs. This along here best and cheapest if this wide bottom above high water continues, 2 1/2 mile tangent on bottom.

At 1:55 stop on point where river turns left for photos.

We start at 2:30. From point of photos 3/4 mile ahead the same low bottom continues to low rock bluff where river turns to right. This is not over 1/4 mile long, has good talus, river very broad, and line can be built at bottom cheaply, or on face. Up to this point the long stretch would have 5-10 foot openings, 5-20 foot openings, 2-50 foot openings.

Beyond this rock bluff the same low sloping bluffs of conglomerate covered with wash of gravel and sand, greasewood and grass. These same low bluffs continue but they [are] more abrupt, 20 feet high, and sloping back from that. At foot of these are low flat bottoms on which line can be located if desired. To end of these low rocky bluffs are 5-10 foot openings, 2-20 foot openings, 1-30 foot opening. Beyond this, low bluffs, as before the rocky ones, with wide flat bottoms below them. Scraper work.

The only objection to building on these bottoms is the openings necessary to be left. They would be much more secure in the bluffs:

3-10 foot spans	1-30 foot span
1-20 foot span	2-50 foot spans

We stop at 3:12 P.M. for photos on right bank about 1 1/2 miles above mouth of Rio Virgin.

We start at 3:34, 1-80 foot span. The same low gravel bluffs to immense flat wash that has run out 1/4 mile into and forced over the river, line will cut across this on tangent for about 3/4 mile to bluffs beyond. Beyond, the slope gradually rises to low gravel bluffs at end of this 3/4+ mile. These bluffs continue to the mouth of Rio Virgin.

At 4:00 P.M. we land at Bonelli's Ferry, about 1/2 mile above mouth of Virgin and go into Camp No. 101. [Photos of] river, Bonelli house, [and] Mrs. Daniel Bonelli and daughter.

We met Mr. [*blank*] Maxwell, C. E., UPRy engineer in charge of UP work in Nevada, who is going down river to Needles exploring; also Daniel Bonelli, Rioville, Nevada.

Salt mines, 6 miles to 20 miles above mouth of Virgin. Eight claims 1500×600, 150+ feet thick.

Raises grapes (10 acres), limes, pomegranates, figs, almonds, pears, peaches, plums, nectarines. Bonelli says he produces as good wines as can be made in Europe. That all these high gravel mesas will grow grapes, with water.

Steamboat 180 feet long made one trip from here at high water, loaded with salt, to El Dorado Canyon, 68 miles, in 3 hours and 10 minutes.[17]

High water 6 years ago was up 21 feet above low water. Mark this in connection with all my high water notes.

WEDNESDAY, MARCH 19, 1890. Cloudy all day and heavy south wind since 10 A.M.

Mr. Bonelli is very much interested in the railroad prospects. He is recorder for this mining district and promises to send me a statement of the resources of this section, etc.

---

[17] Located at the confluence of the Virgin and Colorado rivers, Rioville was the home of Daniel Bonelli, a pioneer prominent in the Mormon thrust southward into southern Utah and to Arizona and Nevada. Bonelli moved to the spot soon ater 1871, built a home, planted garden crops and fruit trees and vines, and staked claims to deposits of rock salt along the banks of the Virgin River. About 1877 he acquired Stone's Ferry, operating nearby. For a good many years Bonelli's Ferry was a major crossing of the Colorado River, much used by mercurial miners rushing about from one mining camp to another, and by Mormon colonists bound for Arizona. A small settlement developed at Rioville, boasted a post office, 1881–1906. Some of the rock salt sold to the mines at El Dorado Canyon downstream was shipped by river barge. On Daniel Bonelli and on commercial navigation, see Melvin T. Smith, "The Colorado River" (1972). The name is preserved in Bonelli Bay on Lake Mead and in other area geographical features.

Major John Wesley Powell ended his 1869 expedition at the Rio Virgen, as he wrote it, a contraction of the Spanish term (Río de la Virgen) commonly in use before his day, and lasting on into the twentieth century. By Stanton's time, however, the Anglicization of the name to Virgin River was in progress.

CHAPTER X

FROM THE RIO VIRGIN TO TIDEWATER

Once through the Grand Canyon, Stanton knew that the most difficult part of the survey was behind him. At that point "our task," he wrote later, is "virtually accomplished." It was open country now. There were few rapids of consequence and the few canyons were short. The mark of other Colorado River pioneers was seen all along the way: ferries, boat landings, steamboats, settlements, mills and mines, army posts, Indian reservations, and railroads. In light of more recent history along the Colorado it is noteworthy that not a single dam had yet been built anywhere along the route of the survey. Passing through the areas now flooded by Lake Mead and Lake Mohave, and after visiting at Fort Mojave, the expedition halted for nearly a month at the Santa Fe Railroad crossing at Needles, California. Then, accelerating the pace, Stanton sailed along through the Lake Havasu area and the Parker, Palo Verde, and Cibola valleys to Yuma, Arizona. From there, in two days, the expedition reached tidewater in Mexico. The grand voyage was over. Altogether, from the confluence of the Colorado and Green rivers, Robert B. Stanton had carried his railroad survey along the river a total of about 985 miles.

WEDNESDAY, MARCH 19 [continued].[1] We start at 8:53 A.M. Stop at 9:07 for photos up the Rio Virgin [and] across the bend to head of Boulder Canyon. Taken about 1 1/2 miles below mouth of Rio Virgin. Start again at 9:28 A.M.

Our line would cut across the point beyond the Rio Virgin.

At 9:40 run light but rocky Rapid No. 25, and 9:53 No. 26.

After reaching point, it would either diverge to left and follow round low bluffs of the river or I think a good line and not heavy grades can be found by turning to right up flat wash and making a straight line for the head of Boulder Canyon. Perhaps to be varied at head of canyon.

At 10:00 run light Rapid No. 27.

---

[1] This chapter is taken from the second half of Stanton's Field Notebook D.

10:30 A.M., it is question which can only be settled by extensive surveys whether line can be continued all the way to head of canyon as the very broken country around the left bend of river above canyon is quite high. Later, I think good and cheap line *can* be had as the *hills* are so cut up by washes that will have to have openings anyhow, that it will be just as cheap to go through these hills as around them.

We stop at 10:40 A.M. for survey and photos, about [a] mile above head of Boulder Canyon, 1/4 mile below last [photo] showing the head of Boulder Canyon.

Up to the Boulder Canyon, 3-50 foot spans, 2-30 foot spans, 4-20 foot spans, 4-10 foot spans.

Start again at 11:27. At 11:34 we enter Boulder Canyon over a swift but light Rapid No. 28 formed by side canyon on right, 80 foot span. The walls of this canyon are of granite rough broken into very bold points, 1-30 foot span. First 1/2 mile has, on the convex side, some real perpendicular walls. High water mark is so low, line can be built in the wide bay. The two points before and after are very high and almost perpendicular, said to be 1800 feet high. On account of steamboat navigation it would perhaps be best to tunnel these two points and build bank with the waste, 1-30 foot span.[2]

Beyond this for 1/2 to 3/4 mile there is good talus above high water which can be built upon. Beyond this one short low point of rock juts out, easy. At this 11:55 run quite sharp Rapid No. 29. The same talus and flats for 1/4 mile, 2-20 foot spans, 1-10 foot span. Then comes wall almost perpendicular for 1/2 mile with small talus at foot. Line can be built along this without interfering with the river.

At 12:08 P.M. small Rapid No. 30 by side wash on left. One 30 foot span on right. Thus to point where river turns to right, better talus at point, and around it. We stop just round first point for lunch at 12:15 P.M.

Photos in Boulder Canyon.

We start up again at 1:25 P.M. Farther around this right bend, broad sand flats, wider canyon, and rock broken down much lower, making easy line to next turn left, 1-20 foot span. Good line on rough slopes round left bend, 1-80 foot opening, 1-50 foot opening. Broad flats, and flat sloping walls.

Good swift water. Six 10 foot openings, 2-30 foot openings, 2-20 foot openings, 1-50 foot opening, to point turn right.

---

[2] By 1890, steamboating up the Colorado to Rioville and the mouth of the Virgin River, practically limited to high-water navigation, had ceased altogether. Rock salt from the mines along the Virgin, the principal item in the commerce, was shipped downstream for use in the mining districts centering at El Dorado Canyon. See Richard E. Lingenfelter, *Steamboats on the Colorado River, 1852–1916* (Tucson, University of Arizona Press, 1978) for a detailed study of the subject.

Boulder Canyon might have been selected as the site for Hoover Dam, but it was passed over in favor of the Black Canyon site about eighteen miles downstream.

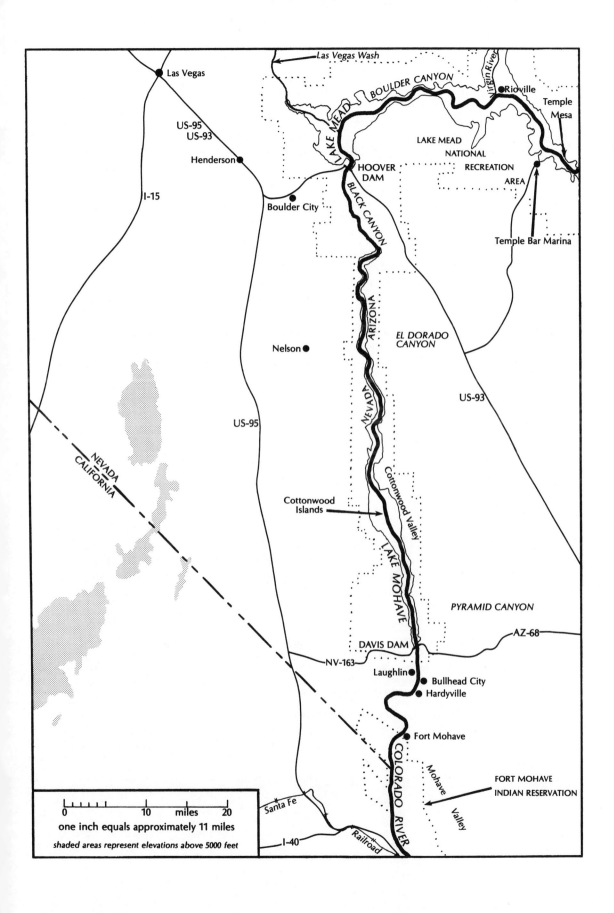

Las Vegas Wash

Las Vegas

US-95
US-93

Henderson

I-15

Boulder City

Nelson

NEVADA
CALIFORNIA

US-95

BOULDER CANYON

Virgin River

Rioville

Temple
Mesa

LAKE MEAD
NATIONAL
RECREATION
AREA

HOOVER
DAM

Temple Bar Marina

BLACK CANYON

ARIZONA

NEVADA

EL DORADO
CANYON

US-93

Cottonwood
Islands

Cottonwood Valley

LAKE MOHAVE

PYRAMID CANYON

AZ-68

DAVIS DAM

NV-163

Laughlin

Bullhead City

Hardyville

Fort Mohave

COLORADO RIVER

Mohave

Valley

FORT MOHAVE
INDIAN RESERVATION

Santa Fe

Railroad

I-40

0   10   miles   20

one inch equals approximately 11 miles

shaded areas represent elevations above 5000 feet

At 2:00 p.m. run sharp little Rapid No. 31, and at 2:03 p.m. land on right side at end of stretch for photo.

Start at 2:17 p.m. At 2:35 we emerge from the canyon, with a great flat wash on right nearly a mile across the flat. Long trestle 300 to 400 feet across the wash proper. Fine gravel in bed, broad, flat, not deep. Beyond this the same low gravel conglomerate bluffs as above Virgin. Four 10 foot openings.

Rounding bend to right pass Old Callville stone ruins.[3]

These low gravel bluffs continue with broad low flats in front of them, 3-10 foot, 2-30 foot, and 1-50 foot openings. A great many washes through them. All of these can be covered with pile work.

We stop at 3:00 p.m. for photos on left bank at end of 1 1/2 miles west stretch, and at left bend.

We start at 3:23 p.m. Ever since leaving Boulder Canyon, line can be built on flat bottom land, *if* sufficient room can be gotten for waterways from side washes.

We have been having a heavy wind up stream all day and now it is blowing a perfect gale. We pass Maxwell, the UP engineer, gone into camp just below Las Vegas Wash on account of storm. The storm increases and it is difficult pulling. After some trouble we land at 4:00 p.m. and go into Camp No. 102, on left bank.

THURSDAY, MARCH 20, 1890. Raining. Rained till 9 a.m. Rained from 12 to 3 p.m. Raining this morning. Hard to get photos, but must try. 7:30 a.m. photos from Camp No. 102 across river towards the Las Vegas Wash [and] across river to south of Las Vegas Wash.

We start in the rain at 7:45 a.m.

The line from Old Callville around this left swing can keep well back on the slopes of the wash ridges and thus gain elevation to go out the Las Vegas Wash; and perhaps in this way can go out through the wash above the Las Vegas and cut through into it above, thus gaining distance. And line down river can branch off on flat above having a good place for town, shops, etc., etc. Mountains covered with snow. Show in the distance up the Las Vegas Wash.[4]

---

[3] Callville, located at the mouth of Callville Wash on the right side of the Colorado, was founded in 1864 by Anson Call for the Church of Jesus Christ of Latter-day Saints, as a river port near the practical head of steamboat navigation. The Mormons hoped to make this a major link in a commercial corridor to the sea, to serve the needs of their inland empire. However, when the transcontinental railroad was completed in 1869 the place was abandoned. Melvin T. Smith, "The Colorado River: Its History in the Lower Canyons Area" (1972), 266–319. The site is now marked by the huge marina on Lake Mead at Callville Bay.

[4] Lake Mead's Las Vegas Bay covers the lower few miles of Las Vegas Wash, which Stanton thought would be a "good place for a town" and "shops." Las Vegas Wash opened out on the river on the outside of a bend, named the "Great Bend" by Lt. Joseph C. Ives,

F<small>IG</small>. 52. Ruins of Callville, now submerged beneath the waters of Lake Mead (1922 Photo). *E. C. LaRue.* U.S. Geological Survey.

At 7:50 A.M. we enter Black Canyon. At first it is very wide and low. Before entering canyon the low conglomerate bluffs continue round right bend. After turning bend to right the rock walls come close to river. Sloping and not difficult. At extreme end of turn, cut back over sand flat to base of bluffs. After right turn, down stretch are some low lava bluffs jutting out into river;

U.S. Army Corps of Engineers, in 1858. Here the Colorado started on its long southward course to the Gulf of California, a distance by river of nearly 500 miles. Ives had been directed to determine the head of steam navigation on the Colorado and to ascertain if the river would be a feasible military supply route. In a steel steamboat of shallow draft, the Ives expedition worked its way slowly upriver to a point near the mouth of Black Canyon where the boat was severely damaged on "Explorer's Rock." In a small skiff Ives and two of his party rowed on up through Black Canyon and on to Las Vegas Wash (which he mistook for the Virgin River), reaching it on March 12. For all practical purposes Ives concluded that the head of Colorado River navigation was the foot of Black Canyon. Ives' *Report Upon the Colorado River of the West Explored in 1857 and 1858* (Washington, Government Printing Office, 1861), with detailed maps of the Colorado River, holds a secure place among the classics of western exploration. Ives added a number of names to the river's nomenclature and his *Report* documented and located accurately those already in use. Stanton was surely familiar with the *Report* and maps, since he uses so many of the Ives names in his notebooks.

cut extreme point well back. From here is a long left swing broken far back into several side canyons, with large low flat in front. Line can follow round on this, or build bank across bend of river, *very wide here*; or perhaps a line can be found up one of these side canyons and tunnel through to river to avoid the very sharp point I see ahead.

As river begins to turn right the high point of rock begins with high sloping talus, to where the turn is very sharp to right, almost 90°. This we pass at 8:25 A.M. and enter Black Canyon proper. At and after this right 90° turn the cliffs are high and bold but not vertical. Down the next stretch which is S 40° W true, the walls are almost vertical for 1 mile. This piece of work for 1 1/2 miles is very difficult and will be very expensive, on account of keeping the river clear for navigation. It is worthy of careful examination for a line back of this point and a tunnel, even long one, to come out at point where river turns left.[5] At this point the walls get lower and have good rock slopes so that line here is good and easy on the slopes or on the talus at this point of left turn.

Stop 8:50 A.M. for photos where river turns right, scene in Black Canyon.

Start again at 9:04 A.M. From point back of this 1 mile, end of *southwest* course, the cliffs are low and broken, making good rock work line. Sixty foot span. Two little right and then left. Long swing left, and the cliffs are much more broken and lower, with flatter rough rock slopes. As we go down this stretch the rock walls are very much lower and broken up into little points with low side canyon on right, 50 foot span.

We stop at 9:26 on left bank at mouth of large side canyon on left for photo.

We start at 9:48 and at once run heavy Rapid No. 32 formed by side canyon on left and at 9:50 run sharp Rapid No. 33. Beyond this side canyon walls low and benched and rough. Not a difficult piece of rock work.

At next turn of river to left side canyon on right, 50 foot span. Around this left bend and down stretch to right turn same broken cliffs but somewhat more bold. At turn to right side wash comes in on left. We pass it at 10:10 A.M. and run light Rapid No. 34 made by it. On right side opposite canyon good sloping talus like walls with little rock bluff next to water. This same character of wall continues round point and down stretch to side canyon on right. Good easy line on the slope, all rock work, and some heavy points to cut. High water mark 10 to 15 feet, 1-50 foot span, and light Rapid No. 35, at 10:20 A.M. One 20 foot opening, 1-60 foot opening side canyon just as river turns to left.

[5] Upper Black Canyon may have been a good place for a dam, but Robert B. Stanton figured that to build a railroad along the canyon wall where the Hoover Dam now stands, and for a mile or so below it, would be "very difficult" and "expensive." Visitors to the dam today can easily visualize the engineer's concern. Stand on top of the dam and look down along the precipitous wall of the canyon on the right (Nevada) side. Build a railroad *there*?

Past it at 10:26 A.M. Ragged *slopes* of rock beyond, 1-20 foot opening, 1-10 foot opening, 2-50 foot openings to where river again turns left.

We stop just at this turn at 10:36 A.M. for photos.

We start at 10:52 A.M. The same slope continues 1/4 mile then cliffs stand vertical 150 feet, practically for 1500 feet. Canyon 200 to 250 feet wide. There would be no difficulty here except for keeping narrow channel open for navigation. Tunnel this and it comes out on good talus slope under cliff with plenty of room.

Beyond here, cliffs broken down and back and cut up by water courses,

4-10 foot openings	1-20 foot opening
1-30 foot opening	1-50 foot opening

to point where river turns southwest which we pass at 11:20 and run rapid, light, No. 36. Around this bend where river begins a southwest course, flat rocky points as above.

We stop about 1/2 mile down southwest course, 11:27, *for lunch.* [Take photos.]

Start after lunch at 12:35 P.M., I note 5-10 foot, 1-20 foot, 1-30 foot, and 1-50 foot openings.

Beyond this good flat rock slopes round left bend. At right bend bluff comes out sharp and bold at point. Cut this heavy at low gap back, perhaps tunnel 300 feet. Then saw-tooth line of flat rock slopes. Four 10 foot, 4-20 foot, and 1-30 foot openings.

At 1:05 run small Rapid No. 37, from long side canyon on right, 80 foot span. Sharp saw-tooth line beyond. 1:04 small Rapid No. 38. Sharp point just beyond. Then very low rock slopes, and low broken country, 1-10 foot and 1-30 foot opening. Then very sharp point into river on sharp turn to right. Go behind this with 1000 foot tunnel on to saw-tooth line round bend and down next stretch. Easier and flatter points, 1-30 foot span. Examine line way back for cutoff. Then beyond flat, a bold cliff with small bench and talus at bottom to sharp right turn. Heavy work to point, 1:25 P.M., 1200 and 200 foot tunnels to good low line beyond. One 10 foot and 1-50 foot opening at left bend.

Down next stretch to where river turns to right with very large side canyon on *left*, cliffs bold but ragged at bottom. Good line but expensive rock work.

At first point of turn, 1/2 mile before side canyon, 300 foot tunnel then saw-tooth line of rock. Directly opposite side canyon, point of rock way out in river. Low gap back of it. Look for line behind this. Pass canyon on left at 1:45 P.M. Later, think can easily get back line. Country much broken up, 1-80 foot and 6-10 foot openings.

Beyond this low saw-tooth line low easy rounded points, 2-10 foot and 2-30 foot openings.

F<small>IG</small>. 53. El Dorado Canyon, river port and milling site for regional mines. The venerable river boat *Gila* appears to the right. *Robert B. Stanton.* Engineering Societies Library.

This long curve to left with low easy rock slopes continues to right turn which is end of Black Canyon; and we pass out of it at 2:10 P.M. Just before going out we stop 2:10 P.M. and take photo.[6]

Start at 2:25 P.M. One 30 foot span. Low bluffs of gravel and cinders. One 200 foot trestle; 3-10 foot, and 2-20 foot openings. At 2:36 run *small* Rapid No. 39, 200 and 300 foot trestles.

This covers notes to El Dorado Canyon.

We reach El Dorado Canyon, Nevada, at 3:00 P.M. and after visiting the mill, etc., go across and make camp No. 103 on left bank directly opposite. Land at El Dorado Canyon at 3:00 P.M.

Photos 4:00 P.M.: [the] river, El Dorado Mills of the Southwestern Mining Company, approach to El Dorado Canyon from higher point.

---

[6] Black Canyon, some twenty-three miles long, with its rough walls of volcanic rock and "sharp points," presented some formidable obstacles to railroad construction, but Stanton was always optimistic. Given enough tunnels and trestles, the line could be built through it.

Anyone studying navigation downstream from Black Canyon will appreciate the *Plan and Profile of Colorado River from Black Canyon, Arizona-Nevada to Arizona-Sonora Boundary* (Washington, U.S. Geological Survey, 1927). The seventeen plans, or maps, were surveyed in 1902–1903 (except the first sheet, A, surveyed in 1920) by the U.S. Geological Survey.

Line approaching El Dorado Canyon would be on the low bluffs before referred to from point where river begins big left swing and, nearer the bluffs, recedes leaving broad flat. Crossing El Dorado Wash it would have to be close to mill as rock bluffs come out close to river on each side, beyond this along the foot of rock bluffs to the flats. Photo [shows] steamer *Gila* in the distance.

Southwestern Mining Company, P. O. El Dorado Canyon, Lincoln County, *Nevada*:

> George Burnham, President — President, Baldwin Locomotive Works; Abram Barker — 125 South 4 Street, Philadelphia; Wharton Barker, son — Secretary and Treasurer; Joseph Wharton — Philadelphia; W. S. Mills, Manager.

Their card reads:

The Southwestern Mining Company

— Mining —

Ore Reducing & Merchandising

Lincoln Co., Nevada

W. S. Mills, Manager

Mr. Maxwell and myself are invited to tea by Mr. W. S. Mills the manager.

FRIDAY, MARCH 21, 1890. Clear all day.

7:45 A.M. from Camp No. 103, photograph El Dorado Canyon and steamer *Gila*. We camped last night on left bank of river directly opposite the mouth of El Dorado Canyon.

After breakfast we crossed back to El Dorado Canyon, and there met the famous Colorado River steamboat Captain Jack Mellon. He is a great brag. Says he can take a small flat bottomed boat and come from Green River Station, Utah, to the Needles in 13 days, distance 865 miles. He took us over the noted steamer *Gila*, stern-wheeler, 180 feet long, engines 16″×5′10″. Four steering rudders hung as centers.

Mr. Mills family came down to bid us good-by.

---

[7] Leaving Black Canyon the Stanton expedition, now in open country, soon reached El Dorado Canyon, the river port and milling site for silver and gold mines located back some miles from the river. Discoveries of precious metals brought a rush of prospectors here in 1861 and 1862, and the district, passing through periods of prosperity and depression, was supplied mainly by Colorado River steamboats. By 1890 the Southwestern Mining Company, the main operator in the district, was still using the steamers at a time when freighting on the river was declining. The *Gila*, tied up at the landing when Stanton arrived, was a venerable river boat, having been launched in 1873. Her captain, John "Jack" A. Mellon, the most famous of the river captains, had been on the river since 1864. Richard E. Lingenfelter, *Steamboats on the Colorado River, 1852–1916* (1978).

This site was covered by the rising waters of Lake Mohave after the completion of Davis Dam in 1953. A landing and marina (Nelson Landing), established at the mouth of

Captain Mellon says find Charles Tyson at Gulf and get his chart of Gulf.

Leave El Dorado Canyon at 9:00 A.M., 2-20 foot openings, 2-10 foot openings.

Line after passing rock points that are on river line can cut across long flat and not follow river by making a high grade.

Turned down wrong channel after duck. Stuck on bar for 15 minutes. Good line round this point on low flats to bluffs on left turn. At beginning of left turn 1-30 foot opening, 1-20 foot opening, and 1-10 foot opening. Stop on left bank for photos 10:08.

Start at 10:30 A.M. and at 10:32 A.M. run light Rapid No. [*blank*].

The whole country here is nothing but one large wash of debris cut through by smaller washes, 1-20 foot, 1-30 foot, 4-10 foot openings. The cheapest line to construct is near the river cutting only the ends of the main banks of wash; but a very much more direct line, and, when distance is considered, perhaps as cheap some little distance back on top of the lower ends of the washes [on] piles. This of course would make cut and fill; but with the openings that will have to be left in either case, I think it would be best, from the appearance. I think that piles can be used.

On this long gentle right swing I estimate 3-200 foot trestles, 2-300 foot trestles, 2-20 foot openings, 6-10 foot openings. End this swing at 10:55 A.M.

Stop at 11:00 A.M. Climb to top of knob in sharp right bend of river on right for photos.

Start at 11:27 and at 11:28 run light Rapid No. [*blank*].

On going up on the knob for photos, I find the country looks quite low. A line nearly tangent for 10 or 12 miles, running back of this knob. The bridging would average about what has been estimated on other work of this kind. Will note end of this line.

Land at 12 noon on right bank for lunch. Start again at 1:25 P.M.

Just after our lunch point a large wash comes in, which to keep the high line would require say a 1000 foot trestle or bank. We go round right side of Round Island, and get stuck on sand bar. At 2:15 run small Rapid No. [*blank*] and get back into main channel.

At 2:30 P.M. pass point where railroad line comes back to the river. Low rock bluffs which would be followed round this left bend, for about one mile, 11-20 foot openings, 1-30 foot opening, 11-10 foot openings. At 2:43 P.M. stop on left bank for photos. The bluffs above referred to show in photo.

Start again at 3:17 P.M. Beyond here the country widens out for several, 20, miles on each side into the great Cottonwood Valley, which is some 15 to 20 miles long. The Cottonwood Islands are very large and seem to be of good soil and would be good land to cultivate.

El Dorado Canyon on Lake Mohave, was destroyed by a flash flood in September, 1974, and the facility has been closed by the National Park Service.

We pass a large but out of order water wheel, formerly used for raising water from the river for irrigating purposes. 4:20 stop at upper end of Cottonwood Islands. Photo from *Cottonwood Islands*.

Start 4:40. At 4:50 P.M. stop on left bank opposite upper quarter of the large Cottonwood Islands and go into Camp No. 104. I have an awful sick headache and go right to bed.

SATURDAY, MARCH 22, 1890. 8:00 A.M. take photos from Camp No. 104 across Cottonwood Islands, Cottonwood Valley, and down river through Cottonwood Valley.

We start at 8:15 A.M.

Our line, from the rock bluffs noted yesterday can follow in a straight line across Cottonwood Valley and over the point of high ground beyond, provided the grades are not heavier than we wish to use. *Or* it can follow around a contour line from the bluffs, around the back of the valley and out towards the river on the high ground beyond. *Or* it can start from the bluffs, build across the islands and strike the river side of the high slope beyond in that way. Or a line somewhere between these. The first line suggested is shortest and best if the grade is right.

FIG. 54. Noon rest, Pyramid Canyon. *Robert B. Stanton.* Engineering Societies Library.

After passing Cottonwood Islands the mountains come in closer to the river. This makes the great gravel slopes steeper and shorter towards the water. This makes the high ground spoken of beyond the Cottonwood Valley. This ground is cut into *flat* ridges by many washes from the mountains. Some of these washes are very wide making large flats about 18 to 20 feet above water; and the tops of the flat ridges are about 20 to 25 feet above these valleys. Stop at 9:25 on left bank for photos showing the valleys or flats referred to [and] showing the ridges and knobs where the mountains come in closest to the river.

Start again at 9:43 A.M.

At 10:05 we run quite a sharp riffle, call it a *light* Rapid No. [*blank*]. The flat from the last bluffs is very even, low, and cheap for construction.

10:10 A.M. quite a wash comes in from the mountains, about 800 feet of trestle or bank with 2-60 foot openings.

At 10:20 we come to sharp left turn. This is entrance to Pyramid Canyon. The base of the mountains come right down to river in low *rock* slopes. Line would be at water's edge on rock slopes 50° + from vertical. This turns left and then right opposite point of right turn. Stop at 10:30 for photos.

Start again at 10:50 A.M. These rock slopes are the easiest and smoothest for railroad purposes we have passed. These low flat rock slopes continue right along, with the usual waterways. Two miles down large side wash pass at 11:10 A.M. 1-60 foot span and 600 foot heavy embankment. Beyond this on turn to right the bluffs are higher but good easy slope to build around, all rock.

Down next stretch the rock slopes are rougher than those above, but not very difficult. A large side wash comes in on right, and high points of rock are left out in river. Line cuts back of these.

We stop at 11:38 for lunch. Photos up river, across river, down river, [and] noon rest in Pyramid Canyon.

We start after lunch at 1:00 P.M. From lunch point on, the rock is in larger points jutting out into river. Some heavy cuts. Around right bend high point of rock, hill, with low gap, 100 feet back from river. Cut back of this and come out on river on flat beyond, 1-50 foot opening. Then on easy rock slope next to river to point of turn to right, 1/4 mile.

At 1:25 P.M. we emerge from Pyramid Canyon[8] and enter the Mojave Valley. Stop at 1:55 on right bank for photos up river showing upper end of Mojave Valley with gravel bluffs at point of right turn.

Start again at 2:15 P.M.

---

[8] Below El Dorado Canyon the Stanton party sailed along easily on quiet water and reached Fort Mojave in two days, a distance of about fifty-five miles. Passage was through the open Cottonwood Valley, past Round Island and the long Cottonwood Island, and through the short Pyramid Canyon (names put on the map by Ives), features inundated by the reservoir behind Davis Dam — Lake Mohave.

The gravel bluffs continue round right bend *all the way to southwest course*. Line would have to come to these and follow around on edge of river. Light drainage.

Pass Hardyville at 2:30 P.M., and stop at mill at 2:32, and start 2:40. And stop at 2:45 on right bank at beginning of southwest course for photos up river, down river, [and] the Mojave Valley.[9]

Start again at 3:15 P.M.

After looking at the country at end of the southwest course, I think a very simple line can be gotten to cut off this great bend. A large wash goes up and the distance is so long I do not think the grade will be too heavy. After line reaches beginning point of left bend, for one mile rough rock slope same as in Pyramid Canyon with a number of water ways cut through it, 5-10 foot, 3-20 foot, and 1-30 foot openings.

After this mile are low bluffs of gravel and clay. Washes cut it all up into ridges. Line would cut these a little way back from river. *Earth work*. This continues for 1 1/2 miles to right bend of river, with 1-30 foot, 3-20 foot, and 6-10 foot openings. At the right turn bluff very low. By keeping line up here a cut off 8 miles long can be run on a tangent back of *Beaver Lake*.

Stop at 4:20 P.M. on right bank for photos about 2 miles above Fort Mojave.

Start again at 4:40 P.M.

Landed at Fort Mojave at 5:00 P.M. Hislop and I went up and called on the commandant Captain Bowman who gave us a most cordial welcome. Gave instructions to his men to give us anything we wished; and later he sent an orderly down to our camp with a large bundle of straw for beds and an invitation to help ourselves to more. We — Travers, Gibson, and myself — called on the captain again in the evening. Had a very pleasant time. At parting the captain went to his own meat box and presented us with a huge roast of beef.

We go into Camp No. 105.

---

[9] Hardyville, near the head of Mohave Valley, dates from 1864, when pioneer entrepreneur William H. Hardy established a ferry and laid out a settlement on the left bank as a rival shipping and supply point to Fort Mojave nine miles downstream. Located at the head of low water navigation on the Colorado, the place prospered until the coming of the railroad to Needles in 1883. Stanton mentions a quartz mill at Hardyville, probably operating at the time of his visit.

Robert Stanton would have some difficulty recognizing this stretch of the Colorado River today. Bullhead City (Lake Mohave has covered the rock formation at the foot of Pyramid Canyon that Lt. J. C. Ives wrote, "looked like the head of a bull") on the left bank just below Davis Dam is a booming recreational and residential town with a number of satellite communities strung out down the valley for some miles. At Laughlin, across the Colorado on the Nevada side, reached by ready one-minute ferries from the Arizona side, a row of hotels and casinos front the river. Of Hardyville nothing remains beyond remnants of the cemetery overlooking the historic site.

SUNDAY, MARCH 23, 1890. Clear.

10:00 A.M. photos across river, [and] down river from bluffs at Fort Mojave.

10:00 A.M. general view of post [and] Capt. A. H. Bowman house and lieutenants.

10:30 A.M. Company "A," Ninth Infantry.

2:00 P.M. Indian group.

3:00 P.M. corporals' group.

4:30 P.M. victorious Shinny Indians.

5:00 P.M. quarters of the "A" Company, Ninth Infantry; [and] Mark L. Hersey, 2d Lt. Company A, Ninth Infantry, [and] Ambrose I. Moriarty, 2d Lt. Company A, Ninth Infantry.

A great day of sport among the Indians. A magnificent game of shinny between two picked sides of seven each.

FIG. 55. The veterans of the second expedition reach Needles. From left: Reginald Travers, H. G. Ballard, W. H. Edwards, George Melick (from Diamond Creek). John Hislop, Langdon Gibson, Elmer Kane, Robert B. Stanton. *R. W. Hildreth.* Engineering Societies Library.

MONDAY, MARCH 24. Captain Bowman, and Lts. Hersey and Moriarty, and many of the soldiers came down to bid us good-by. They all have certainly treated us most royally.[10]

Start at 8:15 A.M. Stop at 11:00 A.M. to wait for No. 2 stuck on a sand bed. She comes up and we start at 11:30 A.M. We land at the Pump House at Needles, California, at 12:10 P.M.[11]

List of goods left with Monaghan and Murphy, Needles, California:

> 1 photo instrument; 1 level, extra legs and tripod; 2 kegs of whisky and brandy; 1 bag sundries, no cover; 2 photo tripods; 1 sack of rubber sacks.

Goods sent to Monaghan and Murphy:

> 4 coils rope; 1 shovel; 3 rubber boots; 2 (1 single and 1 double) blocks.

SATURDAY, APRIL 19, 1890. Clear.

While the men are packing up Kane and I take photos. 8:30 A.M., photos from point 1 mile above new cantilever bridge [and] from west end of bridge.

Start from Camp No. [*blank*] at 10:25 A.M. Land at the bridge camp and make arrangements for going back to Needles.

At 12:07 row down one mile and Camp No. 115. On the water *15 minutes* in all today.

From Camp 115, about 1 mile below Red Rock Bridge. [Photos.][12]

---

[10] Fort Mojave, an army post founded in 1859 to protect travelers passing through Mojave Indian territory, was decommissioned in May 1890, and converted to a government Indian school. Ray Brandes, *Frontier Military Posts in Arizona* (Globe, AZ., D. S. King, 1960). Stanton's visit must have been as pleasant for the post personnel as it was for the surveyors. Life on this remote station during its declining days was surely dreary and dull at best. In writing later about the survey, Stanton remembered with pleasure his genial host at Fort Mojave. Dwight L. Smith, ed., *Down the Colorado* (1965), 221–222.

The engineer planned to run the railroad line west of Beaver Lake, an oxbow lake across the river from Fort Mojave.

"Mojave" is the Hispanicized version of the original Indian name. "Mohave" is the Anglicized form of the Spanish word. Both are in current usage.

[11] Needles, on the California side of the river, was founded in 1883 as a station on the Santa Fe Railroad (then the Atlantic and Pacific). The survey was interrupted here while Stanton and some of the men traveled to Denver for business reasons and for a rest. The progress of the expedition was reported in the press: Denver *Republican*, March 28, 1890; Denver *Times*, April 14, 1890; Chicago *Railway Age*, April 12, 1890.

[12] Having lost three of its bridges built near Needles to flooding by the Colorado River, the Santa Fe Railroad built a fourth at a narrow point ten miles downstream near Topock, Arizona. This was a high cantilever structure known at the time as the "Red Rock Bridge." It was completed in May, 1890.

The railroad town takes its name from The Needles, a group of sharp peaks on the Arizona side of the river about five miles below Topock.

In his report to the DCC & PRR Stanton had to admit that "on account of my small knowledge of the art of photography all the pictures from (Needles) to the end of our journey, were over-exposed, for I was not acquainted with the bright sunlight of open country." The photos could be used to "show the character of the country" but they were not

MONDAY, APRIL 21, 1890.

Camp No. 115 about 1 mile below Red Rock. Broke camp at 7:15 A.M.

Line from Red Rock Bridge down is along very flat sloping rock bluffs to where river first turns right to south course, nearly 1 mile, with 2-10 foot openings. Flat at point. Beyond to [blank] *flat rock* bluffs to point where river narrows up, bluffs rise 50 to 75 feet, side canyon 60 foot opening and bold out to river. River wide enough to handle easily along edge of water. Line to pass bridge is high. Keep it well up to cross this high bluff, 1/2 mile long. This is possibly real entrance to this *Mojave* "Canyon." End of this high bluff is last transit point of survey, then *low* flat rock slopes to the Needles, at 7:40 A.M. Side wash 50 foot span.

In reaching the Needles the line would cut way back of first mountain to avoid two 90° turns and come out of side canyon which flows directly north and south into river as it makes last turn to south. From here on good rock slopes with point out in river and *low* gaps behind.

Stop at 8:05 for photos, at long swing to right, in Mojave Canyon. Start at 8:20 A.M.

These low rock bluffs are very much cut up by side washes and the bridging would be heavy, to here 4-50 foot spans, 1-50 foot opening. Where river turns to left again low *gravel* bluffs all way round long swing with chance of cutting back at point. At end of this sharp left turn with rock at bend for five hundred yards, then low gravel again on long stretch southeast course. This the Chemehuevi Valley line simple and easy all down this valley at cost ready for track of $5000.00 per mile.

Stop at 10:25 for photos from lower end of Chemehuevi Valley. Start at 10:45 A.M.

Beyond this valley low gravel bluffs come down to the river, and at point beyond where river turns to right low enough to make direct line on top, way back from river. Further down broad valleys and easy flats for 3 to 4 miles. Then come in low easy rock bluffs. These rock bluffs soon drop off into smooth hillsides with gravel and earth on top and perhaps rock underneath. The rock bluffs continued only about 1 mile. Gravel bluff and broad flat valleys. The banks of gravel are high and may require following close to river though cutoffs can be made behind the points that come out to river.

Stop at 12 noon for lunch about 25 miles below Red Rock Bridge. Photo. Start again at 1:40 P.M.

[At] the point where we lunched, this gravel bluff continues only a [short distance] when it turns into *rock* slopes like those in Black and Boulder Canyon. These continue for 3 to 3 1/2 miles close to the river.

"artistic pictures," and apparently Stanton removed them from his own files. None of the photographs made by the engineer below Fort Mojave have been seen by the editors.

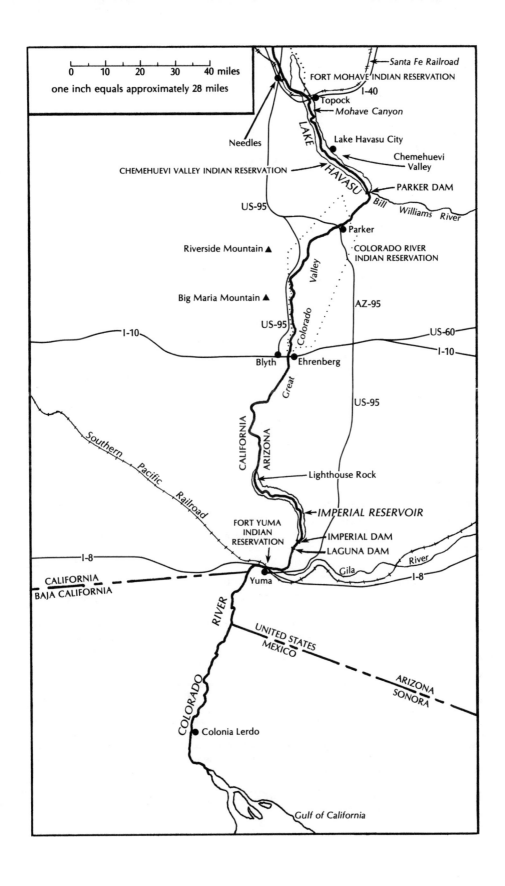

Santa Fe Railroad
FORT MOHAVE INDIAN RESERVATION
I-40
Topock
Mohave Canyon
Lake Havasu City
Chemehuevi Valley
Needles
CHEMEHUEVI VALLEY INDIAN RESERVATION
LAKE HAVASU
PARKER DAM
Bill Williams River
US-95
Parker
Riverside Mountain ▲
COLORADO RIVER INDIAN RESERVATION
Colorado Valley
Big Maria Mountain ▲
AZ-95
US-95
US-60
I-10
I-10
Blyth
Ehrenberg
Colorado
Great
US-95
Southern Pacific Railroad
CALIFORNIA
ARIZONA
Lighthouse Rock
IMPERIAL RESERVOIR
FORT YUMA INDIAN RESERVATION
IMPERIAL DAM
LAGUNA DAM
River
I-8
Gila
I-8
CALIFORNIA
BAJA CALIFORNIA
Yuma
RIVER
UNITED STATES
MEXICO
ARIZONA
SONORA
COLORADO
Colonia Lerdo
Gulf of California

Pass old quartz mill on right. The mountains are close in upon the valley on both sides. The rock bluffs drop back for some distance as river turns left and this opens out into quite a little valley of flat land. Then some gravel bluffs and then 1/2 to 2 miles of flat.

Stop at 2:45 for photos above Bill Williams Fork. Start 3:00 P.M.

After the long flat, extends 1/2 mile beyond, the same low rock bluffs coming out to the river. Pass Bill Williams Fork at 3:23 P.M.

All at once enter quite a little canyon with walls of sloping rock like these above. Side canyon on right, wide bottom below, high water fill, and trestle. Beyond this a very abrupt point coming out into river, which would make some pretty heavy rounding the point. Line built in river for some little distance. River wide, will not interfere with boats. After passing this the big bend of the river is quite low. Think can go back and save sharp turn.

Stop at 3:55 about 3 miles below Bill Williams Fork at point where river turns sharp to right and makes *west* course. [Photos.]

Start at 4:10 P.M. From this point on the bank is low rock bluff and flats between with bold points jutting out into the river. *Some* of these points show low gaps back of them. Possibly line can be found behind and thus save distance and curvature. This class of work for 3 to 4 miles, then *low flat* rock bluffs for one mile. Then for [blank] miles level bottom above ordinary high water. This continues to left turn of river which we pass at 5:25 P.M.

Stop at 5:05 for photos, 1/2 mile above point of left turn at 5:25 P.M. Start at 5:20 P.M.

At 5:30 pass mill on left. Around the "5:25 P.M." turn to left, steep rock bluffs, then long flat for 3/4 mile, then on rock point and bottom again. I think line can go behind this last point. From there on to bend of river to left, opposite old government Headgate, good bottom land line.

We camp No. 116 on left bank at Headgate, at 6:10 P.M. About 55 miles today.[13]

TUESDAY, APRIL 22, 1890. Photos from Camp No. 116.

Break camp and start at 7:55 A.M. Lost time repairing Boat No. 1.

[13] During the days April 21–24, the Stanton party made a rapid, even cursory, survey of the Colorado from Topock below Needles, to Yuma, a distance of about 215 miles. On the first day the men ran through Mojave Canyon-Topock Gorge and the Chemehuevi Valley to the mouth of Bill Williams River, all now covered by Lake Havasu, the reservoir behind Parker Dam.

Lake Havasu City, the center of an expanding resort and residential development on the Arizona side, looks out over the widest part of the lake which broadly outlines the submerged valley, once the tribal home of the Chemehuevi Indians. Below the site of Parker Dam the explorers ran down along a now heavily-used river resort and recreational area — the Parker Strip — and went into camp near the present Parker, Arizona. They were not far from the Headgate Rock Dam which provides irrigation water for the Colorado River Indian Reservation. During the day Stanton noted two riverside quartz mills, evidence of mining activity in the Whipple Mountains west of the river.

From point opposite our last night's camp the gravel bluffs come close to river for about 2 miles. Then line straight across wide bottom flat for 5 to 6 miles to grand bluffs that have been cut away by the river and are in straight lines. Here line would be made well back all in excavation and the material wasted in the river. This for 5 or 6 miles.

Stop at 10:35 for photos. Start at 11:05.

Along this 5 or 6 mile bluff it is necessary to keep up on top which is level and way back. Bluffs are of loose sand and gravel. Back will give good straight line to Riverside Mountains. Skirting this base will be light easy rock work. From Riverside Mountains to Halfway Mountains about 3 miles line would be along top of the bluffs for nearly the whole way thus giving more direct line and keeping away from the unsafe sand bluffs.

Stop at 11:55 A.M. for lunch. Photo [of] the Riverside Mountains from opposite bank. Start at 1:25 P.M.

Beyond the Halfway Mountains the gravel bluffs get higher and perhaps a line would have to run close to the river; but it would be much more direct if it could be built back in a direct line.

Stop at 2:45 for photos. Start at 3:00 P.M.

After getting up on the bank I see line can easily and cheaply be built on direct line on top of these flat bluffs. This flat gravel bluff country continues 12 to 15 miles, then we have 1 to 2 miles of rock slope with gravel bluffs beyond. This rocky point of the mountains that comes out to the river is at the head on right bank of the "Great Colorado Valley."

We camp No. 117 at 6:10 P.M. on right bank about 8 miles below the above noted rock point.[14]

WEDNESDAY, APRIL 23, 1890. Break Camp No. 117 and start at 7:20 A.M.

Stop at 8:10 A.M. Photo, a scene in the Great Colorado Valley. Start at 8:25.

At 8:35 stop at *Ehrenberg*, an old mining camp. Rich gold mines in the neighborhood. English company said to be about putting up a mill. Photos [of] Ehrenberg 125 miles above *Yuma*. Start again at 9:05.[15]

[14] On April 22, Stanton made another good run of about fifty miles, traveling through the open Parker Valley and passing the Riverside and Halfway (now Big Maria Mountains) Mountains on the right. Halfway Mountains? Ives wrote that his Indian informant told him that these mountains were halfway between Fort Yuma and the Mojave villages upstream near Needles. Camp for the night was in the vicinity of the Palo Verde Diversion Dam which supplies water for the Palo Verde Irrigation District. Ives' "Great Colorado Valley" included Parker Valley on the north, Palo Verde Valley, and Cibola Valley on the south.

[15] Ehrenberg, boom town on the left bank of the Colorado, laid out in 1867, became a key point in the economic life of the region. A river port and ferry landing on a major stage route, Ehrenberg eclipsed the older La Paz, a few miles upriver to the north, and enjoyed flush times until 1877 when the Southern Pacific Railroad reached Yuma. When Robert B. Stanton arrived in 1890 the town was still active but decline was evident. Nothing but the

Fig. 56. Lighthouse Rock from a print in J. C. Ives, *Report upon the Colorado River of the West* (1861).

A line through the Great Colorado Valley can be practically straight for 24 to 25 miles of easy light earth and gravel work. Then short cut behind a point of rock.

Stop at 11:35 A.M. for lunch. Photos [of] the Great Colorado Valley. Start again at 12:55 P.M. and sail through the Great Colorado Valley. Stop at 3:20 for photos at lower end of Great Colorado Valley. Start again at 3:40 P.M.

Six to 8 miles of valley bottom lands then 1 mile of gravel bluffs. 4:45 P.M. pass old quartz mill on right, and at 5 P.M. old fort on left. After the last gravel bluffs is an open valley for 4 or 5 miles, then gravel bluffs for say one mile, then open again with the bluffs closer to the river than before, and these continuing all the way to the [*blank*] on right before you come to the Hazard Pass.

Opposite old mining Camp No. 118 on left bank at 5:30 P.M.

THURSDAY, APRIL 24, 1890. Photos from Camp No. 118.
Start at 7:15 A.M.

---

old cemetery remains today to mark the site now covered with mobile home parks. Richard E. Lingenfelter, *Steamboats on the Colorado River, 1852–1916* (1978); Nell Murbarger, *Ghosts of Adobe Walls* (Los Angeles, Westernlore Press, 1964), 22–28.

After the Great Colorado Valley and from our last the rock hills keep in close to the river with a very narrow bottom, not good for line. Line on easy slopes of the gravel and rock.

Stop at 7:45 on Lighthouse Rock for photos. Start at 8:00 A.M.

Our Camp 118 last night was about 4 miles above Lighthouse Rock. From Camp No. 118 the line soon reaches where the bottom between the hills and river is much broader, with points and hills with low gaps behind come to river at long intervals. Good line not 1/4 in rock. Rest earth. As the river first turns east, the rock and gravel bluffs come close to river. Heavy work for 1'/2 mile.

Stop at 9 A.M. for photos. Start at 9:15 A.M. Line all through here is cutting points of rock then over little bottoms and behind points through gaps, with perhaps some short 200 to 300 foot tunnels to save distance.

We pass Red Rock Gate and soon lose the *rock* bluffs and in their place high gravel ones. After passing the two big bends beyond Red Rock Gate, the rock bluffs come in again close to the river with bottoms between the points about 1'/2 rock and 1/2 earth work.

Stop at 10:45 for photos. Start at 11:00 A.M.

Where river turns south again long fine bottom, 5 or 6 miles of earth scraper work.

Stop at 12 noon for lunch. Start again at 1:20 P.M.

After the long bottom, a point, 2 miles of rock. Cut behind by one or other of lines 1:30 P.M. Fine bottom to Explorers Pass then a couple of miles of rock bluffs.

At 5:30 P.M. land at Yuma, just above the railroad bridge. Camp No. 119.[16]

---

[16] Camp on April 23 was probably opposite the Clip Mill and boat landing located about four miles above Lighthouse Rock. Silver and gold ores were milled here during a short boom period in the 1880s. By Stanton's time the mill and the Clip Mine, some miles back from the river, had ceased operation. Nell Murbarger, *Ghosts of the Adobe Walls* (1964), 351; Byrd H. Granger, *Will C. Barnes' Arizona Place Names* (Tucson, University of Arizona Press, 1960), 372. The Granger work is a basic reference for origins of Colorado River nomenclature.

On April 24, the Stanton party made a fast run from Camp 118 to Yuma, a distance by river of about fifty-five miles. Lighthouse Rock was a rock pinnacle in the middle of the river, with channels on either side. In recent times the Arizona channel has silted up. The rock was described by Lt. J. C. Ives, who also named Hazard Pass, a narrow channel in the Colorado in the vicinity of Lighthouse Rock. The quartz mill and the "old fort" noted by Stanton on April 23 have not been identified. Red Rock Gate, another Ives name, was located within California's Picacho State Recreation Area. Explorer's Pass, also named by Ives, was in close proximity to Imperial Dam, diversion gateway for the All American Canal which carries Colorado River water to the Imperial Valley.

Named after the local Indians, historic Yuma at the mouth of the Gila River had been a crossing point on the Colorado since late in the eighteenth century. Spanish colonists had come this way, American troops in the war with Mexico, and California-bound Forty-niners. In 1850 the U.S. Army founded Fort Yuma and thereafter Yuma became intimately associated with steamboat navigation of the Colorado River and with railroad history. Building

FRIDAY, APRIL 25, 1890. Start from Yuma 10:10 A.M. Take photo Yuma from below the bridge.

From point 12 miles above Yuma line follows on bottom 1 to 3 miles back from river, along the foot of the gravel bluffs. The line will cross Southern Pacific Railroad at point directly west of Yuma, where the SP starts to climb the mesa.

Stop at 11:00 A.M. for photos from point just below where SPRR rises to the mesa.

From here for 1/2 mile heavy gravel bluffs, then opens the flat bottom that runs all the way to the Gulf.

12:30 P.M. stop for lunch. Start again at 1:45 P.M. At 6:00 P.M. go into Camp No. 120 on right bank of river in Lower California.

SATURDAY, APRIL 26, 1890. Break camp at 7:15 A.M. Stop at 8:15 to climb bluff and look ahead. Start at 8:30. Stop for lunch at 12:00 noon.

Start at 1:30 P.M. Stop at 3:30. Climb bluff on left. See Upper Lerdo Colony. Start 3:50 P.M.

Stop at 5 P.M. opposite Lower Lerdo Colony and go into Camp 121, in State of Sonora.

SUNDAY, APRIL 27. Spend [the day] in camp. Start at 10 P.M. with 2-4 mule teams and Mexican drivers for Yuma.[17]

TUESDAY, APRIL 29, 1890. Reached Yuma about 4 P.M. Settled with all the men.

---

from California, the Southern Pacific Railroad, headed for Tucson and El Paso, reached Yuma and bridged the Colorado River in 1877. Byrd Granger, *Arizona Place Names* (1960), 388–390; Douglas D. Martin, *Yuma Crossing* (Albuquerque, University of New Mexico Press, 1954); Richard E. Lingenfelter, *Steamboats on the Colorado River, 1852–1916* (1978). During his traverse of the Colorado below Needles, Stanton refers briefly to mining operations here and there. Yuma as a base and supply point for the very considerable mining along the river is the subject of a book by Frank Love, *Mining Camps and Ghost Towns, A History of Mining in Arizona and California Along the Lower Colorado* (Los Angeles, Westernlore Press, 1974).

[17] By the time he reached Yuma Stanton must have been convinced that the fine harbor at San Diego would be a far better terminus for the DCC & PRR than one at the mouth of the Colorado on the Gulf of California. Consequently, his survey below Yuma was little more than a brief reconnaissance. Stanton's "Lower Lerdo Colony," is the one appearing on contemporary maps as "Colonia Lerdo" in 1890, a small agricultural and stock-raising community in the State of Sonora, some ninety miles from Yuma. Lerdo was at or near the head of the tidewater, but some fifty to sixty miles from the mouth of the Colorado. Here, in a "sad parting," Stanton left the boats, the *Bonnie Jean* and the *Lily*. Dwight L. Smith, ed., *Down the Colorado* (1965), 222. Godfrey Sykes, *The Colorado Delta* (Washington and New York, Carnegie Institution and the American Geographical Society, 1937), a classic study, contains a detailed review of exploration and navigation of the lower river. On the basis of his own explorations during the 1890s, Sykes describes the changing Colorado River from Yuma to the Gulf as it was shortly after Stanton's visit.

APRIL 30, 1890. Disbanded party. All men start for Denver, and I go to San Diego, California.[18]

Skeleton Record of Events from April 30th 1890.

After disbanding the Colorado River party at Yuma I went to Coronado Beach, California, where my family was, for a much needed rest.

I remained in California till the end of May. *I* then returned to Denver and went east, where I attended the convention of the American Society of Civil Engineers at Cresson Springs, Pennsylvania, which met June 26th '90, and lectured on my canyon trip. See account in [New York? *Railroad Gazette*, July 4, 1890].

I again went west. Left Denver for California about July 12th. Was in Salt Lake City, July 14th. We all remained at Coronado until early in November. During my summer stay at Coronado I wrote the article ["The Denver, Colorado Cañon & Pacific Railway Project,"] that appeared [in] the *Engineering News* [*and American Railway Journal*], October 18, 1890, and also ["Through the Grand Cañon of the Colorado,"] *Scribner's Magazine*, November 1890.

We returned to Denver early in November where we remained all winter. Just before Christmas '90 Mr. G. W. Holdrege, General Manager, Burlington Railroad sent me to the Black Hills of Dakota to report on the B&MRR's purchase of the Narrow Gauge Railroad in the Black Hills.

1891. About May 1st '91 we left Denver, this time finally, and went to Coronado, California, where I remained until April 7, 1892. I was employed in gathering data for and making field examinations of the railroad route from San Diego, California, to Yuma, Arizona, and in writing.[19]

---

[18] Thus ended Robert Brewster Stanton's historic voyage down the Colorado. The surveyed distance from the confluence of the Colorado and Green rivers to Colonia Lerdo was approximately 984 miles. From Green River, Utah, to Lerdo, the distance covered was about 1104 miles. An extensive press coverage followed after completion of the survey. Some of the articles: Yuma *Times*, April 30, 1890; San Diego *Union*, May 3, 1890; San Diego *Sun*, May 5, 1890; Denver *Republican*, May 26, 1890; Denver *Rocky Mountain News*, June 2, 1890; Salt Lake *Tribune*, July 12, 14, 15, 27, 1890. Some of these notices reflect controversy which developed between Stanton and those who criticized the feasibility of the railroad.

[19] Stanton wrote a number of pieces about the railroad survey. In September, 1890, he submitted a lengthy Report to the president of the Denver, Colorado Canyon & Pacific Railroad, summarizing the work of the survey, presenting arguments in favor of building the line, including cost estimates and observations on business potential. At a meeting of the American Society of Civil Engineers, Stanton read a paper, "Availability of the Cañons of the Colorado River of the West for Railway Purposes," which, together with the discussion following, was published in the Society's *Transactions*, XXVI (April, 1892), 183–361. In three popular accounts Stanton recounted his adventures on the river as he extolled the beauties of the canyons: "Through the Grand Cañon of the Colorado," *Scribner's Magazine*, VIII (November, 1890), 591–613, reprinted in part by Bruce Babbitt, comp., *Grand Canyon, An*

Anthology (Flagstaff, Northland Press, 1978), 37–45. On his pioneer photographic work:
"Engineering with a Camera in the Cañons of the Colorado," *Cosmopolitan Magazine*, XV
(July, 1893), 292–303. In distinguished company he wrote "Engineering in the Depths of
the Grand Canyon," in *The Grand Canyon of Arizona*, a book of appreciative essays by well-
known visitors, published by the Passenger Department of the Santa Fe Railroad, 1902.

In his *Canyon Scrap Book*, 1869–1909, the engineer assembled a mass of news clippings
about the railroad survey and related subjects, including copies of some of his own articles.
Stanton never lost interest in the Colorado River. In 1906 he began to write the story of the
river, substantially completed by 1909, in which his own expeditions were set down in the
perspective of the Colorado's long history. Owing to its great length, this work, entitled "The
River and the Canyon," was never published, but Stanton's narrative of his canyon explorations was rescued and edited by Dwight L. Smith, under the title *Down the Colorado* (1965).

Photographs make up one of the important records of the railroad survey. F. A. Nims
made about 289 photographs; Stanton took the remainder. To accompany his report to the
DCC & PRR, in September, 1890, the engineer prepared an album of some 900 photographs
illustrating the proposed route from the confluence of the Colorado and Green rivers to the
mouth of the Colorado. Another album containing some 700 photographs was presented to
the American Society of Civil Engineers in 1892. This album is preserved in the Engineering Societies Library in New York.

Some of the members of the Stanton railroad survey kept records of the adventure:
Letters by Langdon Gibson; Diary and Scrapbook by W. H. Edwards; Diary by Franklin A.
Nims. These were copied and compiled by the late Otis R. "Dock" Marston. Copy in the
Reference Library, Grand Canyon National Park, Arizona. A brief diary kept by L. G.
Brown, who left the expedition at Diamond Creek, was published in the Denver *Rocky
Mountain News*, March 17, 1890.

Members of the expedition who completed the survey were presented with a medallion
by the DCC & PRR for their participation in the "Explorations & Survey of the Canon of
the Colorado River, 1889–1890." The one inscribed for H. G. Ballard is in the collections of
the Utah State Historical Society, Salt Lake City, Utah.

BIBLIOGRAPHY

Stanton-related bibliography is extensive. The items listed here are limited to the principal ones used by the editors for this project.

STANTON MANUSCRIPTS:

"The Cañons of the Colorado River of the West." Photographs Presented to the American Society of Civil Engineers by Robert B. Stanton, M. Am. Soc. C. E., 1892. Album, Engineering Societies Library, New York.

"Report to H. B. Chamberlin, Esq., President; and the Hon. Board of Directors, of the Denver, Colorado Canyon, and Pacific Railroad Co., San Diego, California, September, 1890." Stanton Papers, New York Public Library. (Cited as "Railroad Report.")

"The River and the Canyon: The Colorado River of the West, and the Exploration, Navigation, and Survey of Its Canyons from the Standpoint of an Engineer." 2 vols., 1920. Stanton Papers, New York Public Library.

BOOKS AND ARTICLES:

Adams, William Y., Alexander J. Lindsay, Jr., and Christy G. Turner, II. "Survey and Excavations in Lower Glen Canyon, 1952–1958." Flagstaff, Museum of Northern Arizona *Bulletin* 36 (1961).

Ashbaugh, Don. *Nevada's Turbulent Yesterdays, a Study in Ghost Towns.* Los Angeles, Westernlore Press, 1963.

Babbitt, Bruce, comp. *Grand Canyon, an Anthology; a Selection of Outstanding Writings.* Flagstaff, Northland Press, 1978.

Belknap, Buzz. *Grand Canyon River Guide, River Map, Historic Photographs, Major Powell's Own Story.* Salt Lake City, Canyonlands Press, 1969.

Belknap, Bill, and Buzz Belknap. *Westwater, Lake Powell, Canyonlands National Park, Canyonlands River Guide.* Boulder City, Nevada, Westwater Books, 1974.

Billingsley, George H. "Mining in Grand Canyon." In William C. Breed and Evelyn C. Roat, eds., *Geology of the Grand Canyon.* Flagstaff, Museum of

[287]

Northern Arizona and Grand Canyon Natural History Association, 1974, 170–178.

Brandes, Ray. *Frontier Military Posts in Arizona.* Globe, Arizona, Dale Stuart King, 1960.

Brooks, Juanita. *John Doyle Lee, Zealot — Pioneer Builder — Scapegoat.* Glendale, California, Arthur H. Clark, 1962.

Chalfant, James M., ed. *Colorado River Controversies,* by Robert Brewster Stanton. Foreword by Julius F. Stone. New York, Dodd, Mead & Co., 1932. Reprint edition, Boulder City, Nevada, Westwater Books, 1982. With Commentaries by Otis R. Marston and Martin J. Anderson.

Cleland, Robert Glass. *This Reckless Breed of Men: the Trappers and Fur Traders of the Southwest.* New York, Alfred A. Knopf, 1952.

Collins, Robert O., and Roderick Nash. *The Big Drops, Ten Legendary Rapids.* San Francisco, Sierra Club Books, 1978.

Crampton, C. Gregory. "Historical Sites in Cataract and Narrow Canyons and in Glen Canyon to California Bar." University of Utah *Anthropological Papers* No. 72 (August 1964).

―――――. "Historical Sites in Glen Canyon, Mouth of Hansen Creek to Mouth of San Juan River." University of Utah *Anthropological Papers* No. 61 (December 1962).

―――――. "Historical Sites in Glen Canyon, Mouth of San Juan River to Lee's Ferry." University of Utah *Anthropological Papers* No. 46 (June 1960).

―――――. *Land of Living Rock, The Grand Canyon and the High Plateaus, Arizona, Utah, Nevada.* New York, Alfred A. Knopf, 1972.

―――――. *Standing Up Country, the Canyon Lands of Utah and Arizona.* New York, Alfred A. Knopf, and the University of Utah Press, in Association with the Amon Carter Museum of Western Art, 1964.

Crampton, C. Gregory, and Dwight L. Smith, eds. "The Hoskaninni Papers: Mining in Glen Canyon, 1897–1902." By Robert B. Stanton, University of Utah *Anthropological Papers* No. 54 (November 1961).

Darrah, William Culp, ed. "Major Powell's Journal, July 2–August 28, 1869." *Utah Historical Quarterly* 15 (1947), 125–131.

―――――. *Powell of the Colorado.* Princeton, Princeton University Press, 1951.

Dellenbaugh, Frederick S. *A Canyon Voyage: The Narrative of the Second Powell Expedition Down the Green-Colorado River from Wyoming, and the Explorations on Land, in the Years 1871 and 1872.* New Haven, Yale University Press, 1926.

―――――. *The Romance of the Colorado River.* New York and London, C. P. Putnam's Sons, 1902.

Dutton, C. E. *Report on the Geology of the High Plateaus of Utah with Atlas.* U.S. Geographical and Geological Survey of the Rocky Mountain Region. Washington, Government Printing Office, 1880.

————. *Tertiary History of the Grand Cañon District with Atlas.* Monographs of the U.S. Geological Survey, vol. 2. Washington, Government Printing Office, 1882. New edition, Santa Barbara and Salt Lake City, Peregrine Smith, 1977.

Euler, Robert C. "The Canyon Dwellers," *American West* 4 (May 1967), 22–27, 67–71.

Farquhar, Francis P. *The Books of the Colorado River & the Grand Canyon, a Selective Bibliography.* Los Angeles, Glen Dawson, 1953.

Fowler, Don D., Robert C. Euler, and Catherine S. Fowler. "John Wesley Powell and the Anthropology of the Canyon Country." U.S. Geological Survey *Professional Paper* No. 670 (Government Printing Office, 1969).

Fradkin, Philip L. *A River No More: The Colorado River and the West.* New York, Alfred A. Knopf, 1981.

Freeman, Lewis R. *The Colorado River: Yesterday, Today and Tomorrow.* New York, Dodd, Mead, 1923.

————. "Surveying the Grand Canyon of the Colorado." *National Geographic Magazine* 45 (May, 1924), 471–548.

Granger, Byrd H. *Will C. Barnes' Arizona Place Names.* Revised and enlarged. Tucson, University of Arizona Press, 1960. New Edition, *Arizona's Names.* Tucson, Falconer Publishing Co., 1983.

Hamblin, W. Kenneth, and J. Keith Rigby. "Guidebook to the Colorado River. Part 1: Lee's Ferry to Phantom Ranch. Part 2: Phantom Ranch to Lake Mead, Arizona-Nevada," Brigham Young University *Geology Studies* 15 (1968–1969).

Hekkers, Jim. "The Colorado River Railroad Survey." *Colorado Outdoors* 29 (January–February 1980), 34–44.

Hughes, J. Donald. *In the House of Stone and Light, a Human History of the Grand Canyon.* Grand Canyon, Grand Canyon Natural History Association, 1978.

Ives, Joseph C. *Report upon the Colorado River of the West Explored in 1857 and 1858.* Washington, Government Printing Office, 1861.

Kelly, Charles. "The Mysterious D. Julien." *Utah Historical Quarterly* 6 (July 1933), 83–88.

Kolb, E. L. *Through the Grand Canyon from Wyoming to Mexico.* New York, Macmillan Co., 1914.

LaRue, E. C. "Water Power and Flood Control of Colorado River Below Green River, Utah," U.S. Geological Survey *Water-Supply Paper 556.* Washington, Government Printing Office, 1925.

Lavender, David. *Colorado River Country.* New York, E. P. Dutton, 1982.

Leydet, François. *Time and the River Flowing: Grand Canyon.* San Francisco, Sierra Club, 1964.

Lingenfelter, Richard E. *Steamboats on the Colorado River, 1852–1916.* Tucson, University of Arizona Press, 1978.

Love, Frank. *Mining Camps and Ghost Towns, a History of Mining In Arizona and California Along the Lower Colorado.* Los Angeles, Westernlore Press, 1974.

Lumholtz, Carl. *New Trails in Mexico.* New York, Chas. Scribner's Sons, 1912.

Marston, Otis R., comp. Colorado River Journals and Diaries, 1889–1951. Typescript, Reference Library, Grand Canyon National Park, Arizona, 1949–1951. 2 vols.

———. "For Water-level Rails along the Colorado River." *Colorado Magazine* 46 (Fall 1969), 287–303.

———. "Separation Marks: Notes on the 'Worst Rapid' in the Grand Canyon." *Journal of Arizona History* 17 (Spring 1976), 1–20.

Martin, Douglas D. *Yuma Crossing.* Albuquerque, University of New Mexico Press, 1954.

Miller, David E. *Hole-in-the-Rock: an Epic in the Colonization of the Great American West.* Salt Lake City, University of Utah Press, 1966.

Murbarger, Nell. *Ghosts of the Adobe Walls.* Los Angeles, Westernlore Press, 1964.

Nims, Franklin A. "Through the Colorado River." *Commonwealth* 3 (Denver, August 1890), 257–272.

———. "Through the Mysterious Cañons of the Colorado." *Overland Monthly*, Second Series 19 (March 1892), 253–270.

Norris, Frank B. *Historical and Architectural Resources Within the Lower Colorado River System.* Boulder City, Nevada, U.S. Water and Power Resources Service, 1980, 4 vols.

Powell, John Wesley. *Exploration of the Colorado River of the West and Its Tributaries Explored in 1869, 1870, 1871, and 1872.* Washington, Government Printing Office, 1875.

Pyne, Stephen J. *Dutton's Point, an Intellectual History of the Grand Canyon.* Grand Canyon, Grand Canyon Natural History Association, 1982.

Reynolds, Ethan A. "In the Whirlpools of the Grand Cañon of the Colorado." *Cosmopolitan* 8 (November 1889), 25–34.

Rusho, W. L., and C. Gregory Crampton. *Desert River Crossing: Historic Lee's Ferry on the Colorado River.* Rev. ed. Salt Lake City, Peregrine Smith, 1981.

Schwartz, Douglas W., Michael P. Marshall, and Jane Kepp. *Archaeology of Grand Canyon: The Bright Angel Site.* Santa Fe, School of American Research Press, 1979.

Smith, Dwight L., ed. *Down the Colorado*, by Robert Brewster Stanton. Norman, University of Oklahoma Press, 1965.

———. "The Engineer and the Canyon." *Utah Historical Quarterly* 28 (July 1960), 262–273.

———. "Hoskaninni: A Gold Mining Venture in Glen Canyon." *El Palacio* 69 (Summer 1962), 77–84.

————. "Hoskaninni: A Gold Mining Venture in Glen Canyon." In *Probing the American West: Papers from the Santa Fe Conference*, edited by K. Ross Toole, *et al.* Santa Fe, Museum of New Mexico Press, 1962, 125–132, 203–204.

————. "The Nims and Czar Incidents in the Denver Press." *Colorado Magazine* 48 (Winter 1971), 49–58.

————, ed. *The Photographer and the River, 1889–1890: The Colorado Cañon Diary of Franklin A. Nims with the Brown-Stanton Railroad Survey Expedition.* Santa Fe, Stagecoach Press, 1967.

————, ed. "Robert B. Stanton's Plan for the Far Southwest." *Arizona and the West* 4 (Winter 1962), 369–380.

Smith, Melvin T. "The Colorado River: Its History in the Lower Canyons Area." Ph.D. Dissertation, Brigham Young University, 1972.

Spamer, Earle E., and others, comps. *Bibliography of the Grand Canyon and the Lower Colorado River, 1540–1980.* Grand Canyon, Grand Canyon Natural History Association, 1981.

Stanton, Robert B. "The Alleged Journey and the Real Journey of James White on the Colorado River in 1861 [1867]." *The Trail* 12 (Denver, September 1919), 7–26.

————. "Availability of the Cañons of the Colorado River of the West for Railway Purposes." American Society of Civil Engineers *Transactions* 26 (April 1892), with discussion, 283–361.

————. *Canyon Scrapbook.* News clips of the Colorado River Survey by Robert B. Stanton and Related Material including articles by Stanton. New York, New York Public Library, 1869–1909.

————. "Col. Stanton's Recent Descent of the Colorado River." *American Naturalist* 24 (May 1890), 463–466.

————. "The Denver, Colorado Cañon & Pacific Railroad Project." New York, *Engineering News and American Railway Journal* (September 21, 1889; October 18, 1890).

————. "Engineering in the Depths of the Grand Canyon." In *The Grand Canyon of Arizona.* Chicago, Passenger Department, Santa Fe Railroad, 1902.

————. "Engineering with a Camera in the Cañons of the Colorado." *Cosmopolitan Magazine* 15 (August 1893), 292–303.

————. "Through the Grand Cañon of the Colorado." *Scribner's Magazine* 8 (November 1890), 591–613.

Stegner, Wallace. *Beyond the Hundredth Meridian: John Wesley Powell and the Second Opening of the West.* Boston, Houghton Mifflin Co., 1954.

————, ed. *Report on the Arid Region of the United States with a More Detailed Account of the Lands of Utah,* by John Wesley Powell. Cambridge, Harvard University Press, 1962.

Stiles, Helen J., ed. "Down the Colorado in 1889." *Colorado Magazine* 41 (Summer 1964), 225–246.

Stone, Julius F. *Canyon Country: The Romance of a Drop of Water and a Grain of Sand.* New York and London, G. P. Putnam's Sons, 1932.

Supreme Court of the United States. *United States vs. Utah.* Number 14, October Term, 1929. Testimony before Charles Warren, Special Master, 1929 (Typescript, Utah State Historical Society, Salt Lake City), 32 volumes.

Sykes, Godfrey. *The Colorado Delta.* American Geographical Society Special Publication No. 19. Washington, Carnegie Institution and the American Geographical Society, 1937.

U.S. Geological Survey. *Plan and Profile of Colorado River from Black Canyon, Arizona-Nevada to Arizona-Sonora Boundary.* Washington, U.S. Geological Survey, 1927.

————. *Plan and Profile of Colorado River from Lee's Ferry, Arizona, to Black Canyon, Arizona-Nevada.* Washington, Government Printing Office, 1924.

————. *Plan and Profile of Colorado River, Lee's Ferry, Arizona, To Mouth of Green River, Utah, and Certain Tributaries.* Washington, Government Printing Office, 1921.

Wheeler, George M. *Report Upon United States Geographical Surveys West of the One Hundredth Meridian.* Volume I, Geographical Report. Washington, Government Printing Office, 1889.

Yates, Richard, and Mary Marshall. *The Lower Colorado River: a Bibliography.* Yuma, Arizona, Arizona Western College Press, 1974.

N E W S P A P E R S :

Chicago *Railway Age.* Aug. 8, 19, 23, 1889; Apr. 12, 1890.

Colorado Springs *Gazette.* Mar. 23, 1891.

Denver *Press.* Jan. 23, 1891.

Denver *Republican.* May 14, 27, June 5, 28, 29, July 23, 28, 30, Sept. 5, Nov. 2, 22, 1889; Jan. 29, 30, Feb. 4, 5, 16, Mar. 4, 11, 24, 25, 28, May 23, 26, 27, June 8, 1890; Jan. 14, 15, 1891.

Denver *Rocky Mountain News.* Mar. 4, July 27, Aug. 5, 11, Oct. 14, 1889; Jan. 29, Mar. 4, 17, 23, June 2, 1890; Jan. 14, 1891.

Denver *Times.* May 14, 20, June 14, 27, July 22, 26, Sept. 4, Nov. 22, Dec. 25, 1889; Jan. 28, 29, Feb. 5, Mar. 3, Apr. 14, 1890.

Kingman, Arizona, *Mohave County Miner.* Mar. 8, 1890; Mar. 5, 1891.

Los Angeles *Miner and Artisan.* Aug. 24, 1889.

New York *Engineering News and American Railway Journal.* June 8, Aug. 31, Sept. 21, 1889; Oct. 18, 1890.

New York *Railroad Gazette.* July 4, 1890.

New York *Scientific American*. June 11, 1892.

New York *Tribune*. Aug. 18, 1889.

Phoenix *Arizona Republican*. Oct. 4, 1892.

Phoenix *Herald*. Oct. 10, 1889; Jan. 28, 1890.

Pittsburgh *Commercial Gazette*. Jan. 20, 1891.

Salt Lake *Tribune*. Mar. 3, 1888; Jan. 4, May 14, 18, 23, July 23, Aug. 4, Nov. 24, 26, 1889; Mar. 4, July 12, 14, 15, 27, 1890.

San Diego *Sun*. May 5, 9, 1890.

San Diego *Union*. May 3, Oct. 18, 1890; Mar. 15, 1891.

San Francisco *Chronicle*. Aug. 25, 1889.

San Francisco *Examiner*. Mar. 4, 1890.

Yuma, Arizona, *Times*. Apr. 30, 1890.

INDEX

Abajo Mountains (Blue Mountains), 62n

All American Canal, 283n

Anasazi Canyon (Mystery Canyon), 53fig., 112n

Anasazi Indian ruins, 43fig., 87, 88n, 109, 109n, 110fig., 142n, 154, 154n, 172, 173n, 184, 185n, 196–197, 198n, 213, 213n

Anderson, M. A., 93

Anderson, William P., 106

Anderson's placer mine, 105–106

Anna placer mine, 109

Atlantic and Pacific Railroad, 1–3, 7, 9, 236–237n. *See also* Santa Fe Railroad

Aubrey Cliffs, 240

Aztec Creek, 51n, 109n, 110fig.

Badger Creek, 69, 70n, 85, 118

Badger Creek Rapid, 70n, 79n

Bailey, I. L., 238

Ballard, H. G. (boatman, Stanton Survey), 98, 102, 103fig., 113fig., 118, 122, 125, 127, 157, 163, 179, 238n, 276fig., 286n

Banks, (unknown), 12

Bass, William Wallace, 197n

Bass Canyon, 197n

Bass Rapid, 175, 197n

"Battery Point", 47, 104

Beal, A. M., 238

Beardsley, Mrs. M. H., 14

Beauty Point, 112

Beaver, Utah, 93

Beaver Creek, 93, 93n

Beaver Lake, 275, 277n

Best, J. D., 185n

"Big Drop" Rapid, 30n, 35n

Bill Williams Fork, 280

Bill Williams River, 280n

Black Canyon, 118n, 264n, 267, 267n, 268, 268n, 270, 270n, 271n, 278

Black Canyon of the Gunnison, 159

Black Granite Gorge, 159. *See also* Granite Gorge

Blackford, F. W., 109

Blake, Utah, 100, 132

Block, Clayton, 91

Bonelli, Daniel, 237, 261–262, 262n

Bonelli Bay, 262n

Bonelli's Ferry, 259fig., 261, 262n

Boucher Rapid, 182n

Boulder Canyon, 263–264, 264n, 266, 278

Bow Knot Bend, 17–18, 18n

Bowman, Capt. A. H., 275–277

"Bridal Falls", 211n, 225

Bridge Canyon, 109n, 244n

Bridge Canyon Dam, 244n

Briggs, George W., 12, 14, 108, 111

Bright Angel Creek, 149, 168, 169fig., 170fig., 171fig., 172–173, 173n, 175–176, 176fig., 177, 182, 183n, 185n

Brown, Frank M. (President of Denver, Colorado Canyon and Pacific Railroad Company Line), 2–3, 10–12, 14–16, 19–20, 22–23, 25–31, 33–35, 35n, 36, 36n, 39, 42, 44, 47n, 51, 51n, 58, 58n, 59, 59n, 62n, 63n, 85, 96n

 death of, 65, 71–72, 72fig., 73–75, 75n, 79, 80fig., 85, 87, 91, 95, 119–121

 notes on Colorado River country resources, 59–64

Brown, L. G. (boatman, Stanton Survey), 98, 102, 103fig., 126–127, 153, 179, 183–184, 238, 238n, 286n

"Brown Betty" rapid, 23n

[295]

MAY 6 88   19